Recommended Bed & Breakfasts™
Mid-Atlantic States

Delaware • Maryland • New Jersey • New York
Pennsylvania • Virginia • Washington, D.C. • West Virginia

HELP US KEEP THIS GUIDE
UP-TO-DATE

Every effort has been made by the author and editors to make this guide as accurate and useful as possible. However, many things can change after a guide is published—establishments close, phone numbers change, facilities come under new management, etc.

We would love to hear from you concerning your experiences with this guide and how you feel it could be made better and be kept up-to-date. While we may not be able to respond to all comments and suggestions, we'll take them to heart, and we'll also make certain to share them with the author. Please send your comments and suggestions to the following address:

The Globe Pequot Press
Reader Response/Editorial Department
P.O. Box 480
Guilford, CT 06437

Or you may e-mail us at:
editorial@globe-pequot.com

Thanks for your input, and happy travels!

Recommended Bed & Breakfasts™ Series

Recommended
BED&
BREAKFASTS™

Mid-Atlantic States

Second Edition

by
Suzi
Forbes
Chase

The
Globe
Pequot
Press

Guilford, Connecticut

Cover and text design by Nancy Freeborn
Cover illustration by Michael Crampton
Illustrations by Mauro Magellan except pages 21, 70, 162, 199, 223, 264, 297, 316, 344, all courtesy of the B&Bs

Library of Congress Cataloging-in-Publication Data

Chase, Suzi Forbes.
    Recommended bed & breakfasts. Mid-Atlantic states / Suzi Forbes Chase.—2nd ed.
    p. cm. — (Recommended bed & breakfasts series)
    "Delaware, Maryland, New Jersey, New York, Pennsylvania, Virginia, West Virginia."
    Includes indexes.
    ISBN 0-7627-0551-5
    1. Bed and breakfast accommodations—Middle Atlantic States—Guidebooks.
    I. Title.   II. Series.

TX907.3.M53 C474 1999
647.9474'03 21—dc21   99-043808

Contents

Acknowledgments

No book is written in a vacuum, and this particular book is the product of a marvelous support system. I especially wish to thank Laura Strom, the Executive Editor of The Globe Pequot Press, who, as my original editor, had so much to do with launching this book in 1998. Her gentle persuasion and sound judgment contributed substantially, then as now, to its success. Paula Brisco, Managing Editor, has been the guiding force in producing this second edition. Her patience, encouragement, clear direction, and sense of humor make her a pleasure to work with. I wish also to thank Mauro Magellan, who is responsible for the engaging line drawings found throughout this book.

Mostly, however, I would like to thank my husband, Dustin, who accompanies me on my quests for B&Bs whenever his work schedule permits but who tolerates my frequent absences from home when he cannot go. Without his support and encouragement, I couldn't write the books I write. Often on my lone trips, if the temperature is warm enough, I am chaperoned by my Lhasa apso, Oreo, who willingly spends nights in his car bed and eats meals in village parks—all for the dubious pleasure of traveling with me. Thanks to you too, Oreo.

Introduction

I'll never forget my first visit to a B&B. It was almost twenty years ago and I was charmed by the turreted, gingerbreaded, multidecked Victorian house, as well as by the antique furnishings and the innkeepers. The couple told me about their interest in saving this grand house that was on the verge of collapsing and how, after a trip to Europe, they decided to buy the house, restore it, and then put it to work to pay for itself.

At the time, I was completing my law school education and I had decided to specialize in historic preservation law, so the restoration of historic houses and buildings and their adaptation to today's uses was extremely appealing to me. Little did I know then that I would one day be privileged to play a role in this great B&B business.

In the 1960s there were probably no more than 200 B&Bs and country inns in America and there was only one guidebook. I've always been an inveterate traveler, so with the guidebook in hand, I made it my mission to stay in a B&B or country inn whenever there was one nearby. Soon I was writing articles for my local newspaper about B&Bs, country inns, restaurants, and travel—and so my career was launched.

I can't imagine a more rewarding job. The lure of a quiet country road is still irresistible to me, and the joy of discovery when I find a new high-quality B&B never gets old. Today, of course, innkeeping is a highly professional business. The number of B&Bs and country inns has increased over the last thirty years some 750 percent, and the American Bed and Breakfast Association now estimates there are about 30,000 B&Bs and country inns in America.

What Is a B&B?

Perhaps a definition is in order here. Over the years, the terms "country inn" and "bed-and-breakfast" have become blurred and are sometimes used synonymously. For the purposes of this book, I have tried to be very clear about the difference. Actually, there are three categories of homes in which guests can stay.

"Home-stay" and "guesthouse" are terms that generally refer to rooms in a private home where the owner either offers rooms seasonally or has another full-time job outside the home. These are not included in this guidebook.

A B&B is generally a home with from three to fifteen guest rooms. The innkeeper lives on the premises, has licensed his business with the town, operates it as his primary means of income, and offers breakfast as well as a room.

"Country" inn, on the other hand, generally refers to an establishment with more than fifteen rooms and one that has a restaurant offering dinner as well as breakfast. It is also a full-time, licensed business for the innkeepers, although larger B&Bs and inns sometimes have a full-time manager who lives on the property. In this book, I have concentrated on B&Bs, but my companion book *Recommended Country Inns of the Mid-Atlantic and Chesapeake Region* describes country inns in the same area.

How Did I Select B&Bs for This Book?

My task is to ferret out the very best B&Bs in the Mid-Atlantic region and to describe them to you in such a way that you can make an informed opinion about where you want to stay. To do that I visited 643 B&Bs and country inns in 1997 and 682 in 1998 and I put more than 10,000 miles on my car each year.

Although I have an enormous database in my computer, I learn about new B&Bs from local innkeepers, from other travelers at B&B breakfast tables, from letters sent by readers and innkeepers, and from the numerous newsletters and publications I review. There is seldom a day that goes by that I don't add a new B&B to my list or note a change in an existing one.

On my first visit to a B&B, I arrive unannounced and do a thorough inspection. I take copious notes in hardbound books that I later index, and I add the dates of my inspections and my overall comments to my computer database. This approach has one major drawback: On occasion, there is no one home, and then I must wait until another visit to review that B&B. On the other hand, the approach works because I know I am seeing the B&B just as it will look to paying guests and not spruced up for a visit by a travel writer. If, after my inspection, I believe the B&B warrants inclusion in my book, I usually schedule a return visit to stay there.

To select merely 200-plus B&Bs from the vast number that are now available, I look for those with the highest standards in each area. I am a stickler for absolute cleanliness, superb maintenance, and friendly on-site innkeepers or managers, so if a B&B is lacking in any of those areas, I generally do not include it. In addition, if a B&B has been in business less than two years, or if there are new owners, I will generally give it time to season.

I believe most travelers today prefer rooms with private baths, so most of the B&Bs in this book have private baths. I also look for B&Bs with comfortable common areas, including verandas, porches, and gardens and those offering something extra—perhaps afternoon tea, or evening wine and cheese, or bicycles to use and maps to follow, or an on-site archeological dig, or an artist in residence. Yet, I also believe I have a responsibility to offer my readers a selection of B&Bs that provide a variety of styles, prices, and amenities and that cover the entire Mid-Atlantic geographic area, although I do concentrate on the most popular tourist destinations.

B&Bs reflect the architectural and decorative styles of the buildings they are located within, as well as the interests of the innkeepers who own them. So whether you're looking for an intimate, romantic retreat with a whirlpool tub and a rose on the pillow at turndown, or an adventure-packed weekend of mountain climbing, you're sure to find what strikes your fancy in these pages. My pledge to you is that each of these B&Bs has been personally inspected by me and, in my opinion, they meet the highest standards of cleanliness, maintenance, decor, and friendliness.

I take my responsibility very seriously and welcome comments from you also. Changes inevitably take place, and your personal experiences add to my knowledge about a B&B. You may write to me at The Globe Pequot Press, P.O. Box 480, Guilford, CT 06437.

Happy traveling!

The prices and rates listed in this guidebook were confirmed at press time. We recommend, however, that you call establishments before traveling to obtain current information.

How to Use This Guidebook

General Information

This guidebook contains more than 200 B&Bs in the geographic area that makes up the Mid-Atlantic region—Delaware, Maryland, New Jersey, New York, Pennsylvania, Virginia, Washington D.C., and West Virginia.

The B&Bs in this guide are alphabetized according to town in each state. You will find a map of the state in front of each chapter. Each B&B is identified by a number on the map, and a legend beside the map indicates the town it's located in. It is usually easiest to decide on your destination and then to read the write-up about each B&B in that area to decide where you want to stay. Several popular geographic areas and the B&Bs located within them are listed in the back indexes.

If you are traveling with children, or with a wheelchair-bound person, or with pets, you will also find an index in the back that identifies B&Bs that offer the necessary facilities that will best accommodate you.

For the most part, I believe travelers today prefer a room with a private bath, so all the B&Bs in this book, with a few clearly identified exceptions, have rooms with private baths. In addition, with each B&B description you will find a list of such important details as size, rates, amenities, and policies.

Some Specifics About Rates

The rates in this book are based on double occupancy, and although innkeepers were asked to provide their 2000 rates, you may find slight differences. It is always best to ask for the exact rate when you book—and be sure to ask if the rate includes all taxes, gratuities, and service charges. B&Bs will often require a deposit to hold the room. You should also ask about and understand the B&B's policy about refunds in case you are unable to go when planned.

 Also for those who would like to stay at a B&B and spend $100 or less for a double-occupancy room, look for the Best Buy icon near the name of the establishment.

What's Nearby

To help you plan your trip, I have identified some of the major attractions near each B&B. In some cases, this information is supplemented by details in the write-up about the inn. Although this data may be helpful when planning your itinerary, be sure to also ask the innkeeper about his or her specific suggestions. In several areas (the Amish/Mennonite section of Pennsylvania and the Gettysburg battlefield area in particular), innkeepers may suggest specific guides to take you on a personalized tour. Often innkeepers will also be able to direct you to local homes where quilts are made, or to an artist's studio, or they can arrange dinner in a local home, or make special arrangements for you to tour a farm or historic house.

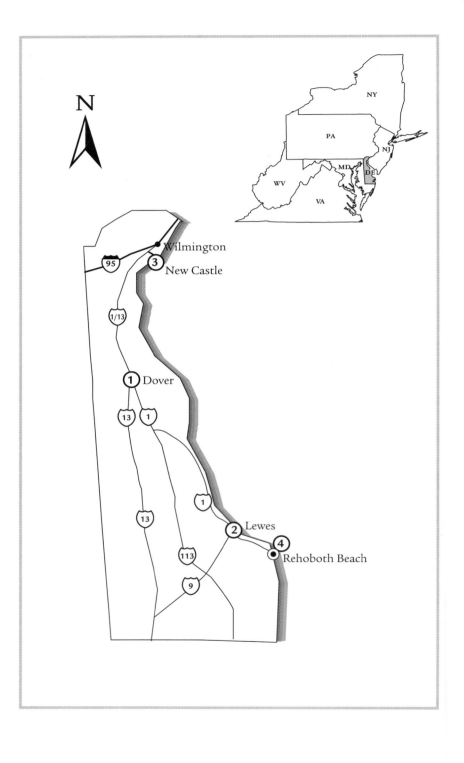

Numbers on map refer to towns numbered below.

Little Creek Inn Bed & Breakfast

2623 North Little Creek Road
Dover, DE 19901
(302) 730–1300

FAX: (302) 730–4070

INNKEEPERS: Carol and Bob Thomas

ROOMS: 4, all with private bath, air conditioning, TV, private line telephone with dataport, desk, and robes; 2 with whirlpool tub

ON THE GROUNDS: On 8 acres, swimming pool, gardens

EXTRAS: Dinner served to B&B guests; parking on premises; fax available; two yellow Labradors, Sir and Spot, on premises

RATES: $100–$125 single occupancy, $200–$225 double occupancy, including full breakfast and dinner with wine; mid-week corporate discounts

CREDIT CARDS ACCEPTED: MasterCard and Visa

OPEN: Year-round

HOW TO GET THERE: From I-95 take exit 4 onto Route 1/13 south to Dover. In Dover take Route 8 east for 2 miles. (In Dover Route 8 is called Division Street, but later it becomes North Little Creek Road.) The house will be visible on the left down a tree-lined drive.

None of this was planned, but then the best things in life often aren't. Carol and Bob Thomas had sold their bed-and-breakfast and restaurant in the Hamptons and had just completed an unsuccessful tour of North

Carolina and Virginia looking for a grand old house to convert to a bed-and-breakfast. A severe thunderstorm had canceled the Cape May-Lewes ferry, so they drove in a pouring rainstorm toward Wilmington. Arriving in Dover, they headed for the nearest hotel to spend the night. The next morning, they awoke to sunshine and decided to do some exploring. During a journey down a side road they spotted a FOR SALE sign on a grand but derelict house. This prompted a call to the realtor, and soon they were the owners.

The house, a gracious 1860 Italianate, sits on eight acres that were once part of William Penn's original land grant. It was the centerpiece of the George Parris Farm and it's still surrounded by verdant farmland. The house is listed on the National Register of Historic Places. The elegant house has wide eaves supported by decorative corbels and tall windows flanked by shutters. There's a lovely front porch supported by columns and containing a wicker swing for two. The Thomases opened it as a bed-and-breakfast early in 1999.

Carol is an interior designer and an antiques appraiser. She's filled the house with fine pieces of antique furniture that give it an authentic mid-1800s ambience. Guests are directed to the handsome lounge by a brass and silver light rescued from Carnegie Hall. The beige-and-taupe room contains elegant upholstered settees and chairs, antique Bombay chests, and rich Oriental rugs on polished pine floors. A gilt, neoclassical mirror with phoenixes on the top rises above the fireplace to the 11-foot ceilings.

Carol has filled the bedrooms with graceful antiques, as well as high-quality reproduction pieces. There are four-poster cherry Amish beds and sleigh beds. The most dramatic room is the appropriately named Blue Room, which has navy blue walls with white trim. A Chinese rug covers the pine floors, and a four-poster bed is dressed in creamy white linens. A beautiful blue-and-white wing chair and ottoman offer a snug reading oasis. The baths are all lavish and modern. They have polished pine floors and pedestal sinks with polished brass fixtures. Two of the rooms have whirlpool tubs as well as glass-enclosed showers. There are plush terry bathrobes and thick towels.

In one respect this is not a bed-and-breakfast at all, but a country inn. Bob is an acclaimed chef who had his own restaurant for thirty years, and it's hard to get a good chef out of the kitchen (why would you want to?). He prepares a gourmet dinner for overnight guests that is served in the pretty soft yellow formal dining room, which also has a fireplace. A pewter chandelier and silver sconces cast diffused light. He might prepare an entree of rack of lamb with roasted vegetables and a dessert of flourless chocolate cake with raspberry coulis topped with shaved white chocolate. Fine red and white wines that complement the dishes are set out so that guests can help themselves.

A full breakfast is also served to B&B guests. Bob is noted for his home-made French bread, so his morning French toast is especially popular.

What's Nearby—Dover

Dover is the capital of Delaware, and the Delaware State House, which dates to 1792, is the second-oldest capitol building in continuous use in the United States. Interesting exhibits tell its history. Dover is also the home of the Delaware State Museum Complex, a group of three museums devoted to Delaware's history. The Meetinghouse Gallery I houses rotating exhibits about life in Delaware, and the Meetinghouse Gallery II is a showcase for turn-of-the-century crafts. The Johnson Victrola Museum offers a tribute to Delaware resident Eldridge Reeves Johnson, who invented the Victor Talking Machine; it is designed to look like a 1920s Victrola dealer's store.

The Bay Moon Bed & Breakfast **Best Buy**

128 Kings Highway
Lewes, DE 19958
(800) 917-2307 (pager) or (302) 644-1802

FAX: (302) 644-1802
E-MAIL: Baymoon@dmv.com
WEB SITE: www.lewes.com/baymoon
INNKEEPER: Pamela J. Rizzo
ROOMS: 4, all with private bath, air conditioning, cable TV, radio, and hair dryer; crib and VCR available
ON THE GROUNDS: Gardens; deck; hot tub; off-street parking
EXTRAS: Evening hors d'oeuvres and wine in bar; telephone and fax available
RATES: $85–$150, double occupancy, including full breakfast; two-night minimum summer and holidays
CREDIT CARDS ACCEPTED: American Express, MasterCard, Visa
OPEN: Year-round
HOW TO GET THERE: From Wilmington, follow Route 13 south to Dover. Then take Route 113 south almost to Milford. North of Milford, take

Route 1 south toward Lewes and follow the signs for the Cape May/Lewes Ferry. At the junction with Route 9E (which is Kings Highway) turn right and follow it east for 1 mile. The B&B will be on the left.

Remember when you were a child and your parents pasted glow-in-the-dark stars on the ceiling to keep the boogeyman away? It's not that you'll be afraid of the dark at The Bay Moon, but you'll appreciate the tranquility of this lovely B&B when you gaze at the constellations on the ceiling of the room called the New Moon.

Due to the happy coincidence of its heritage, this is one of the most impressive inns in Delaware. The first thing you'll notice when you enter the foyer is the abundance of highly polished golden oak found throughout the inn. It's featured in wall paneling, fireplace mantels, flooring, and furniture. Most of the oak was installed by John Paganis, an old-world carpenter who owned the house from 1971 to 1995. He salvaged paneling from banks, mantels from old houses, and other architectural pieces wherever he found them and installed them throughout his home. Today we are all able to appreciate the burnished oak graining as well as Mr. Paganis's craftsmanship. The home became a B&B in 1995.

The common rooms are charming. The living room has an antique oak rolltop desk and an 1800s spinning wheel. A double-sided wood-burning fireplace casts warmth on both the living room and the breakfast room. The den is equipped with games, videos, and books. A TV and VCR are ready to entertain. In the tiny back bar (naturally, of carved oak) wines are enjoyed in the evening as guests become acquainted.

The theme throughout the inn is a celestial one because "it was the moon reflecting over the water" that caused Pamela and her husband Albert to move here. Guest rooms have such names as Full Moon and Blue Moon, and each has its own private bath, although two are off the common hallway. Blue Moon has an entire wall of oak paneling that serves as backdrop for the bed, but other rooms have handcrafted wrought-iron, antique, or wicker beds. Fluffy down comforters cover the beds. Each room has a television, and a VCR is available.

Pamela is a terrific cook (she's also an interior designer). You'll awake to the tantalizing aroma of freshly baked sweet potato biscuits or other quick breads. On the carved dining room table (oak, of course), you'll find juices, as well as gourmet coffee, tea, hot chocolate, and fresh fruits. An entree might consist of blueberry hotcakes with caramel sliced apples served with sugar-cured bacon or herb sausage. As a finale there might be a mixed fresh fruit cup served with a whipped cream brandy hard sauce.

In summer, guests enjoy eating either on the side porch or on the back deck, where they can admire Pamela's rose and flower gardens. An outdoor grill is particularly appreciated by fishermen, as it can be used to prepare fresh-from-the-sea evening meals.

Lewes (pronounced Lewis) offers an abundance of restaurants and activities. Nearby beaches beckon to summer tourists, and Pamela has thoughtfully provided all the equipment: beach chairs, towels, coolers, and even a fully stocked refrigerator from which to fill the cooler.

Following a day at the beach, you might sit on the back deck in the evening as we did, savoring the scent of the roses and watching the rising moon and the stars twinkle above. Or, if you're so inclined, you can don a fluffy terry cloth robe and enjoy the refreshing warmth of the outdoor hot tub while you try to capture a bay moonbeam or two.

What's Nearby—Lewes

Lewes was founded in 1631 by the Dutch, and the Zwaanendael Museum offers an interesting excursion into the Dutch era. It's in a building that is a replica of the town hall of Hoorn, Holland, and contains historical exhibits that trace the history of the area from the first colony to the present. The Lewes Historical Complex is a collection of old buildings furnished to reflect the era in which they were built. In addition, the Queen Anne's Railroad, a steam train, offers rides into the countryside, and a number of excursion boats take groups fishing, whale watching, and sightseeing. At Cape Henlopen State Park, you can swim or sit on the sandy beach, picnic, hike, crab, and fish.

Blue Water House Best Buy

407 East Market Street
Lewes, DE 19958
(800) 493–2080 or (302) 645–7832

FAX: (302) 644–0824
E-MAIL: bwh@lewes-beach.com
WEB SITE: www@lewes-beach.com
INNKEEPERS: Chuck and Karen Ulrich
ROOMS: 6, all with private bath, air conditioning, radio, and balcony; 5 with television; crib available

ON THE GROUNDS: Patios; hammock; picnic table; grill; bicycles; beach chairs; boogie boards

RATES: $80–$160, double occupancy, including Continental breakfast; two-night minimum weekends; three-night minimum holiday weekends

CREDIT CARDS ACCEPTED: MasterCard and Visa

OPEN: Year-round

HOW TO GET THERE: From Wilmington, follow Route 13 south to Dover. Then take Route 113 south almost to Milford. North of Milford, take Route 1 south toward Lewes and follow the signs for the Cape May/Lewes Ferry. At junction of Routes 1 and 9, follow Route 9 (which becomes Savannah Road) into Lewes. Continue on Savannah Road through the traffic light and across the bridge. Turn left at the first intersection onto Angler's Road. Turn right in 1 block onto East Market Street. The B&B is on the right.

The style of Blue Water House is faintly reminiscent of a lighthouse, perched as it is on stilts above the marsh. The house, which has a weathered shingle exterior trimmed with bright gold and turquoise, is surrounded by reeds that shelter a variety of birds. There are patios with picnic tables and benches and also a pond on the ground level. A bevy of bicycles awaits pedalers.

Chuck and Karen Ulrich built their B&B in 1993, and the guestrooms, which are all on the third floor, are spacious and bright. Chuck is an architect and a charter boat captain, and his love of the sea and of fine craftsmanship are intertwined in the B&B he designed. Wide windows flood the rooms with light (sunrises and sunsets are particularly memorable), and each room has French doors that provide access to the wraparound deck, which is encircled by a picket-fence railing.

The spacious rooms are decorated with modern furnishings. You'll find no fancy headboards on the beds here. In fact, there are no headboards at all—merely bright splashes of sherbet colors (one is orange; another lime) defining the placement of the bed. The baths are finished in white tiles.

The Lookout, an enclosed top-floor deck with wraparound windows, is a favorite guest retreat. There's a big-screen TV up here, a selection of books, and wicker chairs gaily covered in bright fabrics. The panorama of the ocean, which seems to stretch "from sea to shining sea," is particularly impressive. You can see the Cape Henlopen lighthouse and the Cape May ferry approaching and departing. The Ulriches have thoughtfully placed a wet bar and refrigerator up here as well. Guests come here to have wine or a cocktail after returning from the beach (or perhaps from a fishing expedition with Captain Chuck) to discuss local restaurants, to read, or just to talk.

Breakfast is served on the second floor, where the Ulriches and their children, Kayla and Charlie, live. An array of freshly made breads (perhaps a coconut-pineapple or an apricot-almond), fresh fruits, juices, and cereals are laid out on the kitchen counter, and guests may help themselves. This very "child-friendly" inn also has an adjoining children's game room with TV, where kids can watch videos or play games while the adults enjoy a more leisurely breakfast.

The B&B is located across the bridge that spans the Lewes-Rehoboth Canal, a short distance from downtown. Lewes is an interesting little seafaring village with a past—it dates to 1631, when the Dutch were the first to land here. The collection of shops in town range from those specializing in fine antiques to clothing, cafes, and bakeries. It's a short bicycle ride to the unspoiled ocean beaches at Cape Henlopen.

This casual, easy-going, bring-the-kids B&B is the ideal place to come when you feel like dressing down instead of up and yet want to enjoy the convenience of modern bedrooms and baths.

What's Nearby

See "What's Nearby—Lewes," page 5.

Armitage Inn

2 The Strand
New Castle, DE 19720
(302) 328–6618

FAX: (302) 324–1163

E-MAIL: armitageinn@earthlink.net

INNKEEPERS: Stephen and Rina Marks

ROOMS: 5, including one suite, all with private bath (2 with shower only) and TV, telephone with dataport, air conditioning, radio, hair dryer, and desk; 2 with fireplace

ON THE GROUNDS: Walled garden

EXTRAS: 3 rooms with whirlpool; fax available

RATES: $105–$150, double occupancy, including full breakfast; two-night minimum from April through October

CREDIT CARDS ACCEPTED: American Express, Discover, MasterCard, Visa

OPEN: Year-round

HOW TO GET THERE: Traveling on I–95, take exit 5A (if coming from the south, take I–295 toward New Jersey and take exit 5A) onto Delaware Route 141 south. At the intersection of Routes 9 and 273, turn north onto Route 9 and travel for ½ mile. Bear right to New Castle via Delaware Street. Continue on Delaware Street through the village to The Strand. The inn is on the right.

The Strand, a grassy common bordering the Delaware River, serves as the spacious backyard of Armitage Inn, a handsome brick Federal house with portions that date to the 1600s. Looking much as it did during the American Revolution when owner Zachariah Van Leuvenigh offered hospitality to post riders bringing news from the battlefront, the house was converted to a gracious B&B by owners Steve and Rina Marks in 1995.

Guests enter a spacious hallway with polished red-pine floors and a sweeping staircase leading to the second floor. The first-floor common rooms include a parlor with a fireplace, which is furnished in fine period antiques. Beyond, there's a handsome library with floor-to-ceiling bookcases on all four walls. The oldest room in the house, dating to the 1600s and still containing the original cooking fireplace and beehive oven, is used as the office. Doors lead from the library to a screened porch and a walled garden, which contains a quaint little cottage where the owners live. On the opposite side of the hall, there's a formal dining room.

In the generous bedrooms guests can enjoy views of the river while snuggled into canopy beds dressed with down pillows and comforters. Televisions are tucked away in period armoires; telephones with modem connections sit beside the beds. Two of the rooms have elegant decorative fireplaces. The private baths (three with whirlpools) are finished with marble and tile. My favorite room is the White Rose Room, which has a nook with windows overlooking The Strand and the Delaware River. I can imagine Mr. Van Leuvenigh watching the river traffic from this spot.

A scrumptious full breakfast is served in the formal dining room each morning. In addition to fresh fruit, juices, and coffee, guests might be treated to an apple-peach crisp or angel cakes (feathery-light little pancakes that incorporate fruit and nuts in the batter and are served with maple syrup) or to maple-cream cheese pastries, a sweet breakfast treat in which a buttery dough is wrapped around a cream cheese mixture, baked, topped with a syrupy maple/brown sugar mixture, and baked a bit more.

New Castle is a gift from the past. It was laid out by Peter Stuyvesant in 1651, and William Penn first landed here in 1681. The narrow brick sidewalks are still lighted by flickering street lamps at night. Antiques shops, restaurants, handsome brick public buildings, taverns, and elegant old houses line the streets just as they did in days of yore. The village green, which was once a parade ground, is bordered by an arsenal built during the War of 1812 that now serves as a fine restaurant.

What's Nearby—New Castle

New Castle has several interesting museums to visit. The Amstel House, a 1730s gem, was the home of Governor Van Dyke, while the George Read II House and Garden dates to the 1840s. Both are furnished with lovely period antiques. The Old Court House once served as the meeting place of the Colonial Assembly before the capital was moved to Dover. Its handsome facade, crowned by a cupola, still dominates the center of town. The Dutch House and the Old Library Museum offer glimpses into New Castle's history.

Fox Lodge at Lesley Manor

123 West 7th Street
New Castle, DE 19720
(302) 328–0768

INNKEEPERS: William and Elaine Class

ROOMS: 3, including 1 suite, all with private bath, air conditioning, radio, coffeemaker, and desk

ON THE GROUNDS: Croquet, bocci, gardens

EXTRAS: A Tonkinese cat named Istuan Sändor and another cat, Elvis Orbeson

RATES: $105–$185, double occupancy, including full breakfast and afternoon snacks; two-night minimum weekends

CREDIT CARDS ACCEPTED: MasterCard and Visa

OPEN: Year-round

HOW TO GET THERE: Traveling on I–95 take exit 5A (if coming from the south, take I–295 toward New Jersey and take exit 5A) onto Delaware Route 141 south. At the intersection of Routes 9 and 273, turn north onto Route 9 and travel for ½ mile. Bear right to New Castle via Delaware Street. Continue to 7th Street and turn right. The B&B will be at the end of the street in 2 blocks on the left.

he grandest house in New Castle, an 1855 Gothic Revival mansion with thirty-three rooms, was built by the Lesley family and is known locally as "The Castle." Its embellishments include a fanciful turret, gingerbread-trimmed gables, a slate roof, and stained glass. Eventually, its condition deteriorated, and it was deserted and neglected when spied by William and Elaine Class in 1994. It took their vision (William loves architectural history) and Elaine's artistic wizardry (she is an interior designer, artist, and gardener) to transform the magnificent but derelict house into the gracious B&B that they opened in 1996.

It also took a tremendous amount of work. The outside is now painted from top to bottom (a considerable distance) in a honey/buff color with rust trim that highlights the angles and arched windows. Frankly, I have been watching the transformation of the mansion for more than two years, and only on my visit in early 1997 did I feel it was sufficiently complete to be recommended to readers. Even then, the entry hall and staircase leading to the guest rooms as well as the dining room had not been restored, but I was assured that they soon would be. Istuan Sändor, the house Tonkinese cat, will see to that.

The first floor parlor, which is entered through a massive pair of faux oak pocket doors, has a bay window with louvered wooden shutters at one end, a majestic carved white marble fireplace, walls color-washed in harlequin diamonds and sparkled with gold, and a massive ornate cast bronze chandelier hanging from the 13-foot ceiling. At check-in time a cute piglet statue may be sitting on the buffet to guard the plate of fruit, meat, cheese, cookies, and wine or beer waiting for her guests.

In the dining room, which has an elaborately carved burled walnut fireplace, the original embossed anaglyphic paper still hangs on the walls. A buffet breakfast of fresh fruit, juice, freshly baked breakfast breads, and cereal is laid out every morning, but if a guest wants a larger breakfast, Elaine might fix a fruit soup (such as chilled cherry), smoked meat or fish, or rice pudding.

The guest rooms and suite are located on the second floor, reached by climbing (there is no elevator) the tall staircase with its elaborate Gothic railing. A room-sized landing at the top contains sofas and chairs and a collection of local menus for perusing.

Each of the spacious rooms is artfully designed for comfort as well as serenity. In Jane, there's an elaborate fireplace mantel (alas, it is decorative only) and a headboard that incorporates peeled yucca poles and rope. A birdcage canopy, draped with gauzy fabric, hangs behind. Even on the second floor the ceilings reach to 12½ feet, creating rooms that seem even larger than they are. Tall windows flood the rooms with light and also offer views of the various gardens.

Gardens ring the house and include a rose, herb, and vegetable variety as well as a medieval privy garden. There are benches for reading or just for watching the bees and butterflies flit from flower to flower. On the front lawn guests may enjoy a game of croquet or bocci.

The inn is approximately 6 blocks from the downtown shops and restaurants, a pleasant stroll along the water or past village houses.

What's Nearby

See "What's Nearby—New Castle," page 9.

The Mallard Guest House

60 Baltimore Avenue
Rehoboth Beach, DE 19971
(888) 872-0644 or (302) 226-3448

E-MAIL: guest@themallard.com

WEB SITE: www.themallard.com

INNKEEPER: Russell Stuckey; manager, Bob Redden

ROOMS: 17, all with private bath, air conditioning, and radio; 4 with private balcony, TV, desk, mini-refrigerator, and whirlpool tub

ON THE GROUNDS: Hot tubs, parking

EXTRAS: A cat named Tiger Ru

RATES: $85–$295, including Continental breakfast; two-night minimum weekends Memorial Day to Labor Day; three-night minimum summer holiday weekends

CREDIT CARDS ACCEPTED: MasterCard and Visa

OPEN: Year-round

SMOKING: On porches and balconies only

HOW TO GET THERE: From Delaware Route 1 turn off onto Rehoboth Avenue (Route 1A) and follow this into Rehoboth Beach. Turn left onto 2nd Avenue and go 1 block. The B&B will be on the right, on the corner of 2nd and Baltimore Avenues.

The Mallard Guest House is not your typical beachy seaside bed-and-breakfast. For one thing, although it's got its casual moments, it is definitely the classiest place to stay in this swinging beachside village. Partly this is because the owners, in their former lives, ran successful real estate and interior design businesses in power-town, Washington, D.C. They know that even when folks relax, they want the creature comforts of modern private baths and comfortable beds dressed in luxurious fabrics.

The Mallard is composed of three turn-of-the-century houses that have been meticulously restored but still retain their old-world character. There are tall ceilings, classical moldings, and decorative fireplaces. The heart of the establishment is a yellow clapboard structure with white trim on the corner of Baltimore and 2nd Avenues—near Rehoboth's finest shops and restaurants—and merely 2 blocks from the boardwalk and the ocean. The other two houses are located side by side in a quiet residential section close to the beach.

Each of the houses has a relaxing living room with upholstered furniture and duck and hunt prints on the walls. The main building has a living room with pine floors and area rugs. Several antique tables and chests mingle with beautiful chairs and sofas clothed in lush fabrics, to offer an inviting place to read, or visit, or perhaps watch a video from the library. A side porch contains an outdoor Jacuzzi, and upstairs there's an expansive private sunporch.

An expanded Continental breakfast is served buffet-style in the stunning open kitchen, which has marble tile floors and granite countertops. Each of the houses has its own kitchen so that guests can have breakfast in the comfort of their own house. You might partake of freshly baked pastries, French toast, fresh fruits, and cereals.

The guest rooms feature antique beds and pretty fabrics. Room #2 in the main house is intimate and sophisticated. It has a four-poster black iron canopy bed and rust-colored walls. Upstairs, Room #3 contains a massive antique oak bed and wardrobe, and it's decorated in pale yellow and rose. One of my favorites, however, is Room #5, which has a private balcony, a Jenny Lind bed, and a lovely yellow needlepoint rug on the floor. All of the baths contain tile floors and tile tub or shower surrounds. Several include Jacuzzi tubs.

What's Nearby—Rehoboth Beach

People come to Rehoboth Beach for, naturally, the beaches and to walk its boardwalk—lined with interesting shops, restaurants, pizza shops, and amusement arcades. But once the sun goes down, what's to do? A lot, it turns out—Rehoboth Beach is a swinging, rocking town. Lighted beach volleyball courts provide nighttime frolicking. The Rehoboth Art League and the Henlopen Theatre Project offer high-class cultural events, and the bars throb with disco and jazz music late into the night. The boardwalk becomes a grand seaside promenade, with people greeting, meeting, and being seen.

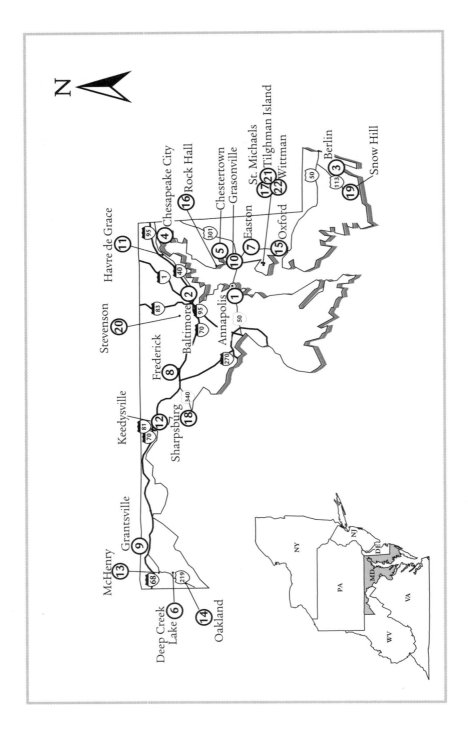

Maryland

Numbers on map refer to towns numbered below.

1. Annapolis,
   55 East Bed and Breakfast, 16
   The Gatehouse Bed &
     Breakfast, 18
   Georgian House Bed
     & Breakfast, 19
   The Jonas Green House Bed
     & Breakfast, 21
   Maryrob Bed and Breakfast, 23
   Two-O-One Bed & Breakfast, 24
   William Page Inn Bed &
     Breakfast, 26

2. Baltimore,
   Ann Street Bed & Breakfast, 28
   Celie's Waterfront Bed &
     Breakfast, 30
   Mr. Mole Bed & Breakfast, 32

3. Berlin, Merry Sherwood
   Plantation, 34

4. Chesapeake City,
   The Blue Max Inn, 36
   Inn at the Canal, 38
   Ship Watch Inn, 40

5. Chestertown,
   Brampton Inn, 41
   Great Oak Manor Bed &
     Breakfast, 43
   The White Swan Tavern, 45

6. Deep Creek Lake, Carmel
   Cove Inn, 47

7. Easton, Ashby 1663, 49

8. Frederick,
   Middle Plantation Inn, 51
   Tyler-Spite Inn, 52

9. Grantsville, Elliott House
   Victorian Inn, 54

10. Grasonville, Lands End Manor
    on the Bay, 57

11. Havre de Grace,
    Currier House B&B, 59
    The Spencer-Silver Mansion, 61

12. Keedysville, Antietam Overlook
    Farm Bed & Breakfast, 62

13. McHenry, Lake Pointe Inn
    Bed & Breakfast, 64

14. Oakland, The Oak & Apple Bed
    & Breakfast, 66

15. Oxford, Combsberry, 68

16. Rock Hall, Moonlight Bay Inn
    & Marina, 70

17. St. Michaels,
    Dr. Dodson House Bed &
      Breakfast, 72
    Hambleton Inn, 74
    The Old Brick Inn, 75
    The Tarr House B&B, 77

18. Sharpsburg, The Inn at
    Antietam, 79

19. Snow Hill, The River House
    Inn, 81

20. Stevenson, Gramercy Mansion
    Bed & Breakfast, 83

21. Tilghman Island, Lazyjack
    Inn, 85

22. Wittman, The Inn at
    Christmas Farm, 87

55 East Bed and Breakfast

55 East Street
Annapolis, MD 21401
(410) 295-0202

FAX: (410) 295-0203

E-MAIL: triciah@erols.com

WEB SITE: www.annearundelcounty.
com/hotel/55east.htm

INNKEEPERS: Tricia and Mat Herban

ROOMS: 3, all with private bath, air
conditioning, radio, hair dryer, robes, and dataport; 2 with fireplace,
private porch, and whirlpool tub

ON THE GROUNDS: Enclosed courtyard with fountain

EXTRAS: Telephone jack in all rooms; fax available; space for small meetings; homemade cookies in evening; half-price coupon for parking in
public garage; West Highland terrier, Mr. Wags, on premises.

RATES: $120-$150, including full breakfast; two-night minimum weekends; discounts for weekday stays of three-plus days

CREDIT CARDS ACCEPTED: MasterCard and Visa

OPEN: Year-round, except for a month in January or February

HOW TO GET THERE: From US Route 50 take exit 24 onto Rowe Boulevard
south. Stay on Rowe Boulevard for 1½ miles until it ends at the Maryland State House. Turn left onto College Avenue and then turn right
onto King George Street. Immediately after passing Gate 1 of the Naval
Academy, turn right onto East Street; 55 East Street is the third house on
the left after crossing Prince George Street.

5 5 East has all the gracious elements that I look for in a great bed-and-breakfast. There are stunning but comfortable common rooms; bedrooms and baths thoughtfully conceived to provide guest serenity; and
friendly, cordial innkeepers who are genuinely concerned that their guests
have a congenial stay.

Located in the heart of Annapolis and an easy walk to restaurants,
shops, and the U.S. Naval Academy, the 1864 Italianate Federal building
was originally a store on the ground floor with lodging upstairs for the family. The main floor bears little resemblance to a store today, however. Guests
enter a wide entry hall with pine floors. To the right a warm living room has
beautiful peach-toned crewel carpets and an ornate fireplace with a mantel

from New Orleans. A Japanese living room, just beyond, is entered through twin columns. The dramatic jade-colored walls are outlined by stark white trim and the walls are hung with Japanese prints. A cypress-wood mantel and a rolltop desk complete the cozy decor. A pretty side deck includes a brick fountain. Throughout the inn engaging examples of Mat's crayon art chronicle the couple's journeys to distant lands and highlight his beautiful interpretations of local landscapes and gardens.

The guest rooms are stunning. The Charles Russell Room has a striking antique Victorian high-headboard bed and a private porch. The bath has a tile floor and a raised tub, as well as a separate shower. An antique dresser with a granite top serves as a vanity. The Mary Slavin Johnson Room includes an antique cannonball bed, a gas stove, and a pine dresser, as well as a private porch. The bath includes another pretty dresser with a granite top that serves as a vanity.

Every amenity for guest comfort has been considered in this classy B&B. Tricia has provided plush lined robes and beautiful padded hangers in the closets. A variety of luxury soaps and body sprays are offered in the bathrooms. There are stemmed glasses and ice buckets beside an ice maker in the hall. In the evening, freshly baked cookies are put out.

Breakfast is served in the formal dining room on one of four sets of china, depending on the entree of the day. Linens are chosen to complement the china, and fine silver and crystal are used as well. Tricia is a fabulous cook. A typical repast might consist of orange juice, followed by toasted pecan/corn waffles topped with strawberry/orange syrup and served with Canadian bacon and sautéed apples.

What's Nearby—Annapolis

The U.S. Naval Academy, covering thirty acres on the banks of the Severn River, was founded in 1845. Visitors can visit the chapel and see where John Paul Jones is buried as well as watch the plebes (new recruits) perform their noontime drill on the quadrangle. In addition, the Maryland State House, which was built in 1772, is the oldest U.S. state capitol building in continuous use in America. It contains a museum devoted to Annapolis history during Colonial times. The William Paca House and Garden, the Hammond-Harwood House, and several other historic homes are open for touring.

The Gatehouse Bed & Breakfast

249 Hanover Street
Annapolis, MD 21401
(410) 280-0024

WEB SITE: www.bbchannel.com

INNKEEPERS: Rene Cunningham and Gerry Van De Velde

ROOMS: 5, 4 with private bath, one with shared bath, all with air conditioning, TV, and robes; portable telephone available on second-floor hallway

ON THE GROUNDS: Enclosed patio

EXTRAS: Parking on premises; basket of fruit and bottled water in rooms; decanter of sherry in living room; chocolates on pillow at turndown; a dog, Gus, and two cats, Scooper and Sam, on premises

RATES: $95–$150, double occupancy, including full breakfast; two-night minimum weekends April–October.

CREDIT CARDS ACCEPTED: MasterCard and Visa

OPEN: Year-round except Easter and Christmas

HOW TO GET THERE: From Route 50 take exit 24 onto Rowe Boulevard south. Follow Rowe Boulevard for 1½ miles until it ends at the Maryland State House. Turn left onto College Avenue and follow this for 1½ blocks to the traffic light. Turn right onto King George Street. Go 1 block to Maryland Avenue and turn left. Go 1 block to Hanover Street and turn left again. The B&B will be on the left.

Unlike many Annapolis B&Bs that trace their building's heritage to the 1700s or 1800s, The Gatehouse was built in 1963. But the brick Georgian-style townhouse blends so seamlessly with its neighbors that it appears to have the same lineage as the rest. It's on a quiet side street across from the U.S. Naval Academy and a block from St. John's College.

Rene, who was formerly an advertising executive in Washington, D.C., and Gerry, who still owns a Washington-based advertising firm, purchased their home in 1993 and have been operating it as a bed-and-breakfast ever since. A sociable parlor includes sofas and chairs and a pretty Oriental carpet on oak floors. The adjacent dining room includes a handsome sideboard and a brick fireplace that covers an entire wall.

The guest rooms, which are located upstairs, are crisp and neat. They are equipped with elegant period reproduction furniture. The Anne Arundel room includes a four-poster rice bed, while the Capitol View room has a Mount Mitchell sleigh bed and a view of the capitol dome, which is lighted at night. The white tile bath is immaculate. I love the feminine confection called Compass Rose, which is all done up in eyelet fabric and rose wallpaper. The white iron bed is perfect for a child traveling with parents, but this room is only rented in concert with College Walk, as these rooms then share the bath. Both Academy and College Walk have private baths in the hall.

Breakfast is a congenial event characterized by lively conversation with a backdrop of classical music. A fire glows in the hearth in winter. Rene prepares a full breakfast. Among her most popular dishes are the cream cheese and ice cream French toast served with fresh berries and bananas Foster, although she often fixes a special quiche or eggs Benedict as well.

What's Nearby

See "What's Nearby—Annapolis," page 17.

Georgian House Bed & Breakfast

170 Duke of Gloucester Street
Annapolis, MD 21401
(800) 557–2068 or (410) 263–5618
(fax same)

E-MAIL: georgian@erols.com

WEB SITE: www.georgianhouse.com

INNKEEPERS: Dan and Michele Brown

ROOMS: 4, including one suite, all with private bath, air conditioning, hair dryer, and robes; 3 with telephone and dataport; 2 with TV and VCR; one with balcony and fireplace

ON THE GROUNDS: Two patios

EXTRAS: Dry bar and refrigerator

RATES: $115–$185, double occupancy, including full breakfast; two-night minimum weekends

CREDIT CARDS ACCEPTED: American Express, MasterCard, Visa

OPEN: Year-round

HOW TO GET THERE: From Route 50 take exit 24 onto Rowe Boulevard south. Follow Rowe Boulevard for 1½ miles until it ends at the Maryland State House. Turn right onto College Avenue and follow the route around Church Circle to Duke of Gloucester Street. Turn right. The B&B is on the left in 2 blocks.

This elegant and refined Georgian house has witnessed much of Annapolis's history. Its walls seem to whisper with the sounds of the past. It was built in 1747 and soon housed the Forensic Club, a gentlemen's organization whose members met every two weeks to discuss the philosophical subjects of the day. Topics ranged from whether it was morally lawful to keep slaves to whether aristocracy or democracy was the best form of government. The meetings included dinner and drink, and they were attended by the leaders of the day, many of whom were later to sign the Declaration of Independence.

The character of this grand old house, which was converted to a bed and breakfast in 1993, has been faithfully retained by Dan and Michele, although they have chosen to decorate with reproduction pieces rather than antiques. Guests enter a handsome living room, where the lustrous original pine floors have recently been refinished. It contains a beautiful fireplace with its original 1770s Annapolis artisans-carved mantel. A table with a marble top and clawfoot feet and a Chippendale-style piece decorate the room. A little sitting room has another fireplace and a secretary that's a reproduction of a James River plantation article. Original artwork by local artists decorates the walls.

There are three guest rooms on the second floor and one on the third. The largest is the Thomas Stone room—a spacious two-room suite. It includes a rice-carved reproduction four-poster bed and a living room with a gas fireplace. The bath has a clawfoot tub, a pedestal sink, and pine floors. The romantically decorated Samuel Chase room has a sleigh bed and a private deck overlooking the gardens. The bath has a tile floor and a pedestal sink.

Depending on the weather, breakfast is served either in the creamy formal dining room beside a glowing fire in the massive fireplace or on the brick patio. It may include a vegetable frittata, a breakfast pizza, or maybe a baked French toast entree.

Dan is a graduate of the U.S. Naval Academy, so he knows all the hidden pathways and gardens of Annapolis, as well as little-known museums and shops. Be sure to ask his expert advice about sights to see during your stay.

What's Nearby

See "What's Nearby—Annapolis," page 17.

The Jonas Green House Bed & Breakfast

Best Buy

124 Charles Street
Annapolis, MD 21401
(410) 263-5892

FAX: (410) 263-5895
E-MAIL: jghouse@erols.com
WEB SITE: www.bbchannel.
com/jghouse

INNKEEPERS: Dede and Randy Brown

ROOMS: 3, 1 with private bath, 2 sharing one bath; all with air conditioning, radio, hair dryer, and robes; 2 with fireplace; telephone available in living room

ON THE GROUNDS: Front porch

EXTRAS: Parking on premises; sherry offered in the living room; two black Labradors, Noel and Ceramic, and one Siamese cat, Kuhfu, on premises; pets permitted with prior permission

RATES: $90–$120, double occupancy, including full breakfast; two-night minimum weekends; three-night minimum boat show weekends

CREDIT CARDS ACCEPTED: American Express, Discover, MasterCard, Visa

OPEN: February–December

HOW TO GET THERE: From Route 50 take exit 24 onto Rowe Boulevard south. Follow Rowe Boulevard for 1½ miles until it ends at the Maryland State House. Turn right onto College Avenue and follow the route around Church Circle to Duke of Gloucester Street. Turn right. In 1 block turn right onto Charles Street. The B&B is on the left in the middle of the first block.

If an authentic Colonial ambience is what you're seeking, then The Jonas Green House is the perfect place for you to stay. Built in the 1690s the house is the second oldest in Annapolis and is on the National Register of Historic Places. Jonas Green descended from a family of printers who migrated from England in 1627; Jonas too was a printer and apprenticed himself to Benjamin Franklin. He and his wife Anne Catherine moved into the house in 1738, and, remarkable as it seems, members of the Green family have lived in the house ever since. Randy Brown is a direct Green descendant.

Because of the respect the Green family has displayed for the historical heritage of their house, many of the original features remain. The huge cooking fireplace in the kitchen dates to the 1690s, and the pine floors, paneled walls, and ten fireplaces throughout the house, are all original. Those in the family living quarters still burn logs, but for safety reasons those in the guest bedrooms have been converted to gas.

The brick and shingle house is a typical center hall Colonial. One side of the house is available for guest use, and the other side is used by the family. The guest living room, which is to the left of the hallway, has red paneling and lovely upholstered pieces mixed with fine antiques that span several periods. Fine oil portraits (a handsome one of an admiral is actually of Randy's father) hang on the walls.

The nicest guest room is the Anne Catherine Green Room, which has a working fireplace and a private bath. There's a rope bed with a wooden headboard and a lovely walnut armoire. The bath has a tile floor. The Frederick Green Room contains several family antiques. There's a beautiful antique bureau and a simple armoire that was once used by Randy's great uncle to hide his stash of liquor. The Boxing Room was originally used to store trunks and boxes. Today this room, which is utterly charming, has painted yellow pine floors and a king-size bed. The Boxing Room and the Frederick Green Room share a hall bath that includes a great old tub and a pedestal sink.

A full breakfast is served in the elegant Colonial dining room, which has a fireplace and dove gray wainscotting. Several popular entrees include an orange French toast casserole and a hearty casserole made with ham, potato soup, mushrooms, cheese, and bread cubes.

Randy is a U.S. Naval Academy graduate and a retired Naval officer, just as his father was. His family association with Annapolis and his chosen occupation give him a unique perspective on Annapolis history—a subject he loves to discuss with his guests.

What's Nearby

See "What's Nearby—Annapolis," page 17.

Maryrob Bed and Breakfast

243 Prince George Street
Annapolis, MD 21401–1631
(410) 268–5438 or (301) 858–5756

FAX: (410) 268–9623

INNKEEPERS: Mary-Stuart Taylor and Robert E. Carlson

ROOMS: 2, both with private bath, air conditioning, TV, hair dryer, robes, iron, and ironing board; 1 with fireplace and whirlpool tub; portable telephone available

ON THE GROUNDS: Parking on premises; boxwood patio garden with fountain

EXTRAS: Two small shih tzu, Jade and Monet, on premises

RATES: $95–$120, double occupancy, including full breakfast

CREDIT CARDS ACCEPTED: MasterCard and Visa

OPEN: Year-round

HOW TO GET THERE: From Route 50 take exit 24 onto Rowe Boulevard south. Follow Rowe Boulevard for 1½ miles until it ends at the Maryland State House. Turn left onto College Avenue. Continue on College Avenue to King George Street and turn right. Go 1 block to the next traffic light and turn right onto Maryland Avenue. Go 1 block to the stop sign and turn right onto Prince George Street. The B&B is on the left almost at the end of the block.

This elegant and impressive brick Victorian Italianate house with aqua trim dates to 1864. Elaborate cornices crown the tall windows, a fan light caps the paneled front door, and heavily carved corbels embellish the eaves. A pretty bay window catches the rays of the sun. The bed-and-breakfast has been owned by Mary-Stuart Taylor and Robert Carlson since 1989. Robert is a retired army colonel, who must sometimes feel like a foreigner among all these navy personnel.

As guests enter the front door, they will immediately notice the beautiful, gracefully curving staircase that sweeps to the second floor. The living room, which has a slate faux marble fireplace, is furnished with elegant period antiques that include an ornately carved walnut Victorian armchair. A fabulous crystal chandelier hangs in the dining room, and there's a marble fireplace here. Original oil paintings hang on the walls.

There are only two guest rooms in the house, but they both have private baths. Queen I has a bed with a fishnet canopy and a pine fireplace mantel. A beautiful armoire from the Andrew Jackson era complements a Queen Anne dressing table and stool. A blue-and-white Ansonia clock and Delft-like vases add decorative touches. The bath has pine floors, Palladian windows, and a huge old tub. Queen II has a bed with a padded headboard.

Breakfast is served in the dining room or in the courtyard garden, depending on the weather. Should the garden get the nod, it is an enclosed enclave of boxwood and fences that includes pretty statuary, garden benches, and a fountain overseen by a statue. Mary-Stuart's breakfasts include interesting entrees such as eggs olé (a dish she prepares with eggs, green chilies, and Monterey jack cheese) or orange-stuffed French toast.

What's Nearby

See "What's Nearby—Annapolis," page 17.

Two-O-One Bed & Breakfast

201 Prince George Street
Annapolis, MD 21401
(410) 268–8053

FAX: (410) 263–3007

E-MAIL: BBat201@aol.com

WEB SITE: www.201BB.com

INNKEEPERS: Graham W. Gardner and Robert A. Bryant

ROOMS: 4, including 2 suites, all with private bath, 27˝ TV, VCR, dataport, hair dryer, air conditioning, mini-refrigerator, robes; 2 with Jacuzzi; 1 with a fireplace and telephone

ON THE GROUNDS: Garden, off-street parking

EXTRAS: Complimentary soft drinks; fresh flowers in room; ironed sheets; Doberman named Franklin, boxer named Sailor, cockapoo named Sandy

RATES: $120–$170, double occupancy, including full breakfast; two-night minimum weekends, three-night minimum boat show weekends

CREDIT CARDS ACCEPTED: American Express, Discover, MasterCard, Visa

OPEN: Year-round

HOW TO GET THERE: From Route 50 take exit 24 (Rowe Boulevard). Follow this to its end and turn left onto College Avenue. At King George Street, turn right. At Randall Street, turn right and take the next right onto Prince George Street. The B&B will be on the left.

If you love dogs, you'll feel right at home at 201. If you don't, you probably should stay elsewhere, although then you'd miss the pleasure of staying in Annapolis's most elegant B&B. The dogs, who are sure to greet you when you arrive, include Franklin, a Doberman; Sailor, a boxer; and Sandy, a cockapoo.

Graham Gardner and Robert Bryant purchased this townhouse shaded by maple trees in 1996. Following a top-to-bottom renovation, they opened it in 1997. It is a beauty. The building's architectural features, its decor, and its antique American and English furniture are all of the finest quality.

Guests enter a formal foyer with a dining room to the left and a living room to the right. An elaborate marble fireplace decorates one wall of the seafoam-green shadow-striped walls of the dining room, while another carved marble fireplace embellishes the persimmon-colored walls of the living room. In the sunny bay overlooking the street, floor-to-ceiling bookcases offer a wealth of reading material. Gleaming oak floors are topped by elegant Oriental rugs.

Upstairs, two exquisite guest rooms and two suites each have private, thoroughly updated baths that include Italian tile floors, glass-enclosed showers, and sinks in elegant antique tables or chests; there are Jacuzzis in some baths. Museum-quality antique armoires or chests-on-chests hold 27" TVs and VCRs, and intricately carved four-poster beds are fluffed with down comforters and pillows. Every detail has been carefully planned. Fresh flowers from the cutting garden in back are placed in each room, and the fine bed linens are lightly starched and ironed.

The Queen Anne Suite is beautiful. There's a gleaming mahogany canopy bed, a 1760s chest-on-chest hiding the TV and VCR, a tiny kitchen with a mini-refrigerator and wet bar, a sitting room with its own fireplace, and a lovely view of the Capitol dome, which is lighted at night. In the Italian-tiled bath, there's a Jacuzzi and a separate glass-enclosed shower.

In 1998 a new suite, the Crow's Nest, was added to the guest rooms. It includes a fabulous carved four-poster bed and a lush sitting area. Architectural elements define the suite. The rooms have peach walls and dramatic Mark Hampton fabrics. The bath is a dream. There's a huge whirlpool tub enclosed in cherry paneling, a separate shower big enough for two, and a pink marble sink.

The spacious one-third-acre walled garden in back includes secluded sitting areas tucked among the flower beds and trees. A fountain spills from an urn into a fish pond where koi reside, and a covered courtyard contains pretty wrought iron furniture.

For breakfast, guests gather in the dining room around an antique mahogany pedestal table overseen by an 1870s crystal chandelier. Fine silverware, Irish linen napkins in silver napkin rings, and silver accessories enhance the ambience. In addition to fresh fruit, juice, and croissants, Robert may have prepared a quiche, a frittata, or his "Sunday best" French toast with orange juice and triple sec.

Annapolis offers numerous museums to visit. The 1763 William Paca House and Garden was the home of one of the signers of the Declaration of Independence. It has thirty-seven rooms decorated in period furnishings and a particularly noteworthy garden. The Hammond-Harwood House, built in 1774, offers a showcase of Georgian architecture and decorative ornamentation.

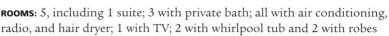

What's Nearby

See "What's Nearby—Annapolis," page 17.

William Page Inn Bed & Breakfast

8 Martin Street
Annapolis, MD 21401
(800) 364–4160 or (410) 626–1506

FAX: (410) 263–4841

E-MAIL: wmpageinn@aol.com

WEB SITE: www.williampageinn.com

INNKEEPER: Robert L. Zuchelli

ROOMS: 5, including 1 suite; 3 with private bath; all with air conditioning, radio, and hair dryer; 1 with TV; 2 with whirlpool tub and 2 with robes

ON THE GROUNDS: Parking

EXTRAS: Wet bar with coffee, sodas, juice; fax, copier; laundry, iron and ironing board available; dog named Chancellor

RATES: $95–$195 double occupancy, including full breakfast; two-night minimum weekends mid-March through November

CREDIT CARDS ACCEPTED: MasterCard and Visa

OPEN: Year-round

HOW TO GET THERE: From Route 50, take exit 24 (Rowe Boulevard). Stay on Rowe Boulevard south until it ends at the Maryland State House. Turn left onto College Avenue and continue to the traffic light. Turn right onto King George Street and continue almost to the Visitor's Gate of the U.S. Naval Academy. Turn right onto East Street. Go 1 block and turn right onto Martin Street. The B&B is on the corner.

The William Page Inn, setting a high standard in Annapolis since it opened in 1987, is in a 1908 brown shingle-style house occupying a quiet corner near the U.S. Naval Academy. For more than fifty years it served as the headquarters for the Democratic Club in Annapolis. This is the closest B&B to the Naval Academy, an easy walk through the gates to view the daily noontime drill of the "plebes" in the quadrangle or to visit the chapel where John Paul Jones is buried.

It seems a modest house from the outside, but as guests enter a tiled foyer, a Victorian crystal chandelier dominates the stairway. In the adjacent living room, a fire may be crackling in the fireplace in winter. Carpeted in beige and with vanilla walls, the living room boasts sofas and chairs upholstered in ivory damask as well as wing chairs in peach. Elegant drapes frame the windows. A lustrous cherry sideboard stands on one wall, while a beautiful antique Chippendale desk with a divided pediment graces another. A wet bar is built into the wall, ready to be put into service for cocktails before dinner.

The guest rooms are named for characters in *Charlotte's Web* by E. B. White. Why? "Because I liked the whimsy," explained innkeeper Robert Zuchelli. One, the Fern Room, which is located on the first floor, has a unique antique Victorian curvilinear bed and an antique Victorian dresser with a marble top. There's a private bath and direct access to a side porch. Three other guest rooms are on the second floor. Each has a carved four-poster bed as well as antique armoires and marble-topped Victorian night stands. Templeton has its own private bath with a whirlpool tub, while Wilbur and Charlotte share a hall bath.

The Marilyn Suite (a name not from *Charlotte's Web*) on the third floor is the most spacious accommodation. There are dormer windows with window seats and a skylight to cast a beam of sunlight across the handsome sleigh bed in the morning. This is the only room with a television. A two-room bath includes a whirlpool tub and a shower.

Breakfast is placed on the buffet in the living room every morning. In addition to fresh fruits, juices, breakfast breads, and a cheese plate, a hot entree (perhaps a quiche) will be available. Small tables can accommodate one or two people in the living room, or, on warm summer days, guests often take their plates out to the porch.

Do you remember Charlotte's children saying, "We take to the breeze; we go as we please?" And so do we. But our breezes are bound to bring us back to the William Page Inn.

What's Nearby

See "What's Nearby—Annapolis," page 17.

Ann Street Bed & Breakfast

804 South Ann Street
Baltimore, MD 21231
(410) 342-5883

INNKEEPERS: Joanne and Andrew Mazurek

ROOMS: 4, including 2 suites, all with private bath, air conditioning, and radio; 3 with fireplace

ON THE GROUNDS: Garden

EXTRAS: Chocolates at turndown

RATES: $85–$110 double occupancy, including full breakfast; two-night minimum holiday weekends

CREDIT CARDS ACCEPTED: None

OPEN: Year-round

HOW TO GET THERE: From Pratt Street in downtown Baltimore, proceed east and turn right onto President Street. Turn left onto Fleet Street and right onto Ann Street. The B&B is on the right just before Thames Street; it is the brick building with twin doors, next to the Robert Long Museum.

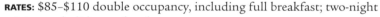

The first shipbuilding facility was established in Baltimore's historic Fells Point area in 1730, and by 1800 there were sixteen shipyards operating along its docks. The handsome pair of brick townhouses occupied by Ann Street Bed and Breakfast were built here in the 1790s, and their history has been intertwined with that of the Mazurek family for many generations. Andrew Mazurek's great-grandmother once owned them, and then in 1945 his mother bought them, but she was forced to sell when they were condemned for a proposed highway. The highway never materialized, and the buildings were boarded up, vandalized, and stripped. In 1978 Andrew and Joanne were allowed to purchase them, but it took five years of painstaking renovation before they were livable. Now they are exquisitely restored to the 1790s era.

The four-story buildings are notable for their symmetry. Individually, they are merely 14 feet wide, but they have lovely mullioned windows, twin-paneled doors, and fourth-floor dormers. Inside there are twelve working fireplaces and handsome hardwood floors.

The Mazureks have decorated their B&B with antiques and period eighteenth-century reproductions. In the parlor, Windsor and wing-back chairs offer places to sit before the fireplace. Oil portraits and hunt scenes from the late 1700s hang on the walls, and bouquets of fresh flowers sit on tables. In summer, guests love to sit in the brick-walled garden in back, which is filled with a cornucopia of flowers from early April to late October.

The B&B has two suites and two bedrooms, and only one does not include a fireplace in the bedroom. The rooms all have either full tester beds or antique rope beds (to remain authentic to the eighteenth-century period, all beds are double-sized). There are lustrous custom-made cherry Windsor chairs, wing back chairs, blanket chests, and fresh flowers on the tables. Each of the rooms has its own private bath.

A full breakfast is served in the dining room-kitchen, which has a woodstove and a bay window overlooking the gardens. Joanne sets individual tables with fresh flowers, country-checked tablecloths, and candles. A typical meal will include fresh juices and fruits (maybe a grapefruit broiled with brown sugar) and fresh blueberry muffins, followed by a German pancake served with powdered sugar, lemon, and maple syrup.

Fells Point is alive with activity throughout the year. In summer, tall ships berth here, street musicians play, and vendors sell everything from antiques to T-shirts. Little Italy is an easy walk, and Baltimore's Inner Harbor is about a mile away. Guests especially enjoy visits to the Aquarium, and the American Visionary Art Museum, which specializes in outsider art.

What's Nearby—Baltimore

The Joseph Meyerhoff Symphony Hall is home to the Baltimore Symphony Orchestra and the Baltimore Chorale Arts Society. Harborplace—a collection of restaurants, shops, and boutiques—is a magnet for tourists, while Baltimore's City Life Museums include numerous historic sites and houses, including the Peale Museum, which contains a collection of paintings by the noted early nineteenth-century painter Rembrandt Peale. Visitors should plan to visit the Baltimore Museum of Art, which holds more than 120,000 paintings. Sports enthusiasts will want to attend a game in Oriole Park, the home of the Baltimore Orioles, and also go to Pimlico Race Course.

Celie's Waterfront Bed & Breakfast

1714 Thames Street
Baltimore, MD 21231
(800) 432–0184 or (410) 522–2323

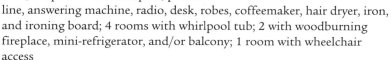

FAX: (410) 522–2324

E-MAIL: celies@aol.com

WEB SITE: www.bbonline.com/md/celies

INNKEEPER: Celie Ives

ROOMS: 7, including 1 suite, all with private bath, air conditioning, TV, VCR, telephone with dataport, private line, answering machine, radio, desk, robes, coffeemaker, hair dryer, iron, and ironing board; 4 rooms with whirlpool tub; 2 with woodburning fireplace, mini-refrigerator, and/or balcony; 1 room with wheelchair access

ON THE GROUNDS: Courtyard garden; rooftop view deck

EXTRAS: Fresh flowers in room; whirlpool tubs; spacious desks

RATES: $120–$220, double occupancy, including Continental breakfast; two- or three-night minimum holiday and special event weekends

CREDIT CARDS ACCEPTED: American Express, Discover, MasterCard, Visa

OPEN: Year-round

HOW TO GET THERE: From Pratt Street in downtown Baltimore, proceed east and turn right onto President Street. Turn left onto Fleet Street and right onto Ann Street. At Thames Street, turn right again. The B&B is in the middle of the block—a gray building with rose trim.

To visit Baltimore's historic Fells Point harborside district is to step back in time—to a time in the 1700s when it was a bustling shipbuilding hub. It was here that sleek clipper ships, schooners, and the first U.S. Navy frigate, the *Constellation*, were built. As you walk along the cobblestone

streets past the rows of brick townhouses, you almost feel as if you're back in the eighteenth century.

Until you walk into Celie's Waterfront Bed and Breakfast, that is. Tucked into a row of townhouses, the tiny entrance and the long brick passageway offer little preparation for the warm contemporary accommodations lying beyond. But when you enter the living room with its fireplace and polished pine floors, you will see the bright brick courtyard with its gentle fountain and iron tables and chairs beyond, and you'll immediately feel at home.

Your guest room will be painted a creamy ivory and enhanced by a bouquet of fresh flowers. If you are staying in #1 or #2, you will enjoy a woodburning fireplace and views of the harbor from your window seat. There will be a whirlpool tub in your spotless and bright bathroom. In a little alcove, a mini-refrigerator, coffeemaker, and microwave will speed your morning journey. If, instead, you have chosen either room #5 or #6, you will have a private balcony with window boxes overflowing with flowers and a table and chairs overlooking the garden courtyard. In your bath, you'll have a whirlpool tub.

Celie has thoughtfully furnished her rooms in crisp pine and wicker furniture. There are TVs and VCPs, telephones with private lines, dataports, answering machines, spacious desks, and coffeemakers.

The favorite retreat in this B&B, however, is the rooftop deck, where the panoramic view of the harbor and its multitude of boats can be mesmerizing. We came up here one warm night to watch the sun dip beyond the horizon, outlining the masts of the historic ships in the harbor in orange and pink. The sounds of rigging slapping against masts mingled with the call of seagulls as we luxuriated in the serenity and beauty of the night.

A help-yourself breakfast is set out each morning on the pine sideboard in the breakfast area. Guests may select breakfast breads, juices, yogurt, granola, and coffee or tea. Then they must make the difficult choice about where to eat it. Will it be on the pine table in the breakfast room or on the rooftop deck or in the courtyard garden or on their private balcony?

From this convenient location, it's possible to walk to excellent restaurants and shops, to take a self-guided walking tour of the Fells Point Historic District, or to ride a water taxi to the Baltimore Convention Center or to Oriole Park to watch the Baltimore Orioles in action.

Or, for several years you might have taken a seat on the rooftop deck and maintained a bird's-eye view of the action below when they were filming the popular TV program *Homicide: Life on the Streets*, which featured the picturesque brick police station directly across the street and the bar just down the block.

What's Nearby

See "What's Nearby—Baltimore," page 29.

Mr. Mole Bed & Breakfast

1601 Bolton Street
Baltimore, MD 21217
(410) 728–1179

FAX: (410) 728–3379

E-MAIL: MrMoleBB@aol.com

INNKEEPERS: Collin Clarke and Paul Bragaw

ROOMS: 5, including 2 suites, all with private bath, air conditioning, telephone with private line, voicemail and dataport, radio, hair dryer, desk, and robes

ON THE GROUNDS: Garage parking with door-opener

EXTRAS: Turndown with chocolates; fax available

RATES: $105–$165, double occupancy, including Continental breakfast; two-night minimum weekends

CREDIT CARDS ACCEPTED: American Express, Diners Club, Discover, Master-Card, Visa

OPEN: Year-round

HOW TO GET THERE: From I-95, take exit 53 to I-395. Bear right onto Martin Luther King, Jr., Boulevard and follow it for 2 miles. Turn left onto Eutaw Street and continue ⁶/10 mile, turning right at the fourth traffic light onto McMechen Street. Bolton Street is the next intersection. Mr. Mole is diagonally across the intersection from the stop sign

Houses in the Bolton Hill Historic District of Baltimore were built by wealthy merchants in the mid-1800s. The quiet, tree-lined streets with their brick row houses retain the air of a genteel suburb even though it is now surrounded by the bustle of Baltimore. Mr. Mole (a character the innkeepers Collin Clarke and Paul Bragaw have adopted to speak for them— a reflection of their droll sense of humor and whimsy and a name taken from *Wind in the Willows*) occupies a handsome 1870s house that was converted to a B&B in 1992.

Mr. Mole's home is a gracious and elegant mansion, reflecting a lifestyle that was fashionable when the house was built. In the most elegant B&B in Baltimore, eighteenth- and nineteenth-century English and American antiques decorate the common rooms as well as the suites. One enters a charming vestibule where the 14-foot ceilings create a sense of spaciousness. The first floor has a living room, a breakfast room, and a drawing room, all painted a bold Kodak yellow. The striking color scheme is complemented by an abundance of large Oriental blue-and-white porcelain pieces. Handsome oil portraits hang beside etchings from the 1830s—all enhanced by bay windows and creamy marble fireplaces.

The guest rooms are equally sumptuous. The Balmoral Suite, for example, is as large as many Manhattan apartments. It has two bedrooms, and in the sitting room bottle-green wainscotting is spiced with cardinal-red walls and softened by white accents. The four-poster bed is lacquered red and swagged with red, green, and white plaids and the sofas and chairs are upholstered in the same manner. The Garden Suite on the third floor has an overhanging garden porch and antique white wicker furniture. The bed is draped with a coverlet and swagged in a soft buttery linen.

One of the treats when staying with Mr. Mole is to become acquainted with Collin and Paul. They are conversant on a variety of topics and will describe Baltimore's museums, theatrical events, and restaurants, as well as their many travels around the world.

A Continental breakfast that includes a variety of sliced meats and cheeses, fresh fruit and juices, freshly baked breakfast breads, cakes, pies, and pastries as well as coffee and tea is served at little tables discreetly dispersed throughout the common rooms. Guests can therefore be as sociable or as reclusive as they wish.

What's Nearby

See "What's Nearby—Baltimore," page 29.

Merry Sherwood Plantation

Best Buy

8909 Worcester Highway (Route 113)
Berlin, MD 21811
(800) 660–0358 or (410) 641–2112

FAX: (410) 641–9528

E-MAIL: info@merrysherwood.com

WEB SITE: www.merrysherwood.com

INNKEEPER: W. Kirk Burbage

ROOMS: 8, including 1 suite; 6 with private bath; all with air conditioning and robes; 1 with Jacuzzi

ON THE GROUNDS: 18 acres of gardens; parking

EXTRAS: Lemonade or tea in the afternoon

RATES: $150–$175 mid-May to mid-October; $95–$125 mid-October to mid-May double occupancy, includes full breakfast; two-night minimum weekends

CREDIT CARDS ACCEPTED: MasterCard and Visa

OPEN: Year-round

HOW TO GET THERE: From Washington, D.C., take Route 50 across the Chesapeake Bay Bridge and continue east to Berlin. In Berlin take the exit for Route 113 south and go 2½ miles to the B&B, which will be on the right side of the road.

The countryside on the southern Eastern Shore of Maryland is rural and sparsely settled. Mostly it is a patchwork of farmland, so the appearance of this magnificent 1859 seafoam-green mansion, dripping with gingerbread from its squared-off wraparound porch, as well as from its overhanging eaves and its cupola, comes as a surprise. You will drive through the ornate gates and along the maple-shaded drive in awe as you admire the lovely home. The meticulous restoration of the twenty-seven-room, 8,500-square-foot mansion was the two-year project of local businessman Kirk Burbage, whose family has lived near Berlin for more than 200 years.

Inside, the main-floor rooms are furnished in elegant good taste. The ballroom has twin ivory marble fireplaces, an ornate square grand piano, and an unusual carved wooden chair somewhat reminiscent of a throne. It has carved lion's head arms and a brass portrait of Queen Victoria, and it's rumored to have been made for an anticipated visit by the queen. Lace curtains filter light at the windows, and damask- and tapestry-covered antique Victorian sofas, loveseats, and chairs are welcoming. Also available for guests to use are a small parlor, a formal dining room with a spectacular brass chandelier and a carved walnut sideboard, and a library filled with rare books and secret closets. A sunporch overlooks the gardens. When we arrived, afternoon tea and lemonade were waiting, so we relaxed on the porch, letting the pressures of the drive melt away.

The bedrooms, which are on the second and third floors, are furnished with museum-quality antiques, including a canopy bed in the Johnson Room, a bed with beehive finials in the Chase Room, and a Gothic Revival bed in the Harrison Room. Six of the rooms have private baths with marble floors and showers, vintage fixtures such as pedestal sinks and clawfoot tubs, and brass hardware. Each room and bath has Victorian light fixtures as well. The Honeymoon Suite also has a Jacuzzi.

Breakfast is served in the dining room, where we feasted on fresh fruit, homemade muffins, juices, and a ham and broccoli strata. The meal is served on linen cloths with silver flatware and fine china around a handsome mahogany table.

The broad wraparound porch of the house is bordered by paneled columns joined by arches. There are comfortable rockers and wicker tables. Ferns and flowers hang in baskets from the arches. The eighteen acres of gardens at Merry Sherwood Plantation are noted for their broad variety of rare specimens. *Southern Living* magazine has been helping with their restoration.

Nearby attractions include the Assateague Island Wildlife Preserve and the beaches at Ocean City, as well as the Globe Theatre in Berlin.

What's Nearby—Berlin

The Assateague Island National Seashore offers miles of beaches and marshland that provide protected homes for waterbirds and wildlife. Hiking, camping, swimming, and fishing along this coastal wilderness are popular pastimes. Berlin is a fetching Victorian town that has antiques shops and restaurants located in historic buildings. Be sure to see the old Globe Theatre, which has an art gallery upstairs and a bookstore, gift shop, and cafe downstairs. Entertainment ranging from folk performers to puppet shows for children takes place year-round. Golfers will appreciate that there are several courses in or near Berlin. (See also Ocean City and Snow Hill.)

The Blue Max Inn

300 Bohemia Avenue
(mailing address: P.O. Box 30)
Chesapeake City, MD 21915
(410) 885-2781

FAX: (410) 885-2809

E-MAIL: bluemax@crosslink.net

WEB SITE: www.chesapeakecity.com/
blue max

INNKEEPERS: Wayne and Wendy Mercer

ROOMS: 7, all with private bath, air conditioning, telephone with data-port, and radio; 4 with TV; 3 with desk; 2 with porch and robes; 1 with whirlpool tub; wheelchair access

ON THE GROUNDS: Parking on premises; garden; two porches; pond; gazebo

EXTRAS: Decanter of sherry in dining room; afternoon tea with cookies and pastries; guest refrigerator with ice and soda water available

RATES: $90–$130, double occupancy, including full breakfast; two-night minimum weekends May to October and holiday weekends

CREDIT CARDS ACCEPTED: American Express, Discover, MasterCard, Visa

OPEN: Year-round

HOW TO GET THERE: From I–95 traveling south, take Delaware exit 1A onto Route 896 (South Middletown). Follow this south for 4 miles to Route 40 west. Turn right and follow this for 4 miles to Elkton. Turn left onto Route 213 south and follow this for 7 miles to the Chesapeake City bridge. Cross over the bridge and immediately turn right at the end. Circle under the bridge to the stop sign. Turn left onto George Street and go to 3rd Street. Turn right. The inn is straight ahead in 1 block. From I–95 traveling north, take Maryland exit 100 and travel south on Route 272 to North East. Turn onto Route 40 and travel east for 8 miles to Route 213 south, then follow directions above.

World War I buffs will recognize the name of this inn as the title of the best-selling book written by Jack Hunter in 1964. It was later made into a movie starring George Peppard. This was Mr. Hunter's home in the 1960s, and his wife named the house after his book when she opened an antiques shop on the main floor.

Originally built in 1854 during the height of Chesapeake City's prosperity, this handsome house was the home of William Lindsay, a local sawmill owner. The sandy-colored clapboard house with white trim and periwinkle-blue shutters is distinctive for its wide double porches across the front—a relaxing spot to sit in the rush-covered rockers while enjoying an interlude in local sightseeing. Occupying almost an acre on the outskirts of this tiny village, the house has generous gardens with brick pathways that slope down to a pond and a gazebo.

The inn boasts a parlor with a pink damask sofa, a lovely tall-case clock, bookcases, and a gas fireplace with a carved plaster mantel. Across the entry hall, the formal dining room has a brass chandelier and another fireplace.

Wayne and Wendy Mercer purchased the bed-and-breakfast in 1998 and immediately began a renovation project that included new furniture, new carpets, and bathroom improvements. The Randall Room, which was Mr. Hunter's study, is a pretty place decorated in blue-and-white checked fabric with accents of yellow floral Laura Ashley prints. The bed has a bookcase headboard, and Mr. Hunter's bookcases still fill the walls. The room has access to the second-floor porch. The Hunter Room has a white iron bed with a heart motif, a new green carpet, and a beautiful tiled bath with Corian counters. French doors lead to the second-floor porch, which is filled with wicker furniture. Two rooms have private baths that are located off the hallway. The Herman Room has lovely green carpeting in a shadowy leaf pattern, a white iron bed, and a tiled bath with a patterned ceiling and a whirlpool tub. The Cleaver Room has a ruby carpet, a bed with an upholstered headboard and spread that coordinate with the drapes, and mustard-colored walls.

Breakfast is served at individual tables in a sunny room with lattice walls that overlooks the gardens. Wendy will prepare either a Continental breakfast or a full breakfast.

What's Nearby—Chesapeake City

The Chesapeake and Delaware Canal, which was completed in 1829, shortened the water route between Philadelphia and Baltimore by more than 300 miles by eliminating the need to "round" the DelMarVa peninsula. It has been widened and dredged numerous times through the years and now annually carries some 1,500 massive freighters and other commercial vessels through the 14-mile trough that connects the Delaware Bay to the Chesapeake Bay. Part of the Intercoastal Waterway, it's said to be the third largest carrier of tonnage in the world, following only the Suez and Panama Canals.

When first opened, the C&D Canal had its own towpath on which mules pulled barges laden with goods. Chesapeake City, Maryland, was the hub of canal traffic. Today you can review this interesting segment of American history at the C&D Canal Museum, housed in one of the original pumphouses. You might also want to take a water tour of the canal or relax while listening to one of the weekend concerts in the park. Afterward, lunch or dinner in one of the seafood restaurants on the banks of the canal might reward you with a view of a towering freighter or an elegant yacht that passes so close you feel as if you can reach out and touch it.

Inn at the Canal

104 Bohemia Avenue
(mailing address: P.O. Box 187)
Chesapeake City, MD 21915
(410) 885-5995

FAX: (410) 885-3585

WEB SITE: www.chesapeakecity.com/innatthecanal/inn.htm

INNKEEPERS: Mary and Al Ioppolo

ROOMS: 7, including 1 suite, all with private bath, air conditioning, TV, telephone with dataport, and radio; 4 with desk; 1 with mini-refrigerator and hair dryer

ON THE GROUNDS: Gardens, antiques shop, porch with view of canal

EXTRAS: Afternoon refreshments; three cats, Chessie, Cali, and Corky, on premises but not in guest areas

RATES: $80–$140, double occupancy, including full breakfast; two-night minimum weekends May to November

CREDIT CARDS ACCEPTED: American Express, Carte Blanche, Diners' Club, Discover, MasterCard, Visa

OPEN: Year-round except Christmas Eve and Christmas Day

HOW TO GET THERE: From I-95 traveling south, take Delaware exit 1A onto Route 896 (South Middletown). Follow this south for 4 miles to Route 40 west. Turn right and follow this for 4 miles to Elkton. Turn left onto Route 213 south and follow this for 7 miles to the Chesapeake City bridge. Cross over the bridge and immediately turn right at the end. Circle under the bridge to the stop sign. Turn left onto George Street and go 3 blocks. Turn right onto 2nd Street and go 1 block to Bohemia Avenue. Turn left. The inn will be on the right.

The historic Brady-Rees House was built in 1870 by one of Chesapeake City's most affluent citizens. Henry Brady owned the mule teams that pulled cargo barges through the C&D Canal. It is a stately house with a lovely covered porch across the front that's filled with wicker furniture, hanging baskets, and planters spilling over with bright flowers. From the broad porch that stretches along one side, guests have mesmerizing views of the passing ships. The house is in the heart of the tiny village's shopping area—an easy walk to art galleries, gift shops, and restaurants.

It's said that Henry Brady built his Victorian home soon after his wife gave birth to the son he had longed for. No expense was spared in the details and many of the original embellishments remain as part of the house today. There are elaborate examples of Victorian fretwork, 12-foot ceilings with handpainted scenes (these are still undergoing restoration), stained glass windows, and slate faux-marble fireplace mantels.

Mary and Al appreciate fine antiques, and they've filled the B&B with some wonderful examples. The dining room, for example, has a gorgeous carved oak sideboard. In the parlor it's possible to spend hours looking through the turn-of-the-century stereopticon at the assorted scenes of people and places (one depicts a state dinner at the White House) or to peruse one of the many historical books. In the kitchen we enjoyed looking at the numerous old baking and cooking implements that hang from the brick fireplace wall.

The guest rooms have either antique or reproduction beds. Room #10, for example, has a four-poster bed with a fishnet canopy and a lovely water view. The bath includes a sink in an old oak dresser. Room #4 has a tub in the bath that is surrounded by walnut paneling and another sink imbedded in an antique dresser. It has a lovely view of the canal.

A full breakfast is served in the dining room, and Mary uses her fine china, linen, silver, and crystal for her guests. One of her most popular entrees is French toast stuffed with cream cheese and topped with a raspberry sauce.

What's Nearby

See "What's Nearby—Chesapeake City," page 37.

Ship Watch Inn

401 First Street
Chesapeake City, MD 21915
(410) 885–5300

FAX: (410) 885–5784
WEB SITE: www.chesapeakecity.com/shipwatchinn
INNKEEPERS: Linda and Tommy Vaughan
ROOMS: 8, all with private bath and porch, TV, telephone with private line and dataport, radio; 4 with whirlpool tub for two; wheelchair access
ON THE GROUNDS: Hot tub on outside porch; garden; porch
EXTRAS: Waterside setting; views
RATES: $95–$150, double occupancy, including full breakfast; $20 surcharge for one-night weekend stay (Friday or Saturday) from May through October
CREDIT CARDS ACCEPTED: American Express, MasterCard, Visa
OPEN: Year-round
HOW TO GET THERE: From I-95 traveling south, take Delaware exit 1A onto Route 896 (South Middletown). Follow this south for 4 miles to Route 40 west. Turn right and follow this for 4 miles to Elkton. Turn left onto Route 213 south and follow this for 7 miles to the Chesapeake City bridge. Cross over the bridge and immediately turn right at the end. Circle under the bridge to the stop sign. Turn left onto George Street and continue to its end. The B&B is the last house on the right.

The Chesapeake and Delaware, an incredible mid-1800s engineering project, is one of the few canals remaining in America. Unlike the greatest of them all, the Erie Canal, however, this one proved so necessary that it has been widened and deepened over the years to accommodate ever larger vessels. Today massive around-the-world freighters use the Chesapeake and Delaware Canal to shorten their voyages between the ports of Philadelphia and Baltimore.

The Ship Watch Inn sits in an advantageous position right at water's edge, where its triple covered verandas offer B&B guests eyeball-to-porthole views of the giant ships. In 1996 Tom and Linda Vaughan, who are lifelong residents of Chesapeake City, renovated a canalside 1920s house that had long been in the family into a bed-and-breakfast. It takes full advantage of its waterside setting. Lawns slope to water's edge and the porches reach out toward the ship decks.

The inn is as shipshape as an elegant ocean liner. There are polished pine floors and the crisp furnishings are interspersed with antique oak pieces. A massive oak buffet in a main floor hallway is especially impressive. A smaller buffet in the living room holds plates of sticky buns, pies, cookies, and drinks in the afternoon. Doors lead from the living room to one of the decks, where a hot tub offers an inviting refuge.

The guest rooms are smartly decorated with sponged walls and designer linens on pretty iron beds. Four of the new tile baths have whirlpool tubs. Every room opens onto a large porch, offering spectacular views. Room #2 has an oak bed and a sink in an oak dresser, but Room #4 has an iron bed, an armoire, and a grey tile bath with a double whirlpool tub and a floral pedestal sink.

A full breakfast is served either on the porch or in the dining room. The entree might consist of a crab omelet, or perhaps baked oatmeal, or maybe eggs Benedict. An excellent seafood restaurant, Bayard House, which has a deck overlooking the water, is a short block away. Schaefer's Canal House, also offering fine seafood and a canalside setting, is on the opposite side of the canal.

What's Nearby

See "What's Nearby—Chesapeake City," page 37.

Brampton Inn

25227 Chestertown Road
(Route 20 South)
Chestertown, MD 21620
(410) 778–1860

FAX: (410) 778–1805

E-MAIL: brampton@friend.ly.net

WEB SITE: www.bramptoninn.com

INNKEEPERS: Michael and Danielle Hanscom

ROOMS: 10, including 2 suites, all with private bath, air conditioning, radio, and hair dryer; 8 with fireplace; 7 with desk; 4 with TV; 3 with coffeemaker and porch; 2 with whirlpool tub and porch; 1 room with wheelchair access; crib available

ON THE GROUNDS: On 35 acres with gardens, woods, and pond

EXTRAS: Afternoon tea, complimentary beverages; fax, copier, and data-port available; dog named Penny, several cats, bunnies, and guinea pigs

RATES: $125–$225, double occupancy, including full breakfast and afternoon tea; two-night minimum if stay includes Saturday night, three-night minimum holiday weekends

CREDIT CARDS ACCEPTED: American Express, MasterCard, Visa

OPEN: Year-round

HOW TO GET THERE: From Washington, D.C., take Route 50, cross the Chesapeake Bay Bridge and continue on Route 301/50 until it splits. Take Route 301 north for 5 miles to Route 213 north. Follow Route 213 through Centreville and into Chestertown. At the traffic light follow Spring Avenue to High Street (Route 20). Continue on Route 20 through town. The B&B is located about 1 mile SW of town on Route 20.

Brampton has evolved. When Michael and Danielle Hanscom first opened their impressive brick mansion as a bed and breakfast in 1987, there were only two guest rooms. On a visit in 1993 the number of guest rooms had grown to seven, but they were still awaiting the arrival of the handsome Sheraton-style sofas they had ordered from a local craftsman for their front parlor. (It took five years.)

By 1996 the number of guest rooms had increased to ten, and the gorgeous sofas were in place. Covered in a rich lemon-yellow damask, they sit before the fireplace in the parlor that now serves as the heart of the inn. Oriental rugs cover glowing pine floors and bookcases reach to the 12-foot ceilings. The windows on all the floors reach from floor to ceiling, flooding the rooms with light and sun.

The seven guest rooms within the main building are spacious, and each has a private bath. My favorite is the Fairy Hill Suite, which occupies the former kitchen. You enter a sitting room that has a large woodburning fireplace and a sofa covered in French Provincial fabric. The bedroom is upstairs, where a queen-sized four-poster cherry bed is covered with a hand-made quilt and a modern bath has cobalt-blue tiles on the floor.

The Smokehouse, a little cottage in back, contains another room with beamed ceilings, a woodstove, and a four-poster bed, but the nicest rooms are the newest ones. These are located in the Garden Cottage, a short walk across the fields. Both spacious and very private suites have woodburning fireplaces, private patios, cherry floors topped with Oriental rugs, and baths with double whirlpool tubs and separate showers.

In the back parlor guests can watch movies on the TV or enjoy the colorful flower garden beyond. In the afternoon freshly baked cookies, tea, and sherry are savored by the guests, often in one of the swings on the spacious front porch.

Danielle is Swiss, and the breakfasts she prepares reflect her heritage. You will feast on fresh muffins or scones and perhaps puffed pancakes with poached pears or cottage cheese waffles with maple syrup as well as fruits, juices, and meats. It's served at individual tables in the formal dining room, which has another fireplace and a 1940s Waterford crystal chandelier.

The tranquil setting, sublimely situated on thirty-five acres, seems so peaceful that it's hard to believe you are only 1 mile from Chestertown. Yet, within five minutes, excellent restaurants, shops, art galleries, and museums may be visited.

What's Nearby—Chestertown

Chestertown is a charming and historic town whose historic district includes several interesting buildings that are open to the public. Concerts, films, lectures, art exhibits, and live theater take place on the campus of Washington College. St. Paul's Church was erected in 1713 and is one of the oldest continuously operating churches in Maryland. The Waterman's Museum in nearby Rock Hall provides a unique perspective into the life of baymen and watermen. Especially during the migratory season, Eastern Neck Natural Wildlife Refuge is heavily populated with waterfowl.

Great Oak Manor Bed & Breakfast

10568 Cliff Road
Chestertown, MD 21620
(800) 504–3098 or (410) 778–5943

FAX: (410) 778–5943
E-MAIL: innkeeper@greatoak.com
WEB SITE: www.greatoak.com

INNKEEPERS: Don and Dianne Cantor

ROOMS: 11, including 1 suite, all with private bath, air conditioning, telephone, radio, and desk; 5 with fireplace; 3 with TV/VCR, and dataport

ON THE GROUNDS: On 12 acres with private beach, bicycle rentals, yard games, gardens, gazebo, benches with bay views. Nearby: marina, tennis, swimming pool, golf course

EXTRAS: Water-views from 7 rooms; coffee, tea, soft drinks, and snacks in the afternoon; port and sherry in evening; yellow Lab named Beau

RATES: $95–$195 double occupancy, including full breakfast; two-night minimum holiday weekends

CREDIT CARDS ACCEPTED: MasterCard and Visa

OPEN: Year-round except two weeks in December and two weeks February/March

HOW TO GET THERE: From Washington, D.C., take Route 50 across the Chesapeake Bay Bridge and continue on Route 301/50 until it splits. Take Route 301 north for 5 miles to Route 213 north. Follow Route 213 through Centreville and into Chestertown. Pass Washington College and turn left at the traffic light onto Route 291 (Morgnec Road). When it dead ends, turn right onto Route 20. Turn right onto Route 514. After crossing Route 298, continue on Route 514 for another $1^8/10$ miles. Turn left onto Great Oak Landing Road. Pass silos, go through first set of brick pillars, continue past golf course, continue straight ahead through second set of brick pillars to large brick manor house.

Great Oak Manor is naughty but nice. One can imagine the wild nights of cognac, cigars, and cash that changed hands at the estate bordering the Chesapeake Bay in the 1950s when it welcomed celebrities such as Arthur Godfrey and Guy Lombardo. They would fly, undetected, into the private airport and then spend a few daytime hours shooting ducks or geese and many after-dark hours playing roulette, blackjack, and poker in the exclusive gaming hall. Those days are long gone, but guests still revel in the stories.

The grand brick twenty-five-room Federal-style manor house was built in 1938 by Russell D'Oench, a W. R. Grace heir. It sat on a 1,100-acre point of land that projected into the Chesapeake Bay. Today, although the estate has dwindled to twelve acres, it still offers marvelous views of the Chesapeake Bay and Fairlee Creek from its bluff-top perch. Inside, the detailed moldings and rich paneling illustrate the craftsmanship that was lavished on this gem.

Dianne and Don Cantor were boating along the East Coast when they fell in love with Chestertown. A realtor told them about a derelict manor house on the water that was for sale. " 'Water' was the operative word," admitted Dianne. "We didn't even hear 'derelict.'" Don had just sold his

California computer company to AT&T They purchased the property in 1993 and began the work of restoring the mansion.

Today we admire the carved icons over the doors and fireplace mantels, the rich paneling, and the sweeping stairway that rises from the massive front-to-back entrance hall. In the Gun Room, a map of the original 1,100-acre estate is handpainted on a panel that pulls down to hide the bar. In the evening guests gather here to watch movies on the large-screen TV.

The guest rooms are furnished with antiques, and five have working fireplaces. One of the most interesting is Russell, which is located in the former gambling hall. It has pine paneling, a brick fireplace, and a cathedral ceiling. D'Oench has a fireplace and a view across the manicured lawns to the bay.

The grounds include flower gardens and a boxwood garden with benches placed in private bowers. More benches line the lip of the bluff, offering wonderful views across the water, especially at sunset.

A full breakfast of fruits, homemade muffins, and perhaps an egg strata or blueberry pancakes is served every morning in the dining room. Guests may help themselves and eat in the dining room, on the brick terrace, or on a bench overlooking the water.

At the little club next door, there's a golf course as well as tennis courts, a swimming pool, a private beach, and a marina—allowing guests to arrive by boat as well as by car. The quiet country lanes are ideal for bicycling. Excellent restaurants will be found in the nearby villages of Chestertown and Rock Hall, as well as numerous antiques shops and art galleries.

What's Nearby

See "What's Nearby—Chestertown," page 43.

The White Swan Tavern

231 High Street
Chestertown, MD 21620
(410) 778-5637

FAX: (410) 778-4543

WEB SITE: www.chestertown.com/ whiteswan

INNKEEPER: Mary Susan Maisel

ROOMS: 6, including 2 suites, all with private bath, air conditioning, mini-refrigerator, hair dryer, desk; 1 with patio; 2 rooms with wheelchair access; crib available

ON THE GROUNDS: Off-street parking, gardens

EXTRAS: Afternoon tea; evening wine and sherry; turndown service; pets occasionally permitted if prior arrangements made

RATES: $110–$185, double occupancy, including Continental breakfast

CREDIT CARDS ACCEPTED: Mastercard and Visa

OPEN: Year-round

SMOKING: In 2 guest rooms only

HOW TO GET THERE: From Washington, D.C., take Route 50 across the Chesapeake Bay Bridge and continue on Route 301/50 until it splits. Take Route 301 north for 5 miles to Route 213 north. Follow Route 213 through Centreville and into Chestertown. At the traffic light turn left onto Cross Street. Follow this to High Street (Route 20). Turn left onto High Street. The B&B will be on the right.

Chestertown's White Swan Tavern is a living history museum as well as a bed-and-breakfast—one of the few places where guests can truly immerse themselves in a historical era. The original tavern dates to 1733, but through meticulous research and archaeological excavations it has been fully restored. Having been returned to its 1793 roots, the center hall now contains paneling that was original to the period, while the Nicholson Room and the Isaac Cannell Room incorporate period cornices, window and door trims, baseboards, paneling, light fixtures, and fireplace mantels.

There are six guest rooms in the tavern, each with its own private bath. A favorite room is located in the original kitchen on the first floor. The Lovegrove Kitchen includes huge posts and beams, stucco walls, a brick floor, a private patio, and a massive kitchen fireplace. There are polished wood tables and a low four-poster bed. The Thomas Peacock Room and the Wilmer Room have reproduction canopy beds, while the Sterling Suite has a queen canopy bed and lovely burnished wood tables and chests. Oil paintings hang on the walls. Unfortunately, the guest room fireplaces cannot be used, but those in the common rooms often are lighted in cool weather.

An afternoon tea of "White Swan cookies," hot mulled cider, and perhaps scones, lemon cake, or carrot cake, and the establishment's signature tea is offered in the Cannell Room or on the terrace every day from 3:00 to 5:00 P.M. People drive from miles around to have tea and look at the artifacts found during the excavations that are displayed in the glass case.

In addition to the common room where tourists often mingle with bed and breakfast guests for afternoon tea, there is a sitting room with a fireplace and a TV for guests. Board games, jigsaw puzzles, books, and a stereo offer additional amusements. In the late afternoon wine and sherry are available to guests, who often retreat to the back of the B&B to sit at the tables and chairs on the brick terrace overlooking the flower-filled garden.

A Continental breakfast, consisting of freshly squeezed juices, fruits, homemade breads, and coffee or tea, is served on a tray on the terrace, in the Cannell Room, or in the room, whichever the guest prefers.

The White Swan is located in Chestertown's historic district, across from a fine restaurant and adjacent to shops and galleries.

What's Nearby

See "What's Nearby—Chestertown," page 43.

Carmel Cove Inn

Glendale Road
(mailing address: P.O. Box 644,
Oakland, MD 21550)
Deep Creek Lake, MD 21561
(301) 387–0067

FAX: (301) 387–2394

E-MAIL: Carmelcove@aol.com

WEB SITE: www.carmelcoveinn.com

INNKEEPER: Ed Spak

ROOMS: 10, all with private bath, air conditioning, telephone with private line, radio, and robes; 4 with patio or deck; 3 with whirlpool tub; 2 with fireplace

ON THE GROUNDS: On 2½ acres with a hot tub, tennis courts, and billiards table; near Deep Creek Lake with swimming docks, canoes, and paddle boats; mountain bike trails, cross-country ski trails, and hiking trails adjacent

EXTRAS: Golf carts, fishing equipment; tea and freshly baked cookies in the afternoon; port and chocolates in the evening

RATES: $80–$160, double occupancy, including full breakfast and afternoon beverages and snacks; two-night minimum most weekends, three-night minimum holiday weekends

CREDIT CARDS ACCEPTED: Discover, MasterCard, Visa

OPEN: Year-round

HOW TO GET THERE: From I–68 traveling west, take exit 14A. Take Route 219 south for approximately 20 miles to Deep Creek Lake. Continue over the Route 219 bridge and along the lake for 2 more miles to Glendale Road. Turn left onto Glendale Road and travel 1 mile, cross over the bridge and bear right at the end. Continue 1 more mile to Carmel Cove. Turn left and then bear left to the inn. From I–68 traveling east, take Maryland exit 4 (Friendsville). Travel south on Route 42 to Route 219 south and continue as above.

The Discalced Carmelite Fathers, who built this serene retreat in 1945, loved the tranquil sounds of the maple and oak leaves rustling in a breeze; the smell of the pine, hemlock, and spruce trees; and the close-up views of God's creatures that included bear, deer, and wild turkeys. A sect who wore no shoes, they would come to this beautiful place to commune with God, undisturbed by worldly sounds. Ever since 1996 when the monastery was converted to a bed-and-breakfast, we have been privileged to enjoy the same calm and halcyon atmosphere as the monks enjoyed.

The monks built their modest shingled retreat with their own hands, assisted by local stonemasons, who donated their time to build the stone foundation for the chapel. This remarkable room, which is today the Great Room of the bed-and-breakfast, has a tall beamed cathedral ceiling but otherwise bears little resemblance to the former chapel. A cast-iron burner heats the entire room. Comfortable sofas and chairs are grouped to form conversation areas. A library offers reading material and an extensive video library holds selections for the VCR. A fabulous sound system surrounds guests with music. A refrigerator holds microbrews and wines and a selection of coffees and teas. Freshly baked cookies await takers in the afternoon and port and chocolates are welcome after-dinner refreshments—perhaps while guests are enjoying a game of billiards.

The guest rooms are a far cry from the tiny cubicles the monks retreated to in the evening. They are spacious and charming. Several of the rooms, including Rooms #1 and #3, have private decks and whirlpool tubs, while others, such as Room #7, have gorgeous mortarless stone fireplaces. They are all furnished with oak beds, dressers, and armoires.

Guests might elect to have their breakfast delivered to their room in the morning, or they can eat in the beamed and pine-paneled breakfast room, which has another mortarless stone fireplace. Ed Spak, the marvelous and friendly innkeeper, will fix a repast worthy of a gourmand. One day it included a sausage-cheese quiche with country ham, as well as bourbon French toast, freshly baked pastries, and fresh fruit and juices. A good hike is definitely in order following this!

What's Nearby—Deep Creek Lake

Deep Creek Lake State Park, which has a 700-foot sandy beach, offers swimming, fishing, and boating throughout the summer; and it's just across the cove. There are cross-country ski trails; mountain biking trails, and an abundance of hiking trails. A nature center was completed in 1999. With its numerous exhibits and a giant IMAX screen, it is designed to sensitize people to the fragility of the environment. A concert amphitheater for performances sponsored by the Garrett Lakes Arts Festival is planned for the future. The Youghiogheny River and the Savage River are among the East's premier whitewater rafting sites. (See also McHenry and Oakland.)

Ashby 1663

27448 Ashby Drive
Easton, MD 21601
(800) 458–3622 or
(410) 822–4235

FAX: (410) 822–9288

WEB SITE: www.ashby1663.com

INNKEEPERS: Cliff Meredith and Jeanie Wagner

ROOMS: 12, including 3 suites and 2 cottages, all with private bath, TV, air conditioning, telephone, desk, and robes; 9 with whirlpool tub; 7 with fireplace; 6 with private porch or patio

ON THE GROUNDS: On 23 acres with swimming pool; lighted tennis court; dock; gardens, canoes, paddleboats

EXTRAS: Exercise room; massage machine, tanning bed, dry sauna; complimentary cocktails and hors d'oeuvres in the evening; turndown with bedside cookies

RATES: $215–$595, double occupancy, including full breakfast, cocktails and hors d'oeuvres; two-night minimum if stay includes Saturday night from April–November

CREDIT CARDS ACCEPTED: American Express, MasterCard, Visa

OPEN: Year-round

HOW TO GET THERE: From Washington, D.C., take Route 50 across the Chesapeake Bay Bridge and follow it to Easton. At Airport Road turn right and travel to the stop sign. Turn right again onto Goldsborough Neck Road and bear left at the fork, traveling past the "No outlet" sign. Turn left again at the sign that reads "Ashby 1663." Continue on the paved road for ¾ mile to the B&B.

It's true that the foundation of this grand white clapboard mansion with its Greek Revival entrance dates to 1663, but its style harks to its 1858 period. When Cliff Meredith and Jeanie Wagner purchased the abandoned estate on 23 acres bordering the Miles River, it was in such disrepair that it was in danger of falling down. Cliff, a realtor and contractor, thoroughly updated the mechanical systems and then rebuilt major portions of the house. There's now a wall of Palladian-style windows in the sun room offering vistas of the Miles River and French doors that provide access to the freeform pool. There's a fireplace at each end and polished antique chests and tables. From the entrance hall, a sweeping stairway leads to the second and third floors. Guests often enter the house through the spectacular kitchen.

The guest rooms are so palatial that you may decide to stay for weeks. The main house includes four rooms and a suite. The Robert Goldsborough Suite has a canopy bed swagged and draped in peach and green. It sits in front of a fireplace and has a view of the river. A dressing room leads to a private porch. The marble bath is positively stunning and utterly romantic. A two-person whirlpool tub sits on a raised platform offering sweeping views of the river. It faces a second fireplace, which casts a seductive glow.

There are additional accommodations in the George Goldsborough House and the Mary Trippe Place. A building at the edge of the river was completed in 1996. The Miles River Cottage contains five more rooms. Each of these has a view of the river, light oak floors, a kitchen, and a sparkling tile bath with a Jacuzzi. Four of these have fireplaces.

Breakfast is served in the formal dining room or the sunroom or on the sunporch. Guests will enjoy freshly baked muffins and breads, fruits, juices, and cereals, as well as such delicious entrees as asparagus in crepes with hollandaise sauce and baked French toast with bananas and walnuts topped with maple syrup. In the evening, guests become acquainted while sampling complimentary cocktails and light hors d'oeuvres.

There are few reasons to leave the grounds of Ashby 1663. There's a dock by which many guests arrive and where canoes and paddleboats are found. A pool and lighted tennis court offer outdoor diversions, while an exercise room has numerous machines. The quiet country lanes surrounding Ashby 1663 are ideal for walking or bicycling.

The activities available on Eastern Shore Maryland are astounding. The Chesapeake Bay Maritime Museum in Easton has a variety of exhibits, while the Talbot County Historical Society includes exhibits in a collection of eight historical buildings. The Academy of the Arts is a regional arts center offering changing exhibits as well as concerts, while the Historic Avalon Theatre is home to performing arts programs that range from a chamber music festival to a waterfowl festival. (See also Oxford and St. Michaels.)

Middle Plantation Inn

9549 Liberty Road
Frederick, MD 21701–3246
(301) 898–7128

E-MAIL: BandB@MPInn.com

WEB SITE: www.MPInn.com

INNKEEPERS: Shirley and Dwight Mullican

ROOMS: 4, all with private bath, air conditioning, TV, and radio; telephone available on request

ON THE GROUNDS: On 26 acres including gardens, walking trails, and Addison's Run Brook

EXTRAS: A miniature poodle, Teddy Bear, on premises

RATES: $90–$110, double occupancy, including Continental breakfast; two-night minimum holiday weekends and all weekends in October

CREDIT CARDS ACCEPTED: American Express, MasterCard, Visa

OPEN: Year-round

HOW TO GET THERE: From I–70 in Frederick, take exit 53 north onto I–270 and follow it to its end at Route 26. Take Route 26 5 miles to Mt. Pleasant. The B&B is in the tiny village of Mt. Pleasant on the right hand side.

*S*hirley and Dwight Mullican, who have deep roots in the village of Mt. Pleasant, found themselves the proud owners of Dwight's grandfather's twenty-six-acre farm in the late 1980s. The farm, which had been known over the years as Middle Plantation, included an 1810 farmhouse composed of hand-hewn logs, beams, and rich old oak and pine floors. Alas, it fronted directly on a busy road. What to do? Like a segment from *This Old House*, they carefully dismantled the home and saved all the materials they could salvage. Then with meticulous care, they constructed a brand-new bed-and-breakfast far back from the road using the old woods and stones.

Middle Plantation Inn is therefore a unique and unusual B&B. The outside is composed of a combination of fieldstone and log walls. Guests enter the inn by way of the Keeping Room, where a large stone fireplace, flagstone floors, and log beams envelop them in a warm, old-time atmosphere. Skylights and beautiful stained-glass windows create a bright but cozy place to read or just to sit and enjoy the fire.

Although the B&B calls itself a "rustic bed-and-breakfast," in my opinion, the four guest rooms are charmingly distinctive and stylish—decidedly not what I would call rustic. The Victorian Room, for example, has a carved walnut Victorian bed with a high head- and footboard and a carved Victorian dresser with a marble top. Dwight embellished the walls with intricate stenciling. An old oak icebox has shelves for storage, and the TV is hidden away in a corner washstand that was also stenciled by Dwight. In the Hunt Room, a white iron-and-brass bed sits on a green carpet, and the bath has a corner cabinet that holds a pottery sink made by a local craftsman. My favorite room, however, is the Log Room, which has its own private entrance. It has log-and-chink-walls and a polished oak floor. The bath includes a clawfoot tub, a mirror made from a harness, and another pottery sink in an old cabinet. A bright quilt covers the blue iron bed.

A Continental breakfast is served in the Keeping Room each morning, where the pastoral views across the fields are a tranquil way to begin any day.

What's Nearby—Mount Pleasant (Frederick)

Mount Pleasant is a small village on the outskirts of Frederick, amid farmland and open fields that are giving way to tract developments, yet the vast array of historic houses and museums in Frederick are only minutes away.

Tyler-Spite Inn

112 West Church Street
Frederick, MD 21701
(301) 831–4455

WEB SITE: www.tylerspite.com

INNKEEPERS: Bill and Andrea Myer

ROOMS: 10, including 4 suites; 7 with private bath; all with air conditioning, desk, robes, hair dryer, iron, ironing board; 6 with woodburning fireplace; 1 room with wheelchair access; telephone available for guest rooms, otherwise telephone at B&B check-in desk

ON THE GROUNDS: Swimming pool; garden with fountain

EXTRAS: Parking on premises; afternoon high tea; decanters of sherry in the room; standard poodle named Mitzi

RATES: $200–$300, double occupancy, including full breakfast and high tea; two-night minimum major holidays

CREDIT CARDS ACCEPTED: MasterCard and Visa

OPEN: Year-round except first two weeks of January

HOW TO GET THERE: From any freeway, follow signs for Frederick National Historic District. Continue to Church Street in the center of town. The B&B will be on the right opposite the old Court House.

In addition to being an innovative doctor (he performed the first cataract operation in America), Dr. John Tyler was a provocative character. When the town decided to cut a road through his vacant property, he hired a crew who worked throughout the night laying a foundation for this grand house. The next morning, when the road crew arrived, they found Dr. Tyler rocking in his favorite chair on his foundation. Town law prohibited seizure of land if there was a significant structure being built.

The three-story Federal-style stucco Tyler-Spite Inn certainly is a significant structure. Inside it has elaborate ceiling moldings surrounding the 13-foot-high walls as well as elaborate columns, arches, chandeliers, and fireplace mantels. The calico marble mantel in the library is matched by the room's burnt-red color, and there are carved marble mantels in the music room, dining room, and parlor that are also noteworthy. Historically furnished by owners Bill and Andrea Myer, the inn has priceless oil paintings, Oriental rugs on polished pine floors, and the mahogany campaign desk on which General Douglas MacArthur signed the peace treaty in Manila.

The spacious guest rooms are equally dramatic, with fireplaces in many, canopy featherbeds, and windows lavishly draped in silk. The walls are dramatically painted in navy or brushed with peach. The Nelson House next door is also part of the inn. It has elegant common rooms (including a terrific back porch overlooking the gardens) and guest rooms furnished in a similar manner. Of the ten rooms, seven have private baths; the rest share. The Nelson Suite in the Nelson House has a marble bath with a whirlpool in an alcove and a separate marble shower entered through fluted columns. For those who prefer a less elegant setting, the Myers Suite in the Nelson House is a garret suite with a painted floor, painted furniture, and a patriotic flag theme. It has a private bath with a double whirlpool.

The lovely formal walled gardens, which have a fountain, are splendidly alive with color in the summer, and there's a brick patio and a swimming pool tucked away in back. A full breakfast is served either formally in the dining room or informally on the patio. Fine linens, china, and silver are used. In addition to fresh fruit, juice, and breakfast breads, there will be a hot entree of perhaps baked apple dumplings, Belgian waffles, a soufflé, or fried green tomatoes. On special occasions, a treat called "kinklings" will be prepared. These are made with a shortbread dough that is deep fried and dipped in powdered sugar. A formal afternoon tea is served on weekends. There will be lemonade, tea, wine, sandwiches, specialty cakes, strawberries, cheese, and crackers. Decanters of sherry are placed in the rooms for a nightcap.

Historic and architecturally important, Frederick is worth a stopover of several days. Take a walking tour of the city to learn about the dramatic events that brought George Washington to town in the eighteenth century and Abraham Lincoln in the nineteenth century.

What's Nearby—Frederick

The Frederick National Historic District includes 33 blocks of buildings of historic and architectural significance. Stop at the visitor center for walking maps. Local museums open for visits include the Francis Scott Key Museum, the Barbara Fritchie House & Museum, the National Museum of Civil War Medicine, and the Schifferstadt Architectural Museum. The Rose Hill Manor Children's Museum, located in a 1790s Georgian mansion that was the home of Maryland's first governor, is a hands-on living museum where children can learn to quilt, comb wool, weave, make soap and candles, and participate in other activities.

Elliott House Victorian Inn

146 Casselman Road
Grantsville, MD 21536
(800) 272–4090 or (301) 895–4250

E-MAIL: edueck@mail.gcnet.net

WEB SITE: www.elliotthouse.com

INNKEEPER: Eleanor Dueck

ROOMS: 7, including 1 suite and 3 cottages, all with private bath, air conditioning, telephone with private line, TV, VCR, mini-refrigerator, coffeemaker, hair dryer, private porch, and robes; 4 with fireplace; 3 with desk; wheelchair access

ON THE GROUNDS: On 7 acres along Casselman River, gardens, nature walks

EXTRAS: Hot tub in courtyard; sodas and wines provided; large meeting/games room with fireplace, pool table and Ping Pong table; bicycles provided

RATES: $85–$135, double occupancy, including sodas and wines (no breakfast is served); two-night minimum major holiday weekends

CREDIT CARDS ACCEPTED: MasterCard and Visa

OPEN: Year-round

HOW TO GET THERE: Traveling west on I–68, take exit 22. Stay in the right lane and continue to the stop light at Alternate Route 40. Turn left on Alternate Route 40 and go 2 miles. The Elliott House will be on the right behind the Penn Alps Restaurant. Traveling east on I–68, take exit 19 and follow the signs to Grantsville. Turn right at the light onto Route 40 and go 1 mile. Just after the bridge, turn left into the Penn Alps Restaurant parking lot. Elliott House is straight ahead through the parking lot.

"The trout fishing is incredible," I heard a guest exclaim, as he came marching up the hill proudly displaying his catch. If he wants, he can prepare his catch for his evening meal at one of the barbecue grills in Casselman Park. Located on seven acres that curve along the picturesque Casselman River, this lovely B&B is the successful accomplishment of Jack and Eleanor Dueck, who were both teachers, lecturers, and consultants before becoming innkeepers. In 1994 they found this 1870 Victorian house bordering the National Pike Road (the first U.S. road built by the government). It had been the home of Eli and Harriett Broadwater Staunton, who operated the Staunton Mill, a building that still stands nearby. Part of a historic village complex, the 1813 Stone Arch Bridge, which was featured in a recent *National Geographic* article, spans the Casselman River steps away from the B&B, the Spruce Forest Artisan Village, and the Penn Alps Restaurant.

Following a thorough renovation of their Victorian house, the Duecks opened their B&B in 1997. It's a beauty. Guests enter through a door with faceted glass and topped by a stained-glass transom. They may choose an afternoon of quiet relaxation here before the gas fireplace while enjoying a book from the extensive library. Or they may crave more active pursuits, in which case they will go downstairs to the game room, which has another fireplace, where they might play pool or Ping Pong or match wits over a board game.

The guest rooms are charming and unique. Each is decorated with a splendid quilt made by a local woman. The baths are sparkling and clean and all are finished in tile. There are pedestal sinks and stencils decorate the walls. Elliott is located in the original parlor of the house. It has a pretty Victorian bed. My favorite accommodations, however, are those in several of the outbuildings. The Audubon House was once the tool house. It has beamed ceilings, a fireplace, a Victorian-style bed, and a deck offering views of the Casselman River. The Drover's House is the B&B's finest suite. This two-story restored house has a living room with a fireplace and a large deck looking down the hill to the river. There's a powder room on this floor, but the bedroom and full bath are one story up.

Breakfast may be taken at the adjacent Penn Alps Restaurant, which somewhat resembles a Swiss chalet. It is the last remaining log tavern on the "Pike." It's a cozy place for dinner or breakfast, with its beamed cathedral ceiling and huge stone fireplace. All meals are served cafeteria-style. Guests may also eat breakfast at several nearby restaurants. A coffeemaker and a mini-refrigerator are located in each guest room.

What's Nearby—Grantsville

Grantsville is located in Maryland's Western panhandle, an area rich with summer arts festivals. The Spruce Forest Artisan Village, which is adjacent to the B&B, is a collection of small log cabins that come alive in the summer when working artists, musicians, and craftsmen come to demonstrate their art and to sell their work. You will see beautiful Amish quilts, hickory rockers, pottery, stained glass—more than one hundred artists, musicians, poets, storytellers, and craftsmen working either in the log cabins or under the spreading spruce trees. The Penn Alps Restaurant, which is housed in an 1818 stagecoach inn, is next door. In addition, there's a local self-guided "history walk," as well as nearby golf courses, downhill ski slopes, cross-country ski trails, and a historic train to ride.

Lands End Manor on the Bay

232 Prospect Bay Drive
Grasonville, MD 21638
(410) 827–6284

INNKEEPER: Elaine Johnson Wheatley

ROOMS: 3, all with private bath and air conditioning, TV, telephone, radio, hair dryer, desk, robes, mini-refrigerator, and tape player; 2 with fireplace; crib available

ON THE GROUNDS: On 17 acres with swimming pool; dock, rowboat, canoe, paddleboat; bicycles

EXTRAS: Afternoon tea by request; evening drinks; turndown with home-made cookies, fruit, and sherry; pets permitted with prior permission; resident dog named Hobo

RATES: $160–$170, double accupancy, including full breakfast, evening drinks; $10 surcharge for one night only

CREDIT CARDS ACCEPTED: MasterCard and Visa

OPEN: Year-round

HOW TO GET THERE: From Washington, D.C., take Route 50 across the Chesapeake Bay Bridge (Route 50/301) to exit 45B (Nesbit Road). Turn right onto Nesbit Road and follow it to the stop sign. Turn left onto Route 18 and continue to the first intersection (Bennett Point Road). Turn right and continue to Perry Corner Road. Turn right again and go to the next intersection (Prospect Bay Road). Turn left and continue to the Prospect Bay Lighthouse. Turn right at the lighthouse and continue to the stop sign. Turn right onto Prospect Bay Drive and continue for 2 miles to Lands End Manor, which will be on the left. You will see a mail-box marked "Lands End" and "#232." The property is surrounded by a split-rail fence.

The rural countryside of Maryland's Eastern Shore is dotted with promontories, inlets, creeks, and rivers that create its jagged coastline. Grasonville, a tiny spot merely fifteen minutes from the Chesapeake Bay Bridge, has yet to be discovered by tourists and therefore offers the ultimate peaceful getaway. Originally called Prospect Plantation, Lands End Manor is located on a seventeen-acre point surrounded by peaceful vistas of Eastern and Prospect Bays and of Greenwood Creek. St. Michael's, Maryland, can be seen across the water on a clear night. Waterfowl nest in the marshes, and the fishing is legendary. That's why, for many years, the manor house served as a private hunting lodge.

Today, it is the home of Charles and Elaine Wheatley and also a delightful bed-and-breakfast run by Elaine, who is an architectural interior designer and a charming innkeeper. One enters a formal entry hall. There's a little library filled with books and a solarium with a flagstone floor and a wall of windows overlooking the gardens. A formal living room has another fireplace and an elaborate molded ceiling. Bouquets of flowers from the garden add splashes of color throughout.

The impressive great room, once the nucleus of the hunting lodge, has oak floors, pine-paneled walls, beamed ceilings with an antler chandelier, and a massive fireplace with eighteenth-century Delft tiles in the surround. There are leather sofas here where guests can sit to enjoy the view, and a large-screen TV for watching videos. The Gun Room has a Tudor feeling with dark beams and stucco walls, another fireplace, a terra-cotta tile floor, and racks of guns.

There are two spacious guest rooms on the second floor. Both have private baths and views of the water. The Heron Room has a feather bed with an upholstered headboard and a woodburning fireplace. In the Swan Room, there's a pencil-post tiger-maple canopy bed and a gorgeous tiger maple chest with twisted spindles. A third bedroom is occasionally used, but it has a private bath downstairs.

Elaine is the perfect pampering hostess. She serves canapés and desserts with afternoon tea whenever guests express an interest. Wine, sherry, and drinks are available prior to going out in the evening. Turndown service includes homemade cookies, sherry, and fresh fruit. A full breakfast is served in the dining room or on the patio. It will include fresh fruit and juice, a homemade coffee cake or other bread, and an entree of perhaps eggs relleños or an apple pancake puff as well as bacon, ham, or sausage.

In a very private setting, concealed from the house by trees, there's a swimming pool. At the private dock, guests may arrive by boat, and there are rowboats, canoes, and paddleboats for guests' enjoyment. Bicycles are available for back-road jaunts. Benches are located by the water, offering an ideal spot for a private picnic.

What's Nearby—Grasonville

In this rural setting near the Eastern Shore end of the Bay Bridge, boating, fishing, and bicycling are pleasant recreational activities. There are miles of untraveled roads to explore. Wye Mills, a nearby restored village, was first settled in the 1600s. It contains an operating grist mill and the restored Wye Church, which dates to 1721 and has its original hanging pulpit and high box pews. The Wye Oak is a venerable 450-year-old specimen that resides in its own 250-acre park.

Currier House B&B

800 South Market Street
Havre de Grace, MD 21078
(800) 827–2889 or (410) 939–7886

FAX: (410) 939–6145

E-MAIL: JaneC@Currier-bb.com

WEB SITE: www.currier-bb.com

INNKEEPERS: Jane and Paul Belbot

ROOMS: 4, all with private bath, air conditioning, TV, VCR, and desk; 1 with robes

ON THE GROUNDS: On 1½ acres with off-street parking, gardens, patio

EXTRAS: Evening tea with cookies or cake

RATES: $85–$95, double occupancy, including full breakfast

CREDIT CARDS ACCEPTED: American Express, Discover, MasterCard, Visa

OPEN: Year-round

HOW TO GET THERE: From I–95 take exit 89 and travel east on Route 155 for 2½ miles to Havre de Grace, where it dead-ends. Turn right onto Juanita Street. Go to the second traffic light and turn left onto Revolution Street. Go 1 block and turn right onto Union Avenue. Go 2 blocks and turn left onto Lafayette Street. Go 2 blocks to Market Street. The B&B is on the corner of Lafayette and Market Streets.

Havre de Grace is located at the mouth of the Susquehanna River, where it spills into the Chesapeake Bay. The first settlers arrived in the 1650s, and as its prominence grew it became the site of a major ferry that was used by George Washington in the Revolutionary War and by Union troops in the Civil War. The Susquehanna and Tidewater Canal was built in 1839, connecting Havre de Grace with Wrightsville, Pennsylvania, along a canal that included a series of twenty-nine locks. Throughout its distinguished history, the town has been noted as a premier fishing and waterfowl hunting center.

The Currier family matches the village in longevity and in prominence. The first Curriers arrived in Maryland in 1648, where they became farmers. Matthew Currier moved to Havre de Grace after the Civil War in 1861 and operated the ferry across the Susquehanna. He built the nucleus of the current Currier House for his family. The present dining room has paneling dating to this period. The walls contain family portraits and newspaper articles, and there's a cabinet holding interesting family memorabilia.

Over the years the Currier House grew. The welcoming wraparound porch was added, as were bedrooms, baths, and parlors. Jane Currier Balbot is a direct descendant of the original owner, and she and her husband Paul are marvelous sources of information about the house and the area. (You might also ask Jane about the ten years she spent in Greenwich Village as a folk singer.) They converted the house to a B&B in 1995.

Guests can enjoy the twin parlors, which contain such interesting pieces as a diabolical solitaire game that uses huge, colorful marbles and is played rather like Chinese checkers and an abundance of books. The guest rooms are charming. The Carroll Room has a brass bed with a chenille spread and a lovely bath with wide pine walls. A blue and white Waverly fabric is used liberally. The Crawford Room has a white iron bed and a huge bath with a black-and-white tile floor, pine walls, and a tub with a pine surround.

A full "waterman's breakfast" (basic food in large portions) is served in the dining room every morning. Jane will fix eggs with bacon, sausage or ham, potatoes, tomatoes and mushrooms, along with hot breads and fresh fruit. You definitely will not go out into the village hungry.

What's Nearby—Havre de Grace

Havre de Grace offers numerous opportunities to learn more about its history. The Concord Point Lighthouse, which has protected ships from the shore for more than 170 years, is at the end of Lafayette Street. The Susquehanna Museum is the place to learn about Havre de Grace's history. It is located in the locktender's house at the southern terminal of the Susquehanna & Tidewater Canal. The Havre de Grace Decoy Museum celebrates the unique craft of decoy carving. The work of local carvers is displayed, and on weekends carvers are on hand to demonstrate. A waterfront promenade offers breathtaking vistas of the water.

The Spencer-Silver Mansion

Best Buy

200 South Union Avenue
Havre de Grace, MD 21078
(800) 780–1485 or (410) 939–1485

E-MAIL: Spencersilver@erols.com

INNKEEPER: Carol Nemeth

ROOMS: 5, 3 with private bath and
two that share one bath; all with
air conditioning, radio, and mini-
refrigerator; 4 with porch or patio
and tape player; 2 with TV, whirlpool tub,
and coffeemaker; wheelchair access

ON THE GROUNDS: On ¾ acre with gardens

EXTRAS: Dishes of candy in each room, bowl of fresh fruit available; two
cats, Ferdinand and Ishmael, on premises

RATES: $75–$150, double occupancy, including full breakfast

CREDIT CARDS ACCEPTED: American Express, Discover, MasterCard, Visa

OPEN: Year-round

HOW TO GET THERE: From I–95 take exit 89 and travel east on Route 155 for
2½ miles to Havre de Grace, where it dead-ends. Turn right onto Juanita
Street. Go to the first traffic light and turn left onto Otsego Street. Go 3
blocks and bear right under the RR bridge onto Union Avenue. Go
through the first traffic light and go 1 block further. The B&B is on the
right on the next corner of Union Avenue and Bourbon Street.

Carol Nemeth has owned her magnificent 1896 stone mansion since 1990,
but she's accomplished its transition to a bed-and-breakfast gracefully
and gently. One by one, as time and funds have permitted, she restored
each room to its former splendor.

The house is located along a broad tree-lined boulevard and is the most
impressive in Havre de Grace. It has a wraparound porch with a copper roof
and multiple turrets and gables. Intricate stone work encircles the house.
Inside the narrow plank oak floors are inlaid with a chain design. There are
two parlors, both with elaborate columned fireplaces, oak woodwork, and
high decorative ceilings. In the entry hall, with its grand oak staircase, wonderful examples of stained glass are enriched by Bradbury and Bradbury
handmade wallpapers, which are also found at the top of the stairs. A small
vestibule has more stained glass and a mosaic tile floor. Carol's extensive
collection of unusual antique lamps are found throughout the B&B.

The guest rooms have been elegantly designed and include some interesting surprises. The Garden Room has an antique brass bed and a marble-topped dresser. The private bath has its original hexagonal tile floor. The Iris Room includes a fabulous carved walnut Victorian high-headboard bed and a bath entered through stained-glass doors. It contains a whirlpool tub and Bradbury and Bradbury border wallpaper. The Swan Room, which has a wonderful decorative fireplace and is in the turret, and Carol's Room, which has another decorative fireplace and a bay window, both have antique oak beds, and they share a bath, with its original embossed tiles and marble sink. Elaborate fretwork caps the doorway.

The most private and romantic accommodation, however, is located in the stone carriage house. It has a living room with an oak fireplace and oak tongue-and-groove walls and a loft bedroom up a spiral stairway. Guests sleep on an oak, high-headboard bed surrounded by more oak tongue-and-groove paneling. In the bath on the main floor, there's a whirlpool tub.

A full breakfast is served in the dining room, where another fireplace with a tile surround and more beautiful stained glass and oak woodwork give the room a warm glow. Among the entrees, guests might have apple French toast, or a quiche, or eggs Benedict.

What's Nearby

See "What's Nearby—Havre de Grace," on page 60.

Antietam Overlook Farm Bed & Breakfast

P.O. Box 30
Keedysville, MD 21756
(800) 878–4241

FAX: (301) 432-5230

E-MAIL: www.antietamoverlookfarm @erols.com

INNKEEPERS: John and Barbara Dreisch

ROOMS: 5, all with private bath, air conditioning, fireplace, balcony, garden tub, and hair dryer; telephone is available for guest room, if requested

ON THE GROUNDS: On 95 acres with hiking and walking trails through the woods

EXTRAS: Complimentary tea, sodas, coffee, wine, and cordials; cocker spaniel named Max

RATES: $115–$165, double occupancy, including full breakfast; two-night minimum on weekends

CREDIT CARDS ACCEPTED: American Express, Diners Club, MasterCard, Visa

OPEN: Year-round

HOW TO GET THERE: Call for directions. Near Sharpsburg and Boonsboro, Maryland, and Shepherdstown, West Virginia

From this eagle's-nest perch high in the Blue Ridge Mountains, with a four-state view and overlooking the Civil War's Antietam National Battlefield, the serenity is almost palpable. Deer graze in the adjacent fields, wild turkeys feed on grain, and migratory birds stop to spend a few days before continuing on their journey. The seclusion and serenity is so zealously guarded that there's an electrically operated gate at the entrance. Once guests reach this 95-acre aerie, their lives change, at least during their stay. The relaxed pace becomes habit-forming—there's no place to rush off to.

Originally, this was the private retreat of John and Barbara Dreisch, and their own home is right next door. The guest portion was newly constructed in 1990. The friendliness and hospitality of the Dreisches—and of their cocker spaniel, Max—and the privacy of the setting have brought guests to their doorstep who return again and again.

The building is constructed of stone and pine. There are rough-sawn yellow pine walls, hand-hewn beams, and posts. The massive stone fireplace in the Country Room is the focal point throughout the winter, while the screened-in porch with its panoramic views is the summer retreat. The decor includes a wagon-wheel chandelier, comfortable sofas and chairs, braided rugs on pine floors, shelves filled with books and magazines, quilts and folk art on the wall, and Civil War memorabilia. There's a wet bar; a full refrigerator stocked with sodas and wine; tea, coffee, an instant hot water tap; and a cabinet filled with cordials and liqueurs. Board games, jigsaw puzzles, and lively conversation take the place of a television.

The guest rooms are unique. Each has its own gas remote-controlled fireplace, a screened-in porch with a top-of-the-world view, fantastically comfortable beds, and a deep, private soaking tub tucked into an alcove that is surrounded by plants and has a view of the valley and of the flickering flames in the fireplace. The Dreisches call this a "garden tub." There's also a shower in each of the baths. One of the advantages of new construction is that central air, thorough soundproofing between walls, and soundless carpeting can be installed. Here, guests feel as if they're in a private cocoon.

A full breakfast is prepared every morning and served at communal tables in the Country Room. On a typical morning, it will include such local fare as fresh fruit; country ham baked with fresh pineapple and cinnamon sugar; fried tomatoes; a three-cheese fluffy egg casserole; battered and fried cranberry nut bread; fresh juices; and homemade jams, curds, and chutneys.

Nearby attractions, in addition to Antietam, include Harpers Ferry National Park, hiking on the Appalachian Trail or on the inn trails, and bicycling on the C. & O. Canal Path. Fine restaurants are nearby, as are antiques and gift shops.

What's Nearby—Keedysville

From this perch high above the Antietam National Battlefield, it's possible to imagine the scene that took place below in September 1862 when 23,000 troops were killed or wounded during the battle following the first Southern invasion of Northern soil in the Civil War. The Appalachian Trail meanders across the nearby mountains, offering interesting day hikes or longer ones. (See also Sharpsburg, Maryland, as well as Charles Town, Harpers Ferry, and Shepherdstown, West Virginia.)

Lake Pointe Inn Bed & Breakfast

174 Lake Pointe Drive
McHenry, MD 21541
(800) 523–LAKE or (301) 387–0111

FAX: (301) 387–0190

E-MAIL: mail@deepcreekinns.com

WEB SITE: www.deepcreekinns.com

INNKEEPER: Caroline McNiece; owners: George and Linda Pettie

ROOMS: 8, all with private bath, air conditioning, TV, VCR, telephone with private line, radio, and hair dryer; 1 with whirlpool tub; Sang Run House, just across the street, is ideal for small conferences or meetings; it has 4 additional rooms, each with private bath, and several meeting rooms

ON THE GROUNDS: On lake with private dock for swimming, kayaks, canoes; bicycles; badminton; hammock; hot tub on deck; gardens; community tennis court

EXTRAS: Homemade cookies, fruit, and snacks always available; sherry and hors d'oeuvres in the evening

RATES: $108–$178, double occupancy, including full breakfast and evening hors d'oeuvres; two-night minimum most weekends; three-night minimum some holiday weekends.

CREDIT CARDS ACCEPTED: Discover, MasterCard, Visa

OPEN: Year-round except Christmas Eve

HOW TO GET THERE: From I-68, take exit 14 onto Route 219 south and continue for 12½ miles to McHenry. Turn right at the Citgo Station onto Sang Run Road. In 2 blocks turn left onto Marsh Hill Road. In ¼ mile turn left onto Lake Pointe Drive and follow the loop road either right or left to the inn.

Tucked into Maryland's western panhandle, the Lake Pointe Inn is one of the most sophisticated but relaxed bed-and-breakfasts in the state. One morning as I sat on the wraparound deck (with its unusual stone pillars) surrounded by the towering spruce trees that date to 1939, I sipped my coffee and basked in the light of the morning sun. I watched birds swoop from trees and saw several chipmunks, bunnies, and woodchucks scurrying along, but most of all I enjoyed the peaceful calm of Deep Creek Lake, which was just steps away. I couldn't imagine anywhere else I'd rather be.

This serene retreat is the result of hard work and unique circumstances. When the stone and wood house was built in the 1890s, it was the centerpiece of a substantial farm. In 1925, however, the local electric company created Deep Creek Lake and suddenly the house sat at the edge of a 3,900-acre recreational lake with 65 miles of shoreline. Over the years the cabin served primarily as a vacation retreat for several owners, but when George and Linda Pettie transformed it into a bed-and-breakfast in 1995, they fully restored it to its turn-of-the-century origins.

The interior of the inn is unique—devoid of fussy decor, just as it should be. The Great Room, with its soaring cathedral ceilings has chestnut posts and beams and wormy chestnut plank walls and ceilings. A fabulous stone fireplace is the focal point. The interior design features furniture and fabrics with an Arts and Crafts motif. A leafy William Morris-style carpet covers the floor, leather chairs with oak frames sit before the fireplace, muslin curtains bordered in red velvet hang on the tall windows that offer views of the lake. Lamps have stained and opaque glass to light the room. Doors lead to the wonderful broad deck that encircles the inn on three sides.

The guest rooms are equally comfortable and snug and all have either a lake view or a view of the ski slopes. There are carpets on the floors, comfy down comforters encased in pretty duvets covering mission-style oak beds, oak armoires, and wicker chairs with bright cushions. The modern baths have hexagonal tile floors and pedestal sinks. The thick chestnut plank doors are original to the house. All rooms have the bath in the room except the two on the third floor, where the private baths are off the hallway.

Caroline is an accomplished innkeeper, who takes great pride in her inn. She fixes fabulous breakfasts for her guests, which are served in the inn's dining room. A typical menu will include fresh mangoes and blueberries in a honey-lime glaze followed by cinnamon bread pudding (French toast with a custard sauce and cinnamon-glazed bananas), as well as fresh grilled turkey sausage. Another day she might prepare an entree of corn and basil egg roulade with yellow tomato coulis or creamy scrambled eggs with leeks served on a puff pastry and topped with mushroom tarragon sauce.

What's Nearby—McHenry

Wisp Mountain Resort, which has twenty-three downhill ski slopes, and an eighteen-hole golf course is just across the highway. In addition, there are mountain biking trails and Nordic ski trails nearby. Fly fishing streams, hiking trails, and boating on Deep Creek Lake offer other recreational experiences. The Garrett Lakes Arts Festival sponsors a series of art performances in the spring and summer that include musicians performing Appalachian and classical music, painters, poets, dancers, and craftsmen. (See also Deep Creek Lake and Oakland.)

The Oak & Apple Bed & Breakfast

208 North Second Street
Oakland, MD 21550
(301) 334–9265

E-MAIL: oakapplebb@mail2.gcnet.net

WEB SITE: www.oak&apple.com

INNKEEPER: Jana Brown

ROOMS: 5, 3 with private bath and 2 that share one bath; 1 with whirlpool tub

ON THE GROUNDS: On ⅔ acre with sunporches and gardens

EXTRAS: Guest refrigerator; a cat, J.C., on premises

RATES: $70–$100, including Continental breakfast; two-night minimum holiday and special event weekends

CREDIT CARDS ACCEPTED: MasterCard and Visa

OPEN: Year-round

HOW TO GET THERE: Traveling west on I–68, take exit 14A onto Route 219 south and travel 25 miles into Oakland. Turn right onto East Crook Street. At the stop sign you will see the B&B across the street on the right corner. Traveling east on I–68, take exit 4 (Friendsville) onto Route 42. This will join Route 219 south in 7 miles. Continue on Route 219 for 14 more miles into Oakland. Turn right onto East Crook Street and follow directions above.

Jana Brown is a current-day example of what innkeeping used to be all about. She is friendly and helpful and truly cares about her guests and their comfort. On the other hand, she is atypical in that, although she has been welcoming guests to her home since 1992, she continues to work full time as an audiologist as well. Therefore, during the week, you are likely to get an answering machine if you call.

Jana's handsome 1915 brick-and-shingle Colonial Revival Victorian sits above the tree-lined street encircled by an inviting wraparound porch. This is where I like to sit at the end of the day, while trying to decide which of the fine restaurants to succumb to. The inside of the house is particularly impressive. The parlor includes a massive, masculine, floor-to-ceiling brick fireplace. A sun porch, where breakfast may be eaten in the morning, has a beadboard ceiling, rounded corners, and fluted columns. The dining room has a fireplace with a tiger oak mantel and a surround of green tiles.

Jana has decorated the guest rooms with flair. The nicest room is the Blue Room, which has a bed with a blue-and-rose tapestry bedspread and a rose carpet. The bath includes a whirlpool tub. The Peach Room, which is also on the second floor, has a green carpet and another private bath. On the third floor, the Rose and Yellow Rooms share a nice bath, and the White Room has a private bath, although it is in the hallway.

What's Nearby—Oakland

Oakland is the county seat of Garrett County, and the Garrett County Historical Museum contains interesting artifacts and exhibits describing local history. Nearby Mountain Lake Park was the site from 1882 to 1942 of a Chautauqua-style resort. Thousands of visitors came every summer to listen to lecturers and orators that included William

Jennings Bryan, William Howard Taft, and Billy Sunday. In 1997 the renowned glass artist Simon Pearce chose this village for his new facility. Visitors can watch the glassblowers creating the beautiful pieces, and they can purchase items as well. (See also Deep Creek Rock and McHenry.)

Combsberry

4837 Evergreen Road
Oxford, MD 21654
(410) 226-5353

FAX: (410) 228-1453

E-MAIL: combsberry@info.com

WEB SITE: www.combsberry.com

INNKEEPERS: Dr. Mahmood and Ann Shariff; manager, Catherine Magrogan

ROOMS: 7, including 2 suites and 2 cottages, all with private bath, air conditioning, robes, and hair dryer; 5 with fireplace; 4 with whirlpool, balcony, or patio; 2 with kitchen; portable telephone for guests to use

ON THE GROUNDS: On 10 waterfront acres with formal gardens; dock, fishing, crabbing, canoeing, paddleboating

EXTRAS: Wine, tea, and cheese on arrival; chocolates at turndown; whirlpool tubs; access to fax; Jack Russell terrier named Katie on premises

RATES: $250–$395, double occupancy, including full breakfast; two-night minimum if Saturday stay included, or $50 surcharge for Saturday stay only

CREDIT CARDS ACCEPTED: MasterCard and Visa

OPEN: Year-round except Thanksgiving and Christmas Day

HOW TO GET THERE: From Washington, D.C., take Route 50 across the Chesapeake Bay Bridge. Stay on Route 50 to Route 322 south, the Easton Parkway. Then take Route 333 south toward Oxford for 6⁸⁄₁₀ miles and turn left onto Evergreen Road. Turn left again at the second driveway through the brick pillars. Drive down a long dirt driveway to the inn.

Were I to choose my favorite spot at Combsberry, I believe it would be the brick patio surrounded by the flower garden and enclosed by a picket fence behind the Oxford Cottage. From this vantage point, I could watch the herons and egrets and swans on Island Creek. My special friend would have picked a magnolia blossom from the nearby tree for my hair, and we would sit here while the sun sank behind the horizon to watch the pink and gold sky fade away. We would be enchanted as the inn's gardens and pathways were illuminated by moonbeams. Can any other place offer such tranquility—such sublime harmony with nature?

The history of Combsberry Plantation actually began in 1649, when one hundred acres were awarded to Josias Cooper. In 1718 the property passed to John Oldham, who began construction of the fine brick manor house that has now been converted to a B&B. The house's history is far from over. Now in the caring hands of Dr. Mahmood and Ann Shariff, the elegant house has been fully restored to the gracious style of the Oldhams.

The house sits on 9½ acres, and it contains some unusual architectural features. Stairs do not rise from a center hall, but within a stair tower, and there are six fireplaces with arched brick openings. The living room has elegant antique furnishings, polished wide-plank pine floors (original to the house) topped with Oriental rugs, and English chintz fabric draped across the windows. Through an archway handpainted with flowers, there's a sunroom offering a stunning view of the river, and French doors lead to a brick-walled garden. Behind the sunroom is a cozy paneled library with a woodburning fireplace and deep-green walls lined with books.

There's a formal dining room where breakfast may be served, but most people prefer to eat in the casual atmosphere of the striking kitchen. The huge space has brick walls, tile floors, and an open island. On the river side, a bay of windows provides views to guests seated at little cafe tables. Breakfast will include fresh breads, fruits, and juices as well as perhaps a ham and broccoli strata or a quiche.

There are seven guest accommodations—all with spectacular views of the water. The Magnolia Suite is in shades of pink and green and includes a canopy bed, a woodburning fireplace, a dresser with flowers handpainted on it, a private deck, and an elegant bath with a double whirlpool and a tiled shower. The charming Victoria Garden Room is in blue and white and furnished with wicker furniture and a wrought-iron bed. It has a private stairway to the English garden, which is softly illuminated at night. Two additional rooms in a building built in 1997 are equally enchanting. These two share a greatroom and a kitchen.

There's a dock that provides access to boaters who wish to arrive by water. A canoe and paddleboat are available, and guests can fish and crab off the pier.

What's Nearby—Oxford

Oxford, which was established in 1694, was the first port of entry on the Eastern Shore. It's still possible to walk its quiet streets to admire the historic old buildings; or to visit the Oxford Customs House, an exact replica of the first one; or to learn more about the town's history at the Oxford Museum. The Oxford-Bellevue Ferry has been traversing the Tred Avon River since 1760.

Moonlight Bay Inn & Marina

6002 Lawton Avenue
Rock Hall, MD 21661
(410) 639–2660

FAX: (410) 639–7739

WEB SITE: www.kentcounty.com/rockhall/moonlightbay

INNKEEPERS: Dorothy and Bob Santangelo

ROOMS: 10, all with private bath, air conditioning, radio, and desk; 5 with balcony and whirlpool tub; wheelchair access

ON THE GROUNDS: On 1½ acres of waterfront with marina, dock, and two 350-foot fishing piers; swimming, bird watching on grounds

EXTRAS: Bicycles available; high afternoon tea with fruit, scones, pastries, and candy; decanter of sherry in guest rooms

RATES: $100–$140, double occupancy, including full breakfast and afternoon tea; two-night minimum weekends; three-night minimum holiday weekends

CREDIT CARDS ACCEPTED: Discover, MasterCard, Visa

OPEN: Year-round

HOW TO GET THERE: From Washington, D.C., take Route 50, cross the Chesapeake Bay Bridge and continue on Route 301/50 until it splits. Take Route 301 north for 5 miles to Route 213 north. Follow Route 213

north for approximately 12 miles and cross the Chester River Bridge. Turn left onto Route 291 and drive ¼ mile to its end. Turn right onto Route 20 and follow Route 20 for approximately 13 miles to its end. Just before the bay, turn right onto Lawton Avenue. Moonlight Bay is the sixth property on the left.

When Dorothy and Bob Santangelo moved south from Long Island, New York, Bob had his heart set on operating a marina and Dorothy wanted to run a bed-and-breakfast. They looked up and down the coast, but nothing quite fit until they spied this property in 1992, really quite by accident. They had come to look at another house, but when they drove past this one with its faded FOR SALE sign, Bob was mesmerized by the water. "He didn't even see the house," said Dorothy. Although the house, which has portions that dated to 1850, had been a ferry terminal, a post office, a restaurant, and a summer boarding house, it was an abandoned

na when they bought it. "It did-
ob, it seems, won that round.
the house, however, the couple
, and creating inviting common
ths, until they were ready to ful-
othly at both the B&B and the
;uest rooms right at the water's
1997 the couple built a brand-
; guest rooms and spectacular

ors. One has oak floors, a fire-
ading alcove filled with books.
but not elegant.
m also. There are wing chairs in
, and a fireplace. The guest tele-
here's a lovely screened gazebo

near the water.

The guest rooms in this building all have whirlpool tubs and private porches. Moon Beam, on the second floor, has pink sponged and glazed walls, a beautiful tiled bath, and a private deck with views of the water. Moon Struck includes an iron canopy bed and a bath finished in black-and-white tiles. Moon Glow has an armoire and an iron bed with a gold spread.

What's Nearby—Rock Hall

The Chesapeake Bay is rich in bird and animal life. The Eastern Neck Island Refuge and Remington Farms are both nearby. Rock Hall has public tennis courts for guests to enjoy. Church Hill is the site of live theater performances in an ornate old movie theater, and on the second and fourth Saturdays of the month there's an antiques and "junque" auction in nearby Galena. On Wednesdays a mammoth flea market in Crumpton brings buyers from a five-state region. From the B&B it's an easy walk to the Waterman's Museum, a potter's shop, restaurants, and gift and craft shops.

Dr. Dodson House Bed & Breakfast

200 Cherry Street
(mailing address: P.O. Box 956)
St. Michaels, MD 21663–0956
(410) 745–3691

E-MAIL: jbuck@bluecrab.org

INNKEEPERS: Janet Buck and Gary Nylander

ROOMS: 2, both with private bath, air conditioning, TV, fireplace, radio, hair dryer, and robes

ON THE GROUNDS: Porches, garden

EXTRAS: Social hour with wine, beer, soft drinks, and gourmet hors d'oeuvres; turndown service with chocolate truffles; complimentary bicycles to use; Tootsie, a Lhasa apso, in owners' quarters

RATES: $130–$185, double occupancy, including full breakfast, evening social hour, and turndown service; two-night minimum most weekends; three-night minimum Labor Day and Memorial Day weekends

CREDIT CARDS ACCEPTED: No credit cards accepted

OPEN: Year-round

HOW TO GET THERE: From Washington, D.C., cross the Chesapeake Bay Bridge and follow Route 50 east. Before Easton, take Route 322/Easton Parkway to Route 33 and follow it into St. Michaels. You will be on Talbot Street. Turn right onto Cherry Street. The B&B is on the corner of Cherry and Locust Streets.

If you're looking for a bed-and-breakfast that's loaded with charm and history and is run by friendly, welcoming innkeepers, then look no further. This is it!

The brick Federal-period house was built in 1799 by Samuel Harrison, a local shipbuilder. It is one of the oldest in St. Michaels. Shortly after the turn of the century, it was in use as a tavern and post office, and perhaps that's how it survived the War of 1812. In the 1860s the Victorian porch was added across the front and in 1878 it became the home and office of Dr. Robert A. Dodson, the local physician. Many of the house's doors, windows, floors, and fireplace mantels are original. Don't be alarmed if you find the exterior trim still needs paint. The innkeepers have concentrated first on the interior.

Respecting the B&B's fine heritage, Janet and Gary have enhanced its historical character by filling it with beautiful period antiques that are augmented by lovely fabrics, needlepoint pillows, and beautiful artwork. The living room has wide-plank pine floors, rose-colored walls, a rose velvet chair, and a fireplace with a brick hearth. The dining room, which is on the opposite side of the entry hall, has rose-colored walls and beautiful quilts, Oriental rugs on the polished pine floors, and another fireplace.

Although there are only two guest rooms, they are so interesting and so charming, guests seldom want to leave. The Dodson Room has pale blue walls and white shutters on the windows. The furnishings include a fireplace, a white iron-and-brass canopy bed, a graceful Victorian ladies' white wicker portrait chair, and an antique marble sink in the room. There are lovely antique quilts and a lively watercolor quilt in a lattice frame. The private bath has a hexagonal tile floor and a marble and glass shower. The Harrison Room has seafoam-green walls, a brass bed, and another brick fireplace. The chairs are upholstered in pink-and-white striped fabric.

Dr. Dodson's pampered guests will receive a carafe of coffee, juice, and a newspaper at their door in the morning. Breakfast, which might include eggs Benedict or waffles topped with bananas and chopped pecans, can be ordered the night before and will be served in the dining room at the hour selected by the guest.

What's Nearby—St. Michaels

St. Michaels is the hub of activity in this section of Eastern Shore Maryland. There are numerous shops, boutiques, and restaurants along the pretty main street. (Don't miss dinner in one of the casual crab houses that overlook the Miles River.) The Chesapeake Bay Maritime Museum consists of a group of eighteen historic buildings that include an authentic 1880s lighthouse, an aquarium, and a boat restoration shop. There's no better way to learn about the seafaring life of the Chesapeake Bay. Charter boats take visitors on fishing excursions, and there's also a narrated sightseeing cruise. (See also Easton, Oxford, Tilghman Island, and Wittman.)

Hambleton Inn

202 Cherry Street
(mailing address: P.O. Box 1007)
St. Michaels, MD 21663
(410) 745–3350

FAX: (410) 745–5709

E-MAIL: furman@dmv.com

WEB SITE: www.hambletoninn.com

INNKEEPERS: Steve and Kimberly Furman

ROOMS: 5, all with private bath and air conditioning; 4 with private porch; 1 with a fireplace

ON THE GROUNDS: On ¾ acre that slopes down to the water, private dock; open porch upstairs with view

EXTRAS: Bicycles for guests to use; turndown with chocolates; golden retriever named Skipper on premises

RATES: $135–$245, double occupancy, including full breakfast; two-night minimum from April–October if Saturday stay included

CREDIT CARDS ACCEPTED: MasterCard and Visa

OPEN: Year-round except Christmas week and two weeks from mid- to late February

HOW TO GET THERE: From Washington, D.C., cross the Chesapeake Bay Bridge and follow Route 50 east. Before Easton, take Route 322/Easton Parkway to Route 33 and follow it into St. Michaels. You will be on Talbot Street. Turn right onto Cherry Street. The B&B is at the end of the block on the right.

The Hambleton Inn, a white-clapboard 1860s inn on a quiet dead-end street and at water's edge, has been owned by Steve and Kimberly Furman since 1995, and they've been making improvements ever since.

They've redecorated the rooms, upgraded the baths, put in new landscaping, added a new kitchen wing, converted the old kitchen into a handsome dining room, and purchased new furniture. The rooms have clean, crisp decor devoid of fussiness, which allows the character of this grand old 1860s house to shine through.

The favorite spot to relax is the great glass-enclosed front porch, where wicker chairs invitingly welcome relaxation. You can sit here mesmerized by the activity in the harbor just below. Should you prefer a seat outside in order to catch some summer rays, you might head to the second-floor porch, which has an even better view. Or you might stroll down to the inn's private dock for an up-close look.

The guest rooms have pine floors and pastel walls with four-poster Shaker-style beds covered with matelassé spreads. The baths are finished with tile floors. Bedroom #1, on the first floor, has pale-green walls and a fireplace with a tile hearth. My favorite room is #5, which encompasses the entire third floor. It has yellow walls with yellow-and-white gingham fabric on the bed. The bath has a fabulous yellow floral paper on the walls.

Breakfast is served in the dining room, which has a brick fireplace. Kimberly might prepare orange French toast, or a strata cheese casserole, or brioche eggs with a basil cheese sauce.

What's Nearby

See "What's Nearby—St. Michaels," page 73.

The Old Brick Inn

401 South Talbot Street
(mailing address: P.O. Box 987)
St. Michaels, MD 21663
(410) 745–3323

FAX: (410) 745–3320

WEB SITE: www.oldbrickinn.com

INNKEEPER: Martha Strickland

ROOMS: 12, including 1 suite, all with private bath, air conditioning, and radio; 4 with fireplace and porch; 1 with VCR and whirlpool tub; wheelchair access

ON THE GROUNDS: Brick courtyard with swimming pool

EXTRAS: Parking on premises; small conference room

RATES: $95–$250, double occupancy, including Continental breakfast; two-night minimum on weekends

CREDIT CARDS ACCEPTED: American Express, Diners Club, MasterCard, Visa

OPEN: February to December

HOW TO GET THERE: From Washington, D.C., cross the Chesapeake Bay Bridge and follow Route 50 east. Before Easton, take Route 322/Easton Parkway to Route 33 and follow it into St. Michaels. You will be on Talbot Street. Turn right onto Mulberry Street. The B&B is on the corner, and another right turn takes you into the B&B's parking lot.

The two handsome brick buildings in the heart of the village of St. Michael's are steeped in history. The corner building, which faces Talbot Street, is a fine example of Federal architecture. It was built as a residence in 1816 and served as the home of the St. Michaels Bank and an antiques store, but it has been known for years as the Old Inn. This building has a dormered roof and double porches. It's on the National Register of Historic Places.

The other brick building, which faces Mulberry Street, was built in 1985 on the site of the former carriage house. Designed to look old, it has three massive sets of French doors topped with fan lights on both the first and the second floors. Boxed columns support roofs across both levels. There's a beautiful courtyard across the first floor with planter boxes filled with flowers and a porch across the second level.

Martha Strickland is much more than an innkeeper. As a part owner of this B&B that opened in 1998, she designed the inn and the decor of its rooms. Furthermore, she's been in the hospitality business all her working life, so she knows what we like the best. The oldest building contains a brick-floored reception room and lovely common room with an emerald-green carpet. This can also be used for small meetings. A brick-walled courtyard with a small pool and a little fountain has a New Orleans ambience. A Continental breakfast is served in this building, also in a pretty brick-floored room that includes brick walls decorated with antique quilts.

The guest rooms in the oldest building contain reproduction four-poster and sleigh beds, and alas, some of the baths have linoleum floors. Nevertheless, they are spacious and bright. The Honeymoon Suite, which has an emerald-green rug and shutters on the windows, has a beautiful bath with a travertine floor and a marble sink. My favorite room in this building, however, is Room #205, which has a nautical flavor. There's a terrific and imposing white four-poster bed dressed with blue-and-white fabrics, as well as wicker furniture.

The most fabulous rooms, however, are the themed rooms found in the Carriage House. For these, Martha let her imagination soar. The Guinevere Suite has brick walls and a brick floor. There's a huge iron bed draped with filmy gold fabric and a suit of armor standing in a corner. The bath has tile floors and another brick wall. The Annie Oakley Room has a Ralph Lauren flannel coverlet on the bed, a plaid sofa, a black-and-white cowhide hanging on the wall, and an old covered-wagon lamp. The Scarlett O'Hara Room has a four-poster bed and two balconies—one in front and one in back.

The Old Brick Inn is steps away from the array of shops and restaurants along Talbot Street—a bustle of activity, especially in the summer. At the end of the block, there's a marina where guests might arrive by boat.

What's Nearby

See "What's Nearby—St. Michaels," page 73.

The Tarr House B&B

109 Green Street
(mailing address: P.O. Box 1152)
St. Michaels, MD 21663
(410) 745–2175 (fax also)

INNKEEPER: Bonnie Baseman

ROOMS: 2, both with private bath, air conditioning, and hair dryer; 1 with a fireplace

ON THE GROUNDS: Gardens

EXTRAS: Decanter of sherry in rooms; Labadoddle (dog) Toby on premises

RATES: $165, double occupancy, including Continental breakfast; two-night minimum weekends

CREDIT CARDS ACCEPTED: None

OPEN: Year-round

HOW TO GET THERE: From Washington, D.C., cross the Bay Bridge and take Route 50 east. Before Easton, take Route 322/Easton Parkway to Route 33 and follow it into St. Michaels. You will be on Talbot Street. Turn right at Christ Church onto Willow Street, which becomes Green Street in 1 block. The B&B will be in 1 block on the left.

Charming, engaging, captivating, and delightful are all adjectives that come to mind when describing the Tarr House B&B. From a little doll's house of brick (circa 1667, making it one of the oldest houses in St. Michaels) that has a new clapboard extension merely 200 years old, innkeeper Bonnie Baseman, an interior designer, has fashioned an enchanting and sweet little B&B. There are green shutters on the windows and window boxes with a cute bunny and rose design that overflow with geraniums in summer. Tucked away on a quiet side street in this village that buzzes with tourists throughout the summer, her sanctuary provides ample space to escape. If you are fortunate enough to have booked one of her two rooms, you'll congratulate yourself throughout your visit.

There are three common rooms for guests to use. Both the living room and the library have woodburning fireplaces, white paneled walls, wide-plank heart pine floors, and English chintz-covered chairs and windows. Floor-to-ceiling bookcases hold a variety of interesting books. The library also contains the house television and a desk with a telephone and fax. Throughout the house, fine European paintings hang on the walls.

At the back of the house, Bonnie added a tile-floored Garden Room with French doors that open to the spacious terrace and a garden filled with an ever-changing kaleidoscope of color from early tulips and iris to daisies and mums. A small natural pond, surrounded with rocks, holds koi.

The dining room, where Bonnie serves an extraordinary Continental breakfast, has another fireplace; there's a sideboard laden with silver; and a glass-topped table set with linen placemats, sterling flatware, and Lenox china. A swan chandelier oversees the bounty. She starts the meal with a plate of fresh fruit (perhaps bananas, kiwi, and melon) decorated with seasonal flowers. This is followed by an array of breakfast breads, from croissants to melt-in-your-mouth blueberry muffins.

The two guest rooms are on the second floor, and they both have private baths. One has a cathedral ceiling, a king-size bed with a headboard upholstered in a brilliant Clarence House fabric, an antique French walnut armoire, an antique French ladies' writing desk, and a tiny "footwarmer" fireplace. The small bath has a shower. The other room has a queen-size bed with a headboard upholstered in a wisteria pattern, an antique German armoire, and a bath with a clawfoot tub and a hand-held shower. A decanter of sherry sits on an antique table in each room.

The B&B is only a few steps from the harbor and an easy walk to the Chesapeake Bay Maritime Museum. Cove Park is across the street.

The Inn at Antietam

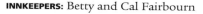

220 East Main Street
(mailing address: P.O. Box 119)
Sharpsburg, MD 21782
(301) 432–6601
Fax: (301) 432–5981

INNKEEPERS: Betty and Cal Fairbourn

ROOMS: 4 suites, all with private bath, air conditioning, desk, robes, and radios; 1 with a TV; 1 with a fireplace; wheelchair access

ON THE GROUNDS: Gardens; parking

EXTRAS: Decanter of sherry in the parlor, cookies in the sun room; dog named Tucker, cat named Rebok

RATES: $150, double occupancy, including full breakfast; two-night minimum weekends and holidays

CREDIT CARDS ACCEPTED: American Express

OPEN: Mid-February to mid-December

HOW TO GET THERE: From I–70 or I–270, go to Frederick. Continue west on I–70 to exit 49 (Braddock Heights). Turn left onto Alternate Route 40 west and follow this through Middletown and Boonsboro. In Boonsboro turn left onto Route 34 and follow this for 6 miles to Sharpsburg. As you approach Sharpsburg, you will see the Antietam National Cemetery on the left. The inn is beside it, also on the left.

The trim white 1908 clapboard Victorian sits high above the road on 7½ acres next to the Antietam Cemetery. From a swing or rocker on the wraparound porch, you can contemplate the tragic events of September 17, 1862, when 23,000 Confederate and Union men lost their lives or were wounded in the Battle of Antietam. Or you can read about them in one of the innkeepers' many Civil War books.

Today the roar of muskets and the thunder of cannons have been replaced by the peaceful sounds of birds chirping. Betty and Cal Fairbourn (he was formerly a vice president of General Motors Acceptance Corporation) restored the house in 1984 and have created a lovely haven.

Guests park at the rear of the house, so the flower-filled gardens and the brick patio with its white wicker and iron furniture are the first view they receive of this fine inn. A bowl of fruit and freshly baked cookies will be waiting in the sunroom, where a magnificent hibiscus tree blooms next to antique wicker furniture. You will surely want to take a cup of tea or a glass of wine to the patio to admire the flowers and the view of the Blue Ridge Mountains beyond. On cooler days, you might sit in the parlor, which is furnished with antique Victorian furniture and has a piano. On a marble-topped Victorian table, there's a decanter of sherry.

The four guest rooms are spacious enough to include sitting areas, and each has a thoroughly updated bath. Each room is decorated with antiques. In the rustic Smoke House, there's a massive brick fireplace, beamed ceilings, barnwood walls, and a large wrought-iron bed in a loft. In the Master Suite, there's a four-poster crown canopy bed dressed in a peach floral fabric that matches the wallpaper, and lace curtains on the windows. The Blue Bird Suite has a white iron bed and whimsical flop-eared bunnies. The Queen Suite has a sleigh bed.

Breakfast is served every morning in the formal dining room, which has elegant pale blue walls. Betty sets the table with a lace tablecloth and her fine silver and china. Candles add a romantic air. She often starts the meal with fresh juice and fruit. Although she may fix coddled eggs or baked apples or poached pears, her specialties are Belgian waffles, blueberry pancakes, and blueberry blintzes.

Many of the Fairbourns' guests are Civil War buffs who come to immerse themselves in Civil War history. They will find many interesting books in the collection at the inn, and they will spend hours walking through the Antietam Cemetery, reading the inscriptions on the marble, bronze, and granite monuments. You can also drive an 8-mile, self-guided audio tour of the site.

What's Nearby—Sharpsburg

A visit to the Antietam National Battlefield should begin at the visitor center, where historical exhibits and an audiovisual program will lay the groundwork for an understanding of the events that took place here. A walk through the Antietam National Cemetery, located next door to the B&B, will have a profound impact. (See also Keedysville, Maryland, as well as Charles Town, Harpers Ferry, and Shepherdstown, West Virginia.)

The River House Inn

201 East Market Street
Snow Hill, MD 21863
(410) 632–2722

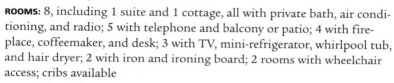

FAX: (410) 632–2866
E-MAIL: innkeeper@riverhouseinn.com
WEB SITE: www.riverhouseinn.com
INNKEEPERS: Larry and Susanne Knudsen

ROOMS: 8, including 1 suite and 1 cottage, all with private bath, air conditioning, and radio; 5 with telephone and balcony or patio; 4 with fireplace, coffeemaker, and desk; 3 with TV, mini-refrigerator, whirlpool tub, and hair dryer; 2 with iron and ironing board; 2 rooms with wheelchair access; cribs available

ON THE GROUNDS: Lawns and gardens down to Pocomoke River

EXTRAS: Wine and snacks in afternoon; soft drinks, coffee, and tea always available; fax available; pets occasionally permitted; two resident standard poodles named Belle and Winner

RATES: $100–$195, double occupancy, including full breakfast; two-night minimum weekends April–October, plus holiday weekends and Pony Penning Days

CREDIT CARDS ACCEPTED: American Express, Discover, MasterCard, Visa

OPEN: Year-round except Christmas Day

HOW TO GET THERE: From Washington, D.C., take Route 50 across the Chesapeake Bay Bridge. Continue on Route 50 east to Salisbury and then take Route 13 bypass toward Norfolk. In 2½ miles, take Route 12 and continue for 16 miles to Snow Hill. Go over the bridge and continue to the light. Turn left onto Market Street and go 1 block. Turn left onto Green Street and then right into the driveway of the B&B.

Although the elaborate beige with white trim clapboard Victorian sits just off the main street of town, its two acres of lawns and gardens slope down to the edge of the Pocomoke River. Built between 1860 and 1890, it is a confection of dripping gingerbread from multiple gables. There's also an overhanging wraparound porch supported by boxed columns, lacy black wrought-iron trim reminiscent of New Orleans buildings, fancy keyhole trim in the gables, and chocolate-brown shutters.

Larry and Susanne Knudsen opened the house to guests in 1991 and have been adding new rooms and buildings ever since. In addition to the main house, which has four guest rooms and one suite, there's also River Cottage, an 1890s carriage barn that has been converted to a deluxe guest room with private porch and a tiny kitchen, and Riverview Hideaway, a new building on the banks of the river with two rooms offering whirlpool tubs and fireplaces as well as sweeping river views from private 28-foot porches.

The River House is still the heart of the B&B. In the entry hall the striking stairway newel is made of lustrous burled walnut. The twin parlors, which are painted cardinal red, have forest green accents in the fireplace surrounds, the carpets, and the upholstered pieces. Guests gather here on winter evenings before the fireplace or on either the upper or lower porch in summer to sip coffee, tea, or wine and nibble on snacks while admiring the view of the river. There's also a TV and VCR and a video library as well as a variety of books and board games.

The guest rooms are furnished with either antiques or period reproductions. The Thebaud Room, for example, has a magnificent antique French bedroom suite and a gas fireplace; the West Room has an early mahogany Chippendale-style bedroom suite with carved phoenixes; and the River Room has local antiques from the 1860s and another gas fireplace. The rooms in the Riverview Hideaway are equally luxurious. The Colonial Room has a Queen Anne-style canopy bed, while the Garden Room has an iron canopy bed.

A full breakfast is served in either the formal dining room or in the breakfast room, where guests sit at individual tables. There will be place mats and linen napkins, silver, and china. The meal will include fruits, juice, and perhaps Susanne's River House eggs—a combination of eggs shirred in cream and topped with herbs and cheese—or her yummy croissant French toast with dried fruits, as well as bacon or sausage.

Were I to plan the perfect day in Snow Hill, I would arise early and walk to the nearby boat rental for a canoe outing on the Pocomoke River, a state-designated wild and scenic river. I would return in time for Susanne's excellent breakfast, and then I'd set out on a walking tour of Snow Hill, or I'd borrow one of the inn bicycles for an afternoon of cycling about the countryside. Larry is also a riverboat captain, and he takes people for tours of the river on his pontoon boat, the *Otter*, so—All aboard!

What's Nearby—Snow Hill

Take a walking tour of historic Snow Hill, board a sightseeing boat for a cruise along the Pocomoke River, or rent a canoe for your own excursion. Visit the Julia A. Purnell Museum to see the exhibits of art and objects related to Worcester County. At Shad Landing State Park you can picnic, boat, or swim in a pool, or you can bask in the sun on the sandy ocean beaches in nearby Assateague State Park. (See also Berlin, Maryland, and Chincoteague, Virginia.)

Gramercy Mansion Bed & Breakfast

1400 Greenspring Valley Road
Stevenson, MD 21153
(800) 553–3404 or (410) 486–2405

FAX: (410) 486–1765

E-MAIL: gramercy@erols.com

WEB SITE: www.angelfire.com/md/
gramercy

INNKEEPERS: Cristin Kline and
Anne Pomykala

ROOMS: 10, including 2 suites, 5 with private bath and the rest shared; all with air conditioning, TV, radio, and robes; 5 with telephone with dataport, VCR, coffeemaker, and hair dryer; 3 with fireplace and whirlpool tub; 1 with porch

ON THE GROUNDS: On 45 acres that include walking trails along Honeybrook Stream, an orchard, an organic farm, gardens, tennis court, pool, croquet lawn, and hiking trails

EXTRAS: Tours of Koinonia Farm, a certified organic farm that's been under cultivation since 1950; a collie, Cookie, on premises

RATES: $165–$275, double occupancy, including full breakfast

CREDIT CARDS ACCEPTED: American Express, Discover, MasterCard, Visa

OPEN: Year-round

HOW TO GET THERE: From downtown Baltimore, follow I–83 (the Jones Falls Expressway) north to I–695. Take the left exit onto I–695 west (Falls Road). Follow Falls Road north toward Brooklandville. At the second light, turn left onto Greenspring Valley Road. Go 1 mile, cross Greenspring Avenue, and then enter the first driveway on the right. The bed-and-breakfast is at the top of the hill.

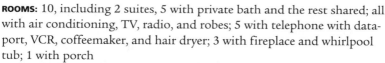ramercy Mansion is one of the sweet surprises that you are almost reluctant to share with others. Yet it's been the special secret of diplomats and naturalists since the 1950s. The undistinguished driveway, with its

tiny sign declaring the presence of an herb garden up the hill, offers no hint of the other pleasures awaiting.

The 1902 brick Tudor mansion was built by Alexander J. Cassatt, the owner of the Pennsylvania Railroad, who was the brother of Mary Cassatt, the wonderful American impressionist painter. He built it as a wedding present for his daughter, Eliza.

In the 1950s the estate became the home of the Koinonia Foundation—a place where President Truman initiated a training program for Christian ambassadors. They learned organic gardening techniques and literacy methods designed to help poorer countries become literate and to produce their own food. The Foundation was the precursor of the Peace Corps. It was on these grounds that seminars on world peace, education, literacy, race relations, hunger, and much more were conducted during the Kennedy presidency. The estate was purchased at auction by the Pomykala family, and they converted it to a bed-and-breakfast in 1987.

The interior of the grand mansion is still replete with dark boxed beams, oak paneling, chestnut floors, and multiple fireplaces. There are beautiful museum-quality antiques throughout. A wide terrace has been enclosed, and it is used as a breakfast room in summer. The elegant formal dining room accommodates breakfast guests in the winter.

Five of the guest rooms are spacious and include their own private baths; the other five are beautifully furnished but small and these "back hall" rooms share hall baths. My favorite room is the Blue Garden Suite, which is furnished in lovely antique Louis XIV furniture. The sitting room has a fireplace and a beautiful ornately carved Victorian walnut bed, and there's a sunporch with lattice walls and views of the garden and pool. In the bath, a whirlpool tub is surrounded by blue tiles, and there's a fabulous marble sink. Aunt Mary's Suite has a parlor with bunny tiles surrounding the fireplace and a king-size canopy bed. The bath has a sink placed in an antique table.

Guests are given the breakfast menu in the afternoon so they can make their preferences known for the following morning. They can choose from a variety of omelets and pancakes.

A stroll along the grounds will take visitors beside Honeybrook Stream, through wooded areas, and to Koinonia Farm, where the organic farming principles established in the 1950s continue to be used.

Lazyjack Inn

5907 Tilghman Island Road
(mailing address: P.O. Box 248)
Tilghman Island, MD 21671
(800) 690–5080 or (410) 886–2215

FAX: (410) 886–2635

E-MAIL: mrichards@bluecrab.org

WEB SITE: www.lazyjackinn.com

INNKEEPERS: Mike and Carol Richards

ROOMS: 4, including 2 suites, all with private bath, air conditioning, clock radio, and hair dryer; 2 with fireplace, whirlpool tub, and robes; 1 with a desk

ON THE GROUNDS: Sailing yacht

EXTRAS: Afternoon tea and snacks; chocolates, bottled water, and sherry in guest rooms; three outside cats

RATES: $145–$200, double occupancy, including full breakfast; two-night minimum weekends April–mid-November and holidays

CREDIT CARDS ACCEPTED: MasterCard and Visa

OPEN: Year-round

HOW TO GET THERE: From Washington, D.C., take Route 50 across the Chesapeake Bay Bridge and continue east on Route 50. Before Easton, take Route 322/Easton Bypass to Route 33. Continue on Route 33 through St. Michaels for another 11 miles to Tilghman Island. The B&B will be on the left.

anguid little Tilghman Island enjoys one of the longest histories in America. It was charted by Captain John Smith in 1608, and it is now the home of the last remaining fleet of skipjacks, historic flat-bottomed sail-boats used for dredging oysters. The lore of the watermen who skipper these craft is laced with romance and adventure—a real-life chapter from James Michener's *Chesapeake*.

The Lazyjack Inn is run by Mike and Carol Richards, who are seafarers and restoration specialists themselves. Not only have they lovingly restored the little house that became their bed-and-breakfast, but they also restored the *Lady Patty* yacht, a splendid 45-foot bronze-and-teak bay ketch built in 1935. Captain Richards takes travelers on two-hour cruises by advance reservation. The champagne sunset sails are particularly popular.

The inn is as bright and pretty as a new penny. Originally a waterman's house built sometime prior to 1855, it has a driveway of crushed oyster shells. The white clapboard house is fronted by a veranda painted pink and filled with white wicker and Adirondack chairs. In the Harbor Room, with its wall of windows offering wonderful views of the interesting old boats in Dogwood Harbor, there's a gas fireplace. The library has an extensive col-lection of maritime books as well as another fireplace.

The guest rooms are spacious and eclectic. The grandest is the Nellie Byrd Suite, which has a magnificent brass bed, a late 1800s Victorian love seat, a fireplace, and lots of duck decoys. The bath has an enclosed whirlpool tub and a sink placed in a marvelous old carved dresser. The stun-ning view reaches up the Choptank River and across Dogwood Harbor. The East Room has exposed beams and heart pine floors covered by a lovely Ori-ental rug as well as sunrise views. The bedroom suite is particularly inter-esting. A complete set of Waterfall furniture with half-shell handles dates from the 1930s. There's a striking handmade quilt on the bed. The tiled bath is small but well designed and includes a glass-enclosed shower. The Garden Room, also with a whirlpool, a fireplace, and a private porch, was added in the spring of 1997.

Afternoon tea is offered daily, and a decanter of sherry is provided in each room. At bedtime you'll find a bottle of water beside your bed and a chocolate on your pillow.

For breakfast Carol and Mike may start with a baked French tart gar-nished with frozen yogurt and freshly baked bran muffins. A hot dish—per-haps a portobello mushroom omelet with cubed red potatoes and sweet red peppers—will follow. This will be accompanied by freshly baked Scottish scones served with home-made strawberry jam.

Just like the residents, you should spend your time on Tilghman Island on the water. There are nature expeditions through the marshes, a trip on a skipjack, and fishing boats to charter as well as the *Lady Patty*. Several restaurants specializing in seafood are located on the island.

What's Nearby—Tilghman Island

Tilghman Island is a laid-back unconventional island reached by bridge across Knapps Narrows and about 15 miles from St. Michaels. Fishing and shellfishing remain the primary activities, and numerous charter and excursion boats offer fishing and sightseeing trips, including a trip on an authentic skipjack. You can watch the watermen bring in their catch of oysters in the evening, rent a canoe or a kayak, or traverse the island by bicycle. The Blackwater National Wildlife Refuge is nearby. Come for the Tilghman Island Seafood Festival in June or for Tilghman Island Days in October. (See also St. Michaels and Wittman.)

The Inn at Christmas Farm

8873 Tilghman Island Road
Wittman, MD 21676
(800) 987–8436 or (410) 745–5312

FAX: (410) 745–5618

INNKEEPERS: David and Beatrice Lee

ROOMS: 6, including 5 suites, all with private bath, air conditioning, and radio; 4 with patio, mini-refrigerator, wet bar, coffeemaker; and 2 with whirlpool tub; wheelchair access

ON THE GROUNDS: 47 acres of waterfront on Cummings Creek; pond, gardens, and farm animals, including peacocks and horses

EXTRAS: Wine and sodas on arrival; three dogs and one cat

RATES: $135–$175, double occupancy, including full breakfast; two-night minimum mid-February–October

CREDIT CARDS ACCEPTED: MasterCard and Visa

OPEN: Year-round

HOW TO GET THERE: From Washington, D.C., take Route 50 across the Chesapeake Bay Bridge. Continue on Route 50 east to Route 322/Easton Parkway and turn right. Turn right again onto Route 33 and follow signs for St. Michaels. Continue on Route 33 past St. Michaels for approximately 6⁷/₁₀ miles (just after the Wittman Market) and turn left into the driveway of Christmas Farm.

Tucked away on forty-seven acres down an unassuming little gravel road, Christmas Farm is a combination of working farm, wildfowl refuge, and elegant B&B. You will see snowy egrets, swans, and blue herons feeding in the marsh grasses, horses, and haughty peacocks with their multi-colored tails fanned on the farmland.

This is no ordinary B&B. In addition to the stately manor house, which contains one suite and one room, there are two suites in a charming 1893 chapel and one more carved out of an 1890s waterman's cottage. The latter two buildings were moved to the property specifically to house guests.

We were charmed by the inn from the moment we walked in. There are enormous happy plants sitting beside red-and-white-checked sofas in the entry. There's a sunporch filled with rustic farm tables where breakfast is served. Beyond the broad windows, there's a swimming pond surrounded by tables and chairs for sunny-weather lounging. When we arrived, a cool glass of wine was waiting, and we welcomed the opportunity to relax by the swimming pond to unwind after our journey. The seclusion is intoxicating. The loudest noise we heard was the crow of a rooster in the morning, the cry of the peacocks, and the distant clang of a buoy in the harbor.

The fetching accommodations at Christmas Farm are decorated with beguiling appeal. The Bell Tower Suite in the 1893 St. James Chapel, which was moved to the farm in 1992, is entered through arched double church doors. There's an iron canopy bed and polished pine floors covered with Oriental carpets as well as a wet bar and a refrigerator. Uncle's Room, an addition to the main house in 1997, has a two-person Jacuzzi on a platform that oversees the spectacular view from a picture window.

Of all the rooms, however, the Christmas Cottage is our favorite. This little two-story gem was formerly a waterman's cottage. We entered the cottage through double Dutch doors. The sitting room has a tile floor with a Jacuzzi tucked behind a screen. The bedroom is upstairs, where a windowed tower fills the room with light.

A farm breakfast is served on the sunporch in the morning. It will include fresh fruits, or perhaps poached pears, and maybe stuffed French toast or an egg soufflé—all served on flowered china. The tables will have red- or green- or yellow-checked tablecloths and napkins, and there will be a huge bowl of fruit in the center.

What's Nearby—Wittman

Wittman is located between St. Michaels and Tilghman Island, offering all the activities and amenities of both. The narrow peninsula is a prime bicycling area with flat roads and exquisite scenery. The inn is next door to a gladioli farm where visitors may purchase bunches of fresh flowers in season as well as bulbs to take home. Canoeing and kayaking in the marshy inlets and bays produce glimpses of waterfowl, animals, birds, fish, and shellfish.

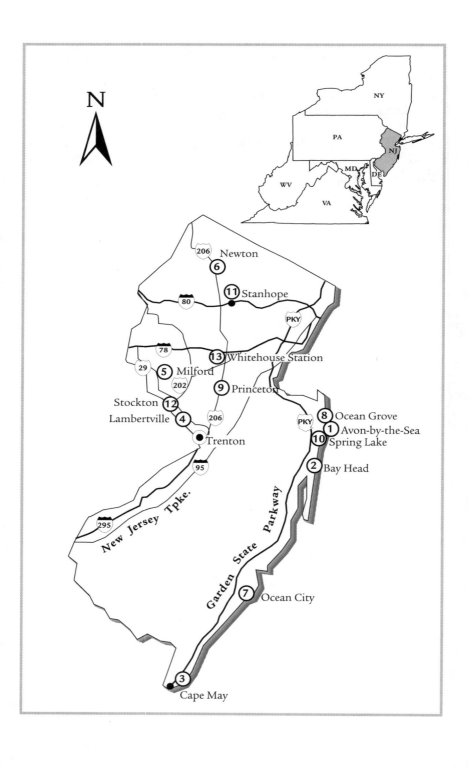

N

NY

PA

NJ

MD

DEL

WV

VA

206 Newton

⑥

⑪ Stanhope

PKY

80

78

29 ⑤ Milford

202

⑬ Whitehouse Station

⑨ Princeton

Stockton ⑫

Lambertville ④

206

⑧ Ocean Grove

PKY ① Avon-by-the-Sea

⑩ Spring Lake

Trenton

② Bay Head

95

New Jersey Tpke.

295

Garden State Parkway

⑦ Ocean City

③

Cape May

New Jersey

Numbers on map refer to towns numbered below.

1. Avon-by-the-Sea,
   Cashelmara Inn, 92

2. Bay Head,
   Bay Head Gables Bed &
      Breakfast, 94
   Conover's Bay Head Inn, 96

3. Cape May,
   The Duke of Windsor Inn, 98
   Fairthorne Bed & Breakfast, 99
   The Humphrey Hughes
      House, 101
   Inn at 22 Jackson, 103
   The Inn on Ocean, 105
   Leith Hall Historic Seashore
      Inn, 106
   The Mainstay Inn, 108
   Manor House Inn, 110
   The Queen Victoria, 111
   The Southern Mansion, 113
   The Summer Cottage Inn, 115
   The Wooden Rabbit, 117

4. Lambertville,
   Chimney Hill Farm Inn, 118
   The Lambertville House, 120

5. Milford, Chestnut Hill on the
      Delaware, 122

6. Newton, The Wooden Duck
      Bed & Breakfast, 124

7. Ocean City
   Castle by the Sea, 126
   Northwood Inn Bed and
      Breakfast, 128

8. Ocean Grove, Ocean Plaza, 129

9. Princeton, Red Maple Farm, 131

10. Spring Lake,
    Hamilton House Inn, 133
    Hollycroft Inn, 135
    La Maison—A B&B and
       Gallery, 137
    Sea Crest by the Sea, 139
    Victoria House Bed and
       Breakfast, 140

11. Stanhope, Whistling
       Swan Inn, 142

12. Stockton, The Woolverton
       Inn, 144

13. Whitehouse Station,
    Holly Thorn House, 146

Cashelmara Inn

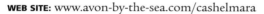

Best Buy

22 Lakeside Avenue
Avon-by-the-Sea, NJ 07717
(800) 821–2976 or
(732) 776–8727

FAX: (732) 988–5819

E-MAIL: cashelmara@
monmouth.com

WEB SITE: www.avon-by-the-sea.com/cashelmara

INNKEEPER: Mary Wiernasz

ROOMS: 14, all with private bath, air conditioning, TV, and radio; 7 with fireplace; 5 with mini-refrigerator; children welcome

ON THE GROUNDS: Front veranda overlooking Swan Lake

EXTRAS: Mulligan's Grand Victorian Cinema, an in-house theater with velvet seats and huge screen, popcorn available; rooms with views of ocean; cookies, candies, tea available all day; a golden retriever, Cody, on premises

RATES: $83–$176, double occupancy, including full breakfast; four-night minimum Fourth of July and Labor Day weekends; three-night minimum summer weekends and Memorial Day weekend; two-night minimum weekends rest of year

CREDIT CARDS ACCEPTED: Discover, MasterCard, Visa

OPEN: Year-round

HOW TO GET THERE: From the Garden State Parkway, take exit 98 onto Route 138 east. Follow this to Route 35 north and turn left. At the first traffic light, turn right onto Sixteenth Avenue and follow this to Ocean Avenue. Turn left onto Ocean Avenue and go about 1 mile. Cross over the inlet bridge in Avon. Go 7 blocks to Lakeside Avenue. Turn left. The B&B will be on the left.

Although Mary Wiernasz has owned Cashelmara Inn (which means "big house by the sea" in Gallic) since 1984, it was in 1996 that she decided to take full advantage of its beauty. Undertaking an overall renovation, she upgraded all the rooms and baths and purchased one fabulous Victorian antique after another to embellish the parlors, dining room, and guest rooms. Every time I visit, I note that she's done more updating such as all new gas fireplaces with pretty mantels, or enlarged and modernized another bath, or added a new suite.

The grand mansion was built in 1907 by William Wilcox, a noted statesman, and at one time, Postmaster General of the U.S. He chose this spot because at the time one side fronted on the ocean and the other on the placid lagoon. Today the lagoon (known as Swan Lake) can be enjoyed from the broad veranda that stretches across one side and, although you cannot step out the door onto the beach, there are still beautiful views of the ocean from the breakfast room and from the guest rooms on the ocean side.

Guests enter the creamy stucco house through massive doors with stained-glass sidelights and step directly into the Victorian age. There are beautiful chandeliers, a foyer with a fireplace, and two intimate parlors (one with a fireplace) equipped with elegant Victorian chairs, loveseats, pier mirrors, a hall tree, and tables. The dining room contains a fabulous new chandelier with cranberry glass shades, a rosewood table, and a heavily carved oak breakfront.

Our favorite common room, though, is Mulligan's Grand Victorian Theater, a posh little theater with soft Victorian theater seats restored with burgundy velvet and an 80" screen. Heavy velvet drapes muffle the surround-sound stereo system as guests enjoy a video from the inn's extensive collection. There's even popcorn!

The guest rooms are as elegant as the common rooms. The newest suite, #11, has raspberry wallpaper and a fabulous Victorian bed with a carved head- and footboard. There's a gas fireplace with an oak mantel. The bath has a marble floor, and there's a small kitchen with a refrigerator. One of the grandest rooms is #12, which has a parlor with a leather sofa facing a gas fireplace and a massive armoire. The canopy bed is swathed in green and yellow fabrics, and there are French doors leading to a private porch with a view of Swan Lake. The bath has a raspberry-colored whirlpool tub and a glass-enclosed shower.

Breakfast is served in a bright room with views of the ocean and a floor painted with flowers. Mary's latest (on my last visit) acquisition, a carved onyx-topped French boudoir dresser serves as a buffet. The sky's the limit for breakfast. You can choose from an omelette, or challah French toast, or pancakes, but the house specialty is Cashel McMara, the house version of eggs Benedict. After this wonderful buffet, you'll be well fortified for a day in the sun.

What's Nearby—Avon-by-the-Sea

Avon-by-the-Sea is a quiet seaside town on the Jersey Shore. It has a sedate and quiet boardwalk that is conducive to casual strolls unencumbered by the honky-tonk of T-shirt shops, pizza parlors, and amusement arcades. It's a place to appreciate and contemplate the beauty of the beach and ocean. In addition to sunbathing, swimming, and surfing, you can go surf fishing or deep sea fishing, or you might go to Monmouth Park to watch the thoroughbreds race or to Freehold Raceway to view the harness races.

Bay Head Gables Bed & Breakfast

Best Buy

200 Main Avenue
Bay Head, NJ 08742
(800) 984–9536 or (732) 899–9844

FAX: (732) 295–2196

E-MAIL: bhgables@monmouth.com

WEB SITE: www.bayheadgables.com

INNKEEPERS: Don Haurie and Ed Laubusch

ROOMS: 11, all with private bath, air conditioning, telephone, and radio; 3 with balcony; 1 with a fireplace (electric)

EXTRAS: Parking on premises

RATES: $95–$195, double occupancy, including full breakfast; two-night minimum weekends spring and autumn, three-night minimum weekends July and August

CREDIT CARDS ACCEPTED: American Express, Discover, MasterCard, Visa

OPEN: April to December

HOW TO GET THERE: From the Garden State Parkway, take exit 98 to Route 34. At the second traffic circle, take Route 35 south through Point Pleasant to Bay Head. The B&B is on the right as you come into town.

Bay Head is a sleepy little Jersey Shore town that was developed in the late nineteenth century by folks from Princeton and Philadelphia. Handsome shingle-style cottages and Victorian houses line the narrow streets, and the beach is unencumbered by high-rise hotels or shops selling saltwater taffy and T-shirts. Most of the bed-and-breakfast establishments are within a block of the beach, making it a pleasant walking town, although Route 35, which is called Main Avenue in Bay Head, can become quite busy in the summer.

Bay Head Gables occupies one of the most distinctive houses in Bay Head, reputedly designed by the firm of McKim, Mead, and White and built in 1914. This wedding present for a young bride has a natural shingle exterior with white columns and railings as well as an expansive wraparound porch and a gabled roof. With such a traditional summer "cottage," one expects a conventional interior, but that is far from the case.

Don Haurie and Ed Laubusch have decorated their inn in a variety of styles, ranging from Art Deco to Oriental. The living room, a composition in Art Deco style, has glass tables; mirrors; chairs with voluptuous curves; and a black, grey, and white color scheme with zesty teal accents. There's a window seat in the bay window and a gas fireplace. The dining room, however, is as traditional as the house in style, with a spectacular crystal chandelier. Even here there are notable exceptions, however. The walls are navy blue, and a fireplace mantel is overflowing with the owners' collection of pigs.

A breakfast room was created by enclosing a corner of the wraparound porch in glass. It contains individual tables that offer glimpses of the ocean a block away. The five-course breakfast will please the hungriest of guests. It begins with a selection of juices. This will be followed by a fruit dish such as poached spiced pears or a fruit compote and a breakfast bread such as banana bread or coffee cake. An entree of perhaps an apple/cheddar strata or an omelette or fruited pancakes will follow.

The guest rooms are as eclectically designed as the common rooms. They range in style from Room #2, which has a Southwestern theme that includes a picture of a steer's skull, a canopy bed, artificial cactus plants, and a carved rooster in the bathroom to Room #4, a contemporary black-and-white room on the front of the inn with a covered porch offering an ocean view. One of the B&B's most distinctive features is the work space incorporated into some of the rooms. The Oriental Room (Room #5), for example, has a pull-out computer shelf, and all rooms have telephones.

East Street, which parallels the ocean, stretches for 2½ miles, offering an excellent place to bicycle (the B&B has bicycles for guests to use), roller blade, jog, and walk. For sunbathers, beach passes, towels, and chairs are provided.

What's Nearby—Bay Head

Bay Head has a marvelous uncrowded ocean beach, and although it's private, most B&Bs provide beach passes. Nearby Point Pleasant has an old-fashioned boardwalk, as does Seaside Heights, and Point Pleasant also has an aquarium. Fishing boats can be chartered here. Other nearby attractions include the Garden State Arts Center, the Red Oak Theatre, and the Strand Theater in Lakewood where the New Jersey Ballet performs.

Conover's Bay Head Inn

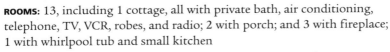

646 Main Avenue
Bay Head, NJ 08742
(800) 956–9099 or (732) 892–4664

FAX: (732) 892–8748

E-MAIL: beverly@conovers.com

WEB SITE: www.conovers.com

INNKEEPERS: Carl, Beverly, and
Timothy Conover

ROOMS: 13, including 1 cottage, all with private bath, air conditioning, telephone, TV, VCR, robes, and radio; 2 with porch; and 3 with fireplace; 1 with whirlpool tub and small kitchen

ON THE GROUNDS: Garden, croquet, lawn games; hot tub, parking

EXTRAS: Package of candies at turndown; snacks and Arizona Tea always available; afternoon tea with cookies and cheese and crackers

RATES: $130–$260, double occupancy, including full breakfast; two-night minimum weekends; three-night minimum July and August; four-night minimum holiday weekends

CREDIT CARDS ACCEPTED: American Express, MasterCard, Visa

OPEN: Year-round

HOW TO GET THERE: From the Garden State Parkway, take exit 98 to Route 34. At the second traffic circle, take Route 35 south through Point Pleasant to Bay Head. The inn is 7 blocks ahead on the right after reaching Bay Head.

Carl and Beverly Conover opened Conover's Bay Head Inn more than twenty-five years ago. Their longevity is remarkable in itself, but what's even more remarkable is that their inn looks and feels as fresh today as it must have when it opened. Furthermore, so do the Conovers. They are as friendly and as refreshing as new innkeepers, exhibiting none of the burnout that you might expect. What's their secret? Their son, Tim, is a full-time assistant and they all love what they're doing.

The house is a pretty shingled cottage with white trim. In summer, awnings shield the front windows from the sun, and you walk through an arched trellis covered with pink roses to reach the front door. A picket fence borders the sidewalk and defines the abundant flower gardens, which are in bloom from early spring through late fall. On the porch, there are white painted tables, a white wicker sofa, and white rocking chairs.

The B&B has a cozy sitting room with a plum-colored floral carpet and a white stone fireplace. Just beyond, the breakfast room has a lovely oak hutch. Guests eat breakfast on individual glass-topped tables. They might start the day with an egg puff accompanied by Canadian bacon, or perhaps baked pancakes. In winter, the Conovers receive citrus fruit directly from Florida, but fresh fruit is served throughout the year. Beverly is noted for the breakfast breads she bakes. She may prepare cheddar cheese biscuits or walnut orange cake or piña colada muffins, and, of course, there will be a selection of juices, coffee, and tea. A little refrigerator in the breakfast room is stocked with a selection of Arizona Tea (Carl is a distributor)—always a welcome treat when returning from the beach. A cabinet here also holds videos for viewing on the VCRs in the rooms.

The guest rooms are spacious, and all have private baths. Room #2, a soothing space in beige tones, has a gas fireplace and a private porch. The bath has a clawfoot tub and a shower as well as a pretty antique wicker vanity dressed with a silver Victorian comb and brush set. Many of the rooms have iron and brass beds, and Beverly has painted some beautiful stencils on the walls and ceilings.

In addition to a large parking area, the B&B is blessed with a spacious side yard shielded from the street by a dense privet hedge. Games of croquet take place here, and lawn chairs offer secluded spots to read, sip an Arizona Tea, or talk. Beach passes, towels, and chairs are available for guests to use. An excellent sports equipment rental shop is located nearby, where bicycles, wind surfing equipment, and roller blades are especially popular.

Nearby Point Pleasant has an active fishing port where it's possible to charter a fishing boat and to watch commercial fishermen bring in the catch of the day. Naturally, there are also some excellent seafood restaurants overlooking Manasquan Inlet.

What's Nearby

See "What's Nearby—Bay Head," page 95.

The Duke of Windsor Inn

Best Buy

817 Washington Street
Cape May, NJ 08204
(800) 826–8973 or (609) 884–1355

FAX: (609) 884–1887

WEB SITE: www.bbianj.com/
dukeofwindsor

INNKEEPER: Patricia Joyce

ROOMS: 10, including 1 suite, all with
private bath, air conditioning, and
radio; 1 with TV and mini-
refrigerator

ON THE GROUNDS: Parking on premises

EXTRAS: Afternoon tea featuring savory and sweet treats

RATES: $95–$220, double occupancy, including full breakfast and afternoon tea; two-night minimum weekends in spring and fall; three-night
minimum weekends in July and August

CREDIT CARDS ACCEPTED: MasterCard and Visa

OPEN: Year-round

HOW TO GET THERE: From the end of the Garden State Parkway or the Lewes
Ferry, take Route 109 south into Cape May. After crossing the bridge
and passing the marina, you will be on Lafayette Street. Turn left at the
first traffic light onto Madison Avenue. Turn right at the next traffic
light onto Washington Street. The B&B is 1½ blocks further on the
right. Enter the driveway to the parking area just before the inn.

When you have a dream, you have to follow it. Patricia had such a dream.
She had been a banker in New York and then in California, but she
wanted to run a bed-and-breakfast. After researching several areas, she
found this beauty in Cape May, and it was love at first sight. No wonder.
The grand first-floor rooms are replete with beautiful stained glass (some
said to be by Tiffany), elaborate oak woodwork, and carved plaster moldings and medallions. The oak glows with the golden hue of wood that has
never been painted. The house had been a bed-and-breakfast since 1982, but
when Patricia bought it in 1998 she knew it needed lots of updating. She
has plans to paint the outside in shades of aqua, teal, and burgundy, and
she's gradually upgrading the baths.

The massive entry hall has a pretty seating area in the turret that's filled
with wicker furniture. A parlor, reached through pocket doors, has a gas

fireplace with an oak mantel and Victorian furniture, while the formal dining room, where breakfast is served, includes a massive buffet along one wall, and the original shoulder-high anaglyphic paper on the walls. Beautiful crystal chandeliers oversee the breakfast festivities when all the guests gather at 9:00 A.M. at the huge center table. Patricia's entree specialties include baked stuffed French toast, baked eggs, blintz soufflés, and much more.

The guest rooms feature antique Victorian beds with high head- and footboards or wrought-iron beds. The nicest is the King George Suite, which has a wonderful carved bed and matching dresser and a charming little sitting room. The bath has wainscotted walls combined with old original tiles and a pedestal sink. The Wallace Simpson Room includes another elaborate Victorian bed on a royal blue carpet.

What's Nearby—Cape May

Cape May has an extensive boardwalk bordering its miles of white sandy beaches. Most B&Bs provide beach passes, and it's possible to rent beach chairs and umbrellas from one of the many stands. Before or after a day at the beach, be sure to take a walking tour or a horse-drawn carriage tour of this very Victorian town, where time seems to be frozen in the late nineteenth century. Fantastic Victorian houses will be seen on every block (there are almost 700 in all). You may tour the Emlen Physick House and Estate, an eighteen-room Victorian mansion designed by Frank Furness. Festivals and special town and house tours take place throughout the year, and many people time their visits to coincide with their favorite. You can obtain a schedule from the Mid-Atlantic Center for the Arts in Cape May.

Fairthorne Bed & Breakfast

111 Ocean Street
(mailing address: P.O. Box 2381)
Cape May, NJ 08204
(800) 438–8742 or (609) 884–8791

FAX: (609) 884–1902
WEB SITE: www.bbianj.com/fairthorne
INNKEEPERS: Diane and Ed Hutchinson

ROOMS: 10, including 1 suite, all with private bath, air conditioning, TV, mini-refrigerator, hair dryer, and radio; 3 with fireplace; 1 with whirlpool tub

ON THE GROUNDS: Gardens

EXTRAS: Afternoon tea with cheese and crackers, sherry, homemade cookies; fax dataport, private meeting room available; cat named Alley Cat

RATES: $140–$230, double occupancy, including full breakfast and afternoon tea; two-night minimum weekends; three-night minimum July, August, and holiday weekends

CREDIT CARDS ACCEPTED: American Express, Discover, MasterCard, Visa

OPEN: Year-round

HOW TO GET THERE: From the end of the Garden State Parkway or the Lewes Ferry, take Route 109 south into Cape May. After crossing the bridge and passing the marina, you will be on Lafayette Street. Turn left at the second traffic light onto Ocean Street. The bed-and-breakfast will be in 3 more blocks on the left.

If you love Victoriana, then you must come to Cape May. This lovely seaside Victorian village somehow escaped the wave of modernization that swept so many towns in the early 1900s. There are still more than 700 Victorian buildings within the town's National Historic District. The Victorian ambience is so complete that you feel as if you should be wearing a long rustling skirt and a bonnet.

The Fairthorne Inn is composed of two buildings. The original building, a natural shingled house with white trim and a broad wraparound porch, has an utterly romantic but welcoming look. Perhaps it's the garden in front, filled with an array of flowers, that you can't help but stop to admire, making you long to sit in the wicker chairs or big rockers on the veranda in the afternoon to watch the butterflies and bees flit from one to the next. The Fairthorne Cottage, which the Hutchinsons purchased and added to the inn in 1998, is a dove-grey clapboard enhanced by hunter green trim, red shutters, and bright yellow accents. It has a handsome clock tower on top. It's separated from the main house by a brick courtyard that's used for parking.

The main Colonial Revival–style house was built in 1892 by a whaling captain. There are elaborate stained-glass and leaded windows throughout. The Fairthorne Cottage is even older, dating to 1880. Diane and Ed Hutchinson, who were both raised in Cape May County and who retired from Bell Atlantic, purchased the first house in 1991.

Patricia's Mini-Suite is one of the most popular rooms. It has a private entrance off the veranda, a fireplace with a painted mantel, and a lovely Eastlake Victorian sideboard. Emma Kate's Suite has a Victorian dresser and a separate sitting room with a view of the water. Each of the bedrooms has its own private bath.

The Fairthorne Cottage has an enclosed porch across the front and a wide entry hall with a rich wine-colored carpet. There's another pretty parlor for guests to enjoy with a rolltop secretary and elaborate ceiling paper. The three guest rooms upstairs all have gas fireplaces, antique beds, and wardrobes. The baths are new and modern.

Breakfast is served in the dining room in winter or on the porch in summer. In the dining room, guests will sit at a common table set with a lace tablecloth, linen napkins, fine china, and silver. The meal will start with fresh fruit and juice. In addition, Diane may prepare a spinach soufflé with bacon and homemade mocha walnut muffins, or perhaps she will fix baked blueberry French toast with country sausage accompanied by cranberry scones. Regardless of the daily fare, it will be delicious and bountiful.

Cape May abounds in antiques shops and art galleries. Or, it's a pleasant bicycle ride out to the restored 1859 Cape May Lighthouse. This is one of the oldest continuously operating lighthouses in the United States, and the panoramic views from its top are breathtaking.

What's Nearby

See "What's Nearby—Cape May," page 99.

The Humphrey Hughes House

29 Ocean Street
Cape May, NJ 08204
(800) 582–3634 or (609) 884–4428

FAX: (609) 898–1845

WEB SITE: www.BBHost.com/
HumphreyHughesHouse

INNKEEPERS: Lorraine and Terry Schmidt

ROOMS: 11, including 4 suites, all with private bath, air conditioning, TV, radio, hair dryer, iron, and ironing board; 2 with telephone, coffeemaker, mini-refrigerator, and robes; 1 suite with wheelchair access

ON THE GROUNDS: Gardens, patio, veranda

EXTRAS: Afternoon tea; cookies and tea in sunroom

RATES: $135–$255, double occupancy, including full breakfast; three-night minimum on weekends, May–October

CREDIT CARDS ACCEPTED: MasterCard and Visa

OPEN: Year-round

HOW TO GET THERE: From the end of the Garden State Parkway or the Lewes Ferry, take Route 109 south into Cape May. After crossing the bridge and passing the marina, you will be on Lafayette Street. Turn left at the second traffic light onto Ocean Street. The B&B will be on the left on the corner of Ocean and Columbia Streets.

aptain Humphrey Hughes arrived in Cape May in 1692 to become one of the town's original landholders. The Humphrey Hughes house was built by a descendant in 1903 on a portion of his property, and it remained a Hughes residence until the death in 1980 of Dr. Harold Hughes. Although there are many fine homes in Cape May, this is one of the most stately. Sitting high above the street, the wide covered veranda stretches across the front on both sides, offering a variety of places to sit on wicker chairs to enjoy the cooling sea breezes.

Lorraine and Terry Schmidt have retained the historical characteristics of their B&B while updating it. Guests enter a living room flanked by carved fluted chestnut columns and admire the ornate grandfather clock that once belonged to Dr. Hughes. The living room has a square grand piano and a fireplace. The dining room has another fireplace, and an elaborate Oriental rug covers the oak floors. An ornate Victorian walnut buffet stands along one wall, and there's a lovely crystal chandelier hanging from a ceiling medallion.

One of the favorite spots in the house to relax is the sunroom, located off the dining room. It's filled with plants and white wicker furniture festively dressed with pink and red cushions. Hot and cold tea, coffee, chocolate, and the overflowing cookie jar are located here.

Every afternoon an elaborate tea is set out for the guests. It will include little tea sandwiches such as cucumber or tomato, cream scones with strawberry butter, and at least two sweets such as Lorraine's chocolate cake with mocha frosting.

The guest rooms have equally beautiful antique Victorian furnishings. In the Rose Room, there's an elaborate Victorian bed with a carved headboard, a lamp with a fringed shade, and a fainting couch. The tiled bath is well designed and spotless. The Ocean View Room has a bay window and an unusual tub in the bathroom that includes a separate footbath in its design. Even though Le Petit is the smallest, it is one of the most charming, with forest-green walls and a white iron bed.

In the morning guests look forward to a bountiful breakfast served around the mahogany dining room table. It's set with placemats and fine china. Guests receive a copy of a printed menu the night before. A typical breakfast might include a toasted bagel with scrambled eggs and cheese sauce accompanied by potato latkes and homemade English muffins.

For a unique trip back in time, it's interesting to visit Cold Spring Village, a twenty-two-acre living history museum. In this restoration of a nineteenth-century farm community, visitors can talk to "locals" dressed in bonnets and long skirts, see bread being kneaded and then baked in a brick oven, watch a flyer being printed, see a spinner twist wool into yarn, and iron being shaped at a forge.

What's Nearby

See "What's Nearby—Cape May," page 99.

Inn at 22 Jackson   Best Buy

22 Jackson Street
Cape May, NJ 08204
(609) 884–2226

FAX: (609) 884–0055

INNKEEPERS: Barbara and Chip Masemore

ROOMS: 5 suites, including 1 cottage, all with private bath, air conditioning, TV, VCR, mini-refrigerator, microwave, coffeemaker, and hair dryer; 3 with porch or deck; 1 with a fireplace

ON THE GROUNDS: Garden

EXTRAS: Afternoon tea with homemade savories, wine, and a nonalcoholic beverage; complimentary off-site parking

RATES: $95–$220, double occupancy, including full breakfast and afternoon tea; two-night minimum weekends

CREDIT CARDS ACCEPTED: American Express, MasterCard, Visa

OPEN: Year-round

HOW TO GET THERE: From the end of the Garden State Parkway or the Lewes Ferry, take Route 109 south into Cape May. After crossing the bridge and passing the marina, you will be on Lafayette Street. Continue on Lafayette Street to the stop sign at its end. Turn left onto Jackson Street. The inn is 1½ blocks further on the right.

Drama, whimsy, and romance create an opera for lovers at Inn at 22 Jackson. The supreme privacy offered to guests amid eclectic furnishings and spiced with Chip's collection of paintings, drawings, photographs, and prints of bawdy women all conspire to create a stage for romance.

The bold exterior of this 1899 Victorian is painted navy blue with striking white trim that defines the double porch railings, turret, and elaborate gingerbread detailing. A wide porch, high above the street, has wicker furniture—the perfect spot to relax after a day at the beach. The inside is as interesting as the outside. A tiny charming foyer has a fireplace with an oak mantel. The walls are covered in a black wallpaper with a rose motif. In the Victorian parlor, Minerva, the chief of housekeeping, greets guests from her Victorian sofa and a barber chair sits in a corner. Examples of Barbara and Chip's collection of toys and games are found in several rooms.

The rooms are sublime oases. The Windward Suite, for example, has a Victorian bed covered with a beautiful quilt and a separate sitting room. The bath has a clawfoot tub and shower and an interesting corner sink with a beautiful marble top. The Turret on the third floor is a terrific place for two couples traveling together. It has two bedrooms—one with a great ocean view—and a sitting room with a wet bar and a private deck. The most private of all the suites, however, is the Cottage. This charming building has a sitting area with a gas fireplace, bar, and small kitchen. Upstairs, there are two bedrooms, each with its own bath, making it the perfect place to stay with children.

A buffet breakfast is served every morning in the dining room, which has a painted floor and rust-colored walls. Barbara's collection of majolica and pottery is on display here. A typical breakfast might include poached pears in chambord, a baked omelette, ham, potatoes, and monkey bread. Believing the beach is a place to relax, Barbara and Chip urge guests to help themselves whenever they get up. They may choose to eat in the dining room, on the porch, or in their room.

What's Nearby

See "What's Nearby—Cape May," page 99.

The Inn on Ocean

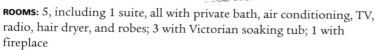

25 Ocean Street
Cape May, NJ 08204
(800) 304–4477 or (609) 884–7070

FAX: (609) 884–1384

E-MAIL: innocean@bellatlantic.net

WEB SITE: www.theinnonocean.com

INNKEEPERS: Jack and Katha Davis

ROOMS: 5, including 1 suite, all with private bath, air conditioning, TV, radio, hair dryer, and robes; 3 with Victorian soaking tub; 1 with fireplace

ON THE GROUNDS: Porches

EXTRAS: Afternoon tea, sherry in the evening

RATES: $199–$299, including full breakfast and afternoon tea; minimum stay requirements vary—please inquire

CREDIT CARDS ACCEPTED: American Express, MasterCard, Visa

OPEN: Mid-February to December

HOW TO GET THERE: From the end of the Garden State Parkway or the Lewes Ferry, take Route 109 south into Cape May. After crossing the bridge and passing the marina, you will be on Lafayette Street. Turn left at the second traffic light onto Ocean Street. The B&B will be on the left in 3½ blocks.

Jack and Katha Davis have created a refined and elegant bed-and-breakfast where Victorian decor is appreciated, but it's used in sublime good taste. The house was built in 1880 in a style that mimics an 1850 house on the site that burned to the ground. Since purchasing it in 1992 the couple has totally updated the house, including installing a new heating system, central air conditioning, and a fabulous stereo system.

The 12-foot-high ceilings on the main floor of the house, which are topped with wide crown moldings, help the rooms achieve an uncluttered and restful ambience. The parlor, which has a library at one end and a fireplace with a marbleized slate mantel, is painted a soft peony pink with white trim. It has its original pine floors. The Billiard Room, which does contain a billiards table, has emerald-green walls and white trim. An empire sofa and a rococo revival love seat sit beneath charming Charles Dana Gibson prints.

The guest rooms are equally genteel. Promenade has a teal carpet and a clawfoot tub in the room. The bath has wainscotted walls and a pretty Victorian chest. The Captain's Quarters has a king-size bed and another clawfoot tub in the room. The bath has a round shower. There's also a spacious sitting room with lace curtains and balloon shades on the windows. Sandpiper has a wonderful big armoire with mirrored doors that hides the TV. It's decorated in a rich sage green.

Breakfast is served in the formal dining room, where a marble mantel surrounds a fireplace. There's a sideboard with a marble top and an oak china cabinet holding the sets of china that Katha changes every day depending on the menu. One of her most popular menus features a breakfast parfait with yogurt and granola, Cape May baked eggs accompanied by bacon and English muffins and garnished with fruit, followed by orange streusel coffee cake.

What's Nearby

See "What's Nearby—Cape May," page 99.

Leith Hall Historic Seashore Inn

22 Ocean Street
Cape May, NJ 08204
(609) 884–1934

INNKEEPERS: Susan and Elan Zingman-Leith

ROOMS: 7, including 3 suites, all with private bath, air conditioning, and radio; 5 with mini-refrigerator; 2 with fireplace; 1 with TV and whirlpool tub

ON THE GROUNDS: Wraparound porch; parking provided

EXTRAS: Afternoon tea with cakes and pastries; sherry available in parlor

RATES: $95–$295, double occupancy, including full breakfast and afternoon tea; three-night minimum weekends Memorial Day–Labor Day and every day late July–August; two-night minimum weekends rest of year

CREDIT CARDS ACCEPTED: MasterCard and Visa

OPEN: Year-round

HOW TO GET THERE: From the end of the Garden State Parkway or the Lewes Ferry, take Route 109 south into Cape May. After crossing the bridge and passing the marina, you will be on Lafayette Street. Turn left at the second traffic light onto Ocean Street. The B&B will be on the right in 3½ blocks.

Elan is a professional historic preservationist, having worked for the New York Landmarks Commission for years, so if you want to stay in a restored Victorian that's absolutely faithful to its period, this is the one. Although the couple have owned their 1880s house since 1989, it continues to be a laboratory of Victoriana and a work in progress. On my last visit in 1999, the porch was being totally rebuilt, and once that was complete, a new paint job would be forthcoming.

When you open the tall front doors you will be in a stunning entry hall embellished with rich examples of Bradbury and Bradbury wallpapers. Immediately you realize that this is a couple who are having a great time garnishing their painted lady. A tiny "Anglo-Japanese" parlor is decorated with Japanese fans, and a huge vase of peacock feathers sits on a cabinet piano. The walls are combed and stenciled. Eastlake sofas and chairs offer places to read a book from the library, a little vestibule off the parlor that is filled with floor-to-ceiling books.

The guest rooms are equally exuberant. Room #1, The Iris Room, is embellished with a fabulous Bradbury and Bradbury iris pattern on the walls and a dragonfly-and-butterfly pattern on the ceiling. There's an ornate Eastlake mantel topped by a mirror and a fancy brass bed. The Highland Room takes its cue from the highlands of Scotland. There's a mural of Scottish castles on the wall and a tartan bedspread on the bed, and Elan has painted a ceiling mural of cherubs dressed in tartans. In 1998 Elan and Susan created the Audubon Suite, a two-room beauty that includes a fireplace, a whirlpool tub, and a TV.

Breakfast is served at individual tables in the parlor and library. Guests help themselves from a buffet that may include a frittata or scrambled eggs with cream cheese and dill, as well as muffins, fruit, granola, sausages, and ham.

What's Nearby

See "What's Nearby—Cape May," page 99.

The Mainstay Inn

Best Buy

635 Columbia Avenue
Cape May, NJ 08204
(609) 884–8690

WEB SITE: www.mainstayinn

INNKEEPERS: Tom and Sue Carroll;
manager, Kathy Miley

ROOMS: 16, including 6 suites, all with private bath,
air conditioning, radio, hair dryer, and desk; 6 with private balcony; 4
with telephone, TV, VCR, mini-refrigerator, coffeemaker, fireplace, iron,
ironing board, and whirlpool tub; 1 room with wheelchair access

ON THE GROUNDS: Gardens

EXTRAS: Parking for 13 cars; afternoon high tea; belvedere; small gift
shop; outdoor cats named Boots and Baby

RATES: $95–$345, double occupancy, including full breakfast and afternoon tea; three-night minimum weekends May–September; two-night
minimum weekends rest of year

CREDIT CARDS ACCEPTED: None

OPEN: Officers' Quarters open year-round; Mainstay and Cottage open
mid-March to December

HOW TO GET THERE: From the end of the Garden State Parkway or the Lewes
Ferry, take Route 109 south into Cape May. After crossing the bridge
and passing the marina, you will be on Lafayette Street. At the first traffic light, turn left onto Madison Street. Proceed 3 blocks and turn right
onto Columbia Avenue. You will see the B&B in 3 blocks on the right.

When Tom and Sue Carroll opened the first B&B in Cape May in the
early 1970s, they started a phenomenon that has now spawned more
than one hundred accommodations in Cape May. They also were in
the forefront of a business that has now swept the United States.

The Carrolls have never looked back. They sold that first B&B when they
purchased The Mainstay, and eventually they also bought the gracious Victorian cottage next door as well as a building across the street known as The
Officers' Quarters. The entire complex is a restoration of the highest cal-
iber, making it the finest place to stay in Cape May.

The original Mainstay Inn, an elaborate Italianate villa with intricate
gingerbread trim, was built as an exclusive gambling hall in 1872. The main
floor rooms have 14-foot ceilings embellished with lustrous Bradbury and

Bradbury wallpapers and furnished with gorgeous Victorian antiques, many of which are original to the building. Across the front of both the Mainstay and the Cottage there are broad verandas filled with green chairs for afternoons at leisure. And there is also the belvedere on top of The Mainstay, where the sound of sea breezes rustling through the sycamore trees mingles with the clip-clop of passing horse-drawn carriages to re-create the sounds of early Cape May.

The guest rooms are as romantic and as elegant as the common rooms. In Henry Clay, for example, there's a magnificent Victorian walnut headboard, an elaborate Victorian chandelier, and a lovely private bath. In the Grant Suite, there's a brass bed and a sitting room furnished with antique wicker. In the Officers' Quarters, the huge suites contain either one or two bedrooms decorated in country pine or country Victorian furniture, living rooms with gas fireplaces, two TVs and VCRs, snack kitchens, telephones, private decks, and large modern baths with whirlpool tubs and separate showers. Stained-glass windows are backlighted for an utterly romantic ambience. These are the only rooms that are open all winter.

Breakfast is a wonderful affair at The Mainstay. Sue may prepare her blintz soufflé with angel biscuits or perhaps her hash brown quiche with baked ham and poppyseed coffee cake. Generally, it's served in formal splendor around the gleaming walnut dining room table, but in the height of the summer a hearty Continental breakfast may be served on the veranda.

The afternoon high tea at The Mainstay is an event that should not be missed. A tour of the main-floor rooms of the house is offered to those not staying at the B&B. (Guests staying here will receive one when they arrive.) This is followed by tea served on the veranda in summer or in the dining room in cooler weather. There will be a selection of tea sandwiches, cheese daisies, and sweets such as almond cake squares and fattening frosted brownies.

What's Nearby

See "What's Nearby—Cape May," page 99.

Manor House Inn

Best Buy

612 Hughes Street
Cape May, NJ 08204
(609) 884–4710

FAX: (609) 898–0471

E-MAIL: innkeepr@bellatlantic.net

WEB SITE: www.manorhouse.net

INNKEEPERS: Nancy and Tom McDonald

ROOMS: 10, including 1 suite, all with private bath, air conditioning, radio, hair dryer, robes, iron, and ironing board; 1 with TV and whirlpool tub

ON THE GROUNDS: Garden

EXTRAS: Afternoon tea, sherry, and baked snacks; cookies in the evening; two dogs, Hanna and Chaucer, keeshonden, in garden at times

RATES: $90–$250, double occupancy, including full breakfast and afternoon tea; two-night minimum all weekends; three-night minimum throughout July and August

CREDIT CARDS ACCEPTED: Discover, MasterCard, Visa

OPEN: February to December

HOW TO GET THERE: From the end of the Garden State Parkway or the Lewes Ferry, take Route 109 south into Cape May. After crossing the bridge and passing the marina, you will be on Lafayette Street. Continue for 8 blocks and then turn left onto Franklin Street. Go 2 blocks and turn right onto Hughes. The B&B will be in the second block on the left.

Tom and Nancy McDonald purchased their dream B&B in 1994. It's tucked down a small side street and has a particularly pretty little back garden. There are brick pathways and abundant flowers (more than 150 varieties of tulips bloom in the spring) and herbs (used in the inn breakfasts and afternoon snacks), and it offers a quieter retreat than many of the nearby bed-and-breakfasts. It's not as grand as some of its neighbors either, but in many ways that makes it more comfortable.

As you enter the spacious foyer, you will notice the polished oak and chestnut floors, woodwork, and stairway. There's an oak window seat on the stair landing and a lovely stained-glass window above. The front parlor has a piano, while the back parlor has a fireplace and an abundance of jigsaw puzzles, games, and books.

In the dining room, which has a lovely breakfront with a marble top, breakfast is served on a table set with placemats, linen napkins, and fine silver. Nancy is a gourmet cook, and her breakfasts reflect her love of food. She may prepare an apple cheddar omelette, or a "Wild and Crazy" waffle with wild rice and pecans, or a tomato and oregano frittata, or maybe a corny egg pie. Each entree will be accompanied by a variety of fruit, juices, and a meat dish such as bacon or sausage. In addition, Nancy always fixes "Mary's sticky buns," a recipe from her predecessor that everyone loves.

This is one inn where you certainly won't leave hungry. In the afternoon, Nancy prepares at least three sweet and savory treats. There may be gourmet pretzels, canapés, pound cake, and pecan bars as well as coffee, tea, lemonade, port, and sherry. In the evening a bowl is filled with cookies straight from Nancy's kitchen that are bound to assure her guests of sweet dreams.

The rooms are continuously being upgraded. All guest rooms now have their own private bath. Room #6, which stretches across the front of the house, has a pretty wicker love seat and chairs. In the bath, which has a painted floor, there's a whirlpool tub. Room #8 has red walls and a beautiful antique Victorian marble-topped dresser.

Visitors to Cape May often like to time their trip to coincide with one of the special Victorian weekends. The month of December is always a special time, as numerous houses are open for tours, and events such as a community wassail party and a gingerbread workshop take place. Other special events are scheduled on weekends in April, May, and October. Regardless of the time of year, a visit to the Emlen Physick Estate, a restored eighteen-room Victorian gem, offers interesting insights into early Cape May life.

What's Nearby

See "What's Nearby—Cape May," page 99.

The Queen Victoria

102 Ocean Street
Cape May, NJ 08204
(609) 884–8702

E-MAIL: Quinn@Bellatlantic.net
WEB SITE: www.queenvictoria.com
INNKEEPERS: Dane and Joan Wells

ROOMS: 21, including 4 suites and 2 cottages, all with private bath, air conditioning, radio, and mini-refrigerator in every room; 8 with whirlpool tub, 6 with TV; 3 with fireplace; one with wheelchair access; cribs available

EXTRAS: Afternoon tea and savories; turndown with chocolates; breakfast in bed available; desks in some rooms; two cats, in owner's quarters only, named Spats and Mugsy

RATES: $95–$300, double occupancy, including full breakfast and afternoon tea; three-night minimum weekends from April–October and in December and on holidays; four-night minimum some weekends mid-summer

CREDIT CARDS ACCEPTED: Personal checks preferred, but MasterCard and Visa accepted

OPEN: Year-round

HOW TO GET THERE: From the end of the Garden State Parkway or the Lewes Ferry, take Route 109 south into Cape May. After crossing the bridge and passing the marina, you will be on Lafayette Street. At the second traffic light, turn left onto Ocean Street. The B&B will be on the right in 3 blocks.

It's hard to imagine how any innkeepers could be better suited to their jobs. Before becoming innkeepers, Joan was the director of the Victorian Society in America, and Dane was manager of Philadelphia's Neighborhood Commercial Revitalization Program. But in 1980 they decided to open their own B&B in America's most Victorian town, and this amazing, energetic couple have been adding to it ever since. They started with the Queen Victoria, a majestic 1881 Victorian house, but soon they added the Prince Albert, and now their enclave includes three houses, a carriage house, a little cottage, and a small hotel. In addition, they have been instrumental in organizing Victorian Weeks in Cape May, Christmas in Cape May, and a three-day extravaganza of Dickens events.

The Queen Victoria, her prince consort, and ladies in waiting are not of the frilly and fussy Victorian variety, as so many in Cape May are. Rather, they are a reflection of the Arts and Crafts period, when straight lines and solid oak tables were the fashion. Each is decorated with elaborate Bradbury and Bradbury papers on the walls and contain some excellent pieces of signed Stickley and Roycroft furniture. Joan has a wonderful collection of Van Briggle pottery in the china cabinet in the dining room. Each of the buildings has its own little pantry stocked with juices and a snack basket, and there are selections of books and games.

All rooms in the Prince Albert building have whirlpool tubs as well as Victorian furnishings that frequently include beds with carved walnut headboards and marble-topped dressers. A tiny private cottage called Regents Park is tucked next to the Prince Albert. Nightly turndown service includes a custom-made chocolate. Rooms in the Queens Hotel are smaller and well suited to business travelers who desire a desk on which to work or to travelers who prefer to get breakfast on their own in the morning.

B&B guests are invited to the Queen Victoria's dining room for a variety of sweets and savories in the afternoon. It's a chance to meet and greet one another and to obtain suggestions from Dane and Joan for dinner destinations and activities.

In the morning, breakfast is served in both the Queen Victoria and Prince Albert buildings. It is an elaborate affair that is generally self-serve from a buffet. There will be a variety of juices, cereals, fruits, yogurt, and breads as well as a hot entree—perhaps Aunt Ruth's baked eggs and cheese served with savory sausage patties or a hash brown potato bake with crisp bacon slices. Before leaving you might want to purchase a copy of the inn's cookbook.

The Wellses have a bevy of bicycles available to get you around town. If your destination is the beach, they provide beach tags, towels, and an outside shower.

What's Nearby

See "What's Nearby—Cape May," page 99.

The Southern Mansion

720 Washington Street
Cape May, NJ 08204
(800) 381–3888 or (609) 884–7171

FAX: (609) 898–0492

E-MAIL: sales@southernmansion.com

WEB SITE: www.southernmansion.com

INNKEEPER: Barbara Wilde; manager, Denise Cortina

ROOMS: 25, all with private bath, air conditioning, TV, telephone with dataport, radio, desk, and robes; 10 with private balcony; 4 with fireplace

ON THE GROUNDS: Parking; gardens

EXTRAS: Afternoon cookies and tea or lemonade; fax, copier, audio-visual equipment, meeting and conference rooms; concierge

RATES: $185–$400, double occupancy, including full breakfast and afternoon refreshments; two-night minimum weekends September–April (longer holiday weekends); three-night minimum weekends May–September (longer holiday weekends)

CREDIT CARDS ACCEPTED: American Express, MasterCard, Visa

OPEN: Year-round

HOW TO GET THERE: From the end of the Garden State Parkway or the Lewes Ferry, take Route 109 south into Cape May. After crossing the bridge and passing the marina, you will be on Lafayette Street. Continue on Lafayette Street through the first traffic light. Turn left at the second street, which is Jefferson. Go 2 blocks. The B&B will be straight ahead on the corner of Washington Street.

For many years visitors and residents of Cape May had shaken their heads sadly when they looked at the George Allen house. Cape May's largest and most elaborate Victorian mansion, a 14,000-square-foot Italianate villa built in the 1850s, had deteriorated into a dismal state by the time Rick and Barbara Wilde spotted the gem in 1994. Rick is a contractor, however, so the couple knew just what to do. They completed the first phase of the renovation in time to have their own wedding there.

Today the B&B probably looks better than when it was new. Ornate crystal chandeliers hang from 15-foot ceilings in the parlor, the elaborate cornice moldings and ceiling medallions have been restored, the twin carved creamy marble mantels in the parlor are repaired, and the walnut, mahogany, and red tulip floor with its center bird's-eye maple star has been cleaned and polished to reveal its luster. Now the parlor walls are painted a teal blue, and the elaborate medallions stand out against a gold ceiling. Bouquets of perfect roses sit on oak tables perfuming the room with their sweetness, and in the afternoon cookies, iced tea, wine, and lemonade await arriving guests on a marble-topped Victorian sideboard.

The guest rooms are massive. The smallest is 300 square feet. On the second floor, there are broad hallways (filled with interesting pictures of old Cape May), and the ceilings reach to 13 feet, giving the rooms a baronial spaciousness and allowing the Wildes to decorate with panache. Rooms are painted in brilliant hues—one in vermillion, another in sapphire. They all have museum-quality Victorian antiques, many of which are original to the mansion. Every room has its own bath, with hand-painted tiles decorating the showers. Sinks are placed in the guest rooms in ornate armoires.

Among my favorites is Room #6, which has sapphire-blue walls, gold brocade covering the bed and pillows, and a spectacular Victorian chandelier hanging in the center. In the bath, a peacock is painted on the tiles in the shower. Room #8 has a four-poster bed and marble-topped dressers against butterscotch walls.

From the rooftop cupola, there's a sensational view of the harbor and town. Guests love to come here to watch the sunset in the evening. For an utterly romantic evening, the staff will serve a five-course dinner up here, complete with wine or champagne.

A new wing was completed late in 1996 that matches the original house in grandeur. There are ten additional rooms, all with private balconies or porches, as well as conference and meeting space. There's a broad wraparound porch across the front of the main house filled with rockers, and a lovely side garden.

Breakfast is served in the parlor. A selection of breakfast breads, juices, and fruits are laid out on the sideboard. An entree of perhaps eggs Benedict or French toast is served at the table.

What's Nearby

See "What's Nearby—Cape May," page 99.

The Summer Cottage Inn

613 Columbia Avenue
Cape May, NJ 08204
(609) 884–4948

E-MAIL: sumcot@bellatlantic.net

WEB SITE: www.summercottageinn.com

INNKEEPERS: Skip and Linda Loughlin

ROOMS: 9, all with private bath, air conditioning, and radios

ON THE GROUNDS: Gardens

EXTRAS: Afternoon tea with treats; complimentary parking provided

RATES: $85–$295, double occupancy, including full breakfast and afternoon tea; three-night minimum weekends June–September; two-night minimum weekends rest of year

CREDIT CARDS ACCEPTED: Discover, MasterCard, Visa

OPEN: Year-round

HOW TO GET THERE: From the end of the Garden State Parkway or the Lewes Ferry, take Route 109 south into Cape May. After crossing the bridge and passing the marina, you will be on Lafayette Street. At the first traffic light, turn left onto Madison Street. Proceed 3 blocks and turn right onto Columbia Avenue. You will see the B&B in 3½ blocks on the right at the War Memorial Monument.

The Victorian houses lining Columbia Avenue between Stockton and Ocean Avenues form a harmonious composition of gingerbread and verandas. All are similarly constructed, and if you were to stand on the veranda of one, you would see straight down the block through the verandas of the rest. It's an unusual study in Victorian architecture. Among this grouping one house stands out from the rest. The Summer Cottage Inn is beautifully and brilliantly painted in goldenrod with straw and dark-red trim. Neat and impeccably maintained, it definitely makes a statement.

Skip and Linda Loughlin purchased their circa 1867 house, which had previously been a restaurant and guest house, in 1993 and they've been upgrading and improving the B&B ever since. The sitting room has navy-blue walls with white trim, a brick fireplace, wicker furniture, and lace curtains. A collection of Cat's Meow painted wooden houses fill multiple shelves. In the parlor the walls and ceiling are lavishly covered with Bradbury and Bradbury wallpaper. Antique Eastlake tables, a pier mirror, and an étagère filled with Linda's cut glass collection complement a grand piano. Columns separate the sitting room from the parlor and also define the stairway. The dining room was also receiving a thorough Bradbury and Bradbury "do" on my last visit in 1999.

I was unable to see any of the rooms on my visit, so I cannot vouch for them, but I was told by guests and by the innkeepers that all of the rooms have been renovated since 1997, and all of the baths have been upgraded. They feature quilts, brass beds, and baths with sinks in antique chests. Judging by the appearance of the outside and of the common rooms, I feel confident in recommending it.

Linda fixes a full breakfast that is served either in the dining room or at individual tables in the living room. One day when I was there, she started the meal with apple salad and prepared an entree of cinnamon stuffed French toast with maple syrup and sausages. She also offered orange chocolate chip bread and bagels. Several of the recipes came directly from the inn's cookbook.

The Wooden Rabbit

609 Hughes Street
Cape May, NJ 08204
(609) 884-7293

FAX: (609) 898-6081

INNKEEPERS: Nancy and Dave McGonigle

ROOMS: 4, including 2 suites, all with private bath, air conditioning, and TV; one with whirlpool tub

EXTRAS: Afternoon tea

RATES: $85–$225, double occupancy, including full breakfast and afternoon tea

CREDIT CARDS ACCEPTED: MasterCard and Visa

OPEN: February to December

HOW TO GET THERE: From the end of the Garden State Parkway or the Lewes Ferry, take Route 109 south into Cape May. After crossing the bridge and passing the marina, you will be on Lafayette Street. Continue for 8 blocks and then turn left onto Franklin Street. Go 2 blocks and turn right onto Hughes. The B&B is in the second block on the right.

The joy of this charming little haven is that it is not—I repeat not—Victorian. Tucked away on a peaceful and quiet side street, and yet within a five-minute walk of the beach and shopping, it harks to its Federal roots. Built in 1838 and listed on the National Register of Historic Places, the building was here before any of its neighbors.

Respecting its heritage, Nancy and Dave, who purchased the inn in 1998, have furnished it in the simple, uncluttered style of the Federal period. Yet, with a touch of whimsy, they named it after one of Beatrix Potter's storybook characters. In the living room an 1840s settee sits before a gas fireplace, and the wide-plank pine floors glow with the mellow confidence of age. A beautiful Oriental Heriz softens footsteps. A pretty garden room has shutters on the windows, wicker furniture, and radiant heat in the floor.

The dining room, where breakfast is served by candlelight, has a huge Amish farm table and another fireplace. Nancy serves the meal on Dedham pottery with a rabbit motif. She's a fabulous cook who loves to entertain and to bake. A typical repast might include upside-down French toast with a mixed berry coulis and sausage or bacon, or maybe herb and cheese eggs in a flour tortilla on a bed of cheese with homemade salsa. Naturally, there will be freshly baked breads, fruit, juices, and homemade granola as well.

The guest rooms are comfortably furnished in the Federal period as well. The pine-floored hallways have charming patchwork quilts hanging on the walls. One room has a rabbit border stenciled along the wall and a Pennsylvania jelly cupboard. Another has a yellow-and-white striped sofa and yellow gingham curtains. A braided rug sits on the natural pine floors. The beautiful bath has tile walls and an Italian porcelain tile floor. A third room has a cherry four-poster bed and a former fireplace opening that's stenciled with a colorful basket of flowers.

What's Nearby

See "What's Nearby—Cape May," page 99.

Chimney Hill Farm Inn   Best Buy

207 Goat Hill Road
Lambertville, NJ 08530
(800) 211–4667 or (609) 397–1516

FAX: (609) 397–9353

E-MAIL: chbb@erols.com

WEB SITE: www.chimneyhillinn.com

INNKEEPERS: Terry Ann and Richard Anderson

ROOMS: 12, all with private bath and air conditioning; 9 with fireplace, 4 with whirlpool tub; 4 with TV, telephone with dataport, radio, mini-refrigerator, coffeemaker, and robes; 3 with porch or patio; wheelchair access

ON THE GROUNDS: On 8½ acres with gardens and natural areas

EXTRAS: Pantry with snacks, cookies, sherry, and port; fax, copier, dataport

RATES: $145–$250 weekends with full breakfast; $95–$145, weekdays with Continental breakfast, both double occupancy; corporate rate available; two-night minimum if Saturday stay included

CREDIT CARDS ACCEPTED: American Express, MasterCard, Visa

OPEN: Year-round except Christmas

HOW TO GET THERE: From New York take the New Jersey Turnpike south to exit 14 and follow I–78 west to exit 29. Follow I–287 south to Route 202 south. Follow Route 202 for approximately 20 miles to Route 179 south. Stay on Route 179 until you reach a traffic light. Route 179 turns right here, but you go straight ahead. Take the second left onto Swan Street. Turn right onto Studdiford Street, which will change to Goat Hill Road. The B&B is at the top of the hill on the left.

This grand stone manor house began as a humble farmhouse but was expanded in 1927 to its present proportions. It sits on 8½ acres where deer, rabbits, and wild turkeys will frequently be seen.

The original farmhouse, with its low-beamed ceiling and massive fireplace, now serves as the dining room for the inn. A full breakfast of fresh fruits, sweet breads, and perhaps oven-baked French toast with apples and brown sugar is served on weekends; during the week a Continental breakfast is set out on the mahogany table in the bay window that overlooks a little side courtyard with a pretty fountain. Individual tables are set with placemats and silver candelabra.

The magnificent living room has wide-plank pine floors topped by exquisite Oriental rugs. A fireplace graces one wall, and sofas and chairs are upholstered in wine-colored tapestry. A multitude of books fills cases, and a baby grand piano sits at one end. The adjacent Stone Room, aptly named because of its stone floor and stone fireplace, is a favorite retreat. Splashy floral chintz covers the chairs, beautiful English oil paintings hang on the walls, and French doors lead to the gardens.

In 1988 the house was host to a decorator showhouse, and many of the wall treatments and light fixtures date from that period. Terry and Rich Anderson acquired the house in 1994. One of the grandest guest rooms is in the home's original library on the main floor. The shelves are still lined with books, and there's a canopy bed and a huge fireplace with a wooden mantel. The walls are covered with a grey-and-white toile. A lovely tiled bath is in the hallway.

The remaining rooms are upstairs. In the Hunt Room a splashy red fabric with green trees is festooned across the windows, table skirt, and bed canopy and skirt. There's a lovely antique dresser with spiraled arms holding the mirror. The bath has oxblood walls and elaborate tasseled stenciling. Every room has its own private tiled bath, but some are located in the hallway. To provide additional rooms with fireplaces, the Andersons have installed units with gorgeous mahogany mantels that use cans of Sterno for flame.

In 1999 the couple converted their big old post-and-beam barn into four elegant suites that include fireplaces and spacious baths with whirlpool tubs and incredible showers. There are four-poster, mission-style, and pencil-post beds. A common room has a terrific stone fireplace. The suites on the top floor feature cathedral ceilings, where the beauty of the exposed beams, posts, and rafters can be appreciated. The most elaborate suite includes a double-sided fireplace that can be seen from a sitting area and from a Jacuzzi lounge. The bed is in a loft reached via a spiral stairway.

There's a nice butler's pantry off the breakfast room with a mini-refrigerator. Port and cream sherry are available as well as a selection of teas, coffee, a basket of snacks, and home-baked cookies.

The gardens are spectacular, offering lovely secluded spots for reading and relaxing. Hushed classical music is piped outside in the summer.

What's Nearby—Lambertville

Although located in New Jersey, Lambertville is just across the Delaware River from New Hope, Pennsylvania, the shopping and cultural center of Pennsylvania's Bucks County. The Lambertville Chamber of Commerce has prepared a walking tour of the historic sites and buildings along the village streets, and there are marvelous shops and restaurants in town. In addition, there are picnic sites and other activities in New Jersey's longest park, the Delaware and Raritan Canal State Park, which borders the Delaware River. (See also Stockton, New Jersey, and New Hope, Pennsylvania.)

The Lambertville House

32 Bridge Street
Lambertville, NJ 08530
(888) 867–8859 or (609) 397–0200

FAX: (609) 397–0511

E-MAIL: innkeeper@lambertvillehouse.com

WEB SITE: www.lambertvillehouse.com

INNKEEPERS: George and Jan Michael; managers: Brad Michael and Traci Ambrose

ROOMS: 26, including 8 suites, all with private bath, air conditioning, TV, telephone with dataport, whirlpool tub, radio, hair dryer, desk, robes, iron, and ironing board; 23 with fireplace; 8 with porch; wheelchair access

ON THE GROUNDS: Courtyard with tables and fountain; parking on premises

EXTRAS: Small lounge on premises; turndown with chocolates on request; meeting rooms

RATES: $205–$350, double occupancy, including Continental breakfast

CREDIT CARDS ACCEPTED: American Express, Discover, MasterCard, Visa

OPEN: Year-round

HOW TO GET THERE: From I-95, take New Jersey exit 1 and travel north on Route 29 for 10 miles to Lambertville. Turn left onto Route 179 toward New Hope. The inn is on the right in 2½ blocks.

Landmarks of this vintage and stature are definitely worth saving, but finding someone to do the job right is often the problem. In this case all the pieces fit perfectly into place and we are all the beneficiaries.

The Lambertville House was built in 1812 during the height of stagecoach travel. Visitors to the hostelry included such dignitaries as Andrew Johnson and General U. S. Grant. But as with so many stagecoach stops, when its usefulness diminished, it became a cherished relic and eventually an eyesore. Yet the Lambertville House was located in the heart of an up-and-coming village, and its restoration could be the catalyst that gave the village a competitive edge over its across-the-river neighbor, New Hope, Pennsylvania.

When George and Jan Michael purchased the stone-and-stucco building in 1995, they had a goal—to give the building a useful life and to make it an integral part of Lambertville again. Since George is a local custom builder, the couple had the resources and expertise to make it work, and they accomplished their purpose admirably. It's now listed on the National Register of Historic Places.

More like a small boutique hotel that you would expect to find on the Upper East Side of Manhattan than a traditional B&B, Lambertville House offers casual elegance with a historical flavor. The heavy stone walls in the lobby impart a timelessness that contrasts with the smooth mustard-sponged walls. A masculine and intimate common room has a gas fireplace and both leather- and tapestry-covered furniture.

The guest rooms are furnished with high-quality reproduction furniture and decorated with art by well-known local artists. Several rooms, such as the Daniel Garber and the Randolph Bye, feature works by those artists on the walls. The Daniel Garber is decorated in shades of red and has a gas fireplace, while the Randolph Bye features a fabulous bath with a marble floor and granite counters and a two-person whirlpool tub. My favorite accommodation, however, is the Spire Suite, which has a fireplace with an original stone hearth and a wonderful enclosed porch where the whirlpool tub resides.

A Continental breakfast is served downstairs every morning in a room that has a tile floor and another fireplace.

What's Nearby

See "What's Nearby—Lambertville," page 120.

Chestnut Hill on the Delaware

Best Buy

63 Church Street (mailing address: P.O. Box N)
Milford, NJ 08848
(908) 995-9761

FAX: (908) 995-0608

E-MAIL: chhillinn@aol.com

INNKEEPERS: Linda and Rob Castagna

ROOMS: 6, including 1 suite and 1 cottage; 4 with private bath; all with air conditioning, radio, hair dryer, and robes; 5 with telephone; 4 with TV; 2 with balcony or porch; 1 with whirlpool tub; cottage with fireplace; 1 room with wheelchair access

ON THE GROUNDS: Gardens, patio with picnic tables; parking

EXTRAS: Afternoon tea with homemade snacks; fax available

RATES: $90–$150, double occupancy, including full breakfast; two-night minimum weekends

CREDIT CARDS ACCEPTED: None

OPEN: Year-round

HOW TO GET THERE: From I–78, take exit 11 (Pattenburg). Follow Route 614 for 8 miles south to Spring Hill. Turn left onto Route 519 and travel 3 miles south to Milford. In Milford turn right onto Bridge Street and then right onto Church Street. At the end of Church Street turn left; the inn's parking lot is straight ahead.

The first thing you'll notice when you drive up to Chestnut Hill is the spectacular view of the Delaware River. The next will be the lovely 1860s Victorian house handsomely painted in shades of green to highlight its numerous gables and gingerbread. There's an elaborate grapevine wrought-iron trim that parades across the porch and down the columns. You may find the collection of antique rockers on the porch so inviting—they offer views of the river over the abundant rhododendron bushes—that you will forego your trip inside until you have relaxed here with a glass of iced tea that Linda will bring to you.

When you eventually venture inside, you will be welcomed by a mannequin dressed in a nineteenth-century dress. The drawing room to the left of the entrance is furnished with a pump organ and an upright piano. An ornately carved walnut fireplace mantel is overseen by Bradbury and Bradbury wallpaper borders. Along one wall, there's a black walnut apothecary cabinet filled with Linda's unique gift shop. She has an artist's eye for exquisite craft items: wooden boxes painted to look like charming English cottages that hold tissues and intricate hair clips she purchased from an artist in Costa Rica. Linda also sells some of the jewelry she makes.

The guest rooms are decorated with Victorian flair—each with its own theme. In the Rose Garden, there's a window seat offering a terrific view of the river, rose motif paper on the wall, and a bath with lovely tile work and a whirlpool tub. Teddy's Place on the third floor has a brass-and-iron bed, a TV, a telephone, and a bath with a sink in a Victorian chest. There are more than 150 teddy bears marching up the stairs and enjoying the spacious room with the guests. The Country Cottage by the River, located next door, has its own private porch (complete with a carousel horse) and a fireplace in the bedroom. When guests return to the inn after dinner, they'll find a goodnight note waiting on the stair newel and chocolates and warm cookies in their rooms.

Linda prepares an elegant gourmet breakfast and serves it in her formal dining room, which has a magnificent crystal chandelier. She sets her black walnut table with fine china, crystal, silver, and candles. Linda will start with a fresh fruit cup and freshly baked breads. This will be followed by an entree such as macadamia/banana pancakes with fruit or maple syrup.

To allow their guests to enjoy the river even more, Rob built a riverwalk and a 40-foot deck at river's edge. There are benches for watching the river up close; guests are often mesmerized by the endless parade of ospreys, swans, and otters.

Milford has the small-town ambience of an earlier time. Its shops and restaurants are refined and upbeat but not as utterly sophisticated as those across the river. Popular activities in this section of the Delaware River Valley include canoeing and rafting on the Delaware River and walking along the towpath that borders it. (See also Erwinna, Kintnersville, Ottsville, and Upper Black Eddy, Pennsylvania.)

The Wooden Duck Bed & Breakfast

140 Goodale Road
Newton, NJ 07860
(973) 300–0395 (fax also)

WEB SITE: www.bbianj.com/woodenduck

INNKEEPERS: Bob and Barbara Hadden

ROOMS: 7, including 1 suite, all with private bath, air conditioning, TV, VCR, telephone with data-port, hair dryer, radio, desk, robes, iron, and ironing board; 2 with fireplace and whirlpool tub; 3 with balcony

ON THE GROUNDS: 17 acres with gardens, swimming pool surrounded by brick patios, horseshoes, hiking, cross-country skiing

EXTRAS: Parking; tea, fruit drinks, snacks, and chocolate chip cookies available 24 hours

RATES: $100–$175, double occupancy; including full breakfast; two- or three-night minimum holiday weekends

CREDIT CARDS ACCEPTED: American Express, Discover, MasterCard, Visa

OPEN: Year-round

HOW TO GET THERE: From I–80 eastbound, take exit 19 to Route 517 north and travel for 6³/₁₀ miles to Andover Center. From I–80 westbound, take exit 25 to Route 206 north and travel for 6²/₁₀ miles to Andover Center. Continue on Route 206 for 1⁶/₁₀ miles to Goodale Road. Turn right (at Lakeland Rescue Squad) and travel for 1⁵/₁₀ miles. The Wooden Duck is on the left.

New Jersey is known as the "Garden State," and when you reach northern New Jersey, you understand how the state got its moniker. Here there are still fields of pumpkins and strawberries, forests, horse farms, and houses with spacious lawns and gardens of flowers.

When Bob and Barbara Hadden retired from the corporate world, they began a search for a smaller retirement house with a little land. But when they saw this huge house, their plans changed.

The Wooden Duck is located on seventeen acres of utter serenity. The first thing you're likely to see in the morning is deer feeding in a field or wild turkeys foraging for seeds or cardinals, woodpeckers, and humming-birds feeding at the numerous feeders.

The gracious rooms of the manor house have tall, beamed ceilings and rooms that flow together. The living room is brightened by a bay window and it has a double-sided fireplace that can be enjoyed in the Game Room also. Display shelves hold exquisite examples of hand-carved duck decoys. The Game Room has a selection of jigsaw puzzles, games, bumper pool, and a video library. An 1860s map of the United States covers one whole wall.

Each of the guest rooms is named for a type of duck. There are five in the main house and two in the carriage house, and they all have sitting areas with TVs and VCRs tucked into armoires, as well as telephones with dataports. Ruddy Duck is decorated in cheerful yellows with pine furniture, including a high four-poster bed. Mallard is in hunter green and has pine furniture, including a pine four-poster bed. One of the favorites is Pintail, which is located in the carriage house. It has knotty pine walls with built-ins, pine furniture, and a huge picture window that looks out on the fields. Guest often awake to see deer grazing nearby.

In 1998 Bob and Barbara completed an addition to their B&B that added two new luxury guest rooms. Both feature cathedral ceilings, private balconies, and double-sided fireplaces that can be enjoyed from the bedroom as well as from a two-person soaking tub in the bathroom. Cherry furniture (Harlequin has a homestead bed and Golden Eye has a sleigh bed) is used throughout.

Breakfast is served in the formal dining room on fine china with sterling silver and crystal glassware. Barbara is a marvelous cook. She starts the meal with freshly squeezed orange juice and perhaps a warm apple crisp, along with maybe applesauce/oatmeal muffins or banana bread. She may fix pancakes with bananas or with fresh strawberries for an entree.

Castle by the Sea

Best Buy

701 Ocean Avenue
Ocean City, NJ 08226
(800) 622–4894 or (609) 398–3555

FAX: (609) 398–8742

E-MAIL: castle701@aol.com

WEB SITE: www.castlebythesea.com

INNKEEPERS: Renee and Jack Krutsick

ROOMS: 9, including 1 suite, all with private bath, air conditioning, TV, VCR, hair dryer, and iron, and ironing board; 2 with fireplace; 1 with whirlpool tub

ON THE GROUNDS: Parking on premises

EXTRAS: Afternoon tea with baked cakes and sweets, herbal teas, flavored coffees

RATES: $99–$239, double occupancy, including full breakfast and afternoon tea; two-night minimum weekends April–October

CREDIT CARDS ACCEPTED: American Express, Discover, MasterCard,Visa

OPEN: Year-round

HOW TO GET THERE: From the Garden State Parkway, take exit 30 and follow the signs for Ocean City, traveling around the traffic circle and onto Route 52, which becomes Ninth Street in Ocean City. Cross over the Ninth Street bridge and continue on Ninth Street for 7 blocks to Ocean Avenue. Turn left onto Ocean and go 2 blocks. The B&B is on the corner of Seventh Street and Ocean Avenue.

When Renee and Jack Krutsick purchased the building that is now known as Castle by the Sea in 1996, it was nothing but a shell. The amount of work necessary to turn such a structure into a beautiful bed-and-breakfast is mind-boggling. The upside, however, is that you are free to put in the most modern electrical, plumbing, air conditioning, and heating systems that you want. And you can also put in soundproof walls, spiffy modern bathrooms, and all the other amenities that blend to create a high-quality bed-and-breakfast. And that's what Renee and Jack have done.

The outside is a fanciful confection of Victorian gingerbread that is reminiscent of a tiered wedding cake. The Krutsicks have given it a lively interpretation by painting it teal and pink with white trim. Inside there are polished pine floors and beautiful stained glass. The decor of the common rooms is only slightly less flamboyant than the outside. In the parlor there are pink-and-white striped love seats on a purple carpet, and the breakfast room has peacock wallpaper on the walls.

The guest rooms are well designed for comfort and leisure. One of the nicest, An Affair to Remember, has a pine sleigh bed and a bath with a whirlpool tub for two. It's got wallpaper and decor featuring hearts, angels, and cupids. Romantic Rose offers a beautiful stained-glass window and a cherry four-poster rice-carved bed. An electric fireplace lends a romantic air. Budding Countryside is done in Laura Ashley fabrics and there's a beautiful antique white four-poster bed and a Victorian mirror.

Renee gives her guests a pretty hand-printed menu when they check in to let them know the fare for breakfast the next morning. It includes such interesting items as honey-corn muffins with apricot-honey glaze, breakfast rice pudding, and stuffed French toast with fresh berries and Canadian bacon, or perhaps an apple crisp and a three-cheese egg bake or orange-chocolate chip muffins and a broccoli-cheese pie.

What's Nearby—Ocean City

Ocean City is just 8 miles from the bright lights, casinos, and nightclub shows of Atlantic City, which makes it a great place in which to escape to a quieter setting. The town was built as a Christian summer resort in 1879, and the sale of liquor has been prohibited throughout the town's history (read: few teens on school breaks). This family-friendly town offers concerts on the Ocean City Music Pier in the summer. Also Wonderland and Playland offer a variety of rides and arcades. There's a 2½ - mile boardwalk for jogging, biking, and walking.

Northwood Inn Bed & Breakfast

401 Wesley Avenue
Ocean City, NJ 08226
(609) 399-6071

E-MAIL: nwoodinn@bellatlantic.net

WEB SITE: www.northwoodinn.com

INNKEEPERS: Marj and John Loeper

ROOMS: 7, including 2 suites, all with private bath, air conditioning, TV, VCR, radio, and hair dryer; 2 with whirlpool tub; 1 with porch

ON THE GROUNDS: Hot tub on roof deck

EXTRAS: Afternoon tea and treats; complimentary bicycles; billiard table

RATES: $95–$210, double occupancy, including full breakfast; three-night minimum weekends in summer and holidays; two-night minimum weekends rest of year

CREDIT CARDS ACCEPTED: American Express, MasterCard, Visa

OPEN: Year-round

HOW TO GET THERE: From the Garden State Parkway, take exit 30 and follow the signs for Ocean City, traveling around the traffic circle and onto Route 52, which becomes Ninth Street in Ocean City. Cross over the Ninth Street bridge. At the fifth traffic light, turn left onto Wesley Avenue. Follow Wesley for 5 blocks to Fourth Street. The B&B is on the right on the corner of Fourth Street and Wesley Avenue.

The house John and Marj Loeper now own has been an inn or a boarding house since it was built in 1894, although those first guests certainly wouldn't have lived as elegantly as John and Marj's guests do. The couple purchased the Victorian in 1988, and it doesn't seem as if they've stopped rebuilding and restoring long enough to take a deep breath. John is a wooden boat builder and also a member of the local historic preservation commission so he knows what he's doing. Marj, a photographer, has chronicled it all.

The beige shingle-and-clapboard house with coral and seafoam green trim sits high above the broad boulevard, and it has a terrific wraparound porch. When it was built, the land to the north was heavily treed—thus giving it the moniker Northwood.

Guests enter a foyer that leads to a billiards room and also a library with floor-to-ceiling books and videos, and an abundance of games. A parlor contains a TV/VCR. Pretty Victorian chairs are covered in green fabric. The place most guests retire to, however, is the sundeck on the roof, where they can luxuriate in the outdoor hot tub.

Each of the guest rooms has individually controlled heat and air conditioning (the house has central air), and there are central sprinklers. A complete renovation of the Tower Suite in 1999 created a fabulous tiled bath with a whirlpool tub and a large sitting room. There are extravagant sunset views. The Rose Room has pink rag-treated walls, a white iron bed, and a bath with faux lattice work painted on the walls. Lovely antiques are used throughout.

A breakfast buffet is served in the morning. It might include fried bananas or Chambord pears, as well as French toast with Canadian bacon or oatmeal cake with broiled brown sugar and almond glaze.

What's Nearby

See "What's Nearby—Ocean City," page 127.

Ocean Plaza

Best Buy

18 Ocean Pathway
Ocean Grove, NJ 07756
(888) 891–9442 or (732) 774–6552

FAX: (732) 869–1180

E-MAIL: JVJJGreen@aol.com

INNKEEPERS: Valerie and Jack Green

ROOMS: 18, including 2 suites, all
with private bath, air conditioning,

TV, VCR, telephone, and radio; 2 have private porch, mini-refrigerator, and coffeemaker; wheelchair access

ON THE GROUNDS: Vegetable garden

EXTRAS: Mints on the pillow at night; afternoon tea, coffee, and cookies; cat named Stubby

RATES: $80–$185 July through September, two-night minimum weekends; $65–$150 October through June, except Memorial Day weekend, all double occupancy including Continental breakfast

CREDIT CARDS ACCEPTED: MasterCard and Visa

OPEN: Year-round

HOW TO GET THERE: From the Garden State Parkway south, take exit 100B; from the Garden State Parkway north, take exit 100. Follow Route 33 east to Ocean Grove. At the end of Route 33, take a left, then take the second right onto Main Avenue and go east. Turn left onto Beach Avenue, which is 1 block before the ocean. Travel 4 blocks. The B&B is on the corner of Beach Avenue and Ocean Parkway.

Ocean Grove is a lovely secret treasure—a village still immersed in the traditions by which it was founded. During the last half of the nineteenth century, the Methodist Episcopal Church established communities throughout the United States where open-air religious revivals were held in seaside or woodland settings. Cottages and houses were built in the elaborate Victorian style of the day. Although several other communities have survived, no other is as complete as Ocean Grove, which harks back to 1869. Many of the original cottages with their tent-like projections have been handed down from generation to generation. The entire town is listed on the National Register of Historic Places.

Camp Meeting Weeks are still held here every summer—in 1999 it enjoys its 130th season. Throughout July and August, there are Bible hours, band and organ recitals, family picnics, and a variety of events ranging from craft shows to concerts by popular artists to revivals led by recognized evangelists—all interspersed with walks along the beach and bicycle and roller blading jaunts along the boardwalk.

The Ocean Plaza Hotel was built in 1870 by one of the founders of the Ocean Grove Camp Meeting Association, and it served as a summer boarding house for many years. The building has a distinctive facade that includes fanciful railings enclosing broad porches. When purchased by Jack and Valerie Green in 1993, the hotel had thirty-five tiny rooms and six bathrooms. Jack had summered in Ocean Grove as a child, and when he and Valerie married shortly after college, they became summer tenters. Jack owns a construction company, so the task of restoring the big old building was not overly daunting. It opened as a classy B&B in 1996.

There are Tennessee rockers on the first-level wraparound porch. Inside, a sunny common room has an Oriental rug on a polished oak floor, wing chairs covered in bright yellow floral chintz, and flowers painted above the windows. Pretty watercolors of local scenes, such as the restored Asbury Park carousel, grace the walls, and happy ferns wave from pedestal stands.

The guest rooms are equally bright, with floral spreads, wicker chairs, pine armoires holding TVs and VCRs, and carpeted floors. Each of the rooms has a private bath in black-and-white tiles, and both the guest rooms and the baths have ivy and flowers handpainted on the walls. Several rooms have private porches. The two suites on the top floor are especially spacious, and they each have a private porch with a lovely ocean view.

A Continental breakfast is served on the second-floor porch, which is outfitted with wicker tables and chairs or in a pretty room with a garden enclosed by a picket fence and gate painted on the wall. The B&B is merely a block from the ocean.

What's Nearby—Ocean Grove

Especially in July and August when the Ocean Grove Camp Meeting Weeks take place, there are many things to do for the entire family. There are spiritual hours; band and organ concerts and recitals; events ranging from craft shows to revivals led by recognized evangelists; and concerts by big-name performers. No matter what time of the year you come, however, the pristine white sandy beach bordered by a boardwalk is an inviting place to walk, bicycle, rollerblade, or just to sit and contemplate the ocean's vastness. (See also Spring Lake.)

Red Maple Farm Best Buy

211 Raymond Road
(mailing address: RD4)
Princeton, NJ 08540
(732) 329-3821

INNKEEPERS: Roberta and Lindsey Churchill

ROOMS: 3, all with private bath and air conditioning; 1 with fireplace

ON THE GROUNDS: Swimming pool, gardens, orchard

EXTRAS: Tea, espresso, cookies on sideboard all day; outside cat named Jill

RATES: $75–$85, double occupancy, $65–$75, single occupancy, two night minimum holiday and special Princeton University weekends

CREDIT CARDS ACCEPTED: American Express, Discover, MasterCard, Visa

OPEN: Year-round

HOW TO GET THERE: From Route 1 north of Princeton (Route 1 is a Princeton bypass that runs east of the city) watch for Stouts Lane. After Stouts Lane, take the next left onto Raymond Road. The B&B will be on the left. Look for "Red Maple Farm" on the mailbox.

Princeton is one of the most sophisticated university towns in America, yet there are few country inns or bed-and-breakfast establishments nearby. Red Maple Farm is the exception. Located on a back road about 4 miles from the university, the 2½-acre property is made up of a white clapboard farm house, an 1850s barn/carriage house, a smokehouse, a chicken house, and a pool house (this was once a playhouse). There's an orchard, an organic vegetable garden, and a berry garden. A swimming pool is sequestered behind the pool house. The historic house and property are on the National Register of Historic Places, and a secret room and tunnel to the barn suggest that it may have been a stop on the Underground Railroad.

Both Lindsey and Roberta Churchill are academics, and their collection of books is impressive to say the least, but the eclectic decor of their inn reflects their worldwide travels and interest in folk art as well. Peruvian, Navaho, Georgian (in former USSR), and Finnish rugs hang on the walls and lie on the wide-plank floors in the parlor. There's a fireplace in the parlor as well as in the small room where the inn's only TV and VCR are located.

There are three guest rooms, and they all have private baths. Two of the bedrooms open off a large center hall that Roberta stenciled with cascades of ivy. The Strawberry Room has a huge fireplace and a lovely pine cupboard. There's a brass bed with an Amish quilt and a braided rug on the polished pumpkin-colored pine floor. A charming bath has a green tile floor and pretty handpainted stenciling on the walls. The Blue Room has a four-poster bed with pineapple finials. The occupants of this room use a hall bath with an antique "slipper" tub.

The cherry sideboard in the dining room is set with coffee, tea, and homemade cookies so that guests may help themselves in the afternoon. Roberta was formerly the chef of a Princeton restaurant that a *New York Times* critic acclaimed as one of the five best in New Jersey. As one might imagine, her breakfasts are terrific. Guests sit at the huge walnut table that will be set with the Churchills' lovely Limoges or Noritake china and fine silver. A Tiffany-style lamp hangs overhead. In winter the fireplace will be glowing. Roberta may offer a cheese and bread pudding, homemade muffins or breads, perhaps bacon or sausage, and a crumble made with fruits of the season.

The Churchills have bicycles for their guests to use. The grounds include glorious beds of flowers—some in the stone circle where the farm's massive red maple tree used to reside.

What's Nearby—Princeton

Sophisticated and urbane, Princeton has lovely shops and innovative restaurants. Princeton University offers a wealth of cultural events throughout the year ranging from lectures to concerts. The Westminster Choir College performs during the year also. Nearby Washington Crossing State Park on the Delaware River has picnicking, hiking trails, and historic exhibits.

Hamilton House Inn

15 Mercer Avenue
Spring Lake, NJ 07762
(732) 449-8282

FAX: (732) 449-0206

E-MAIL: relax@hamiltonhouseinn.com

WEB SITE: www.hamiltonhouseinn.com

INNKEEPERS: Bud and Anne Benz

ROOMS: 8, including 1 suite, all with private bath, air conditioning, and hair dryer; 3 with fireplace; 1 with TV, VCR, and balcony

ON THE GROUNDS: On ½ acre with swimming pool

EXTRAS: Coffee, tea, and cookies always available; a golden retriever, Sandy, on premises

RATES: $135–$250, double occupancy, including full breakfast; two-night minimum weekends in the summer

CREDIT CARDS ACCEPTED: American Express, MasterCard, Visa

OPEN: Year-round

HOW TO GET THERE: From the Garden State Parkway, take exit 98 onto Route 34 south. Follow Route 34 to the traffic circle and then take Route 524 east for 4 miles to Ocean Avenue in Spring Lake. Turn right. Go 11 blocks and turn right onto Mercer Avenue. The B&B is on the left on the next corner.

Anne and Bud Benz, a gregarious and friendly couple, were born and raised right here—she in Spring Lake and he in nearby Belmar. They are both "retired" from AT&T, but running their inn can hardly be called retirement—it's a new career.

Their house was built in 1877 by William C. Hamilton, a thrifty Philadelphia businessman, who used timbers from the Centennial of 1876 in the construction. He certainly didn't stint when it came to room sizes, however. The living room measures 27 feet by 27 feet, offering space for numerous conversation areas. A Pennsylvania stone woodburning fireplace is the focal point of the room. The house has some lovely examples of stained glass, especially in the skylight above the stairs.

In addition to the living room, guests enjoy the use of a solarium, which has another fireplace and is furnished with wicker tables and chairs. A TV and VCR are located here. There are also double porches where the soft sea breezes are refreshing after a day beside the pool. There's a huge case of books in the upstairs hallway for guests to read and an extensive gift shop as well.

Although Anne and Bud have owned the house since 1993, they totally renovated it in 1997. You will find some baths with their original tile walls but thoroughly updated fixtures. The Carousel Room has a merry-go-round theme. There are beautiful little statues of carousel horses and a fabulous stained-glass window featuring a carousel. A Victorian dresser and a carved four-poster mahogany bed complete the decor. Garden Party has an ornate antique brass bed, while Memory Lane has a sleigh bed and a view of the ocean. It's decorated with rose floral wallpaper, an antique Stickley rocker, and a vintage radio/tape player with tapes of old radio programs.

Breakfast is served in a bright breakfast room, where Anne pampers her guests with entrees that might feature oven-baked French toast, or a mushroom and cheese omelette accompanied by freshly baked bread or scones or muffins.

What's Nearby—Spring Lake

Pretty Spring Lake has a shopping street lined with antiques shops and interior design studios. At the PNC/Garden State Arts Center there are concerts year-round, while the Spring Lake Historical Museum offers interesting historical exhibits. Spring Lake has a lovely boardwalk that's perfect for walking, rollerblading, and bicycling and there's a jogging/walking trail around the lake. (See also Ocean Grove.)

Hollycroft Inn

506 North Boulevard, South Belmer
(mailing address: P.O. Box 448)
Spring Lake, NJ 07762
(800) 679–2254 or (732) 681–2254

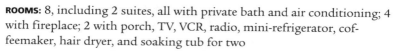

FAX: (732) 280–8145

WEB SITE: www.hollycroft.com

INNKEEPERS: Linda and Mark Fessler

ROOMS: 8, including 2 suites, all with private bath and air conditioning; 4 with fireplace; 2 with porch, TV, VCR, radio, mini-refrigerator, coffeemaker, hair dryer, and soaking tub for two

ON THE GROUNDS: On ¾ acre of wooded grounds; hammock for two

EXTRAS: Sherry in living room; Perrier and imported chocolates in room; two cats named Bouncer and Pip

RATES: $100–$295, double occupancy, including full breakfast; two-night minimum weekends mid-May through September; three-night minimum holiday weekends

CREDIT CARDS ACCEPTED: American Express, MasterCard, Visa

OPEN: Year-round, except Thanksgiving and Christmas days and Christmas Eve

HOW TO GET THERE: From the Garden State Parkway, take exit 98 onto Route 34 south. At the traffic circle go ¾ of the way around and exit onto Route 524 east (Allaire Road). Go 3³⁄₁₀ miles to the fourth traffic light and turn left onto Route 71. Make an immediate right onto Church Street and continue for half mile to Third Avenue. Turn left and go 2 blocks. Turn right at the lake onto North Boulevard. Go 2½ blocks and you will see the Hollycroft sign on the right. Drive up the driveway. The B&B is the house on the left. Proceed around the house to the parking area.

What do you do if you want a cottage by the sea but your wife longs for the smell of evergreens in the mountains? You find the highest point near the ocean, plant it with pine and oak trees, rhododendrons, holly trees, azaleas, and mountain laurel, and build a log and stone Adirondack-style mountain lodge overlooking a lake. Surprisingly, this solution worked beautifully in 1908 for the original owners, and it works for us, too.

The first floor and the chimneys are made of local ironstone, which is turning a lovely reddish color with age, while the second story is of half-timber and stucco construction. The house was purchased in 1985 by Mark and Linda Fessler from descendants of the original owners. Mark is an architect, and Linda is an expert artist and craftsperson. Together they have preserved the unique characteristics of the house, while creating a charming and comfortable getaway.

You enter a living room with yellow pine floors and a massive fireplace and chimney made of jagged pieces of ironstone. An extension of the living room has a brick floor and a view of Lake Como. A decanter of sherry sits on a table as encouragement for winding down to enjoy this special place. Throughout this floor, there are massive cedar log beams and pine-paneled walls. Beyond the living room, French doors lead to an enclosed sunroom with a brick floor, a wall of stone, and a lattice ceiling.

The guest rooms are equally distinctive. The Lord of the Manor Suite is stunning. The small sitting room includes a wet bar and refrigerator hidden in a corner cupboard charmingly handpainted by Linda. A massive ironstone fireplace casts a glow across the iron canopy featherbed. The walls are sponged in pale yellow and the ceiling in a pale blue that creates the illusion of clouds. A large private porch offers views of the lake. The bathroom, however, is the tour de force. A double soaking tub sits by a picture window, offering treetop views of the lake.

The latest addition is the Windsor Suite, which has a bedroom with a cathedral ceiling that accommodates a half tester featherbed and a tiled fireplace. The sitting room has a window seat and offers views of the lake. In the bath a stained-glass window separates the shower from a soaking tub for two.

Linda sets out a buffet-style breakfast in the dining room, which has another ironstone fireplace. There will be juice, fresh fruit such as bananas and oranges layered with honey, freshly baked nut bread and Irish soda bread, an entree such as a sweet pepper and caramelized onion frittata with sage sausage patties, and also a dessert such as a four-berry crumble served with chantilly cream.

Perhaps a relaxing day at the beach with a book will beckon, or maybe the hammock in back will call. If you seek other diversions, follow the advice on the Hollycroft brochure. "You can swing a fishing rod, a golf club, or a tennis racket. You can ride a wave or a trolley, a horse, or a ferris wheel."

What's Nearby—Spring Lake

See "What's Nearby—Spring Lake," page 134.

La Maison—A B&B and Gallery

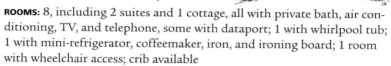

404 Jersey Avenue
Spring Lake, NJ 07762
(800) 276–2088 or (732) 449–0969

FAX: (732) 449–4860

INNKEEPERS: Barbara Furdyna and
Peter Oliver; assistant: Paula Jordan

ROOMS: 8, including 2 suites and 1 cottage, all with private bath, air conditioning, TV, and telephone, some with dataport; 1 with whirlpool tub; 1 with mini-refrigerator, coffeemaker, iron, and ironing board; 1 room with wheelchair access; crib available

ON THE GROUNDS: Side garden

EXTRAS: Fresh flowers in the room; afternoon "happy hour" with wine, cheese, and hors d'oeuvres

RATES: $100–$325, double occupancy, including full breakfast and afternoon "happy hour"; three-night minimum weekends July and August; two-night minimum weekends rest of year

CREDIT CARDS ACCEPTED: American Express, Diners Club, Discover, MasterCard, Visa

OPEN: February to December

HOW TO GET THERE: From the Garden State Parkway, take exit 98 onto Route 34 south. Follow Route 34 to the traffic circle and then take Route 524 east for 4 miles to Spring Lake. After crossing the railroad tracks, take the second right onto Fourth Avenue. Proceed for 5 blocks and turn right onto Jersey Avenue. La Maison is the second house on the right.

Spring Lake is home to scores of distinctive artists. Peter Oliver, one of the innkeepers, is a fine watercolorist, and Paula Jordan, the assistant innkeeper, paints in watercolors and oils. Barbara Furdyna, the vivacious owner/innkeeper, is a superb artist as well. Not only has she created a unique art gallery (all the artwork is for sale) on the first floor and stairway of her B&B, she has decorated it with exceptional taste and style.

Barbara is an acknowledged Francophile. She was a French major in college and lived in France, where she studied at the Sorbonne, and she never really left France spiritually. Therefore, her B&B is infused with a French mood that includes French antiques, champagne buckets filled with fresh flowers, and French music playing in the background. The cozy parlor has a fireplace, a lovely Persian rug, shelves filled with books about France,

French chairs and tables, and a huge painting of poppy fields in Provence. Every afternoon cheeses, pâtés, fruits, and wine are set out on an antique buffet.

You'll find light, airy, and romantic guest rooms with French sleigh beds, iron beds, ornate French iron chairs, carved armoires, and pots of blooming orchids, which can be purchased to serve as a living memento of your stay. There are colorful balloon shades on the windows and white duvets on the beds. Unfortunately, on my last visit I detected several maintenance problems that I sincerely hope are already remedied. The baths are adequate, although several are quite small. I especially like the King Juan Carlos Room, with its sexy bath that contains a two-person whirlpool tub and a skylight in the cathedral ceiling, through which we could view a full moon. A little cottage in back has its own private garden.

Breakfast is served in the formal dining room, which has two pine trestle tables overseen by two brass and crystal chandeliers. Red walls and ladder-back chairs give it a French country appeal. The relaxed *en famille* atmosphere begins with glasses of mimosas. Barbara may serve a menu of poached pears in orange sauce followed by crème brûlée French toast and a dish of fresh fruit, all accompanied by oversized cups of coffee, tea, or cappuccino.

Spring Lake is a peaceful and charming seaside Victorian village unaffected by the fast-food emporiums and honky-tonk dives that characterize other sections of the New Jersey shore. Stately mansions with broad lawns line the well-kept wide streets, and the village has an impressive collection of antiques shops, decorator showrooms, and cafes.

Barbara offers complimentary beach, pool, and tennis passes to her guests (chairs and umbrellas, too) as well as membership in a full-service health club. She also has bicycles for her guests to use.

What's Nearby

See "What's Nearby—Spring Lake," page 134.

Sea Crest by the Sea

19 Tuttle Avenue
Spring Lake, NJ 07762
(800) 803–9031 or (732) 449–9031

FAX: (732) 974–0403

E-MAIL: JK@seacrestbythesea.com

WEB SITE: www.seacrestbythesea.com

INNKEEPERS: John and Carol Kirby; managers, Terri and Arthur Thomson

ROOMS: 11, including 2 suites, all with private bath, air conditioning, TV, VCR, telephone, hair dryer, and robes; 8 with gas fireplace; 6 with whirlpool tub for two

ON THE GROUNDS: On 1 acre with parking and gardens

EXTRAS: Afternoon tea and desserts; chocolates at night; one dog named Daisy

RATES: $165–$265 mid-May through September; $145–$249 October to mid-May, double occupancy, including full breakfast and afternoon tea; three-night minimum weekends and two-night minimum weekdays from June through September, two-night minimum weekends from October through May

CREDIT CARDS ACCEPTED: American Express, MasterCard, Visa

OPEN: Year-round

HOW TO GET THERE: From the Garden State Parkway, take exit 98 onto Route 34 south. Follow Route 34 to the traffic circle and then take Route 524 east for 4 miles to Ocean Avenue in Spring Lake. Turn right. Go 1 block and turn right again onto Tuttle Avenue. The B&B will be on the left in 1 block.

We love the turrets and gingerbread, the bay windows, the ornate fireplace mantels, and the broad porches of fine Victorian homes. So naturally, we love Sea Crest, a Victorian gem that has furnishings as Victorian as its architecture.

John and Carol Kirby fled corporate life for innkeeping in 1989, purchasing this 1885 home that has been welcoming guests for more than one hundred years. We walked across the wraparound porch to the ornate front door and were immediately immersed in the spell of the late 1800s. Tea and freshly baked cookies and cakes (it was a white chocolate cheese cake when we last visited) were waiting in the dining room when we arrived, and we relaxed while John told us about the history of Spring Lake.

The guest rooms are fantasy retreats designed for adults who are seeking a romantic escape. Take the Casablanca Room, for example. You will enter through a bead curtain, sleep on a rattan bed, and be surrounded by lamps and artifacts that John collected in Africa when he was an officer in the merchant marine. A trench coat hangs behind the door, and "the" movie is available in the video library to watch on the VCR in your room. The Queen Victoria Suite has a four-poster canopy featherbed, pictures of the queen, a sitting room with a fireplace, and a Jacuzzi. Several of the baths are small, but adequate.

Individual touches abound at this inn that is infused with the personalities of the creative innkeepers. There's a wonderful gift corner just inside the entrance where unusual jewelry, paintings, and craft items are sold. Also, when guests return from dinner they will be greeted by "James the Butler," a charming wooden gent who will be standing on the stairway holding a tray of delectable homemade chocolates.

Breakfast is an elaborate affair that is served in the formal dining room and also in a cozy addition that boasts a woodstove. We started with breads, including freshly baked buttermilk scones, juices, and cereals that we selected ourselves from a corner cupboard. This was followed by Carol's popular featherbed eggs, a baked soufflé of eggs and bread, spiced with her seasonings of choice. She might use ham and cheese, or spicy peppers and herbs for a Mexican flavor. A side dish of fresh fruit is included as well as freshly roasted and ground coffee that guests rave about. It's all served on pretty china on placemats.

Although guests are often reluctant to leave the lively table conversations that begin around John and Carol's table, John might suggest a spritely walk along the 2-mile boardwalk, which he claims "is guaranteed to use up at least 400 calories." Or, there is a fleet of English three-speed bicycles for guests to use.

What's Nearby

See "What's Nearby—Spring Lake," page 134.

Victoria House Bed and Breakfast

214 Monmouth Avenue
Spring Lake, NJ 07762
(888) 249–6252 or (732) 974–1882

FAX: (732) 974–2132

E-MAIL: victoriahousebb@worldnet.att.net

WEB SITE: www.victoriahouse.net

INNKEEPERS: Robert and Louise Goodall

ROOMS: 9, 7 with private bath and 2 that share 1 bath, all with air conditioning and hair dryer; 2 with fireplace and robes; 1 with a whirlpool tub

ON THE GROUNDS: On-site parking, gardens

EXTRAS: Afternoon tea in winter; beverage-stocked refrigerator year-round; bicycles available; complimentary beach towels and badges

RATES: $125–$250, double occupancy, including full breakfast and afternoon tea (winter only); two-night minimum weekends mid-May–September and holidays, and throughout year for deluxe rooms; three-night minimum holidays mid-May–September

CREDIT CARDS ACCEPTED: American Express, Discover, MasterCard, Visa

OPEN: Year-round except Christmas Eve and Christmas Day

HOW TO GET THERE: From the Garden State Parkway, take exit 98 and follow the first exit onto Route 138 east. Stay on Route 138 for about 5 miles and then bear right onto Route 35 south. At the second traffic light turn left onto Allaire Road. Go 1³/₁₀ miles and turn right onto Fifth Avenue. Turn left onto Monmouth Avenue. The B&B will be on the left in 3 blocks.

Victoria House is a distinctive Victorian confection of gingerbread, shingles cut into unusual shapes and sizes, a square turret, and vintage stained-glass windows. Built in 1882 it retains all of its fancy work. The Goodalls have painted their elaborate Queen Anne home in soft shades of taupe and greige. The wraparound porch is a wonderful spot to relax in the afternoon, and breakfast is served here also in sunny, warm weather.

An elaborate tin ceiling distinguishes the entry hall and a gorgeous stained-glass window with a turquoise background highlighted with red and gold jewels, shines from the stair landing. The parlor of the house is welcoming and snug. There's a gas fireplace with a marble face and an 1880s Eastlake carved walnut mantel. A sofa is upholstered in rose-colored damask.

The guest rooms are lovely and the baths are some of the nicest in Spring Lake. The Turret Room has a wonderful antique Victorian walnut dresser and an elaborate king-size bed. The Eastlake Room has a brass bed dressed in wine-colored fabric and a beautiful antique Eastlake armoire. The dark walls create an intimate cocoon. My favorite, however, is Victoria's Hideaway, a suite that has an iron bed in the corner, an antique dresser, and a gas fireplace. The generous bath has a whirlpool tub.

Breakfast will include such delectable main courses as Grand Marnier French toast with bacon or Mexican eggs with corn bread and sausage. This is served in a dining room with a lovely carved European sideboard and chairs.

What's Nearby

See "What's Nearby—Spring Lake," page 134.

Whistling Swan Inn

110 Main Street
Stanhope, NJ 07874
(973) 347-6369

FAX: (973) 347-3391

E-MAIL: wswan@worldnet.att.net

WEB SITE: bbianj.com/whistlingswan

INNKEEPERS: Joe and Paula Williams Mulay

ROOMS: 10, including 1 suite, all with private bath, air conditioning, telephone with dataport, TV, radio, hair dryer, mini-refrigerator, iron, and ironing board; 7 with desk; 6 with VCR; 4 with soaking tub

ON THE GROUNDS: Parking, side yard with swings, picnic table, hammocks, gardens

EXTRAS: Afternoon refreshments, including lemonade and freshly baked cookies; fax, copier, light typing available

RATES: $95–$150, double occupancy, including full breakfast and afternoon snacks; two-night minimum holiday weekends and all weekends in September and October

CREDIT CARDS ACCEPTED: American Express, Diners Club, Discover, MasterCard, Visa

OPEN: Year-round

HOW TO GET THERE: From I–80 take exit 25 eastbound or exit 27B westbound and follow Route 206 north until it becomes Route 183. Continue on Route 183 to the Hess gasoline station in Stanhope, where you will turn onto Main Street. The B&B will be on the left.

When the Erie Canal opened in 1825, it linked the huge population on the East Coast with the industrial products and the agricultural produce further west. Soon feeder canals were built as well. The Morris Canal, a link between the Hudson and Delaware Rivers, was of primary importance, and Stanhope became a major stop along this great canal. Eventually, Stanhope blossomed into an industrial town itself.

Joe and Paula Mulay decided to leave the corporate world of AT&T when they realized they saw more of each other in airports than at home. Operating a B&B was something they considered, so when they found a Whistling Swan sign in an antiques store, they bought it and looked for a house to hang it on. The swan and this house are symbolic. Swans mate for life and are elegant, both elements that apply here as well.

The Whistling Swan sits on a stone foundation that creates a wide wraparound porch across the front and side. It's filled with wicker chairs and rockers and a wicker porch swing. Inside, there's a fireplace in both the foyer and one of the parlors. Red walls create a rich backdrop for the warm tiger oak floors, columns, fretwork, and fireplace mantel. Some interesting antique pieces furnish the rooms, much of it from Paula's grandmother's home. In one parlor, there's a player piano and an old Victrola as well as a TV, a VCR, a movie library, games, and jigsaw puzzles. In the dining room, there's a tiger oak china closet with dolphin handles.

There are ten guest rooms in this spacious house, and each is enhanced by a working antique radio and a colorful afghan made by Joe's mother. Waterloo Village is one of our favorites. It has a bed with a lace canopy and an oak wardrobe. The bath is seductively painted in red and has a pedestal sink and brass fixtures. On the third floor there's a magnificent 7-foot stained-glass window at the end of the hall and an oak halltree with twisted spindles on the landing.

The room that is most unique, however, is not a guest room at all, but the original bathroom. All rooms have private baths with showers, but off the second floor hallway, there's a separate bath with twin clawfoot tubs painted blue to match the walls. Joe and Paula call this their Victorian Jacuzzi. All guests are welcome to use the room.

Breakfast is served in the formal dining room. The meal will start with freshly baked breakfast breads and a cold soup, perhaps a peach soup made with tapioca or yogurt. The main course might be a quiche or perhaps a potato-apple dish with turkey sausage.

What's Nearby—Stanhope

This rural northwest region of Sussex County, New Jersey, is called "the Skylands" because of its low-lying mountains and abundance of rivers, streams, and lakes. Lake Hopatcong is nearby. Historic Waterloo Village is a charming complex of restored eighteenth-century stone buildings, boat locks, and mills in a peaceful setting on the Morris Canal in Allamuchy Mountain State Park, just west of Stanhope. During the summer months, there are craft demonstrations as well as craft, antiques, and art exhibits and concerts. In addition, guests can go horseback riding or hiking or visit a local winery. (See also Newton.)

The Woolverton Inn

6 Woolverton Road
Stockton, NJ 08559
(888) AN INN 4U or (609) 397–0802

FAX: (609) 397–0987

E-MAIL: woolinn@voicenet.com

WEB SITE: Woolvertoninn.com

INNKEEPERS: Carolyn McGavin, Mark Smith, Matthew Lovette

ROOMS: 10, including 2 suites, all with private bath, air conditioning, radio, and robes; 3 with fireplace; 2 with whirlpool tub; 1 with private porch; wheelchair access

ON THE GROUNDS: On 10 acres with parking; gardens, croquet lawn, horseshoes pit; pastures with sheep named Betty and Pâté

EXTRAS: Afternoon refreshments

RATES: $105–$225, double occupancy, including full breakfast and afternoon refreshments; two-night minimum weekends; three-night minimum some holiday weekends

CREDIT CARDS ACCEPTED: American Express, MasterCard, Visa

OPEN: Year-round

HOW TO GET THERE: From New York take the New Jersey Turnpike south to exit 14 and follow I–78 west to exit 29. Follow I–287 south to Route 202 south. Stay on Route 202 to the second Lambertville exit. Then take Route 29, traveling north to Stockton. Travel through the village to the fork. Turn right onto Route 523 and go $^2/_{10}$ mile. Turn left onto Woolverton Road. The inn is reached along the second driveway on the right.

The Woolverton Inn is one of my favorite bed-and-breakfasts. The setting on ten pastoral acres high above the Delaware River is so serene that cares seem to melt away. The magnificent eighteenth-century stone manor house, with its lacy porch railings and wrought-iron roof crest, is impressive but welcoming at the same time. Sheep graze in the meadow, and sweeping lawns encompass stands of apple and oak trees, flower gardens, and a pretty pergola.

Although the bed-and-breakfast has been welcoming guests since 1980, Elizabeth and Michael Palmer purchased the inn in 1993 and worked continuously to create the special retreat we enjoy today. Private baths were added to every guest room, and in two rooms, there are two-person whirlpool tubs. There are canopy beds, lush fabrics, fireplaces in three rooms, and walls charmingly handpainted with flowers or pastoral scenes. Note: In 1999, they sold the inn and the new innkeepers have added featherbeds as well.

My favorite room is Amelia's Garden, which has a four-poster cherry bed with a fishnet canopy, a pretty sitting room, and an elegant bath with pink walls and a walnut dresser outfitted with a sink. In Letitia's Repose, a pink-and-green confection with a fireplace, the bath has a dreamy mural on the wall beside the Jacuzzi tub. The Stockton Quay Suite has a twig bed and chair and a bath with a corner Jacuzzi tub and a woodland scene painted on the ceiling. Caroline's Balustrade has its own private second-floor porch, and although the bath is across the hall, it's the most charming of all. It has a painted garden scene, complete with abundant flowers cascading along a stone wall.

Every afternoon Carolyn prepares light refreshments that will include hot and cold drinks and a fruit and cheese tray, or perhaps crudités and a dip, as well as freshly baked cookies.

Breakfast is served in the formal dining room, which has another fireplace, or on one of the porches or the veranda in summer. Carolyn may prepare cinnamon sticky buns, a special juice such as strawberry/orange, fresh fruit, eggs Benedict with pan-fried potatoes, and brandied raisin bread pudding with caramel sauce or it may be zucchini and pineapple muffins, fresh fruit, yogurt crepes with cider sauce, and a peach-and-blueberry cobbler.

There are a stone spring house, a picturesque barn that may one day contain additional rooms, and a carriage house with two guest rooms. Hiking trails meander about, and there's a croquet lawn and a horseshoes pit.

Stockton, located on the Delaware River, is near Point Pleasant, Pennsylvania, where you can rent canoes and rafts for trips down the river. Walking along the old tow path that borders the Delaware River is also a popular activity. The Bucks County Playhouse offers theatrical productions year-round. Stockton has several interesting shops and restaurants, including Phillip's Fine Wines, one of the best wine shops in the state with about 5,000 labels and stocking about 200,000 bottles. The Mt. Airy ski area is located nearby. (See also Lambertville, New Jersey, and New Hope, Pennsylvania.)

Holly Thorn House

143 Readington Road
Whitehouse Station, NJ 08889
(908) 534–1616

FAX: (908) 534–9017

WEB SITE: www.bbian.com/hollythorn

INNKEEPERS: Anne and Joe Fosbre

ROOMS: 5, including 1 suite, all with private bath, air conditioning, telephone with dataport, radio, hair dryer, and desk; 1 room with fireplace; 1 room with wheelchair access

ON THE GROUNDS: On 3 acres with parking; swimming pool with cabana; herb garden; lawn games

EXTRAS: Snacks, wine, soft drinks, coffee, and cookies; fax, telephones with modems; cat named Lilly

RATES: $110 weekdays, $125–$160 weekends, double occupancy, including full breakfast

CREDIT CARDS ACCEPTED: American Express, Discover, MasterCard, Visa

OPEN: Year-round

HOW TO GET THERE: From I–78, take exit 26 and turn left onto Lamington Road. At the T, turn left and go 700 yards; turn right onto Orr Drive and follow this across Route 22. You are now on Readington Road. Follow Readington Road south for 3 miles to its end. Turn right at the church and go 300 yards. The Holly Thorn House is on the left.

I t's hard to imagine that this elegant, rambling, beige stucco bed-and-breakfast began life as a cow barn, but the exposed beams and grand first-floor open space continue to give it a distinctive character. Anne and Joe Fosbre raised their children in this unique structure that they redesigned to replicate an English manor house. When the children were grown, they converted it to a bed-and-breakfast.

One enters a great room encircled by a balcony encompassing several comfortable sitting areas with fireplaces. There's a darkly paneled billiards room with plaid carpeting. A wet bar and a refrigerator stocked with soft drinks are located here. Up the spiral stairs and at the end of the second-floor hall, a library contains a gas fireplace and a TV and VCR as well as an extensive video library and a multitude of books and games. Overstuffed chairs welcome relaxation, and the snack bar is stocked with snacks, coffee, fruit, and a filled cookie jar. Another refrigerator holds soft drinks, beer, and wine. A fax machine keeps you in touch, if you must.

The open kitchen becomes a gathering spot, especially in the morning. Guests may eat breakfast at a table in front of a fireplace while admiring Anne's collection of more than 125 monks. They are found on steins, carved wooden statues, and glassware. Breakfast will consist of juice, fruit, and homemade breads and rice puddings. The main course might be a cheese and ham strata or fruit-filled crepes.

The guest rooms are sophisticated and unique, and each has a private bath. The suite has black-and-white French toile on the walls, a gas fireplace with a magnificent carved mantel, and a tall carved headboard. The Hunt Room has a masculine feel with large hunting prints on brown walls, a massive armoire, and an antique four-poster bed.

The three acres of the property include a fragrant "herbary walk," where guests may pick samples; a pool with a poolhouse and changing room; and sunny lawns and patios.

What's Nearby—Whitehouse Station

For sports enthusiasts, there are several golf courses in the area, while for adventurers, hot-air balloon expeditions can be arranged. History buffs will want to visit Washington's winter headquarters during the Revolutionary War in 1778–1779, which was located in nearby Somerville. Those with a green thumb can visit Wallace House as well as Duke Gardens, a group of eleven gardens enclosed in a glass conservatory.

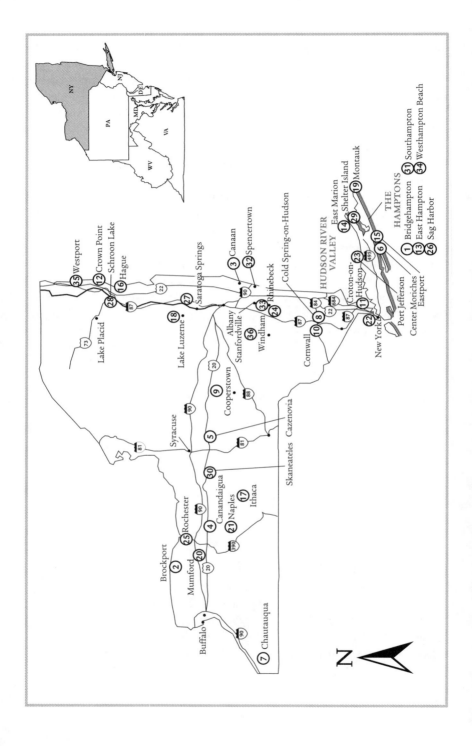

New York

Numbers on map refer to towns numbered below.

Bridgehampton Inn

2266 Main Street
(mailing address: P.O. Box 1342)
Bridgehampton, NY 11932
(516) 537–3660

FAX: (516) 537–3589

INNKEEPERS: Anna and Detlef
Pump; manager: Maureen Brown

ROOMS: 8, including 1 suite, all with private bath, air conditioning, TV, telephone, hair dryer, and robes; cribs available

ON THE GROUNDS: Parking; gardens, covered veranda

EXTRAS: Wine, beer, cheeses, cakes, offered in the afternoon; fresh flowers throughout; breakfast in bed available; beach towels provided

RATES: $250–$390 May through September; $190–$290 October, March, and April; $140–$250 November through February, double occupancy, including full breakfast; two-night minimum weekends mid-May to mid-October; three-night minimum holiday weekends

CREDIT CARDS ACCEPTED: American Express, MasterCard, Visa

OPEN: February to December

HOW TO GET THERE: From New York City take I–495 (the Long Island Expressway) to exit 70 (Manorville) and follow Route 111 south to Highway 27 (Sunrise Highway). Follow Highway 27 (which becomes the Montauk Highway) east. It becomes Main Street as it reaches Bridgehampton. The B&B is on the left ½ mile beyond the traffic light at the entrance to Bridgehampton Common shopping center and before reaching the village of Bridgehampton.

The Bridgehampton Inn sits on the edge of a fashionable village, where it enjoys the best of all worlds. It's close to wonderful shops and restaurants and yet is far enough from the bustle of pedestrian traffic to offer a peaceful country feeling. The mansion was built in 1795 and served as the Boxwood Inn for many years, but when Detlef and Anna Pump purchased it in 1993, it needed considerable attention. Detlef is a builder, however, and he appreciates a challenge. Today, the inn is a reflection of its historic past and of the Scandinavian heritage of its owners.

The large white clapboard house has a handsome facade. There's a gabled roof in the center portion and wings projecting from both sides. It sits on an acre behind a picket fence surrounded by gardens. Inside, the style is crisp but warm. There are Oriental rugs on polished oak floors. The reception area has a fireplace. The living room, which has French doors to the back garden and to a side veranda, has a Victorian sofa upholstered in forest-green velvet and a fireplace where a fire will be glowing in winter. A glass bowl of fresh fruit sits on an antique table, and a pitcher of fresh flowers graces the mantel.

Anna is the owner of one of the Hamptons' premier catering firms, Loaves and Fishes, so guests find a tray of cheeses or perhaps some hors d'oeuvres or cakes to accompany the carafes of wine waiting in the afternoon in the bright breakfast room, which has a third fireplace. Breakfast is served here featuring homemade blueberry (or another variety) muffins, scones, and croissants, fresh juice, and fruit. This may be accompanied by Swedish pancakes with warm blueberry sauce, or perhaps eggs with bacon or ham.

The guest rooms are unique—all are decorated in a warm European country ambience, and each is furnished with a custom-crafted four-poster bed and elegant antiques. There's wall-to-wall carpeting, burnished antique chests and tables, and a serene and restful atmosphere. The most alluring room is Number 6, a suite that is furnished with an extraordinary, eight-piece antique Biedermeier bedroom ensemble that includes a bed, chests, dressers, and tables. The gray marble baths have deep European sinks with wide countertops. The glass showers are big enough for two and have the practical European feature of a center showerhead—something one sees frequently in Anna and Detlef's native Denmark.

Some of the Hamptons' finest restaurants are located right here in Bridgehampton, so there's no need to travel far for dinner.

The Victorian Bed & Breakfast

320 Main Street
Brockport, NY 14420
(716) 637-7519 (fax also)

WEB SITE: www.victorianbandb.com

INNKEEPER: Sharon M. Kehoe

ROOMS: 7, all with private bath, air conditioning, TV, telephone, radio, and desk; 3 with VCR; 1 with whirlpool tub

ON THE GROUNDS: Gardens; parking on premises

EXTRAS: Afternoon and evening tea, cookies, and fruit

RATES: $65–$100, double occupancy, including full breakfast; two-night stay on special event weekends at State University College at Brockport

CREDIT CARDS ACCEPTED: None

OPEN: Year-round

HOW TO GET THERE: From I–90 (the New York State Thruway) take exit 47 onto Route 19 north. Follow Route 19 for 12 miles to Brockport, where it becomes Main Street. Cross Route 31 and then continue on Main Street through 3 more traffic lights. The B&B is on the left corner of Main Street and Centennial.

How does she do it all? Sharon Kehoe is a college professor, an attorney, a town justice of Brockport, a developer, and the innkeeper of this wonderful bed-and-breakfast. Arriving early one morning, I found Sharon busily preparing garnished plates of French toast and bacon for her guests, who had already feasted on home-baked muffins, fresh fruit, and juices.

Sharon bought the main house, an 1891 Victorian beauty with two turrets, in 1989. It has elaborate corbels under the eaves and fancy fishscale shingles on the second and third floors. She painted it a lilac color with peach trim. Shortly after, she added a house across the street to her enterprise. She painted the clapboards of this one a pretty pink.

Sharon's guests have a lovely parlor to sit in with oak floors and a Victorian fireplace. There's a rose-colored Victorian sofa on which to repose. A bright and cheerful solarium has a colorful Waverly chintz on the windows and a green sofa.

The guest rooms are equally inviting. The Loft Room has a green carpet and peach walls and a bed with a beige spread. The skylit bath is bright and new. All of the rooms have TVs and telephones. The Rose Room, in the former master bedroom of the house, has a canopy bed and a whirlpool tub in the bath.

What's Nearby—Brockport

Brockport, which at one time was located at a lock on the old Erie Canal, is 20 miles from Rochester. Many of the historic buildings in the village remain much as they were when the canal was functioning. Brockport is the home of a branch of the State University of New York, and numerous cultural events including theatrical productions, concerts, dance performances, and sports events take place year-round. An arts festival is held once a year that attracts more than 300 vendors. Tour boats then ply the canal again, much as they did in days of old.

The Inn at Silver Maple Farm

Route 295
(mailing address:
P.O. Box 358)
Canaan, NY 12029
(518) 781–3600

FAX: (518) 781–3883

E-MAIL: info@silvermaplefarm.com

WEB SITE: www.silvermaplefarm.com

INNKEEPERS: Meg and Bill Stratton

ROOMS: 11, including 2 suites, all with private bath, air conditioning, TV, and radio; 8 with telephone with dataport; 3 with desk and mini-refrigerator; 2 with soaking tub and hair dryer; wheelchair access

ON THE GROUNDS: On 10½ acres with whirlpool spa and gardens, hammock in trees

EXTRAS: Afternoon tea and cookies

RATES: $75–$250, double occupancy, including full breakfast; two-night minimum weekends May–October; three-night minimum some holiday weekends

CREDIT CARDS ACCEPTED: American Express, Discover, MasterCard, Visa

OPEN: Year-round

HOW TO GET THERE: From the Taconic State Parkway traveling north, take the exit for Route 295. Follow Route 295 east for 6 miles. The B&B will be on the left. From I–90 (the New York State Thruway) take exit B2 and turn right after the toll booth. Follow the signs to Route 295 and turn left onto Route 295 east. Follow Route 295 east for 4½ miles. The B&B will be on the left.

The trees were bright with leaves of red and orange and yellow as we drove up the drive to the pristine white farmhouse and barn. At the entrance to the barn, a round stone-rimmed planter was filled with colorful flowers and encircled by the entry drive. First impressions are important and we were enchanted by this B&B before we even entered the building.

Meg and Bill Stratton have owned their 10½-acre farm since 1995, and they have done a spectacular job of converting the barn to a B&B. They live in the adjacent farmhouse. The barn has wide-plank pine floors and cathedral ceilings offering views of the heavy posts and beams. There's a fireplace along one wall with cozy wing chairs in which to enjoy the flame. Whimsical artistic touches and interesting decor are found throughout. Look for the chickens painted on the door of the old hayloft. Along one wall beside tall windows, tables are made from sewing machine bases. This is where breakfast and afternoon tea will be enjoyed.

The guest rooms are casual and wonderful—most feature Ralph Lauren bed dressings, antique trunks, and pine cupboards, and the modern baths have pine floors. The King Room has a bed with a headboard made from old shutters and a separate sitting room. The Cottage Room has a fabulous mural of roses trailing along a split-rail fence painted along the wall and a bed with a headboard made of old porch posts. Lower Lodge features an apple tree painted around a wall and a bed made with antique pine which has a vibrant red plaid patchwork duvet.

Two new rooms were added in 1998. One features a sitting area with a fireplace and a bath with a wonderful big soaking tub, while the other, The Pine, is a two-level suite. There's a sitting room with a fireplace on the first floor and a bedroom and bath with a soaking tub upstairs.

Meg and Bill have a background in hotel and resort management, so they have experience in pleasing guests. They can arrange breakfast at a flexible hour, for example, or provide a Continental breakfast for those who prefer one. On the other hand, most guests appreciate the array of fresh fruit, yogurts, granola, and homemade muffins in the morning, as well as a frittata or Meg's popular baked apple French toast.

What's Nearby—Canaan

Canaan is tucked into the Berkshire foothills just west of the Massachusetts border. The countryside is peaceful and bucolic—an area that fostered several Shaker communities in the past. You might visit the Shaker Museum in Old Chatham to appreciate some of their craftsmanship, or, for a total immersion in Shaker life, a trip to Hancock Shaker Village in nearby Hancock, Massachusetts, will be most rewarding. The B&B is about 13 miles from Tanglewood in Lenox, Massachusettes, and about 15 miles from the Norman Rockwell Museum in Stockbridge, Massachusettes. (See also Spencertown.)

Acorn Inn

4508 Route 64 South
Canandaigua, NY 14424
(716) 229–2834

FAX: (716) 229–5046

WEB SITE: http://acorninnbb.com

INNKEEPERS: Joan and Louis Clark

ROOMS: 4, all with private bath, TV, VCR, telephone with dataport, radio, hair dryer, and robes; 2 rooms with fireplace and tape player; 1 room with private porch and whirlpool tub

ON THE GROUNDS: On ½ acre with Jacuzzi spa in garden

EXTRAS: Hospitality closet stocked with mineral water, soft drinks, fruit juices, ice; turndown with chocolate acorns; afternoon tea on request; a standard poodle, Terra Cotta, on premises

RATES: $105–$200, double occupancy, including full breakfast; two-night minimum weekends July–October and holiday weekends

CREDIT CARDS ACCEPTED: American Express, Discover, MasterCard, Visa

OPEN: Year-round

HOW TO GET THERE: From I–90 (the New York State Thruway) traveling west, take exit 43 (Manchester/Canandaigua) and follow Route 21 south past Canandaigua. At the junction with County Road 32, follow that for 7½ miles to Route 64. Turn left (south) onto Route 64, and the inn is the fourth house on the right. From I–90 traveling east take exit 45 (Victor) onto Route 96 east to Victor. In Victor take Route 444 south to Routes 5/20. Turn left (east) and continue one mile to Route 64. Turn right (south) and continue on Route 64 for 5½ miles to the inn, which will be on the left.

In 1785 Ephraim Wilder built this dark grey shingled structure with its rust trim to serve as a tavern at Bristol Center, a crossroads on the dusty trail that carried stagecoach passengers south from Rochester. When Joan and Louis Clark purchased the building in 1988, they turned it into a fine antiques shop specializing in beautiful Oriental rugs.

In 1990, however, they decided to convert the building into an upscale B&B, and we are certainly glad they did. The wonderful old Federal-style building retains its mellow heart-pine floors, floor-to-ceiling windows, and exposed beamed ceilings. The Rumford fireplace, with its brick hearth, warms B&B guests just as it did tavern guests of old. The room is now decorated with Oriental rugs, Windsor chairs, a sofa with a red toile fabric, and wing chairs upholstered in blue-and-white check, giving it a much more elegant appearance than it ever had before. Original oil paintings by Hudson River Valley artists hang on the walls and Staffordshire statues line the mantel. Bookcases hold a multitude of books.

The guest rooms are charming. The Bristol has a canopy bed and a woodstove. A window seat in a bay overlooks the gardens, and the bath has acorn stenciling and a large soaking tub plus a separate shower. The Hotchkiss Room features a fireplace and French doors leading to a private terrace with views of the gardens and the woods beyond. There's a whirlpool tub in the bath.

The B&B gardens are superb. In spring the spreading dogwood tree offers an abundance of blooms, and from spring through fall there's a constant array of changing colors and patterns. A hot tub is a great place to unwind throughout the year. The latest addition to the B&B is the conversion of the barn to a "smoking room," which is complete with a Franklin stove.

Joan fixes a full breakfast, which is served in the formal dining room. One of her most popular entrees is French toast crème brûlée.

What's Nearby—Canandaigua

Canandaigua, an Indian word meaning "chosen spot," is in the Finger Lakes Region of New York State—an area known for its wineries—there are some forty to visit. Sonnenberg Gardens, a 50-acre estate featuring a forty-room Victorian mansion and formal gardens dotted with sculptures is nearby, as is Granger Homestead, a lovely 1816 mansion and a carriage house with more than fifty horse-drawn vehicles on display. Bristol Mountain offers downhill skiing and fall foliage chairlift rides. The Bristol Valley Theatre and the Finger Lakes Performing Arts Center are home to concerts and other cultural performances. (See also Naples.)

Habersham Country Inn Bed and Breakfast

6124 Routes 5 and 20
Canandaigua, NY 14424
(800) 240–0644 or (716) 394–1510

E-MAIL: habershamm@aol.com

WEB SITE: www.habershaminn.com

INNKEEPERS: Raymond and Sharon Lesio

ROOMS: 4, including 1 suite, all with private bath, air conditioning, and TV; 1 with fireplace, whirlpool tub, robes, and tape player

ON THE GROUNDS: On 12 acres with pond for skating and fishing, pretty flower gardens, hills for sledding, and nature walks on premises.

EXTRAS: Cheese and crackers in the afternoon; two bichons frises, Muffin and Josie, on premises; guest pets permitted with prior permission

RATES: $105–$160, double occupancy, including full breakfast

CREDIT CARDS ACCEPTED: MasterCard and Visa

OPEN: Year-round

HOW TO GET THERE: From I–90 (the New York State Thruway) traveling west, take exit 43 (Manchester) onto Route 21 south. Follow this to Route 488 south, which will lead to Route 5/20. Turn right (west) onto Route 5/20 and travel through the village of Canandaigua. Continue on Route 5/20 for approximately 4 miles to Centerfield, where you will see a caution light. The B&B is on the right. From I–90 traveling east, take exit 44 (Canandaigua) onto Route 332 south. Follow this for 9 miles to Route 5/20. Turn right (west) to Centerfield. The B&B will be on the right at the caution light.

When you arrive at this handsome B&B, you will probably be greeted by Muffin and Josie, two adorable white bichons frises, who are absolutely sure it's their job to graciously welcome their guests. Of course, Ray and Sharon will be right behind—unless Ray is tending to his chef duties at their restaurant, Raymond's Balley Inn, in nearby Honeoye Falls.

The house, an ivory-clapboard Federal-style Colonial with black shutters, was built in 1840. It was converted to a B&B in 1992, and Ray and Sharon have been the owners since 1998. Its site high above the road and its pristine, neat appearance give it a commanding presence, as if important events have taken place here and will do so again.

The house is entered from an ample covered porch, which is furnished with green iron tables and chairs and comfortable rockers, offering spots for quiet contemplation. The living room has a rose-colored carpet and a floral sofa, and features a fireplace, which has a stenciled cover in the summer. Folk art, including a collection of duck decoys, decorates the room and there's a little gift shop. A room that everyone especially enjoys, however, is the Williamsburg-style tavern and dining room, which has mellow pine floors, a high-backed bench, and a bar faced with beadboard.

The guest rooms are decorated in a country style that features canopy, four-poster, and white iron beds. The Hillview Suite includes a marble fireplace and a four-poster bed with a checked bedskirt and canopy, as well as a sitting area with wing chairs and a Victorian sofa. The tiled bath has a two-person whirlpool tub. The Southwood has a more feminine appeal with a white iron bed, floral paper on the wall, and a pastel spread and pillows.

With a chef in the house, a fine breakfast is assured. Ray prepares a full repast of fruit and juice plus perhaps eggs Florentine with potatoes and sausage, all accompanied by freshly baked breads or muffins.

Morgan-Samuels Inn

2920 Smith Road
Canandaigua, NY 14424
(716) 394–9232

FAX: (716) 394–8044

E-MAIL: Morsambb@aol.com

WEB SITE: www.morgansamuelsinn.com

INNKEEPERS: John and Julie Sullivan

ROOMS: 6, including 1 suite, all with private bath, air conditioning, fireplace, radio, hair dryer, tape player, and robes; 4 with private porch; 2 with whirlpool tub, mini-refrigerator, and desk; portable TVs, VCRs, and telephones available

ON THE GROUNDS: On 46 acres that include pastures for a special breed of Holstein cows, beautiful gardens, and small creek; tennis court

EXTRAS: Evening tea with hors d'oeuvres and beverages; turndown with chocolates; a dalmatian, Tasha, on premises

RATES: $109–$255, double occupancy, including full breakfast and evening snacks; two-night minimum weekends May–mid-November

CREDIT CARDS ACCEPTED: MasterCard and Visa

OPEN: Year-round except Christmas Eve and Christmas Day

HOW TO GET THERE: From I–90 (the New York State Thruway) take exit 43 (Manchester/Canandaigua) and turn right (south) onto Route 21. Proceed to Route 488 and turn left. At the first intersection (which will be in 400 feet), turn right onto East Avenue and go to the first stop sign (County Route 4). Proceed through the intersection for ¾ mile to the B&B driveway, which will be on the right.

This beautiful stone mansion is always a source of amazement and surprise to me, as it's so unexpected. Amid fields of gently grazing Holstein cows (John is a Cornell graduate in agriculture) lies this sophisticated and splendid house. The house was built in 1810 by Judson Morgan, a playwright whose family owned the highly respected Morgan Department Stores of Canada. These stores are now part of the Hudson Bay Company chain. Later the house was purchased by Howard Samuels and his wife Bobbie. Mr. Samuels is noted for his invention of the plastic clothesline and the plastic bag.

John and Julie Sullivan have been the owners of the farm since 1988, and the care and attention they have lavished on their house and grounds, coupled with their solicitous concern for the well being of their guests, make this one of the finest places to stay in the Finger Lakes region.

Located on a rise at the end of a maple-lined driveway, the mansion is truly impressive in its sylvan setting. The English-style house is composed of stone, brick, hand-hewn beams, and multiple fireplaces. The B&B is still a working farm, so in addition to grazing Holsteins, you may see chickens, ducks, and turkeys roaming the grounds.

The mansion has a number of common rooms. The glassed-in Victorian porch has a fireplace. The living room also has a fireplace—a huge stone one. This room is filled with antique furniture and elegant oil paintings hang on the walls. The cozy library, with its shelves laden with books, has yet another fireplace, as well as a TV, VCR, video library, and game table. The Tea Room has 16-foot windows overlooking the gardens, a wall of stone, and a potbellied stove.

The grounds surrounding the mansion have been as thoughtfully planned out as the rooms themselves. There are several beautiful patios— one with a pond, another reached through an antique steel gate and archway, and a third with a well and a statue. Beyond the walls, there are majestic 250-year-old trees, acres of lawns, and abundant flower beds.

The guest rooms are delightful. The Morgan Suite features an eighteenth-century French antique suite enhanced by inlaid woods and a fireplace. There are views of the gardens from two sides, and in the bath, a whirlpool tub awaits. The Gothic Room has a cathedral ceiling with a tall Gothic window draped in black and rose Laura Ashley fabric. Each of the rooms has a fireplace, and the Victorian Room has another whirlpool tub as well.

Breakfast is served in either the Dining Room, which has beamed ceilings, a bay window, and another fireplace or in the Tea Room. John prepares a full breakfast that might include an omelette or French toast, in addition to an impressive array of fresh fruits. He obtains some of the B&B's breads from the nearby Trappist monastery.

What's Nearby

See "What's Nearby—Canandaigua," page 157.

Sutherland House Bed and Breakfast Inn

3179 State Route 21 South (Bristol Street Extension)
Canandaigua, NY 14424
(800) 396–0375 or (716) 396–0375

FAX: (716) 396–9281

E-MAIL: goodnite@frontiernet.net

WEB SITE: www.sutherlandhouse.com

INNKEEPERS: Cor and Diane Van der Woude

ROOMS: 5, including 1 suite, all with private bath, air conditioning, TV, VCR, and radio; 3 with private-line telephone and dataport, fireplace, and robes; 2 with whirlpool tub, desk, and tape players

ON THE GROUNDS: On 5 acres with gardens

EXTRAS: Afternoon tea, coffee bar, guest refrigerator stocked with water, soda, and fruit juices; a boxer, Lady Tyson, on premises

RATES: $110–$185, double occupancy, including full breakfast; two-night minimum weekends Memorial Day–Thanksgiving

CREDIT CARDS ACCEPTED: American Express, Discover, MasterCard, Visa

OPEN: Year-round

HOW TO GET THERE: From I–90, take exit 44 (Canandaigua) onto Route 332 south. Follow this for about 5 miles into Canandaigua. At the second traffic light after the railroad tracks, turn right onto Bristol Street, which becomes Route 21. Continue on Bristol about 2 miles, crossing Route 5/20. Sutherland House will be on the left. Look for the sign.

Sutherland House, a 6,000-square-foot Victorian mansion with a square turret, fancy shingles, porches, and gingerbread corbels, was built by Henry Sutherland in 1885, to joyfully reflect the exuberant architectural style of the era. Henry raised beef cattle on his land, became vice president of the Canandaigua Tin Company, and was on the board of directors of the Canandaigua First National Bank. More than one hundred years later, when in 1993 Cor and Diane spotted the house, it was known locally as "the haunted house" because of its deplorable condition. Cor describes it as "structurally challenged." But he is an expert carpenter by trade and the couple had previously renovated six homes, so they were undaunted.

They purchased the home and immediately began renovations, welcoming their first guests in 1994. But that was just the beginning. They've continued to make improvements every year. Today the clapboard is painted a mellow taupe and there are four colors of trim—sand, midnight blue, sky blue, and burgundy.

The B&B has a lovely parlor with a fireplace with a marbleized soapstone mantel and tall windows flanked by antique cherry shutters. Lace curtains diffuse the view of a majestic two-hundred-year-old copper beech tree. In the afternoon tea is set out here on an antique Dutch table. The dining room is equally impressive. It has its original carved cherrywood mantel, pocket doors, and woodwork. A solid cherry dining room table seats ten guests at breakfast.

The guest rooms are nicely furnished with antiques and reproductions, and all have private baths. The Dutch Treat Suite has a black iron bed with a canopy and spread in a Waverly ivy pattern, and ivy is also stenciled on the walls. It sits on a light green carpet. A gas woodstove provides a romantic ambience, as does the whirlpool tub for two in the bath. Lillian's Lodge has a navy carpet and another gas woodstove. A blue-and-white love seat offers a place to curl up to enjoy the warmth. Among the country decor, you will find red tulips stenciled on the walls and a uniquely sculpted mural made of carved pieces of wood.

Breakfast will not only include an array of freshly baked muffins, breads, and coffee cakes, but also a breakfast casserole, or pancakes, or perhaps "romance waffles"—waffles in the shape of hearts and topped with fresh strawberries.

What's Nearby

See "What's Nearby—Canandaigua," page 157.

Notleymere Cottage

4641 East Lake Road
Cazenovia, NY 13035
(800) 704–4753 or (315) 655–9419

FAX: (315) 655–8110

E-MAIL: notleymere@aol.com

WEB SITE: www.dreamscape.com/
notleymerecottage

INNKEEPERS: John and Susan McCarvill

ROOMS: 5, including 1 suite, all with private bath, air conditioning, TV, telephone, hair dryer, and desk; 3 with fireplace; 2 with private porch; 1 with whirlpool tub

ON THE GROUNDS: On 2 acres on Cazenovia Lake, with large English garden that leads to the lake, where dock, canoe, Windsurfer available; horseshoes, croquet, and badminton available

EXTRAS: Cookies and sodas in evening; fire built in fire pit down by dock evenings in summer

RATES: $70–$150, double occupancy, including full breakfast

CREDIT CARDS ACCEPTED: American Express, Diners Club, MasterCard, Visa

OPEN: Year-round

HOW TO GET THERE: From I–81, south of Syracuse, take exit 15 (Lafayette) onto Route 20 east. Follow Route 20 for 17 miles to Cazenovia. At the traffic light stay on Route 20 and turn left (north) onto Forman Street. Stay on this road, which becomes East Lake Road (through the flashing caution light) and for 1½ miles more to the B&B, which will be on the left.

Anyone who is familiar with Teddy Roosevelt's Sagamore Hill or with FDR's Hyde Park will recognize Notleymere Cottage, an 1888 shingled summer cottage with a broad wraparound porch, multiple chimneys, and Victorian turrets, gables, bays, balconies, and stained glass. Designed to take advantage of the breezes off Cazenovia Lake, it is a comfortable and hospitable home. The house is on the National Register of Historic Places and was built by Frank Norton. An Episcopal minister, Norton, it is said, was a friend of Teddy Roosevelt. President Roosevelt is said to have stayed in a third-floor guest room here several times.

Guests enter the house through a porte cochere of hand-hewn stone and wood. The entry has rich oak wainscotting and a stone fireplace with an oak mantel surmounted by a mirror. A grand oak stairway sweeps to the upper floors and window seats offer places to view the lake. A wraparound veranda is a relaxing place to sit in the afternoon to watch the sun set on the lake.

The guest rooms are spacious and charming. The romantic Master Suite has two fireplaces—one in the sitting area and one in the bedroom—and two captivating balconies with views of the lake. The room is decorated in soothing colors of rose, mauve, and green and the wrought-iron bed has a lacy head- and footboard. Queen Lake 2 and King Garden both also have fireplaces, and Queen Lake 2 and Queen Lake 3 have beautiful views of the water.

The dining room, which has a coffered mahogany ceiling and another fireplace, provides a gracious setting for breakfast, but in summer guests often choose to eat on the veranda. Susan's Canadian bacon frittata and homemade breads and muffins are especially popular.

What's Nearby—Cazenovia

You might tour Lorenzo State Historic Site, the estate and mansion of John Lincklaen, the founder of Cazenovia. This gracious 1808 mansion, which overlooks Cazenovia Lake, has most of the original oil paintings, furniture, chandeliers, family photographs, silver, and china of the founding family. The grounds and gardens are the site of numerous art shows and equestrian events throughout the summer. The grounds of Stone Quarry Hill Art Park are home to changing sculptural exhibits. Artists in residence offer workshops and demonstrations. Chittenango Falls State Park, a 192-acre park, has fishing and picnic sites. Its center-piece is Chittenango Falls, a 167-foot cascade that is taller than Niagara Falls.

The Lindenmere Estate B&B

16 Sedgemere Road
Center Moriches, NY 11934
(516) 874-2273

FAX: (516) 878-5445

WEB SITE: www.lindenmere.com

INNKEEPER: Jennie Magaro

ROOMS: 12, all with private bath, air conditioning, TV, VCR, telephone jack, hair dryer, and robes; 6 with water view; 4 with whirlpool tub

ON THE GROUNDS: On 13 acres bordering Moriches Bay with private beach, swimming pool, pool pavilion, lighted Har-Tru tennis court, boardwalk, gardens, nature trail, fishing

EXTRAS: Wine, cheese, and fruit in afternoon

RATES: $150–$275, double occupancy, including full breakfast; two-night minimum weekends mid-May–mid-September; three-night minimum holiday weekends

CREDIT CARDS ACCEPTED: American Express, MasterCard, Visa

OPEN: Valentine's Day through September

HOW TO GET THERE: From I–495 (the Long Island Expressway) take exit 69 (Wading River). At the stop sign at the top of the ramp, turn right onto Wading River Road. Travel approximately 3 to 4 miles and turn right at the second stop sign onto Chichester Street. Go 1 mile to its end and turn left onto Main Street in Center Moriches. At the first traffic light, turn right onto Union Street. Follow Union Street for 1 mile to Sedgemere Road. Turn left onto Sedgemere Road and cross a small bridge over the creek. The inn is the first right turn after the bridge. Ring the bell at the wrought-iron gates and announce yourself, then proceed ¼ mile to the main house.

Lindenmere is a secret surprise—at one time so secret that Imelda Marcos only shared it with her closest friends. But now I'm going to share the secret with you.

The setting is spectacular. Located on Moriches Bay, the house was designed to capture all the beauty of its waterfront backdrop. Stretching along the water, a broad, colonnaded, covered veranda and an expanse of green lawn focus attention on the view. Down at water's edge, a boardwalk has benches for even closer contemplation of the majesty of the bay. Reached via a one-quarter-mile-long lane flanked by one-hundred-year-old linden trees, you understand why the Marcoses treasured their visits here so much.

The twelve-bedroom house was built as a private residence in 1905. The classic, shingle-style mansion is rumored to have been designed by Stanford White, who left a legacy of other similar houses on Long Island. The hurricane of 1938 destroyed much of the mansion, and for a number of years it was abandoned. After World War II, however, it was rebuilt and opened as the Lindenmere Hotel, but eventually that closed too. Local residents remember when Philippine president Ferdinand Marcos and his wife Imelda purchased the estate in the early 1980s. Imelda lavished attention and wealth on the mansion, restoring it to a beauty it had never known before. She installed grand staircases and remodeled the baths to include marble floors and twenty-four-carat gold and onyx fixtures. When the president was deposed in 1987, the government seized the house and put it on the market. In 1996 Dr. Peter Magaro and his wife, Jennie, purchased the thirteen-acre estate; they opened it as a bed-and-breakfast in 1997.

Today guests enter a foyer with a piano and shelves of books and videos. A living room contains a fireplace, a cardinal-red velvet sofa, and puffy chairs upholstered in a Ralph Lauren fabric of yellow and rose. The oak floors are covered by Oriental rugs and modern oil paintings hang on the walls. A dining room has an elegant Victorian walnut marble-topped sideboard and a fabulously carved oak buffet.

The guest rooms are spacious, classic, and simple. Half have views of the water. Room #2 has a Shaker-style four-poster bed and a huge bath with emerald trim. Folk art hangs on the walls and an Indian rug covers the oak floors. Room #8 has two brass beds and a bath with a whirlpool tub.

The grounds include a lighted Har-Tru tennis court and a fabulous waterside pool adjacent to a pool pavilion with a pagoda-like cathedral ceiling. What a pool house! It has marble floors, a giant barbecue grill and walls of glass that look out to the water. Jennie caters weddings and parties here, as the building can easily accommodate seventy-five seated guests for an elegant dinner.

A full breakfast is served either in the beautiful dining room or in the pool pavilion. It may include an entree of quiche Lorraine with home fries and fried apples, or perhaps corn cakes with maple syrup and bacon, ham, or sausage.

What's Nearby—Center Moriches

The beautiful bay and the activities on the inn's thirteen acres might entice guests to stay put, but there are golf courses nearby, and the flat roads offer wonderful places to bicycle. There are places to horseback ride, sail, and hang glide within a few minutes. In addition, the beaches of Fire Island and Westhampton Beach are not far away. For shoppers the Tanger Factory Outlet Center has more than 150 stores offering discounted merchandise. There are excellent restaurants within an easy drive. (See also Eastport.)

The Maple Inn

8 Bowman Avenue
(mailing address: P.O. Box 46)
Chautauqua, NY 14722
(716) 357–4583

FAX: (716) 357–4583
INNKEEPERS: Tom and Linda Krueger

ROOMS: 11, including 5 suites, all with private bath, air conditioning, small kitchen, coffeemaker, and private porch

EXTRAS: All facilities of Chautauqua Institution available to guests

RATES: $85, double occupancy, per night off season; $1,100, double occupancy, per week during 9 weeks of Chautauqua Institution season

CREDIT CARDS ACCEPTED: None

OPEN: Year-round

HOW TO GET THERE: From I-90, take exit 60 (Westfield) onto Route 394 south and follow this for 10 miles to the main gate of the Chautauqua Institution. Enter the property and turn right. Go 2 blocks and turn left onto Bowman Avenue. The B&B is in 2 more blocks on the left.

The Chautauqua Institution was founded at the height of the Victorian era. As the popularity of the concerts, lectures, and classes grew, visitors built a plethora of charming Victorian cottages side by side on the campus, separated only by narrow, tree-studded streets. Most of these cottages have remained in the same family through the years—passed along from generation to generation. Interspersed along the Victorian village's streets are the Amphitheater, Norton Hall, and the Hall of Philosophy. The entire village is on the National Register of Historic Places.

In our opinion, the Maple Inn offers the best on-campus alternative to staying with family or friends. It was built in 1894 and has been an inn since 1909. It's a pristine white clapboard structure with a double deck across the front, giving it a more Colonial than Victorian appearance.

The smartly decorated reception room has a neat and comfortable appearance with overstuffed chairs and a navy blue carpet. The guest rooms come in two sizes. The two-room suites have a combination living/dining room and a kitchen with a separate bedroom and bath, while the studios have a bedroom with an efficiency kitchen occupying one wall. White is the predominant color with accents of blue and green, and the furniture includes old dressers, tables, and chests painted in white. Each room has a private deck.

When you have your own kitchen, breakfast can be as simple or as elaborate as you wish. The refrigerator allows you to store fresh fruit for daylong munching, as well as a variety of beverages. In addition to folks such as you and I, Paul Newman, Robert Redford, and President Bill Clinton have enjoyed their stays here.

What's Nearby—Chautauqua

The Chautauqua Institution, which was founded in 1874 as a summer training conference for Sunday school teachers, soon developed into the nation's premier intellectual retreat. It continues to offer cultural activities that include an incredible array of classes, lectures, concerts, and performances. In addition, the beautiful campus on Chautauqua Lake includes twelve tennis courts, three beaches, a boat dock, a thirty-six-hole golf course, and numerous restaurants. (See also Westfield.)

Pig Hill Inn

73 Main Street
Cold Spring-on-Hudson, NY 10516
(914) 265–9247

FAX: (914) 265–4614

E-MAIL: pighillinn@aol.com

WEB SITE: www.enjoyhv.com/pighill

INNKEEPER: Kim Teng; proprietors: Henry and Vera Keil

ROOMS: 9, including 5 with private bath and 4 sharing 2 baths; all with air conditioning; 6 with fireplace; cribs available; telephone available

ON THE GROUNDS: Parking for 4 cars; garden

EXTRAS: Afternoon tea or cider, plus homemade breads and cookies; breakfast available in guest rooms; fax available; pets sometimes permitted with prior permission

RATES: $110–$160, double occupancy, including full breakfast; two-night minimum weekends mid-May to October; three-night minimum holiday weekends May to November

CREDIT CARDS ACCEPTED: American Express, MasterCard, Visa

OPEN: Year-round

HOW TO GET THERE: From New York City, cross the George Washington Bridge and travel north on the Palisades Parkway. Cross the Hudson River again on the Bear Mountain Bridge, making the first left after crossing the bridge onto Route 9D. Follow Route 9D north to the light at the corner of Route 9D and Route 301 (Cold Spring's Main Street). Turn left onto Main Street. The B&B will be on the left in 2 blocks.

Main Street in Cold Spring is as quaint and "country" as an upscale Hudson River town can be. Boutiques, bookstores, cafes, and restaurants share space with classy antiques shops—including the Pig Hill Inn. But there's an interesting spin here. Although an antiques shop occupies most of the first floor of the brick building, each of the guest rooms on the second and third floors are mini-showrooms, as they are decorated with antique beds, tables, and dressers as well.

Not only that, but each of the rooms is decorated in a distinctive style, ranging from Southwestern to chinoiserie, and most have fireplaces. On the nightstand beside each bed there's a description of each antique and collectible in the room and its price.

Why name a B&B "Pig Hill"? The former owner grew up on a farm where her family raised pigs, and her collection of pigs was extensive. You'll still see numerous pigs lurking about the antiques shop. So, the name seemed a natural extension.

The hallways of the B&B are bright and sunny, thanks to a large window wall in the stairwell and a balcony at the top of the stairs. The walls and door frames were stenciled with cascades of ivy by a local artist. Room #1 has an eclectic Western feeling. There's an adobe kiva-style fireplace in the corner, American Indian blankets and rugs, and birch-branch furniture. The headboard is made from wooden fence posts. The room overlooks the garden. Room #6 is Victorian in style. It has a four-poster Victorian bed with lace draped above, sage-colored walls, yellow Chinese-patterned chintz on the windows and custom-made spreads, and a large taupe enameled woodstove. On each floor two guest rooms have private bathrooms, and the two remaining guest rooms share one bath. The only exception is a new room that was added on the first floor in 1998. Although this room does have a private bath, it is located across from the dining room.

There's a pretty two-tiered garden with a brick-and-stone courtyard in back. Somehow, although they are merely steps from the street, a calm pervades these little spaces. Enclosed by trees and flowers, guests enjoy lounging on the white garden-and-twig furniture.

Breakfast is served in the guest's room, the garden, or downstairs in the dining room every morning. Typically, it will include fresh fruit and freshly baked breads such as blueberry muffins, spice cake, or herb biscuits. This is followed by a hot dish, such as asparagus soufflé, and bacon.

Cold Spring's Main Street ends at the Hudson River with a little park filled with benches. We love to sit here to watch the tugs, barges, sailboats, and yachts slip by.

What's Nearby—Cold Spring-on-Hudson

Get a glimpse of how the wealthy lived in a bygone era by visiting the numerous historic mansions in the area, including Boscobel, an exquisite nineteenth-century jewel in nearby Garrison. The Foundry School Museum has a collection of Hudson River paintings and a re-created country store. West Point, home of the United State Military Academy, is just across the river. You can visit the museum, which contains a collection of military art and artifacts, or watch a cadet parade, or listen to a concert. (See also Croton-on-Hudson.)

The Cooper Inn

Corner of Main & Chestnut Streets
(mailing address: P.O. Box 311)
Cooperstown, NY 13326
(607) 547–2567 or reservations only (800) 348–6222

FAX: (607) 547–1271

E-MAIL: reservations@cooperinn.com

WEB SITE: www.cooperinn.com

MANAGER: Stephen C. Walker

ROOMS: 15, including 5 suites, all with private bath, air conditioning, TV, telephone with dataport, radio, hair dryer, desk, iron, and ironing board

ON THE GROUNDS: On three acres with outside terrace with umbrellas

EXTRAS: Wine and beer honor bar in parlor; afternoon tea at Otesaga Resort in season; facilities of Otesaga Resort Hotel available to all guests, including Leatherstocking Golf Course, tennis courts, pool and lake swimming, canoes, power boats, fishing; discounted passes available to Clark Sports Center, a full exercise and fitness center

RATES: $100–$250, double occupancy, including Continental breakfast and afternoon tea (in season); two-night minimum holiday weekends

CREDIT CARDS ACCEPTED: American Express, MasterCard, Visa

OPEN: Year-round

HOW TO GET THERE: From I–90 or I–87 (both New York State Thruway), take exit 25A to I–88 south toward Oneonta. Travel about 60 miles to exit 17 and take Route 28 north for 20 miles to Cooperstown. Route 28 becomes Chestnut Street. The inn is on the corner of Chestnut and Main Streets.

Location, location, location, they say in real estate, but sometimes that's true for B&Bs too. The Cooper Inn in Cooperstown, for example, has a superb location.

James Fenimore Cooper's father founded Cooperstown in 1786, a few years before James was born. The boy undoubtedly played in the streets where the Cooper Inn now stands—well before baseball was invented here by Abner Doubleday in 1839. The handsome Federal brick building was built in 1812 by publisher Henry Phinney and expanded in 1936, when it first became an inn. There's a columned portico, white shutters, and elegant corbels that support wide overhanging eaves. In 1998 a top-to-bottom renovation reduced the room count and created fifteen rooms that are spacious and elegant.

The inn, which is owned by the proprietors of the Otesaga Resort Hotel, is located on three secluded acres in the heart of town. You can walk to the National Baseball Hall of Fame and Museum, as well as all the shops and restaurants. Or you might sit in one of the handsome twin parlors, with their unusual and elaborate moldings and elegant oil paintings, to enjoy the warmth of the fireplace among the company of friends. Or perhaps an evening of TV or a jigsaw puzzle will entice you to the game room before retiring. On sunny summer days a roof deck offers umbrellaed tables.

The guest rooms are beautifully appointed with damask and chintz fabrics and period reproduction furnishings. All the baths are fresh and new with tile floors and walls. The rooms I visited were spacious, and all had peach walls and lovely drapes and spreads. If Cooperstown is your destination, I can't imagine a nicer place to stay.

What's Nearby—Cooperstown

The charming town of Cooperstown, on the banks of Otsego Lake, was founded by Judge William Cooper, the father of James Fenimore Cooper, who immortalized his hometown and the surrounding area in his *Leatherstocking Tales*. Cooperstown is noted as the home of the National Baseball Hall of Fame and Museum and the town where Abner Doubleday devised the original rules for the game that became "America's Pastime." Don't miss the museum. It's packed with interesting exhibits and ephemera. The Farmers Museum and Village Crossroads is a collection of salvaged and restored buildings where various farming demonstrations such as shoeing horses, spinning thread, baking bread, etc., are performed. The Glimmerglass Opera has an excellent and widespread reputation for its fine productions.

Thistlebrook B&B Inn

316 County Highway 28
Cooperstown, NY 13326
(800) 596–9305 or
(607) 547–6093 (fax also)

FAX: (607) 547–6093

INNKEEPERS: Jim and Paula Bugonian

ROOMS: 5, including 2 suites, all with private bath, air conditioning, radio, and hair dryer; wheelchair access

ON THE GROUNDS: On 6 acres with walking trails

EXTRAS: Port, sherry, chocolates, and cookies in the evening; a cat named Kashka on premises

RATES: $125–$160, double occupancy, including full breakfast; two-night minimum weekends

CREDIT CARDS ACCEPTED: None

OPEN: May through October

HOW TO GET THERE: From I–90 or I–87 (both New York State Thruway), take exit 25A to I–88 south toward Oneonta. Travel about 60 miles to exit 17 and take Route 28 north for 20 miles to Cooperstown. Route 28 becomes Chestnut Street. Remain on Chestnut Street for one block beyond Main Street and then turn left at the stop sign onto Lake Street (Route 80). Continue on Route 80 for 2 1/10 miles past the golf course and Farmers' Museum. Bear left and go up the hill on Otsego County Highway 28. (Note: this is *not* the same as Route 28.) Follow Highway 28 for 1 1/10 miles to the B&B, which will be on the right.

The ambling country road leads past fields and wooded plots. The simple (but expansive) red barn looks beguiling but unexceptional, so the sophistication and elegance are an unexpected surprise. Jim and Paula Bugonian have been caring for their circa 1866 work-in-progress since 1989, and although it looks perfect to us, in 1999 they informed me they will be expanding the gardens and improving the decks and outside sitting areas.

The living room with its 16-foot ceilings is extraordinary. A creamy white fireplace wall includes antique sconces and built-in bookshelves. Round fluted columns define sitting areas featuring antique French and American chairs and loveseats covered in elegant damasks and tapestries. Oriental rugs cover the floors. An antique Chinese china cabinet that reaches to the ceiling is stunning. French doors lead to a spacious deck that overlooks the fields, as well as a pond and a little waterfall. This peaceful and tranquil setting often yields views of deer, wood ducks, and an occasional blue heron. At night the croak of bullfrogs in the pond will lull you to sleep.

The five guest rooms are as elegant as the common areas. Dramatic antiques, beds dressed with lovely fabrics, and baths that contain all the comforts we enjoy are included. Each of the rooms is sequestered away in a different part of the barn to ensure complete privacy, and each has a sitting area as well as a sleeping section. The Loft Suite, located in the former hayloft, has cathedral ceilings and beautiful views across the fields.

Breakfast is one of Paula's specialties. She might fix orange pancakes with fresh blueberries or a vegetable omelette, but it will always include fresh seasonal fruits and berries.

What's Nearby

See "What's Nearby—Cooperstown," page 171.

Cromwell Manor Inn

Angola Road
Cornwall, NY 12518
(914) 534–7136

FAX: (914) 534–3709

INNKEEPERS: Dale and Barbara O'Hara

ROOMS: 13, including 3 suites and one cottage, all with private baths, air conditioning, and radio; 7 with fireplace; 1 with a private balcony and a whirlpool tub; 1 with wheelchair access

ON THE GROUNDS: On 7 acres with parking and gardens

RATES: $135–$295, double occupancy, including full breakfast; two-night minimum summer weekends

CREDIT CARDS ACCEPTED: MasterCard and Visa

OPEN: Year-round

HOW TO GET THERE: From New York City, cross the George Washington Bridge and follow the Palisades Parkway north. Stay on the Palisades Parkway to its end at Bear Mountain. At the traffic circle, take 9W north for 11¼ miles to the Angola Road (Cornwall) exit. At the end of the exit ramp, turn left onto Angola Road and continue for ³⁄10 miles. The B&B will be on the right.

No, Oliver Cromwell did not stay here, but his descendant, David, did. David Cromwell built Cromwell Manor, a brick Greek Revival mansion with massive white boxed columns across the front, in 1820. The majestic house sits on seven serene acres that include formal gardens, a croquet lawn, a pond, and an even earlier cottage built in 1764. It's directly across the street from the 4,000-acre Black Rock Forest and adjacent to the Museum of the Hudson Highlands, which includes an additional 200 acres.

Innkeepers are the most fascinating people I know. They must be risk-takers, caretakers, and astute business people. In this case, Dale O'Hara was driving along a back country road in 1984 when he spotted a crumbling mansion with a FOR SALE sign out front. The next day he owned it. Just like that. Over the next six years, he scraped, painted, fixed, repaired, and got married. Eventually, the couple decided to become innkeepers, and that required another two years to get the necessary permits and to put in thirteen new bathrooms. But in 1993 they opened the doors.

This grand manor house is perfect in every detail. The elegant formal parlor has a fireplace with a marble mantel. There's a bronze chandelier, an antique coffee table with a lyre base, and an antique secretary with a rolltop desk. The chrysanthemum yellow walls provide a stunning background for the white-on-white Empire sofas and chairs.

The guest rooms are filled with antiques as well. The Darby Room has a sleigh bed and a bath with vibrant raspberry tile. The Cromwell Suite has a canopy bed and a marble fireplace mantel. The bath is enormous. It has a bidet, a double whirlpool tub, and two pedestal sinks. The Wellington Room is in the former parlor, and it has another fireplace with a marble mantel. There are yellow walls and a bed covered in green tapestry as well as a Federal couch and dresser. The Canterbury Room is in the former dining room. It has floor-to-ceiling windows and a fireplace. There are four additional rooms in the cottage.

Breakfast is served in the country breakfast room, which was formerly the kitchen. It has a relaxed, cozy feeling highlighted by a collection of intricate models of square-rigged galleons that sit atop the natural wood cabinets. There are various-sized individual tables for guests to use. Breakfast will include yogurt or baked apples, perhaps French toast or a zucchini quiche, and a crumb cake or mini-cheese cakes.

There are numerous things to do locally. The Museum of the Hudson Highlands, located in a rustic building, has natural history and art exhibits as well as live animals and nature trails. There are wineries nearby to visit, and the Jones Farm Country Store is just down the road. Locally made jams, preserves, maple syrup, cider, baskets, and craft items are displayed in an old barn.

What's Nearby—Cornwall

Visitors to Orange County should not miss Storm King Art Center in Mountainville. This 200-acre sculpture park includes work by Nevelson, Noguchi, and Calder. There are hiking trails and swimming possibilities in nearby Harriman State Park as well as in Bear Mountain State Park, where in winter there are also facilities for ice skating and ski jumping. The Appalachian Trail bisects nearby Bear Mountain.

Alexander Hamilton House *Best Buy*

49 Van Wyck Street
Croton-on-Hudson, NY 10520
(914) 271–6737

FAX: (914) 271–3927
E-MAIL: alexhouse@bestweb.net
WEB SITE: www.alexanderhamiltonhouse.com

INNKEEPER: Barbara Notarius; manager: Maggie Moore

ROOMS: 7, including 4 suites, all with private bath, air conditioning, TV, radio, fireplace, telephone with dataport, robes, and hair dryer; 3 with mini-refrigerator and desk; 2 with whirlpool tub, CD player, and VCR

ON THE GROUNDS: Swimming pool; gardens; parking

EXTRAS: Gift/antiques shop and art gallery on premises; cookies, candy, and fruit available all day; also cheese and crackers in the afternoon; answering machine available

RATES: $95–$250 double occupancy; $75–$150 single occupancy (plus 9.75% tax and 10% gratuity), including full breakfast; two-night minimum weekends; three-night minimum holiday weekends

CREDIT CARDS ACCEPTED: American Express, Diners Club, Discover, Master-Card, Visa

OPEN: Year-round

HOW TO GET THERE: From Manhattan take the Saw Mill River Parkway north to Route 9A. Continue north on Route 9A for approximately 10 miles to Route 9 and continue to Croton-on-Hudson. Exit Route 9 at Route 129 and go east to the traffic light on Riverside Avenue. Turn left onto Riverside and go 1 block. Turn right onto Grand Street and go 1 block. Turn left onto Hamilton, which will intersect with Van Wyck in front of the B&B.

When Barbara Notarius decided to buy a house, she knew specifically what she wanted. It had to be big, with multiple fireplaces, and it had to have a view and a pool. She got all she wanted—and more. The 1889, 7,000-square-foot Victorian has ten bedrooms, eight bathrooms, seven fireplaces, and much of its original woodwork and moldings. She scraped, painted, and repaired the house and soon realized she would have to put it to work. When she opened her B&B in 1982, there was just one room, but she quickly added the rest. As with other things this energetic, enthusiastic woman does, she soon was totally immersed in her new occupation. She became the manager of a bed-and-breakfast reservation service, and then she wrote a book describing how to open and operate a B&B. Although she no longer runs the reservation service, her book is now in its fourth printing.

Today her B&B occupies all her time, especially since she never stops adding to, and improving the house. It seems she's forever adding a new bathroom, upgrading an old one, or adding a new fireplace (all rooms now have their own).

The parlor has a mix of antique furnishings that range from a carved French rococo baby grand piano to a Victorian platform rocker. There's a creamy striped paper on the walls. In the adjoining dining room, which has a Queen Anne–style table and chairs, the color scheme is in peach tones. Breakfast is served on the sunporch, which has an eclectic mix of oak and wicker furniture. A TV and VCR are here also.

The guest rooms are furnished primarily with floral fabrics, white and brass iron beds, or beds in verdigris wrought iron. The Master Suite is extraordinary. It has a green marble fireplace mantel, silk Oriental rugs on hardwood floors, a private entertainment center, and a view of the river. The bath includes a two-person whirlpool tub and a huge stained-glass window that is backlighted for the ultimate in romantic impact. The most requested room, however, is the stunning Bridal Chamber, located on the third floor. It has an iron-and-brass bed, Victorian furnishings on wall-to-wall carpeting, and a marble-fronted fireplace—all overseen by multiple skylights. It has its own entertainment center also, and in the bath there's a two-person whirlpool tub.

Breakfast is a formal event in the dining room, where Barbara may prepare her popular apple blintzes with sour cream and a hot fruit compote, along with juices, fresh fruit, and freshly baked muffins such as chocolate chip or blueberry. Throughout the day she has fresh fruit, coffee, tea, cookies, and candy available, and in the afternoon, she also offers cheese and crackers.

The grounds contain informal vegetable plots and formal flower gardens as well as a swimming pool with sundecks surrounding it. The patio has a barbecue area.

What's Nearby—Croton-on-Hudson

Historic Croton-on-Hudson offers several fine museum house restorations, including Van Cortlandt Manor, Philipsburg Manor, and Sunnyside (once the home of author Washington Irving). Lyndhurst, which is also nearby, is a National Trust property. The latest historic home to be opened to the public is Kykuit, the former Rockefeller compound, established by John D. Rockefeller. The Hudson River Museum of Westchester County includes a nineteenth-century mansion and a planetarium. (See also Cold Spring-on-Hudson.)

The village of Croton-on-Hudson is 45 minutes from Grand Central Station on Metro North. Union Church of Pocantico Hills, which contains stained glass by Marc Chagall and Henri Matisse, is nearby, as is Caramoor estate, which is noted for its outstanding summer concert series.

Crown Point Bed & Breakfast

Route 9 North, Main Street
(mailing address: P.O. Box 490)
Crown Point, NY 12928
(518) 597–3651

FAX: (518) 597–4451

E-MAIL: mail@crownpointbandb

WEB SITE: www.crownpointbandb.com

INNKEEPERS: Hugh and Sandy Johnson

ROOMS: 6, including 2 suites, all with private bath, massage shower, and robes; 1 with fireplace, whirlpool tub, and porch

ON THE GROUNDS: On 5½ acres including wooded areas with hiking trails and gardens with fountain; volleyball, badminton, horseshoes, bocci ball, croquet, and bicycles built for two on premises

EXTRAS: Port and sherry available; popcorn machine, homemade cookies, tea and coffee or iced tea in afternoon; turndown with chocolates; small dog named Gizmo on premises

RATES: $70–$140, double occupancy, including full breakfast; two-night minimum holiday weekends

CREDIT CARDS ACCEPTED: American Express, Discover, MasterCard, Visa

OPEN: Year-round; but by appointment only November–March

HOW TO GET THERE: From I–87 (the Northway) take exit 28 Schroon Lake. Turn right at the end of the ramp onto Route 74 east. Continue on Route 74 for 19 miles to the intersection of Route 9N. Turn left onto Route 9N and follow this for 7 miles to the B&B, which will be on the left.

One afternoon after reaching Crown Point via beautiful Route 9N—it meanders along the banks of Lake George and Lake Champlain—we needed more strenuous activity. But the Johnsons had anticipated that. Hugh suggested a ride over to Lake Champlain on the B&B's bicycle built for two. It proved the perfect antidote to hours of car driving. After a leisurely ride, we sat on benches overlooking Monitor Bay and marveled at the beauty of this countryside.

This splendor was certainly not lost on Richard Wyman, the local banker who built the grand Victorian house in 1886 that is now Crown Point Bed & Breakfast. He spared no expense. He embellished the outside with elaborate gingerbread, gables, and a wraparound porch and included stained glass as well as a variety of elegant woods in the interior decor. Hugh and Sandy Johnson purchased the elaborate house in 1988 and converted it into a warm and elegant B&B.

You'll have no trouble finding the B&B. Its elaborate exterior is painted in ten refined and subdued colors and shades that include beige, taupe, pink, mauve, burgundy, and blue-gray. Pretty white wicker waits on the front porch. Oak predominates the main floor. A beautiful stairway with oak spindles, newels, and paneling rises from the entry hall. Oak is found in both dark and light versions, as well as chestnut, butternut, cherry, walnut, and pine in the inlaid floors. Three parlors have wonderful Victorian fireplace mantels, antique Eastlake furniture, and oak floors covered with Oriental rugs. An informal Adirondack Game Room has pine-paneled ceilings and walls and a woodburning stove. This is the place to watch a video or TV.

The guest rooms are equally inviting, and they're filled with elegant antique furnishings. The Master Suite is the most elaborate. The Victorian walnut bedroom suite includes a highback double bed and a matching mar-

ble-topped dresser. An adjoining sitting room is large enough to accommodate two children. Although the bath is in the hallway, it includes a modern
whirlpool tub and a Victorian pull-chain toilet and washstand. For pure
romance, however, I love the Crown Room. Its wonderful queen-sized brass
bed has ceramic ball finials. A bay window is topped by Victorian fretwork,
and an adjoining oak-paneled sitting room has a fireplace.

Breakfast is served in the oak-paneled dining room, where candles burn
in silver candlesticks and a fire may be lit in the fireplace. Sandy's menu
might include pumpkin cheese-filled muffins, oven puffed pancakes,
banana-blueberry bread, and papaya breakfast cake.

What's Nearby—Crown Point

Monitor Bay on Lake Champlain is just ½ mile away. Fort Ticonderoga,
located at the strategic and narrow point where Lake George meets Lake
Champlain, is just seven miles south of Crown Point. This is the fort
Ethan Allen and his Green Mountain Boys captured from the British in
1775 in a significant early encounter of the Revolutionary War. In the
summer there are fife-and-drum marches and battle reenactments. A
museum includes many interesting eighteenth century artifacts. (See
also Hague, Schroon Lake, and Westport.)

Centennial House

13 Woods Lane
East Hampton, NY 11937
(516) 324-9414

FAX: (516) 324-0493

E-MAIL: centhouse@hamptons.com

INNKEEPERS: David A. Oxford and Harry Chancey, Jr.

ROOMS: 6, including 1 cottage rented by the week only, all with private
bath, air conditioning, TV, VCR, telephone, hair dryer, and robes; 2 with
fireplace; 4 with private deck

ON THE GROUNDS: Swimming pool; gardens; parking

EXTRAS: Soft drinks, bottled water, snacks, port, and sherry; one Lhasa
apso, Edwinna, on premises; exercise equipment; beach passes, beach
towels, and chairs available; fax, copy machine, business services available

RATES: $200–$395, double occupancy, mid-May to mid-October;
$225–$295, double occupancy, mid-October to mid-May, including full

breakfast; two-night minimum weekends in spring and autumn; three-night minimum weekends in summer; longer minimum stays holiday weekends

CREDIT CARDS ACCEPTED: MasterCard and Visa

OPEN: Year-round

HOW TO GET THERE: From New York City take I–495 (the Long Island Expressway) to exit 70 (Manorville) and follow Route 111 south to Highway 27 (Sunrise Highway). Follow Highway 27 (which becomes the Montauk Highway) east for another 32 miles to East Hampton. The B&B is on the right, just before the light at the intersection of Main Street and the Montauk Highway. (If you pass Town Pond, you have gone too far.)

As David Oxford and Harry Chancey were renovating their classic Hamptons shingle-style cottage, they found a board with an inscription dated 1876—and this became the inspiration for their B&B's name. It's perfect. A century isn't that old in a village that was founded in 1648, yet it signifies a house that has character and longevity.

The house sits well back from the road on 1½ acres. A large porch runs across the front, but most guests retreat to the backyard, where the spacious lawns are studded with abundant flower beds and there's a pool that is surrounded by roses and day lilies. The property is completed by a cottage and a barn that contains an exercise room.

We think Centennial House perfectly captures the country elegance of the Hamptons without being overdone. David and Harry, the ideal hosts, have seen to it that everything is flawless. The living room has twin crystal chandeliers and European oil paintings on the walls. There's a piano at one end and a tall-case clock. At the other, a fireplace is flanked by sofas and chairs covered in damask or chintz.

Upstairs in the hallway, there's a refrigerator filled with bottled waters, soft drinks, and ice. A marble counter holds stemmed glasses and a decanter of sherry. A basket of snacks is available for guests—a tempting nibble while they watch a video from the inn's collection on their in-room VCR.

The guest rooms are as elegant as the main floor. The Bay Room holds an antique four-poster carved rice bed in a bay window overlooking the side gardens. A fireplace provides a cozy warmth, and an Oriental rug covers the wide-plank pine floors. Beside the French provincial secretary, the exposed board reading "April 22, 1876, T.E.B." has been carefully preserved. The step-down bath is huge. It has a clawfoot tub, a sink in an antique pine pulpit, an antique vanity table, and a glass-enclosed shower. The Lincoln

Room, done in shades of green and burgundy, has an ornate Victorian bed similar to the one in which Abraham Lincoln died, as well as a matching armoire. The bath has a marble sink with brass legs.

Breakfast is served on gilt-edged china in the elegant formal dining room. The lovely Italian dining room table has floral marquetry inlays. In one corner, sage green bookshelves reach to the ceiling filled with interesting books for guests to read.

Breakfast is an event. The guests and innkeepers carry on a spirited banter while eating fresh fruits and juices, and an entree of perhaps eggs Benedict or pancakes and ham as well as homemade biscuits and other breads.

The B&B is equidistant from East Hampton's Main Beach and the downtown shops and restaurants. It's a pleasant bicycle ride or walk in either direction. In addition, a nice restaurant (open in the summer only) is just across the street.

What's Nearby—East Hampton

East Hampton has one of the prettiest ocean beaches of any town, and it also is endowed with the most amenities. There's an excellent snack bar; you can buy suntan lotion and sunglasses; you can rent beach chairs or umbrellas; there are changing rooms and restrooms; and there's plenty of bicycle and auto parking (although you must pay for the latter). In addition, the village has wonderful shops and restaurants as well as cultural activities that range from the movie theater to the John Drew Theatre and Guild Hall, where name entertainers perform throughout the year. Historic attractions include the Mulford Farm, Home Sweet Home, and the historic Hook Windmill. (See also Amagansett and Bridgehampton.)

The J. Harper Poor Cottage

181 Main Street
East Hampton, NY 11937
(516) 324–4081

FAX: (516) 329–5931
E-MAIL: info@jharperpoor.com
WEB SITE: www.jharperpoor.com
INNKEEPERS: Gary and Rita Reiswig

ROOMS: 5, all with private bath, air conditioning, TV, VCR, two or three telephones with dataports, and robes; 4 with fireplace; 3 with whirlpool tub and desk; 1 with private balcony

ON THE GROUNDS: Parking; parterre garden, wisteria arbor

EXTRAS: Turndown with chocolates; cheeses, fruits, crudités, or little pizzas, and wine (small additional charge) in the afternoon; one dog named Ashley; beach passes, beach towels, and chairs available

RATES: $195–$450, double occupancy, including full breakfast; two-night minimum weekends throughout the year, except in July and August, when there's a one-week minimum

CREDIT CARDS ACCEPTED: American Express, MasterCard, Visa

OPEN: Year-round

HOW TO GET THERE: From New York City take I–495 (the Long Island Expressway) to exit 70 (Manorville) and follow Route 111 south to Highway 27 (Sunrise Highway). Follow Highway 27 (which becomes the Montauk Highway) east for another 32 miles to East Hampton. At the traffic light, turn left. You will now be on Main Street; continue to #181, which will be on the left.

Hidden away behind a stucco wall lies one of the secret treasures of East Hampton. This lovely mansion, a medley of rich woods, multiple fireplaces, and William Morris-inspired furniture and decor, was transformed into the Hampton's finest B&B in 1996. Experienced innkeepers/owners Gary and Rita Reiswig owned the Maidstone Arms for many years, but their latest venture tops anything else in the Hamptons.

The "cottage," said to incorporate the oldest continually occupied structure in East Hampton, has a distinctly Arts and Crafts design due to a renovation that took place in 1910. It boasts Elizabethan gables, mullioned windows, and a soft buff stucco exterior made especially charming by the guardian angels that oversee the front door.

There's a large entry hall with comfortable seating areas and a library filled with interesting books. In the breakfast room, the low beamed ceilings are from the house's earliest era. A woodstove offers warmth and a cozy country ambience. In the living room, the molded patterned plaster ceiling and massive tiled fireplace are examples of designs inspired by William Morris, as are the patterned fabrics on the chairs and sofas and the frieze atop the wall. Mullioned windows on both sides create a light and bright space for reading, conversation, or playing the piano.

The guest rooms are spacious and sophisticated. One room combines floral and plaid fabrics in yellow and green with pine furniture. The bath is lavish in its use of patterned tile, and there's an elegant whirlpool tub as well as a glassed-in shower. Another room has paneled walls, a fireplace (with a cache of wood ready to be put to use), an iron bed, and beamed ceilings. A private balcony overlooks Main Street, and there is a tiled bath (all the tilework was expertly laid by Gary's son). Every room has not only a TV and VCR but at least two telephones with dataports. The two largest rooms each have three telephones.

Guests enter the B&B, not through the front door, but through a lovely carved wooden door in the solid stucco wall behind the B&B, which hides an acre of courtyards and gardens. A purple wisteria is a cascade of blooms in May, and the courtyard offers both secluded and open spaces. A sunken parterre garden is lush and tranquil. Beyond the garden, there's plenty of parking space, a scarce commodity in East Hampton.

A full breakfast is prepared every morning. It is served in either the breakfast room or in the courtyard, depending on the weather. Guests start with freshly baked breads, juices, and fruits. Entrees will include perhaps a salmon and scallion frittata or cinnamon-swirl French toast. In addition, there will be a fruit salad or a fruit dish such as apples with custard.

Away from the crowds, and yet close enough to encourage a walk to town, the B&B is near the John Drew Theatre and Guild Hall. Art exhibits, classes, and exhibitions take place throughout the year here, as well as lectures, theatrical productions, and concerts. The B&B is also within walking distance of the beach.

What's Nearby

See "What's Nearby—East Hampton," page 181.

Lysander House

132 Main Street
East Hampton, NY 11937
(516) 329–9025

FAX: (516) 329–2265

INNKEEPERS: Larry and Leslie Hillel

ROOMS: 3, including 1 suite, all with private bath, air conditioning, radio, and hair dryer; a private telephone may be connected in the suite

ON THE GROUNDS: On almost 2 acres with parking, gardens

EXTRAS: Bag of fresh cookies on departure; one cat named Persie in owners' quarters; beach passes, beach towels, and chairs available

RATES: $200–$350, double occupancy, May–October; $195–$270, double occupancy, November–April including full breakfast; two-night minimum weekends spring and fall; three-night minimum weekends from July 4th to Labor Day; four-night minimum holiday weekends

CREDIT CARDS ACCEPTED: None

OPEN: Year-round

HOW TO GET THERE: From New York City take I-495 (the Long Island Expressway) to exit 70 (Manorville) and follow Route 111 south to Highway 27 (Sunrise Highway). Follow Highway 27 (which becomes the Montauk Highway) east for another 32 miles to East Hampton. At the traffic light, turn left. You will now be on Main Street; continue to #132, which will be on the right.

The one thing you learn when writing about B&Bs and country inns is that each one is a wonderful reflection of the creativity and imagination of its innkeepers. The outside may be identical to that of its neighbors, but inside you'll find Early American, Country French, or an eclectic combination of styles and patterns that are so unique, and yet blend together so harmoniously, that you are eager to meet the people who chose these items and placed them so perfectly.

That's what you feel when you see Lysander House. The Hamptons are filled with houses sheathed in weathered shingles and trimmed in white. Most of them have porches across the front (Larry and Leslie added one to theirs), and they reach to two or three stories. This one, a rather unremarkable Victorian farmhouse, was built in 1885 on land that was used for growing flax during the Civil War. Larry (formerly a banker) and Leslie (formerly a school teacher) Hillel had lived in Mexico and Japan prior to migrating to the Hamptons, so their furnishings include an unusual blend of three distinctive cultures. But it's more the style in which they're used than the pieces themselves that give this B&B its character.

The couple painted and repaired and fixed and decorated their house after purchasing it in 1995. All the floors are white. In the parlor there are masks from Mexico and Japan, mixed with an engaging New England folk art scene painted on a plank that hangs over the fireplace. There's a TV and VCR here. Leslie has mixed interesting antique furniture with old painted tables and chairs. The spacious sitting/dining room, painted a sunny yellow with white trim and white shutters on the windows, provides a comfortable area with lots of books. The most unusual item in the house is a Japanese step *tansu,* a clever device that served as a movable set of stairs and also as storage space, as there's a drawer under each stair.

Each of the three guest rooms is unique. Liza's Suite is the largest. It has an iron headboard and a Victorian cottage dresser. On one of the pale lavender walls of the bedroom hangs a contemporary watercolor, but in the pale pink sitting room, there's another folk art painting and a pine bookcase. The bath is done in a stunning Ralph Lauren stripe. Alexander's Master Bedroom is painted a buttercup yellow, and it includes an iron and brass bed, a pine wardrobe, and several more folk art paintings. Everyone raves about the mattresses here, and it's no wonder. They're Dux beds, which are imported from Sweden and are the Rolls Royce of the field. There are no telephones in the guest rooms, but guests may use one in the kitchen.

Leslie and Larry serve a full breakfast that will include homemade scones and breads and perhaps orange French toast or oatmeal/yogurt pancakes as well as fresh fruits, juices, cakes, and cookies. The meal is served in the sitting/dining room, where guests eat at a common table. Leslie provides a bag of biscotti or cookies for guests to enjoy on the trip home.

The house sits on 1½ acres in the heart of the historic district of the village. Gardens surround the house, and the lawns stretching behind the house lead to two individual cottages that are rented year-round to long-term tenants.

The B&B is near Guild Hall and the John Drew Theatre and only three blocks from downtown. The Hillels have storage space for guests' bicycles and in-line skates. Excellent golf courses are nearby, as well as tennis courts and cross-country skiing.

What's Nearby

See "What's Nearby—East Hampton," page 181.

Mill House Inn

33 North Main Street
East Hampton, NY 11937
(877) 324–9753 or (516) 324–9766

FAX: (516) 324–9793
E-MAIL: millhouse@worldnet.att.net
WEB SITE: www.millhouseinn.com

INNKEEPERS: Dan and Katherine Hartnett; manager: Robin Goldfarb

ROOMS: 8, with private bath, air conditioning, TV, VCR, telephone with voice mail, radio, and hair dryer; 6 with fireplace; 4 with whirlpool tub; 3 with desk and 2 with robes; 1 room with wheelchair access; cribs available

ON THE GROUNDS: Parking; garden

EXTRAS: Afternoon snack; fax, voice mail, and small conference area available; beach passes, beach towels, and chairs available

RATES: $275–$475, double occupancy, mid-May to October; $175–$375, double occupancy, November to mid-May, including full breakfast and afternoon snacks; three-night minimum weekends May–October; four-night minimum holiday weekends

CREDIT CARDS ACCEPTED: MasterCard and Visa

OPEN: Year-round

HOW TO GET THERE: From New York City take I–495 (the Long Island Expressway) to exit 70 (Manorville) and follow Route 111 south to Highway 27 (Sunrise Highway). Follow Highway 27 (which becomes the Montauk Highway) east for another 32 miles to East Hampton. At the traffic light, turn left. You will now be on Main Street; continue through town and straight ahead at the next traffic light. Approximately 150 feet beyond the light, bear left onto North Main Street, traveling left of the Hook Windmill. The B&B is the fifth house on the left.

Resting on a knoll that overlooks East Hampton's famed Hook Windmill, the Mill House Inn has been welcoming guests since 1973, but it has virtually been rebuilt since Dan and Katherine Hartnett purchased it in 1994. The enclosed front porch with its cool tile floor is inviting for afternoon relaxation (and views of the windmill). Wonderful white rockers with cutwork and spindles beg you to sit, and the exterior of the house sports a fresh layer of shingles.

The inn's decor has a country sophistication. The living and dining rooms have exposed beams, and the living room also has a fireplace. There's a tall-case clock that formerly belonged to an early East Hampton family.

My favorite room is the Hampton Holiday on the third floor. It's done in shades of green and plum. A Mission-style sleigh bed faces the fireplace, and in the large bath, there's a skylight over the whirlpool tub and a separate tiled shower. Emerald green carpet and French toile wallpaper decorate the Patrick Lynch Room, which has an oak dresser and an antique bed with acorn posts. The Rose Room has rose carpeting, an iron bed, a pine wardrobe, and a gas fireplace. In the sparkling new bath, there's another whirlpool tub.

Behind the B&B, there's plenty of parking space for guests' cars as well as a lawn with Adirondack chairs and tables.

Katherine used to be a chef at the Pierre Hotel in New York, and one of the first things the couple did was to install a commercial kitchen. Obviously, the breakfasts are terrific. A sample menu includes a potato and smoked Gouda frittata as well as several breads—such as an Irish soda bread and peasant bread—and also maple granola cereal with bananas. All the baking is done right here, so guests can also look forward to chocolate chip cookies or lemon bar squares with their afternoon tea or lemonade. Katherine recently authored a cookbook featuring Mill House Inn breakfast recipes, as well as those from leading East Hampton restaurants. *Tasting the Hamptons* is available at the inn.

The B&B is located in the North Main section of East Hampton, where several of the village's premier restaurants, such as Nick and Toni's and Della Femina, are located. From the B&B it's also an easy walk to other restaurants and the shopping area in the heart of town. It should be noted that a train infrequently rumbles past the backyard. Those who want a quieter night's repose should ask for a room on the street side.

What's Nearby

See "What's Nearby—East Hampton," page 181.

The Pink House

26 James Lane
East Hampton, NY 11937
(516) 324–3400

FAX: (516) 324–5254

E-MAIL: RoSo@Hamptons.com

WEB SITE: www.thepinkhouse.net

INNKEEPER: Ron Steinhilber; manager: Mercedes Dekkers

ROOMS: 5, all with private bath, air conditioning, TV, telephone, hair dryer, and robes; 1 with a patio, and 1 with a whirlpool tub; 1 room with wheelchair access

ON THE GROUNDS: Parking; swimming pool; gardens

EXTRAS: Chocolates at turndown; fax available; bar with beer and wine; three dogs named Brindle, Max, and Ginger; beach passes and beach towels available

RATES: $145–$385, double occupancy, including full breakfast; three -four-night minimum spring and summer; five-night minimum holiday weekends; two-night minimum weekends rest of year

CREDIT CARDS ACCEPTED: American Express, MasterCard, Visa

OPEN: Year-round

HOW TO GET THERE: From New York City take I-495 (the Long Island Expressway) to exit 70 (Manorville) and follow Route 111 south to Highway 27 (Sunrise Highway). Follow Highway 27 (which becomes the Montauk Highway) east for another 32 miles to East Hampton. At the traffic light turn left and drive past Town Pond, which will be on the right. Turn right at the first street, and the B&B's driveway will be directly ahead across James Lane.

Yes, it is pink—not a shocking bright pink, but a subdued cotton candy pink—pretty enough to eat. It's trimmed in white, and a flock of white wicker chairs rest on the front porch interspersed with planters of pink geraniums, hydrangeas, and impatiens. The entire effect is charming. Ron Steinhilber, an architect and builder, renovated the 1850s house in 1990 and opened it to guests. It's located on a half acre on a quiet side street across from Town Pond and beside the spacious lawns of St. Luke's Episcopal Church. But even if this didn't assure its quiet repose, the tall privet hedge and fences surrounding it give it a feeling of utter seclusion and privacy.

The living room and dining room are low key and Country Hamptons in feel but spiced with some unusual pieces. You may spend hours studying the lively watercolors painted by Walter Steinhilber, Ron's grandfather. He was a peripatetic traveler who chronicled his journeys in his paintings, capturing wonderful details that make each one come to life. Also note the lamp in the living room made from a street lamp Ron rescued when Brooklyn's Myrtle Avenue El was being demolished. Both the living room and dining room have fireplaces.

There are five guest rooms—four on the second floor and one on the ground floor. All have private baths. The roomy Blue Room has a pencil-post pine canopy bed and a window seat offering views of Town Pond. The bath has a marble shower. The Garden Room, which is located on the first floor, has a four-poster bed and its own private patio with pots of flowers—a welcome hideaway. The most-requested room, however, is the spacious Elk Room on the top floor. It has a distinctive look that includes a moose head and cowboy hats on the wall, a TV and VCR , and a bath with a whirlpool tub.

Surrounded by a tall hedge and a wide slate terrace, the pool in the back-yard—with its abundance of chaise lounges, chairs, and umbrella-shaded tables—is a popular retreat. Frosty cold soft drinks, beer, and wine stock a refrigerator, and guests frequently relax here after a day at the beach, spent shopping in town, or at the Hamptons Classic Horse Show.

Ron prepares a full breakfast every morning, which he serves in the dining room in cool weather or on the back porch when it's warm. If guests are lucky, he may prepare his popular batter-dipped sourdough French toast. Homemade granola will always be available, and if it isn't a French toast day, he may prepare Belgian waffles or a frittata.

The B&B is within a block's walk of Mulford Farm, Home Sweet Home, and fine restaurants. The East Hampton Library is also nearby. Bicycling, in-line skating, golfing, and tennis are all popular activities.

What's Nearby

See "What's Nearby—East Hampton," page 181.

The Plover's Nest

199 Main Street
East Hampton, NY 11937
(516) 329–1120 (fax also)

INNKEEPERS: Fred and Adele Filasky

ROOMS: 4, including 1 suite, all with private bath, air conditioning, and TV; 3 with desk; 2 with fireplace

ON THE GROUNDS: On 1 acre with gardens; parking

EXTRAS: Beach passes and towels available; a boxer named Baron and a dachshund named Ginger in owner's quarters

RATES: $225–$285, double occupancy, Memorial Day to Labor Day, $165–$200, double occupancy, rest of year, including Continental breakfast; two-night minimum May, June, September, and October; three-night minimum July and August; four-night minimum holiday weekends

CREDIT CARDS ACCEPTED: American Express, MasterCard, Visa

OPEN: Year-round

HOW TO GET THERE: From New York City take I–495 (the Long Island Expressway) to exit 70 (Manorville) and follow Route 111 south to Highway 27 (Sunrise Highway). Follow Highway 27 (which becomes the Montauk Highway) east for another 32 miles to East Hampton. At the traffic light, turn left. You will now be on Main Street; continue to #199, which will be on the left.

red and Adele Filasky have been renovating old houses for some time, so when they bought this beauty, they were prepared to make the improvements it needed. Thankfully, they retained its interesting character in the process. Although the weathered shingle house was built in 1774, its foundation dates to 1650, merely two years after East Hampton was first settled. It's shielded from Main Street by a tall privet hedge.

The house still feels and looks as it might have during Colonial times. It has low, hand-hewn beamed ceilings and a multitude of fireplaces. In the living room, there are beige-colored walls and a wooden fireplace mantel with a marble face. Sisal rugs cover the random-width pine floors. Down-filled chairs covered in red damask and a down-filled sofa in a bright chintz are so comfortable you may snuggle in for the evening. The Filaskys have thoughtfully outfitted a guest office with a desk, telephone (there are none in the rooms), and a fax for those who need these items.

For travelers who are tired of the fuss and frills of many B&Bs, this is the antidote. The guest rooms are charming but uncluttered. They have wide-plank pine floors covered with sisal or Oriental rugs and simple, well-designed furniture. The Blue Room has its own fireplace and a sleigh bed. The Green Room has a four-poster bed and another fireplace. My favorite, however, is the Raspberry Room, which has a beamed ceiling, an antique white iron and brass bed, and green wicker furniture. It's cozy and utterly romantic. All the baths are fresh and sparkling with new tilework, and all the baths are in the guest rooms except the one for the Blue Room, which is in the hall.

Breakfast is served buffet style in the gracious dining room, and there's a brick fireplace here as well. There's an English-style wallpaper in yellow and blue on the walls and a blue wash on the paneling. Guests are seated at individual tables before the fireplace in winter. In nice weather, guests often choose to eat on the brick patio, which is under the canopy of a magnificent old beech tree. Dutch doors lead there from a little anteroom just off the dining room. The B&B is on an acre of land, and beyond the patio and parking area, there's a private, lush lawn enclosed by forsythia. Here wait Adirondack chairs and an iron table that provide a restful place for relaxing with a good book.

Breakfast will consist of homemade fruit scones, muffins, or perhaps hot cross buns as well as fresh fruit, juices, berries in season, and cereals.

The B&B is located across from Town Pond and near fine restaurants. Mulford Farm, Home Sweet Home, Guild Hall, and the John Drew Theatre are nearby.

What's Nearby

See "What's Nearby—East Hampton," page 181.

The 1770 House

134 Main Street
East Hampton, NY 11937
(516) 324–1770

FAX: (516) 324–3504

INNKEEPERS: Wendy Van Deusen and Adam Perle; manager: Burton Van Deusen

ROOMS: 8, including 1 suite and 1 cottage, all with private bath, air conditioning, and telephone; 7 with desk; 2 with fireplace and private porch

ON THE GROUNDS: Parking; gardens

RATES: $120–$325, double occupancy, including full breakfast; three-night minimum in July and August; four-night minimum summer holiday weekends; two-night minimum weekends rest of year

CREDIT CARDS ACCEPTED: American Express, MasterCard, Visa

OPEN: Year-round

HOW TO GET THERE: From New York City take I–495 (the Long Island Expressway) east to exit 70 (Manorville) and follow Route 111 south to Highway 27 (Sunrise Highway). Follow Highway 27 (which becomes the Montauk Highway) east for another 32 miles to East Hampton. At the traffic light, turn left. You will now be on Main Street; continue to #134, which will be on the left.

It appears as if the name of this inn may be a bit of a misnomer. For years it was thought to have been built in 1770, but the wonderful walk-in fireplace with its beehive oven actually predates the 1770s. Research indicates the last time they were built in the Hamptons was in the 1740s, so the building must be at least thirty years older than previously thought. No matter. The handsome white-clapboard Colonial was acquired by Sid and Mim Perle in 1977, and although it was in deplorable shape, they soon found pecan paneling beneath layers of paint in the library, which includes a fireplace, and a wonderful shell corner cabinet. They filled their inn with gorgeous antiques and with their collection of regulator clocks.

Mim was a Cordon Bleu–trained chef and caterer when they opened the inn, and she soon started serving romantic dinners in the warm dining rooms that still feature elaborate stained-glass windows, a wonderful fireplace, and the interesting clocks. The 1770 House became one of East Hampton's most celebrated inns. Alas, both Sid and Mim have now passed away, but their daughter and son now run the inn, ably assisted by Wendy's husband, Burton. Although they no longer serve dinner, the inn continues to feature some of East Hampton's most romantic and atmospheric guest rooms.

One of my favorites is the separate carriage house in back, where the living room has walls lined with books and a stairway leads to the loft bedroom. In the main B&B, I've stayed in several of the rooms over the years. Most feature canopy beds and all have unique antiques. My particular favorite, however, is Room #2, which has a fireplace in a handsome paneled wall, comfortable chairs upholstered in pretty fabrics, and a canopy bed.

Wendy, like her mother before her, is also a professionally trained chef, and for many years she was the executive chef of the inn. Her breakfasts are as inventive and interesting as the inn's dinners used to be. One morning she might fix waffles with brown sugar and fresh berries accompanied by bacon, and on another there may be vanilla French toast made from challah bread or an omelette.

This is one B&B where it pays to poke around. Be sure to visit the office to see the remnants of East Hampton's original post office. The ornate window and counter, as well as several banks of oak boxes, are reminders of how our post offices used to look.

What's Nearby

See "What's Nearby—East Hampton," page 181.

Treasure Island Bed & Breakfast

14909 Main Road
(mailing address: P.O. Box 337)
East Marion, NY 11939
(516) 477-2788

INNKEEPER: Norman Whitehead

ROOMS: 3 suites, all with private bath, air conditioning, TV, radio, desk, hair dryer, and robes; 2 with decorative fireplace

ON THE GROUNDS: On 6 acres with private beach and pond

EXTRAS: Waterfront; waterviews; refrigerator stocked with nonalcoholic drinks, snacks; cocoa, tea, cakes, and cookies winter afternoons; iced tea, lemonade, cheese, crackers, and fruit summer afternoons; beach passes provided

RATES: $190, double occupancy, including full breakfast and afternoon snacks; two-night minimum

CREDIT CARDS ACCEPTED: American Express, MasterCard, Visa

OPEN: Year-round

HOW TO GET THERE: From New York City take I–495 (the Long Island Expressway) east to its end at exit 73 (Riverhead). You will now be on Route 58 (Old Country Road). Continue east for about ½ mile (going beyond the traffic circle) and then turn left (north) onto Northville Road. Follow Northville Road to its end at Sound Avenue. Turn right onto Route 48 (Sound Avenue) and travel east for about 20 miles to the junction with Route 25 (there will be a flashing light). Route 48 now becomes Route 25. Continue east on Route 25 for about 2½ miles to the causeway (stone barriers and seawall). The B&B is up the first driveway on the left on the causeway.

Norm Whitehead summered here at his grandparents' estate while he was growing up. What an idyllic existence it must have been. He remembers swimming in Long Island Sound, exploring the nearby coastline in a rowboat, and watching the birds nest in the marsh grasses.

The shingled house, with a cedar-shake roof pierced by dormers, has a grand porch across the front. The estate sits on a piece of land that is almost surrounded by Dam Pond. Located high on a hill, it has glorious views of Long Island Sound and Truman Beach to the north and of Gardiner's Bay and Orient Harbor to the south. Norm doesn't remember exactly why his grandmother named it Treasure Island, but he thinks it was either because she found numerous antiques in the attic (the beautiful and ornate wicker furniture is all original to the house) or because they found some money buried in the yard.

Norm and his wife, Marjorie, made extensive renovations to the house before opening it to overnight guests. In addition to updating the baths with Corian counters, backsplashes, and tub or shower surrounds, they created three suites with separate sitting rooms. Each has antique furniture, including Victorian beds that have been converted to accommodate queen-size mattresses.

The B&B has a spacious common room filled with interesting antiques and paintings. A fireplace at one end is a focal point before which guests gather for convivial warmth in the afternoon when Marjorie brings out her specialty hors d'oeuvres. (Guests often bring their own wine, which they may have picked up from one of the local wineries.) A columned porch contains much of the wonderful old wicker, and it offers spectacular views. On a clear day you can see as far as Connecticut from the terrace in back. A glass-enclosed porch offers a vantage point for viewing the myriad birds and animals that parade past.

The guest rooms include a suite on the first floor that has a bedroom with views of Long Island Sound and a sitting room overlooking the bay. There's a matching Victorian Eastlake bedroom suite. The other two suites are upstairs. Each has a private bath, as well as a bedroom and a separate sitting room.

A full buffet breakfast is served in a corner of the common room. It will include fresh fruits, homemade muffins and breads, plus perhaps French toast or a quiche with bacon or sausage or some special concoction that Marjorie has dreamed up.

What's Nearby—East Marion

The North Fork of Long Island is noted for its fine wines and expansive farms. You can visit eighteen wineries along the narrow strip of land that stretches from Aquebogue to Southold to take a tour and to sample the wines. In addition, excellent farm and flower stands sell the bounty of the fields from early spring to late fall. Definitely plan to pick up a fruit pie at Briermere Farms in Riverhead. One of the most interesting museums in the area is near the B&B in the charming hamlet of Orient. Oysterponds Historical Society is a collection of nineteenth-century buildings that includes a former village inn, an old schoolhouse (now the museum shop), and a building actually slept in by George Washington. Pay a visit to the Orient Country Store, where the atmosphere of old worn wooden floors and the prices (a huge Reuben sandwich for $2.50) hark to an earlier era.

A Victorian on the Bay

57 South Bay Avenue
Eastport, NY 11941
(888) 449–0620 or
(516) 325–1000

FAX: (516) 325–9659

E-MAIL: rbarone@hamptons.com

WEB SITE: www.bbonline.com/ny/victorian

INNKEEPERS: Rosemary and Fred Barone

ROOMS: 5, including 3 suites, all with private bath, air conditioning, TV, VCR, telephone with dataport, whirlpool tub, radio, hair dryer, and featherbed; 3 with balcony or porch; 2 with fireplace and robes

ON THE GROUNDS: Golf driving range; gardens; parking

EXTRAS: Exercise room with treadmill, free weights, bicycle, and universal; bicycles, including a bicycle built for two available to rent; Godiva chocolates and liqueurs in all rooms; fishing 400 feet away; views of water; nearby marina allows guests to arrive by boat

RATES: $150–$450, double occupancy, including full breakfast; two-night minimum weekends; two-four-night minimum holiday weekends

CREDIT CARDS ACCEPTED: American Express, MasterCard, Visa

OPEN: Year-round

HOW TO GET THERE: From New York City take I–495 (the Long Island Expressway) east to exit 70 (Manorville) and follow Route 111 south to Route 55 (Eastport Manor Road). Turn right and follow Eastport Manor Road beyond Route 27 (Sunrise Highway) to its end at Route 27A (Montauk Highway). Turn left (east) onto Montauk Highway and go ⁷⁄₁₀ mile to South Bay Avenue. Turn left and follow this almost to its end to #57. The B&B will be on the right.

Most innkeepers fall in love with an old, historic house and embark on a massive renovation project to create their bed-and-breakfast. Not so with Rosemary and Fred Barone. Instead, they found a beautiful 3½-acre parcel of property with views of Moriches Bay, and they created a brand new Victorian B&B, complete with gables, a turret, and a wonderful wraparound porch. This gave them the opportunity to install soundproof walls, large closets, central air conditioning, and heat with individual in-room controls.

The B&B opened in 1998 and it's a beauty. I chanced upon it on a sunny summer day and the white Victorian glowed in the afternoon light. A circular drive leads to a pride of stairs that climbs to an expansive covered porch. Inside there's an entry with a cathedral ceiling and an oak staircase. To the right an intimate living room is decorated in a soft yellow. There's a fireplace and an overstuffed sofa and wing chairs offering cozy spots for reading or talking to friends. The piano room has a piano and shelves of books for borrowing. To the left of the entry, a breakfast room adjoins the bright kitchen. French doors lead to the deck and its views of the bay.

The guest rooms are located upstairs and all have views of the water. They are spacious and elegant without being fussy. The Sunset Suite is one of my favorites, as the views of the setting sun at night are enchanting. There's a four-poster featherbed and a fireplace as well. The Master Suite, all done in pink lavender, is my other favorite. It also has a water view, as well as a porch from which to enjoy it even more. There's a four-poster featherbed here as well. All of the baths have whirlpool tubs.

A full breakfast of perhaps vanilla challah French bread, fresh fruit and juices, and homemade breads will also include Rosemary's Victorian Sweet Secret, a pastry with a sweet center.

What's Nearby—Eastport

A short ride to Westhampton Beach will take you to ocean beaches and also to the Westhampton Beach Performing Arts Center, which offers a variety of plays, musical performances, concerts, art shows, and much more throughout the year. There's an excellent bayside restaurant at the end of South Bay Avenue. Fishing boats can be hired nearby, and there are several golf courses. Tanger Factory Outlet Center, which has more than one hundred shops, is in Riverhead. (See also Center Moriches.)

Ruah Bed and Breakfast

Best Buy

9221 Lake Shore Drive
Hague, NY 12836
(800) 224–7549 or (518) 543–8816

FAX: (518) 543–6913

E-MAIL: ruahbb@aol.com

WEB SITE: www.ruahbb.com

INNKEEPERS: Peter and Judith Foster

ROOMS: 4, including 2 suites, all with private bath, fireplace, and robes; 3 with private porch and desk

ON THE GROUNDS: On 6½ acres with gardens and hiking trails

EXTRAS: Wonderful lake views; one dog, a Lab mix, named Sassy on premises

RATES: $105–$150, double occupancy, June–October (plus $20 supplement per weekend night in July and August); $90–$135, double occupancy, November–May; two-night minimum weekends in summer; three-night minimum holiday weekends

CREDIT CARDS ACCEPTED: American Express, Discover, MasterCard, Visa

OPEN: Year-round

HOW TO GET THERE: From I–87 (the Northway), take exit 25 onto Route 8 east. Follow this for 20 miles to the intersection of Route 9N (Lake Shore Drive) in Hague. Turn left onto Route 9N and travel approximately 1 mile. The B&B is on the left.

Ruah is a Hebrew word meaning "gentle breeze/breath of life," a name selected for the house by Peter and Judy's son, who was studying the Old Testament at his prep school when they purchased it, and that's exactly what Judy and Peter Foster found in their wondrous 1907 mansion. A gentle breath of life that seems to restore the soul by offering spectacular panoramic views of upper Lake George and a quiet peaceful setting. From the 80-foot veranda of the mansion, the water of Lake George seems to dance in the sun, and it's possible to watch sailboat races and other boating activity from this elevated perch.

The house was built by famed turn-of-the-century artist Harry Watrous as his summer retreat, and it's said that he employed Stanford White as his architect. Nestled among stately trees, the first floor of the inn is composed of fieldstone salvaged from the excavation of Route 9N, as are the picturesque ice house, water reservoir, and the massive fieldstone fireplace in the 30-foot by 50-foot living room. Watrous called his home "Camp Hill," and he apparently held an adult summer camp for many years, organizing parties for his guests that featured gambling, pranks, and practical jokes. Ask about his Lake George monster.

Peter and Judy are the perfect caretakers for this treasure. Peter is a landscape architect and Judy a floral designer, so they have carefully enhanced the grounds of the estate. They are intimately familiar with the Lake George area, as they are long-time area residents who formerly owned a nursery, garden center, floral design, and gift shop locally. They purchased the home in 1985 and converted it to a bed-and-breakfast in 1994.

The house has spacious common rooms with tall windows that offer wondrous views of the lake and the mountains beyond. Incredibly, some of the original furniture, including a lovely grand piano, remain in the house.

The guest rooms are amply proportioned, and all are furnished with antiques. They have working fireplaces and views of the lake. The grandest is The Queen of the Lakes. It has a king-size bed, an antique fainting couch, access to the balcony, and a distinctive bath with a coral bath and shower. The Waltonian features a king-size bed and two balconies, both with wonderful views. Flirtation and Asas have private baths, but they are accessed off the hallway.

Breakfast is served in the dining room, which has a coffered ceiling and large bay windows. The repast may include an entree of German cheese oven pancakes, a strata or frittata, or French toast with a hot fruit sauce.

What's Nearby—Hague

Fort Ticonderoga is just nine miles north of the B&B. Here you'll find a museum displaying interesting eighteenth-century artifacts and the fort that Ethan Allen and his Green Mountain Boys captured from the British in a significant early Revolutionary War battle. The B&B overlooks Lake George, where boating, sailing, swimming, and fishing take place, as well as outdoor concerts in the summer. (See also Crown Point.)

Buttermilk Falls B&B

Best Buy

110 East Buttermilk Falls Road
Ithaca, NY 14850
(607) 272–6767

INNKEEPER: Margie Rumsey

ROOMS: 5, including 1 cottage,
all with private bath, air
conditioning, radio, hair
dryer, and robes; 2 with TV,
private deck, mini-refrigerator,
and desk; 1 with fireplace, whirlpool tub, VCR, and tape player; wheelchair access

ON THE GROUNDS: On 2 acres adjacent to Buttermilk Falls; expansive lawn
and gardens

EXTRAS: Afternoon snacks offered; walking sticks provided for ambling
along the forest trails; yoga mats, meditation pillows provided

RATES: $95–$250, double occupancy, including full breakfast and afternoon snacks; two-night minimum some weekends

CREDIT CARDS ACCEPTED: None

OPEN: Year-round

HOW TO GET THERE: From I–90 (the New York State Thruway) take exit 40
onto Route 34 south and continue for approximately 38 miles to Ithaca.
Continue south through Ithaca to the junction with Route 13. Follow
Route 13 to East Buttermilk Falls Road. Turn into Buttermilk Falls State
Park. The B&B is the second house on the left.

Margie has lived in her wonderful brick farmhouse beside Buttermilk
Falls since 1952, when she arrived as a young bride. Actually, members
of her family have lived here since 1825, and her grandfather operated
a dairy farm on the property. Margie is the sixth generation to occupy the
land and her granddaughter Kristen is the eighth. Margie converted the
house and cottage to a B&B in 1983, and with her keen decorating skills
she's filled it by incorporating objects from her round-the-world travels
alongside interesting antiques and thoroughly modern conveniences.

One gets a sense of her use of found objects in the dining room, where
breakfast is served at a plank table that has a buckboard seat at both ends.
Wide-plank pine floors are covered by Oriental rugs, giving the rooms a
crisp, uncluttered, Shaker-style simplicity. In the living room, which has a
fireplace, you'll see folk art peeking out of an Amish-style cupboard and a

high-backed love seat, where one might sit to play one of the many old games that are available. Fresh flowers grace windowsills, tables, and counters.

The bedrooms feature pretty, handmade quilts on the beds and more fresh flowers. The suite includes a full kitchen. My favorite is the Jacuzzi suite, which occupies the former sunporch. It has a fireplace and a Jacuzzi in the room and a wonderful old pine armoire that's covered by a quilt.

For breakfast, Margie might fix baked French toast or an omelette, as well as apple crisp, a breakfast meat, and fresh fruit and juices.

Guests can walk across the lawn to Buttermilk Falls, which cascades with a tumultuous roar from a 500-foot elevation onto two terraces before arriving at the pool at its base. In the summer guests can swim in the pool, and in any season they can walk the gorge trails in the adjoining 750-acre state park.

What's Nearby—Ithaca

Ithaca is situated at the southern tip of Cayuga Lake in the beautiful Finger Lakes region of New York. In addition to fishing, boating, and swimming, exceptional wineries along the Finger Lakes Wine Trail offer tours and tastings. Ithaca is the home of Cornell University and Ithaca College. Numerous concerts, plays, and lectures associated with the schools take place throughout the year. The Herbert F. Johnson Museum of Art on the Cornell campus was designed by I. M. Pei and includes examples of Asian, nineteenth- and twentieth-century American art. There are excellent restaurants in the area, including the famed Moosewood Restaurant, a mecca for vegetarians.

The Hanshaw House Bed & Breakfast

15 Sapsucker Woods Road
Ithaca, NY 14850
(800) 257–1437 or (607) 257–1437

WEB SITE: www.wordpro.com/hanshawhouse

INNKEEPER: Helen Scoones

ROOMS: 4, all with private bath and air conditioning; 3 with desk

ON THE GROUNDS: On 1⅔ acres with gorgeous gardens, two stone patios, pond, pergola, Monet bridge, hammock

EXTRAS: Brownies, biscotti and cookies, plus hot or cold drinks every afternoon until 10:00 P.M.; turndown with Perugina chocolates; two beagles in owners' quarters only

RATES: $77–$155, double occupancy, including full breakfast and afternoon snacks; slightly lower rate for singles; two-night minimum if Saturday night stay included from March–November

CREDIT CARDS ACCEPTED: American Express, MasterCard, Visa

OPEN: Year-round

HOW TO GET THERE: From I-90 (the New York State Thruway) take exit 40 onto Route 34 south and continue for approximately 37 miles. At the junction with Route 13 (north of Ithaca) turn east onto Route 13 and go to Warren Road. Turn south (right) onto Warren Road, traveling away from the airport. Go to the stop sign at Hanshaw Road and turn left. Go approximately 7/10 mile to Sapsucker Woods Road and turn left. The B&B is the second house on the right.

There is absolutely nothing commonplace about Hanshaw House B&B. Helen (who was formerly an interior designer) has such a wonderful eye for design and color, and a commitment to the artistry of local talents, that she has infused her entire B&B with unusual and engaging painted furniture, artwork, pottery, and paintings.

From the moment you drive up to the immaculate white-clapboard 1830s Colonial, which is fronted by an overflowing English country flower garden surrounded by a white picket fence, you know you've arrived at a very special place. Butterflies and bees light on the flowers as if caressing them gently. What you cannot see from the road is the even more wonderful gardens in back, which feature two stone patios, a pond, a Monet bridge, and a pergola. Interspersed among the abundant perennials that bloom from early spring through late fall are bird feeders that entice woodpeckers, cardinals, and many of their friends.

Guests enter a parlor where white wicker sofas are covered with imported English chintz. The focus, however, is through the tall windows, which act as a frame to the gardens beyond. This is a wonderful place to sit with a cup of tea in the afternoon while trying to decide on a restaurant destination. In the TV room Helen has combined white wicker with colorful green cushions and a pretty French high-backed bench that has pink-striped fabric. A local artist, Nancy Ternasky, has painted elaborate scenes on several wooden pieces.

In the dining room, which has an unusually long table and a glass-fronted chest at one end, Helen sets a breakfast table using hand-crocheted place mats and the whimsical pottery created by MacKenzie-Childs (they are headquartered nearby in Aurora). Her breakfasts are as inventive as her decor, and she's often assisted by her husband, Bill, who is an administrator at Ithaca College. She might prepare her popular baked French toast with caramel and walnuts or Scandinavian pancakes with sautéed apples, which are actually more like individual soufflés than pancakes.

Naturally, the guest rooms are equally alluring. Room #1 is on the first floor and has a wonderful view of the gardens. The four-poster bed is covered with a matelassé spread. Room #4, which is upstairs, has a massive pine four-poster bed covered with a cutwork spread and a sofa effectively upholstered in ticking. An antique oak sewing machine sits in a corner. All of the rooms have immaculate private baths.

What's Nearby

See "What's Nearby—Ithaca," page 200.

The Lamplight Inn Bed & Breakfast

231 Lake Avenue
(mailing address: P.O. Box 70)
Lake Luzerne, NY 12846
(800) 262–4668 or (518) 696–5294

FAX: (518) 696–5256

E-MAIL: lamp@netheaven.com

WEB SITE: www.lamplightinn.com

INNKEEPERS: Linda and Gene Merlino

ROOMS: 17, all with private bath, air conditioning, telephone with dataport, and radio; 12 with fireplace; 7 with TV; 4 with whirlpool tub, desk, and private porch; wheelchair access

ON THE GROUNDS: On 10 acres with parking; walking and hiking trails, cross-country ski trails; gardens

EXTRAS: Fax and copier available; a husky/shepherd named Toto

RATES: $95–$225, double occupancy, including full breakfast; corporate rate available; two-night minimum weekends; three-night minimum holidays and special event weekends

CREDIT CARDS ACCEPTED: American Express, MasterCard, Visa

OPEN: Year-round except December 24th and 25th

HOW TO GET THERE: From I-87, take exit 21 (Lake Luzerne/Lake George). At the end of the ramp bear left onto Route 9N south. Follow 9N for 10 miles. The B&B will be on the right.

It sits serenely on a hill just outside the small village of Lake Luzerne, and its daffodil yellow clapboard facade with white trim is as welcoming as a sunny smile. But so are the friendly innkeepers. Warm and outgoing, Linda and Gene Merlino are the ideal innkeepers. Gene was the manager of a textile engraving plant for twenty years, and Linda was a textile artist and fashion illustrator. They bought the 1890s Victorian in 1985 and immediately began the creation of their bed-and-breakfast by painstakingly renovating the dilapidated house. And they just never stopped. In 1996, Gene built a new carriage house that has five luxury rooms with fireplaces, private porches, and whirlpool tubs. The new carriage house allows the bed-and-breakfast to appeal to two very different types of guests.

For those who enjoy Victoriana, the main inn is literally stuffed with Victorian furniture and decorative items, all embraced by warm chestnut and oak paneling and floors. There are 12-foot beamed ceilings and fireplaces in both the great room and in one of the parlors. Several of Linda's collections are on view here. Her doll collection, which includes a number of Madame Alexander dolls, is located in cabinets and on tables throughout the entrance and the huge 20- x 40-foot great room as well as in the three large sitting areas. A large gift shop offers soaps, dolls, stationery, and gift items for sale. A small service bar is nearby where guests may purchase wine and beer. There's also a wraparound porch with porch swings, rockers, and wicker furniture.

The guest rooms in the main inn are as Victorian as the common rooms. They have canopy or white iron beds, oak dressers, and small private baths. Victorian lamps, quilts on the beds, Victorian pillows, lace curtains at the windows—all add to the Victorian ambience. The rooms here tend to be small, but the baths sparkle with fresh new tile.

For guests who prefer more privacy and a less fussy Victorian decor, the Brookside Cottage, which was originally the caretaker's cottage, and the new Carriage House offer modern rooms furnished with wicker, and all have gas fireplaces. The Carriage House also has whirlpool tubs in the rooms and private decks surrounded by trees. They are crisp, clean, and spacious rather than luxurious.

Breakfast is served in the large oak-floored dining room, which has a sunny exposure. Linda decorates the room seasonally with abundant plants and fresh flowers. Guests are seated at individual glass-topped tables, where they are presented with a daily menu. They help themselves to a buffet of fresh fruit, breads, coffee cakes, juices, and Linda's homemade granola. Gene then prepares the main course. It may consists of an omelette—perhaps with cheddar, Swiss, and American cheese or with peppers, onion, ham, and cheese. On the side, he serves spicy home-fried potatoes and bacon or sausage.

The bed-and-breakfast is located on ten acres in the Adirondack Mountains, 10 miles from Lake George and 18 miles from Saratoga Springs. The village of Lake Luzerne is tucked between the Hudson River and pretty Lake Luzerne. Scenic Rockwell Falls, the narrowest point on the Hudson, is located in town, and the lake has been an Adirondack summer resort since the nineteenth century.

What's Nearby—Lake Luzerne

Lake Luzerne is located on the southern fringe of the Adirondack State Park. You can visit the Frances Garner Kinnear Museum of Local History, the Pulp Mill Museum, and the School House Museum to see interesting exhibits. At Bennett's Riding Stables you can take guided trail rides for varying lengths of time.

In summer, there's boating, swimming, fishing, and golfing; in winter, there's plenty of snowmobiling and cross-country skiing. Summer concerts, museums to explore, and a championship rodeo that attracts rodeo stars and country singers offer alternative activities.

Peri's Bed & Breakfast

206 Essex Street
Montauk, NY 11954
(516) 668–1394

FAX: (516) 668–6096
E-MAIL: peris@concentric.net
WEB SITE: www.concentric.net/~peris
INNKEEPER: Peri Aronian
ROOMS: 3, all with private bath, hair dryer, and robes; 1 with balcony
ON THE GROUNDS: On 1 acre with patios and gardens; badminton
EXTRAS: Spa therapy and massage packages available for treatments on premises; evening munchies such as veggies with dip, nuts, cheese, soda or beer; Rhodesian ridgeback dog named Sirus on premises

RATES: $150–$200, double occupancy, including full breakfast and after-noon refreshments; two-night minimum year-round except three-night minimum holiday weekends

CREDIT CARDS ACCEPTED: MasterCard and Visa

OPEN: February through December

HOW TO GET THERE: From New York City take I–495 (the Long Island Expressway) east to exit 70 (Manorville) and follow Route 111 south to Highway 27 (Sunrise Highway). Follow Highway 27 (which becomes the Montauk Highway) east for another 47 miles to Montauk. Continue through the village of Montauk to the last cross street, which is Essex Street. Turn left onto Essex Street and go up the hill for ½ mile to #206. The B&B will be on the right.

Expect the unexpected at Peri's. Peri is an artistic, enthusiastic, and caring innkeeper who has designed an unusual and eclectic bed-and-breakfast that reflects her previous life as a fashion designer, as well as the wonderful eccentricities of her home. Where to start?

Perhaps with the house itself. In 1926 a dreamer by the name of Carl Fisher ventured to Montauk with a grand scheme in mind. He was the developer responsible for Miami Beach, and he proposed creating a "Miami of the North" at Montauk. He built numerous buildings and houses in a vaguely Tudor style of stucco, brick, and half timbers. But economic conditions, including the stock market crash of 1929, a decline in Florida real estate prices, a hurricane in Florida, and the Great Depression, conspired to halt his plan long before it was completed. Nevertheless, many of his buildings remain. One of them is Peri's.

Guests drive into a cobblestone courtyard with lush lawns and flower gardens beyond—all secretly hidden away behind a 12-foot privet hedge. The house is composed of steep gabled roofs and unusual windows. You will enter an arched door and find yourself in a living room with a fireplace containing a fabulous, heavy carved wood mantel. There's a leather sofa and an Oriental rug on the oak floor.

There are three guest rooms—two of which are named for Peri's favorite cities. I love Marais, partly because it's reminiscent of my favorite city, Paris. There's a French bed, a French marble-topped dresser, and a tiny deck with a view of the water. This wonderful package is wrapped in walls of lime green. Fez has azure blue walls and an iron canopy bed draped with an Oriental rug. The private bath for this room is in the hallway. The largest room is Millenium, which has silvery walls and a bed draped in gauzy mosquito netting. Dramatic Helmut Newton photographs line the walls, and Peri's grandmother's art deco vanity adds interest.

Peri has installed a great art deco bar in the massive billiards room, where guests gather in the evening for wine and hors d'oeuvres. French doors lead to a spacious flagstone patio and the gardens. The house was once owned by restaurateur Henri Soulé, and I can just imagine the wonderful dinner parties he held in this room.

The dining room of the house is painted a dramatic "wake-up call" red. Gourmet breakfasts consisting of fresh fruit and perhaps a crepe dish or baked French toast might be followed by an apple soufflé.

Peri has a staff of licensed massage therapists and facialists that she calls upon to administer to her guests. The treatments might take place in the garden or in the privacy of the guest room.

What's Nearby—Montauk

Montauk is the easternmost point in New York State and the launching point for fabulous deep-sea fishing charters. A variety of marinas offer trips that range from several hours to all day or all night. There are sightseeing excursions and whale watching expeditions as well, and also ferries to Block Island and elsewhere. Wonderful seafood restaurants abound. A visit to the Montauk Lighthouse, with its spectacular views and fine museum, offers an interesting change of pace. In addition, there are miles of sandy beaches to sun on, or you might join a local horseback riding party for a trot along the beach next to the crashing waves.

Genesee Country Inn

948 George Street
Mumford, NY 14511
(mailing address: P.O. Box 340)
(800) 697–8297 or (716) 538–2500

FAX: (716) 538–4565
E-MAIL: gbarklow@aol.com
WEB SITE: www.geneseecountryinn.com
INNKEEPER: Kim Rasmussen; proprietor: Glenda Barcklow

ROOMS: 9, all with private bath, air conditioning, TV, telephone, and radio; 3 with fireplace; 2 with private deck and hair dryer

ON THE GROUNDS: On 8 acres that include a stream and waterfall, beautiful gardens, walking trails

EXTRAS: Afternoon snacks of tea, cheese, crackers, and cookies; dinner occasionally on Friday and Saturday nights

RATES: $85–$140, double occupancy, including full breakfast; two-night minimum special event weekends

CREDIT CARDS ACCEPTED: American Express, Discover, MasterCard, Visa

OPEN: Year-round

HOW TO GET THERE: From I–90 (the New York State Thruway), take exit 47 (Le Roy) onto Route 19 and travel south for 4 miles to Le Roy. In Le Roy, at the junction with Route 5, turn left (east) and follow Route 5 for 5 miles to Caledonia. At the intersection with Route 36, travel north for 1 mile to Mumford, turning left onto George Street. The B&B is 1½ blocks further on the right.

Glenda Barcklow began her restoration of this wonderful old 1833 plaster and paper mill in 1982, and if the walls could talk they'd be singing her praises, just as her guests do. The mellow stone building has walls that are 2 feet thick, creating an exceptionally quiet and peaceful interior. Glenda has painstakingly stenciled them in intricate designs. The Old Mill Shop, her unusual gift shop, is rich with needlecraft items. The maple floors gleam, and the wide moldings speak of an earlier era.

The setting is as distinctive as the building. Two streams converge beneath the building to form Spring Creek, which once gave power to a waterwheel that operated the mill. Today the lawns behind the mill dip away in a cascade of flower beds. Brick walkways lead to a gazebo and also to the banks of the creek, which offers sustenance to ducks and birds and even an occasional egret or crane. Deer come to drink, and guests often spot muskrat, fox, and other small animals as well. A pathway leads to a waterfall, where guests can enjoy a picnic lunch on a balmy summer day. The stream is also noted for its trout fishing.

The guest rooms are as elegantly stenciled as the common rooms, and each is distinct and interesting in its own right. Those that overlook the creek are particular favorites, as it's possible to open the windows at night to allow the rustle of the trees, the songs of the birds, and the soft sounds of the creek to filter in. In the Stewart, Glenda has used Laura Ashley fabric against the pine-paneled walls. There's a beamed ceiling, a gas fireplace, and a private deck overlooking the stream. A four-poster bed has a fishnet canopy. The tile bath includes an antique oak chest. In the Skivington, which has another gas fireplace and a private deck, the old raceway continues to course beneath, and there are beautiful views of the stream.

A full breakfast is offered in the dining room. Glenda or Kim might fix strawberry waffles or a ham and cheese omelette. Guests enjoy the warmth of another gas fireplace, beamed ceilings, and pine floors.

What's Nearby—Mumford

One of the "don't miss" attractions of the state is the Genesee Country Village Museum, which is about a mile down the road from the B&B. It's a fully restored nineteenth-century village of fifty-seven buildings that includes churches, schools, barns, and even the house where George Eastman was born. A village green with grazing sheep and cattle, and flower and herb gardens beside museum houses, give the museum an authentic early American flavor.

The Vagabond Inn

3300 Sliter Road
Naples, NY 14512
(716) 554-6271

INNKEEPER: Celeste Stanhope-Wiley; manager: Mica Pierce

ROOMS: 5, including 3 suites, all with private bath, TV, VCR, mini-refrigerator, coffeemaker, and tape player; 4 with whirlpool tub and private patio; 3 with fireplace

ON THE GROUNDS: On 100 acres with hiking and cross-country ski trails; swimming pool; 9-hole golf course; gardens; and hot tub

EXTRAS: Extensive gift shop on premises; large, fully equipped guest kitchen; hot coffee and cocoa center open 24 hours; a cat named Mama on premises

RATES: $125–$200, double occupancy, including full breakfast

CREDIT CARDS ACCEPTED: MasterCard and Visa

OPEN: Year-round

HOW TO GET THERE: From I–90 (the New York State Thruway) take exit 42. Turn right and then right again onto Route 96 north. Watch for the Log Cabin Tavern on the right. Just beyond, take County Road 6 (on the left)

to Route 5/20. Turn right (east) onto Route 5/20 and then turn left (south) onto Route 14A. Stay on Route 14A until you reach Route 245. Bear right onto Route 245 and stay on this for about 20 miles to Middlesex. Turn left in Middlesex onto Route 364 and go uphill for ½ mile to Shay Road. Turn right onto Shay Road and continue for 4²/10 miles to Sliter Road, which will be on the left. Take Sliter Road to The Vagabond Inn (the last ³/10 mile will be on gravel).

If you're seeking absolute privacy, serenity, and seclusion, as well as a dramatic setting, I can't imagine a more suitable choice. Did I hear the word romance? The Vagabond Inn offers the ultimate in that category.

The inn is high, high on a hilltop aerie, and one must climb and climb up one hillside after the next to reach it. Views of Canandaigua Lake and of hills lined with grapevines recede into the distance. After traversing the final ³/10 mile on a gravel road, the contemporary grey board-and-batten house may initially be a disappointment, but be not dismayed, for the drama lies within.

You will enter a 60-foot great room with a massive fieldstone fireplace at both ends. A wall of windows offers panoramic views of even higher mountains, a swimming pool, a nine-hole golf course, and beautiful gardens. Linger awhile to inspect the exquisite blown-glass dishes, wind chimes, unusual fine-art jewelry, candles, and much more in the gift shop that literally covers tables, shelves, and windowsills here.

The guest rooms are sybaritic cocoons, complete with everything a couple may desire. My favorite is The Lodge, which has a stone floor, fieldstone walls, and a massive river-rock fireplace. The pine bed is stenciled in a tulip design, and it sits under huge boxed beams. The "bathing chamber" has a tile floor and pine walls, and includes a private hot tub. The Mahogany has a green carpet and a four-poster bed with a red-and-purple spread, as well as a mahogany chest and lovely oil paintings on the walls. The views across the fields are wonderful. The Bristol features a gas stove and a bed with a fishnet canopy. This fabulous bath has a raised redwood whirlpool tub with views of the mountains, a private dining porch, as well as a sundeck. A 400-video library offers a variety of selections for viewing on the VCRs that are found in every room. For those who so desire, an outdoor hot tub can be reserved also.

Celeste is so solicitous of her guests' comfort that she arranges a flexible breakfast hour and will prepare whatever is requested. She has also learned that her guests hate to leave her secluded hideaway once they arrive, so she suggests they pick up a gourmet dinner and wine in the afternoon. She has thoughtfully provided a full kitchen so that her guests can prepare dinner at their leisure.

What's Nearby—Naples

Naples is in the Finger Lakes region, near numerous fine wineries. Most have daily tours and wine tastings. Bristol Mountain offers downhill skiing and fall foliage chairlift rides. The Bristol Valley Theatre and the Finger Lakes Performing Arts Center are home to concerts and other cultural performances. (See also Canandaigua.)

Bed & Breakfast on the Park

113 Prospect Park West
New York (Brooklyn), NY 11215
(718) 499–6115

FAX: (718) 499–1385

E-MAIL: lianap@bigfoot.net

WEB SITE: www.bbnyc.com

INNKEEPER: Liana Paolella; manager: Donal Ward

ROOMS: 7, including 3 suites, 5 with private bath, all with air conditioning, TV, telephone, radio, hair dryer, 2 with fireplace and patio or deck

ON THE GROUNDS: Garden

EXTRAS: Cookies beside bed; Shiva, a shepherd, on premises; fresh flowers in rooms

RATES: $125–$275, double occupancy, including full breakfast; two-night minimum

CREDIT CARDS ACCEPTED: MasterCard and Visa

OPEN: Year-round

HOW TO GET THERE: From Manhattan, take the Brooklyn Bridge. After crossing the bridge, turn left onto Atlantic Avenue at the Mobil station. Turn right onto Fourth Avenue and continue for about 1 mile. At Fifth Street, turn left and continue to its end. Turn right onto Prospect Park West. Go 2 blocks to #113.

Liana Paolella was an antiques dealer when she purchased this grand limestone townhouse in 1985. It needed a tremendous amount of work, but she knew what to do. Stripping the paneled walls, doors, stair railings, detailed fretwork, and window frames, she converted a Victorian derelict into a rare emerald. She then filled it with antiques that might have been used when George Brickelmeier, a liquor merchant, built the house in 1892.

There are fringed sofas and chairs and an elaborate floor lamp with a beaded fringe in one parlor. In the front parlor, there are massive oil paintings (one that is exceptionally fine was painted by Liana's step-father, William Earl Singer) and a Pairpoint lamp (it has a blown-glass shade that is reverse-painted with poppies). The rich African mahogany woodwork stands out against the frothy lace curtains that shield the windows from the street. More paintings line the stairway, and the oak-lined foyer hides a lovely powder room behind paneling.

The guest rooms are elegant and refined, just as Victorian boudoirs should be. My favorite is the Park Suite, a jewel that overlooks Prospect Park. It has a bed with an antique Brussels lace crown canopy that cascades down the wall and a crocheted coverlet. Handmade Brussels lace curtains hang at the windows, and there's a spectacular stained-glass window. The dressing room is fully paneled with bird's-eye maple and includes mirrored doors and even a built-in vanity. The Lady Liberty Suite has a canopy bed and ornately carved marble-topped dressers as well as French doors leading to a private deck. Another set of stairs leads even higher to a rooftop perch offering a view that stretches from the Empire State Building to Lady Liberty herself.

Breakfast is served in the most Victorian room in the house. The dining room has a bay of stained-glass windows defined by Victorian fretwork, and the walls are lined with china cabinets filled with elaborate Victorian silver and china. Liana sets her table with a lace tablecloth, sterling silver flatware, cut-glass crystal, and gold-rimmed china. Silver teapots and other serving pieces grace the table. The setting is as Victorian as a scene from a Merchant/Ivory period movie. I always feel as if I should be attired in a long, flowing dress. Breakfast will include fresh fruits and cereals, homemade muffins and breads, and an entree such as German pancakes or a frittata with a sweet potato crust.

Park Slope is a lovely section of Brooklyn. Tree-lined streets are faced with elegant townhouses and brownstones, and there are fine restaurants nearby.

What's Nearby—Brooklyn

Directly across the street from the B&B is Brooklyn's crown jewel, the 526-acre Prospect Park, created by Frederick Law Olmsted and Calvert

Vaux, designers of Manhattan's Central Park. You can ride on a restored carousel, visit the excellent Brooklyn Museum, or walk through the Brooklyn Botanic Gardens—all within its confines. Just around the corner, the Brooklyn Academy of Music offers a potpourri of music, dance, and theater year-round.

The Inn at Irving Place

54 Irving Place
New York (Manhattan), NY 10003
(800) 685–1447 or (212) 533–4600

FAX: (212) 533–4611

WEB SITE: www.inatirving.com

INNKEEPERS: Shawn Rettstatt and Susanne Sarwaryn

ROOMS: 12, all with private bath, air conditioning, TV, VCR, telephone with dataport, desk, stereo, mini-refrigerator, CD player, hair dryer, robes, and non-functioning fireplace; wheelchair access

EXTRAS: Afternoon tea, bar service available (there is a charge); fresh flowers in the rooms; fax, laptop computers with internet access, cellular telephones, and pagers available

RATES: $300–$450, double occupancy, including Continental breakfast

CREDIT CARDS ACCEPTED: American Express, Diners Club, MasterCard, Visa

OPEN: Year-round

SMOKING: Smoking permitted; some rooms designated nonsmoking

HOW TO GET THERE: Irving Place is an extension of Lexington Avenue, separated from it by Gramercy Park. The B&B is between East 17th and East 18th Streets.

Like a page from *Time and Again*, The Inn at Irving Place seems to have emerged from an earlier era. It's possible to imagine Elsie de Wolfe arriving at her house across the street by horsedrawn carriage to prepare for one of her salons or O. Henry scurrying along in the chilly winter air to reach the warm, convivial atmosphere of Pete's Tavern to finish writing "Gift of the Magi." The street has changed little over the years, and the two townhouses where this sumptuous bed and breakfast are located retain their original stoops, wrought-iron balustrades, and elegant entrances. The inn is so discreet that there isn't even a sign outside announcing its presence.

An earlier time pervades the inside as well. Imagine walking up the stairs, pressing the bell, and then being escorted into a gracious parlor filled with antique sofas, chairs, and tables. A fire glows in the fireplace; oil paintings hang on the walls. There is no reception desk or visible sign that this is not someone's home. An innkeeper warmly greets you and offers you tea. You relax, knowing you're in good hands, and feeling as if you've left the brisk pace of New York far behind.

The guest rooms, which are named for well-known Victorian personalities, are as refined and urbane as the parlor. Although each is furnished with fine antiques, they are all decorated with a restrained dignity that is the antithesis of the fussy Victorian homes of its age. Yet we're sure Elsie would smile approvingly. The room named for Stanford White (who certainly trod this street) has a carved walnut bed, elaborate ceiling moldings, an inlaid floor, and a magnificent armoire. Washington Irving's room has a bed and matching armoire inlaid with a musical instrument motif, while the O. Henry room has a brass bed and a carved armoire. Each of the rooms has a private bath with a black-and-white tile floor, pedestal sink, and a tub or shower (or sometimes both).

The parlor in one of the townhouses is now Lady Mendl's Tearoom (née Elsie de Wolfe). Afternoon tea, evening drinks, and Continental breakfast are served here. Reminiscent of a French *salon de thé*, the tiny *boîte* is furnished with Victorian cast-iron tables and colorful chairs. Wooden shutters cover the windows.

A wonderful restaurant, Verbena, is located on the ground floor of one of the townhouses. It has a pretty garden in back and several fireplaces to warm chilly winter evenings. It is leased to the chef and not managed by the B&B. The Cibar Lounge, on the ground floor of the other townhouse, was opened by the B&B in 1998, however. This warm and convivial bar features light appetizers, wines and drinks, and a selection of fine cigars.

A Continental breakfast of fresh fruit, freshly baked pastries, and coffee can be delivered to guests' rooms, or guests may eat in Lady Mendl's Tearoom or in the Parlor.

Irving Place is the business street of the Gramercy Park neighborhood. The park, from which the neighborhood takes its name, is encircled by a high wrought-iron fence. Keys for the gate are available to full-time residents only. Pete's Tavern is still as busy today as in O. Henry's time, and it even looks the same. There are numerous other restaurants on the block as well as shops and boutiques.

Inn New York City

266 West 71st Street
New York (Manhattan), NY 10023
(212) 580–1900

FAX: (212) 580–4437

WEB SITE: www.innnewyorkcity.com

INNKEEPERS: Ruth Mensch and Elyn Mensch

ROOMS: 4 suites, all with private bath, air conditioning, TV, VCR, telephone with dataport, CD player, kitchen; 2 with fireplace and 2 with whirlpool tub; 1 with a balcony

EXTRAS: Chocolates by the bed; soft drinks, bottled waters, wine, quiche, cheeses in refrigerators; basket of snacks, candy bars, fresh fruit, port, and sherry in hallway

RATES: $350–$415, double occupancy, including Continental breakfast; two-night minimum

CREDIT CARDS ACCEPTED: American Express, MasterCard, Visa

OPEN: Year-round

HOW TO GET THERE: The B&B is located on the south side of West 71st Street, between Broadway and West End Avenue.

When a guest calls the innkeeper in the morning and says, "Ah, this was a night in Paradise," the innkeeper knows she's doing things right.

Located on a charming side street of townhouses and brownstones on Manhattan's Upper West Side, Inn New York City is a unique treasure. It's a little bit of "country" in the heart of the city—an easy walk from Lincoln Center, Central Park, and Riverside Park, and near the upscale Upper Broadway shopping area. Ruth Mensch and her daughter Elyn converted this townhouse to a four-suite bed-and-breakfast in 1989, and it's seldom had a vacancy ever since.

The four-story brownstone, which has an ornate wrought-iron door flanked by sandstone pillars, has such an archetypal New York ambience that guests feel right at home—so much so, in fact, that some make it their home-away-from-home for extended visits. Broadway and Lincoln Center performers have found the ambience and the location ideal.

The vestibule and front parlor of the B&B are charming. They have high ceilings, inlaid hardwood floors, elaborate moldings, carved cabinetry, and crystal chandeliers—all evocative of the nineteenth century. Guests often invite friends over to have a drink in the parlor before departing for a local restaurant or a concert at Lincoln Center.

The suites are spacious and alluring. Ruth is a genius at salvaging discarded architectural treasures and turning them into striking pieces of furniture. Her creativity is found throughout the B&B. The Spa Suite, for example, on the second floor has a king-sized bed with a beadboard headboard. The sybaritic bath, however, is the pièce de résistance. It has a double Jacuzzi on a platform in the center of the room, a fireplace with a carved mantel, an old barber chair, a cast-iron foot bath, a Victorian dresser with a sink set into its marble top, a sauna for two, and a glassed-in shower.

The Opera Suite has a living room with a 12-foot-high ceiling. The foyer has a stained-glass ceiling, and there's a baby grand piano in the living room. The bedroom has a balcony, a fireplace, and a queen-size bed with a headboard made from wrought-iron estate gates. The bath has a Jacuzzi. Every room has a small kitchen and such personal touches as private libraries, fresh flowers, and fluffy robes.

Every evening after guests leave for dinner, Ruth or Elyn stock their refrigerators with morning food, such as freshly baked muffins or other treats, coffee, fruit, and juice. A copy of *The New York Times* is left at the door every morning.

What's Nearby

Lincoln Center for the Performing Arts—home of the New York Philharmonic, the Metropolitan Opera, the American Ballet Theatre, the New York City Opera, Juilliard School, and so much more—is within walking distance of this B&B. Riverside Park is virtually across the street, and the Museum of Natural History and the New York Historical Society are also nearby.

The Inn on 23rd

131 West 23rd Street
New York, NY 10011
(212) 463–0330 or (877) 387–2323

FAX: (212) 463–0302

WEB SITE: www.innon23rd@aol.com

INNKEEPERS: Annette, Barry, Kenneth, and Lewis Fisherman

ROOMS: 11, including 1 suite, all with private bath, air conditioning, TV, two-line telephone with dataport, desk, radio, and hair dryer; wheelchair access

EXTRAS: Library on second floor; free local calls, fax and copy machine in room on request

RATES: $150–$250, double occupancy, including Continental breakfast; two-night minimum

CREDIT CARDS ACCEPTED: American Express, MasterCard, Visa

OPEN: Year-round

HOW TO GET THERE: The B&B is located on the West Side of Manhattan between Sixth and Seventh Avenues in the Chelsea/Flatiron district.

Walking along the streets of Manhattan one day, I was amazed to see a freshly painted sign on a newly renovated nineteenth-century town-house. Since the sign identified the building as an about-to-open B&B, I couldn't resist an inspection.

Annette and Barry Fisherman had lived on Long Island with their sons Kenneth and Lewis, where Barry was an opthalmologist and Annette owned an art gallery, but for this new venture, they sold their family home and transported their lovely antiques to the spacious rooms in their beautifully converted B&B. Each room is unique, and those on the top floor have the distinction of cathedral ceilings and studio-style skylights.

Guests enter the B&B and find themselves in a formal living room with a maple floor covered by Oriental rugs. It's furnished with antiques, including an unusual Victorian rocker. Breakfast is served buffet-style from a carved oak table in the room beyond. On the second floor, a spacious library with brick walls features shelves of books, an antique pool table, and a round antique oak clawfoot table—the ideal place to relax with a cup of tea.

The guest rooms have brick walls and modern baths with pedestal sinks and tile floors and tub surrounds. Each is decorated with a theme. The

Cabin has Adirondack-style furniture, while Nevada features an antique slot machine and an enormous skylight. The Rosewood Room features rosewood furniture and the Victorian Room has a four-poster bed, an antique wardrobe, a Victorian tapestry, and a Victorian lamp with porcelain flowers. The Suite has some wonderful furniture including a walnut Victorian bed with a carved head and footboard.

Breakfast consists of fresh fruit, yogurt, bagels, and freshly baked croissants from a nearby French bakery. This B&B combines the best of both old and new New York.

What's Nearby

The Flatiron Building, built in 1902 to fit into the triangle created by the junction of Broadway and Fifth Avenue, gives this district of Manhattan its moniker. You'll find a potpourri of restaurants, shops, and designer boutiques. Madison Square Park offers a leafy greensward nearby. A walk along 23rd Street will take you past the Chelsea Hotel, with its delightful exterior of lacy ironwork balconies and red brick. Plaques at the entrance identify many famous personalities who have lived here.

The Golden Pineapple

201 Liberty Avenue
Port Jefferson, NY 11777
(516) 331–0706

FAX: (516) 474–5311

WEB SITE: www.portjeff.com/gp

INNKEEPERS: Ron and Grace Fitterer

ROOMS: 3, all with private bath, air conditioning, radio, hair dryer, robes, iron, and ironing board

ON THE GROUNDS: Gardens; parking

EXTRAS: Evening cordials, soft drinks and sweets; bottled water in all rooms

RATES: $110–$150, double occupancy, including full breakfast and evening sweets and cordials; two-night minimum weekends May–September; three-night minimum holiday weekends

CREDIT CARDS ACCEPTED: American Express, MasterCard, Visa

OPEN: Year-round except one week at Christmas

HOW TO GET THERE: From New York City take I–495 (the Long Island Expressway) east to exit 64 north (Port Jefferson) onto Route 112 north. Follow this for approximately 6 miles to Port Jefferson. Turn left onto Liberty Avenue. The B&B is at the top of the hill on the left.

Ebenezer Jones was one of the founding fathers of Port Jefferson. A leading shipbuilder, he built his home in 1828 high on a commanding hill. It was built not to impress but rather to offer comfortable shelter for his family. One can only imagine how pleased he would be to see his home today. When Ron and Grace purchased the house, they began an extensive renovation project, and today the B&B shines. There are new baths, a bright new kitchen, and new wide moldings, but the elegant old touches were left in place. The B&B opened for business in November 1997.

Guests enter a handsome entry hall that leads to a living room defined by fluted columns. A gas fireplace has a distinguished mantel. There's a floral sofa and a needlepoint rug that partially covers the oak floor. Ron and Grace have collected some wonderful artwork over the years, and some of it hangs on the living room walls.

The guest rooms are located upstairs, where a vibrant needlepoint picture of poppies hangs in the hall. The Blue Room at the top of the stairs has a blue-grey iron and brass bed with a white spread and a new tile bath. The Yellow Room includes an iron bed and a pretty bath with a pedestal sink. Guests especially enjoy the Bunny Room, which has bunnies hidden in the pictures on the walls. There's an iron sleigh bed with a wisteria-patterned spread. The bath for this room is off the hallway.

One of the features of this B&B that's especially nice is the Front Room, a special guest parlor that's filled with books and games. A TV and VCR provide entertainment, and sweets and cordials are set out here in the evening. A tiny gift shop features jewelry, Christmas ornaments, and other items with a pineapple motif.

Breakfast may be served in the bright breakfast room or on the deck that overlooks a wooded area. Grace will prepare homemade muffins and breads, as well as a hot entree. Perhaps it will be an egg casserole using herbs from the kitchen garden. There will be fresh fruit from one of the local farmstands and tea imported from Sweden and England.

What's Nearby—Port Jefferson

Port Jefferson is the embarkation point for ferries to Bridgeport, Connecticut, so it's an easy drive from New England points to this B&B. In town you might take a paddlewheel boat cruise for dinner or sightseeing or visit the Mather Museum, which describes the history of the Port Jefferson area. You could also drive to picturesque Stony Brook to see The Museums at Stony Brook, a collection of three buildings housing a carriage museum, an art museum featuring the work of Stony Brook native William Sidney Mount, and the Blackwell History Museum. The Staller Center on the campus of the State University of New York at Stony Brook offers a full complement of music, theater, dance, and art programs.

Veranda House Bed & Breakfast

82 Montgomery Street
Rhinebeck, NY 12572
(914) 876–4133

FAX: (914) 876–6218

E-MAIL: veranda82@aol.com

WEB SITE: www.verandahouse.com

INNKEEPERS: Linda and Ward Stanley

ROOMS: 4, all with private bath, air conditioning, and telephone

ON THE GROUNDS: Parking; gardens

EXTRAS: Decanter of sherry on sideboard in dining room; chocolates in room; Saturday night reception with appetizers and beverages; one calico cat named Katerina in owner's quarters only

RATES: $90–$130, double occupancy, including full breakfast; two-night minimum weekends May–October and all holiday weekends

CREDIT CARDS ACCEPTED: None

OPEN: Year-round

HOW TO GET THERE: From New York City, take the Hudson River Parkway north to the Saw Mill River Parkway north and then follow the Taconic Parkway north. Take the exit marked Red Hook/Pine Plains/Route 199 and follow Route 199 west. At the traffic light, continue straight ahead onto Route 308 west. Continue on Route 308 for approximately 6 miles to the traffic light in Rhinebeck. Turn right onto Route 9 north (Montgomery Street). Go 3 blocks and turn left onto Locust Grove Road. Turn right at the first driveway into the B&B parking area.

Named for the broad veranda across the front that's filled with wicker furniture in the summer, the house was built in 1845 as a humble farmhouse. It later served as the parsonage for the Episcopal Church of the Messiah for some ninety years. It was probably during this period that the elaborate brackets under the eaves and the front veranda were added. It was purchased by the Stanleys in 1993, and they converted it to a B&B.

The house has several interesting architectural features that were of particular interest to Ward, a former college professor of art and architectural history. The doorways are topped by elaborate cornice brackets, and there are unusually pretty oak parquet floors with mahogany border inserts.

The gracious living room has a painted wood mantel over the fireplace and comfortable sofas and chairs. The adjoining library, where the B&B's TV and VCR are located, has floor-to-ceiling shelves filled with art, history, and architectural tomes (and, of course, Ward loves to tell guests about local history and architecture as well), and numerous happy plants basking in the light that streams in the windows. There are French doors here that lead to a bluestone patio where breakfast is often served in the summer. The dining room also has a parquet floor covered by an Oriental rug, a crystal chandelier, and another set of French doors to the patio. There are several handsome oak hutches and chests here also.

The guest rooms are simple and comfortable, and they all have private baths. One room has predominantly green colors with a cherry pencil-post four-poster bed, a window seat, and a Victorian marble-topped dresser. The small bath has wainscotted walls. Another room is decorated in blue-and-white gingham and has built-in bookcases. This room has a bath that was original to the house and includes a handsome sink with a marble countertop and twisted nickel-plated legs.

Breakfast is served in the dining room unless the weather is nice enough to eat on the terrace. Ward and Linda added a professional kitchen to the house in 1996, and Linda prides herself on her three-course breakfasts. Guests will begin the meal with a fresh fruit plate such as pear slices with kiwi and raspberries, as well as homemade breads. Among the favorites are French fruit braid, maple walnut coffee cake, and orange date muffins. For an entree, she may serve crepes filled with feta cheese and sautéed zucchini in a light cream sauce and topped with a pesto sauce, or orange yogurt pancakes.

The lawns of Veranda House slope away from the house in back, and there are stately trees and overflowing flower beds. The house is merely a three-block walk from the center of town.

The Hudson River Valley is a treasure trove of places to see and things to do. Near Rhinebeck you can visit a number of historic homes: Clermont, the Vanderbilt Mansion, the Mills Mansion, Montgomery Place, and Wilderstein are all nearby, as is the Roosevelt home and library in Hyde Park. The Culinary Institute of America is also located in Hyde Park. Visit the kitchens in this training ground for America's finest chefs, and then stay to sample the food in one of the on-site restaurants (but be sure to make reservations because they are often booked months in advance). (See also Stanfordville.)

428 Mt. Vernon—A Bed & Breakfast Inn

428 Mt. Vernon Avenue
Rochester, NY 14620
(800) 836–3159 or (716) 271–0792

FAX: (716) 271–0946

WEB SITE: virt.cities.com/inns/outs

INNKEEPERS: Philip and Claire Lanzatella

ROOMS: 7, all with private bath, air conditioning, TV, telephone with dataport, radio, hair dryer, and desk; 3 with fireplace; wheelchair accessible; children over the age of 11 welcome

ON THE GROUNDS: On 2½ acres adjacent to Highland Park

EXTRAS: Coffee or tea room service; turndown with fresh cookies and chocolates; a parrot, Nicky, on premises

RATES: $110, double occupancy; $90, single occupancy, including full breakfast; two-night minimum weekends May–October

CREDIT CARDS ACCEPTED: American Express, Diners Club, MasterCard, Visa

OPEN: Year-round

SMOKING: Limited smoking permitted; designated nonsmoking room

HOW TO GET THERE: From I–90 (the New York State Thruway) take exit 46 onto I–390 north. Proceed to exit 16 onto Route 15A. Stay to the right after turning right and follow the right lane to South Avenue (about ½ mile). Stay on South Avenue through 2 traffic lights. After passing Highland, turn right in 2 more streets onto Alpine Street, which bears to the left and becomes Mt. Vernon. Go 1 block to Doctors Road and turn

right. Then turn immediately to the left and go up the hill through the inn's gates, which are on the left.

It's hard to imagine that this wonderful sequestered B&B is actually in the heart of a major city, but here it is, secluded among stately trees—a brick hilltop mansion circa 1917, displaying all the elegant architectural characteristics that were prevalent just after the turn of the century. Located on 2½ peaceful acres, and adjacent to 150-acre Highland Park, the property appealed to the Sisters of Mercy, who had their nunnery here for thirty-six years.

Phil and Clair Lanzatella lived in a neighborhood nearby when they were raising their family, but when this property became available in 1986, they welcomed the opportunity to preserve it. Phil is a general contractor who specializes in the restoration of older buildings, so this was a natural for him.

The house has generous common rooms that are distinguished by the use of beautiful woods. There are narrow-plank oak floors, tall ceilings, oak moldings, and oak window seats. There's a wonderful leaded- and stained-glass window in the stair landing.

In the living room an Oriental rug complements a pretty Victorian sofa, an ivory tapestry love seat, and a blue shadow-stripe fainting couch. A square grand piano is often the focus of impromptu musical events, and there's a beautiful maple fireplace mantel. An adjacent solarium is decorated with bird-motif plates and mission-style furniture. This leads to a brick patio and the gardens.

The guest rooms, which are on the second and third floors, are decorated with antiques. Room #3 features a bed with an oak headboard and a wonderful oak table with glass ball feet, while room #1 has a walnut Victorian bed. Maxfield Parrish prints decorate the walls. In the baths the old hexagonal tile floors have been retained, and they are lovely, but I noticed on my last visit that the baths and linens covering the beds are now ready for refurbishment.

Guests order their breakfast from a menu that is presented the night before. It is served in the lovely dining room that features a fireplace with a stunning oak mantel. There are more Maxfield Parrish prints covering the walls, and an oak buffet displays antique silver and china.

What's Nearby—Rochester

The B&B is located adjacent to Highland Park, a 150-acre park laid out by Frederick Law Olmsted in the 1880s. There are numerous hiking trails in summer and cross-country ski trails in winter that thread past rare trees and shrubs and whimsical nineteenth-century buildings. Rochester is New York's third largest city and it offers a variety of cultural events. Spread along both sides of the Genesee River, it is a waterborne city of bridges. It is home to Eastman Kodak, and you can visit the George Eastman mansion on "millionaires' row," where the evolution of photography and cameras is traced. The Strong Museum is noted for its 20,000-plus doll collection, as well as textiles, furniture, and toys from the nineteenth and twentieth century.

Lighthouse on the Bay

59 Mashomack Drive
Sag Harbor, NY 11963
(516) 725-7112

FAX: (516) 725-7112

INNKEEPERS: Regina and Stephen Humanitzki

ROOMS: 4, including 2 suites, all with private bath, air conditioning, telephone, radio, hair dryer, and robes; 1 with TV, VCR, private porch, and whirlpool tub

ON THE GROUNDS: On 2 acres with decks overlooking Shelter Island Bay; boardwalk to private beach; gardens; hiking trails

EXTRAS: Beautiful views; mineral water and fruit in rooms; bicycles, beach chairs provided; tennis available on nearby private courts

RATES: $150–$300, double occupancy, including full breakfast; two-night minimum

CREDIT CARDS ACCEPTED: None

OPEN: Year-round

HOW TO GET THERE: From New York City take I–495 (the Long Island Expressway) to exit 70 (Manorville) and follow Route 111 south to Highway 27 (Sunrise Highway). Follow Highway 27 (which becomes the Montauk Highway) east to Bridgehampton. At the monument and traffic light in the center of town, turn left onto the Bridgehampton-Sag Harbor Turnpike. In the village of Sag Harbor, this becomes Main Street. Follow Main Street through the village to its end at the windmill. Turn left onto Route 114 and cross the bridge. You are now in North Haven. Continue on Route 114 for about ½ mile. At the pillars marked North Haven Manor, turn right. Specific directions from this point will be given to those with confirmed reservations.

I dream about Lighthouse on the Bay. Honest. It's got that kind of hold. Once you've seen it, you know you must return again and again for the peaceful solitude it offers. The only sounds are those of the marsh grasses whispering in a breeze and the cry of an occasional seagull. You can watch the ospreys on their wooden perches in the springtime and the herons and egrets on their nests in the marsh.

Lighthouse on the Bay is not one of those old and historic structures—it was built by Regina and Stephen Humanitzki in 1997. They fell in love with the waterfront setting and thought they would renovate an old house on the property, but instead they ended up tearing it down and building anew. They created a house that sits high on the land on a stone foundation. It has two lighthouse-style towers clad in natural shingles and surrounded by wonderful broad decks so that their guests can take full advantage of the views.

Guests enter a bright entry with a flagstone floor. A powder room has a slab of fieldstone for a counter and a black sink. The open floor plan and walls of glass draw guests toward the views beyond. Regina is a fabulous cook and she makes muffins or bread fresh daily. The open kitchen allows her to fix an entree of perhaps a soufflé or her popular blueberry baked French toast while talking to her guests. They might choose to eat on the deck or at the table inside.

The guest rooms are spectacular. The Tower Suite, one of my favorites, is a six-sided room with a fabulous view from the bedroom; by climbing a spiral stairway to the observation room guests will have a 360-degree view. There are sofas up here for fully appreciating the view. Little touches like an end table made from a sewing machine base are interesting. This suite has a TV. Another room has a pine sleigh bed. The Round Bedroom (yes, it really is round) is another of my favorites. This one has a private deck and an iron canopy bed draped with gauzy fabric that sits beneath a tower with celestory windows—a wonderful opportunity to wish upon a star. The bath has mahogany cabinets and a whirlpool tub.

A boardwalk leads from the house down to the private beach, and Regina and Stephen are happy to provide beach chairs and towels.

What's Nearby—Sag Harbor

Sag Harbor, an old whaling town, is charming and eccentric. There are fabulous restaurants as well as funky dives; upscale and classy antiques shops, as well as flea market-type shops. The Sag Harbor Whaling

Museum chronicles the village's whaling history, and The Old Custom House offers a fascinating history into early village life. Best of all, however, is the Bay Street Theatre Festival, a year-round professional theater company that offers live theatrical performances that often feature recognized Broadway stars.

The Batcheller Mansion Inn

20 Circular Street
Saratoga Springs, NY 12866
(800) 616–7012 or (518) 584–7012

FAX: (518) 581–7746

E-MAIL: batman@interpcs.net

WEB SITE: www.batchellermansioninn.com

INNKEEPER: Susan McCabe;
manager: Frank Burns

ROOMS: 9, all with private bath,
air conditioning, TV, telephone, radio, mini-refrigerator, hair dryer, desk, iron, ironing board, and robes; 4 with fireplace; 3 with whirlpool tub; 1 with a balcony

ON THE GROUNDS: Parking; gardens

EXTRAS: Turndown service with chocolates; tea and cookies in afternoon during racing season

RATES: $125–$265, except during racing season from late July through Labor Day weekend, when rates are $220–$395, all rates double occupancy; including Continental breakfast Monday–Friday and full breakfast Saturday, Sunday, and during racing season; two-night minimum weekends April–November; four-night minimum during racing season

CREDIT CARDS ACCEPTED: American Express, MasterCard, Visa

OPEN: Year-round

HOW TO GET THERE: From I–87 (the Northway) take exit 14. At the end of the ramp, turn right onto Union Avenue (Route 9P). Traveling west for 2 miles, follow Union Avenue to its end. Turn left onto Circular Street. The B&B is located straight ahead after 1 long block.

This twenty-eight-room High Victorian Gothic mansion narrowly escaped the wrecker's ball when it was abandoned in 1966 and then condemned by the city in 1972. Fortunately, it was purchased in 1973, and a twenty-year restoration began that concluded in 1994. Today this mélange of minarets, towers, and turrets takes its place once again as the showplace of Saratoga Springs—an opulent and extravagant B&B.

The house was built by George Sherman Batcheller, a brigadier general in the Union Army and ambassador to Portugal, among other things. He spared no expense when he built his summer "House of Pleasure" in 1873. Today the outside is painted a creamy ivory with grey-green and burgundy trim.

In the foyer there are magnificent walnut and tiger maple inlaid floors and a grand stairway leading to the second floor. The living room has an 1800s Czechoslovakian chandelier with milky-blue glass arms that hangs from the 12-foot-tall ceiling. Massive oil paintings by Stuart Williams, a copy artist and a former innkeeper of the B&B, cover the walls. There's also a baby grand piano and a fireplace with a marble mantel. Ingenious Victorian double-hung windows rise to create a doorway to the porch. The library has parquet floors and paneled bookshelves that have intricately carved details. Here guests will find a huge library table in a turret, wine velvet sofas and chairs, and a large-screen TV. Classical music plays in the background.

There are nine guest rooms on the second and third floors of the house. Even on the second floor the ceilings reach 12 feet. The Katrina Trask Room is often used as a bridal chamber. It has a lacy canopy bed, a blue carpet, a marble fireplace mantel, a marble-topped dresser, and a private balcony with wicker tables and chairs entered by way of a double-hung window. The bath has a pedestal sink and paneling painted blue. The most incredible room, however, is Diamond Jim Brady. This 18- x 28-foot room has a king-size canopy bed and a sitting area with a full-sized pool table. In the bath, there's a Jacuzzi tub.

The kitchen is fantastic. It has 26-foot-tall ceilings and a tile floor. One entire wall above the countertops is composed of a massive glass window salvaged from the Shawmut Bank in Boston. On the opposite wall, paintings by Williams climb to the ceiling. Breakfast is prepared here and served to guests seated in the dining room or on the porch. Individual tables are set with fine linen, Royal Doulton china, silver, and fine crystal.

During the week a Continental breakfast is offered consisting of fresh fruit, freshly baked pastries, juice, and coffee. On weekends, guests may also have their choice of an egg or pancake entree.

Behind the house there's a lovely and very private garden overseen by a back porch. The house is across the street from Congress Park, a park that contains Saratoga's famed brick casino building. The famous and the infamous gathered there in the late nineteenth and early twentieth centuries to gamble the night away amid opulent splendor. It is said that solitaire originated here and that the club sandwich was first made in the casino kitchens. Today a gift shop, an art gallery, and a museum are open to the public.

What's Nearby—Saratoga Springs

Saratoga Springs, known as "the Queen of Spas," was once the most fashionable of summer resorts. The 1940 WPA guide speaks nostalgically about the 1890s, when the resort was in its prime. "It stirs with anticipation in June, swings into preparatory activity in July, and rushes headlong into the full tumult of its summer season in August." There were grand hotels where glamorous balls and dinners took place, and the casino was filled with the notables and the notorious. Saratoga Springs is still a beehive of activity in the summer, especially from late July through Labor Day weekend, when the thoroughbreds race at the Saratoga Flat Track. Visit the National Museum of Racing and Hall of Fame located across the street. Saratoga Springs is also the summer home of the Philadelphia Orchestra and the New York City Ballet, who perform, along with popular artists, at the Saratoga Performing Arts Center. At the Saratoga Spa State Park, you can still enjoy a soothing therapy bath just as in days of old.

Union Gables Bed & Breakfast

55 Union Avenue
Saratoga Springs, NY 12866
(800) 398–1558 or (518) 584–1558

FAX: (518) 583–0649

E-MAIL: 73752.645@compuserve.com

INNKEEPER: Jody Roohan

ROOMS: 10, including 1 suite, all with private bath, air conditioning, TV, telephone, large desk, and minirefrigerator; 2 with balcony; cribs available

ON THE GROUNDS: Parking; tennis court; hot tub; gardens; hammock

EXTRAS: Exercise room; fax, modem, copier, small meeting space available; one dog named Max, one cat named Oreo; guest pets allowed

RATES: $110–$265, double occupancy, including Continental breakfast

CREDIT CARDS ACCEPTED: American Express, Discover, MasterCard, Visa

OPEN: Year-round

HOW TO GET THERE: From I–87 (the Northway) take exit 14. At the end of the ramp, turn right onto Union Avenue (Route 9P). Union Gables is about a mile farther on the right.

When Skidmore College decided it no longer needed to use Furness House as a dormitory, Tom Roohan, a local realtor, saw the perfect opportunity. It had all the makings of an elegant bed-and-breakfast. Massive renovation was necessary to create spacious rooms with a private bath in each, but in 1992, when the construction was complete, Tom and his wife Jody opened the house to local designers for a Decorator Showhouse, and the B&B was appropriately launched.

The grand 1901 Victorian is located on Saratoga Spring's finest street—a broad tree-lined esplanade with stately mansions on both sides. The house features gables, turrets, fanciful gingerbread trim, and a huge wraparound porch. It's set on spacious lawns bordered by overflowing flower beds.

One enters a wide foyer with boxed beams and a fireplace flanked by oak paneling and benches. One unique feature of the house is visible in the turret room that the Roohans use as an office. The room is paneled in curly maple with bamboo trim, and the living room is fully trimmed with curly maple also. There's another fireplace in the living room, as well as a baby grand piano and a chess set on a table in the turret.

The guest rooms are spacious and dramatic, and each has a TV, telephone, and mini-refrigerator stocked with the area's famed Saratoga Springs water. Cindy (all the rooms are named for family members), a suite, has inlaid oak floors and navy blue walls with white trim. There's a massive pine cannonball bed in the main room and another room with twin beds—an ideal arrangement for families. The bath is tiled, and there's a private screened-in porch overlooking the back. Kate has a horsey theme with plaid walls and bedspread, a handpainted chest of drawers featuring the Victorian houses of Saratoga, and a clever bath that has a mirror over the sink that's framed in a massive leather horse yoke.

A Continental breakfast is served in the dining room, which has another fireplace with a wonderful carved mahogany mantel, a bay window, and lincresta ceiling trim. Guests sit at the large dining room table, but they eat whenever they are ready. Breakfast will include a variety of bakery rolls, fresh fruit, and juices.

The house has one of the largest wraparound porches you'll ever see, furnished with wicker tables and chairs interspersed with verdigris metal pieces. The B&B has bicycles for guests to use, a tennis court, an outdoor hot tub, and an exercise room.

What's Nearby

See "What's Nearby—Saratoga Springs," page 227.

Schroon Lake Bed & Breakfast   **Best Buy**

Route 9
(mailing address: RD1, Box 274)
Schroon Lake, NY 12870
(800) 523–6755 or (518) 532–7042

E-MAIL: schroonbb@aol.com

WEB SITE: www.schroonbb.com

INNKEEPERS: Rita and Bob Skojec

ROOMS: 4, including 1 suite, all with private bath, air conditioning, hair dryer, and robes

ON THE GROUNDS: On 3 acres with parking; gardens

EXTRAS: Complimentary sodas and juices; computer access and fax available

RATES: $80–$105, double occupancy, including full breakfast; two-night minimum weekends; three-night minimum holiday weekends July–October

CREDIT CARDS ACCEPTED: American Express, MasterCard, Visa

OPEN: Year-round

HOW TO GET THERE: From I–87 (the Northway) take exit 28. At the end of the ramp turn right and go ²/₁₀ mile to the flashing red light. Turn right onto Route 9 south. The B&B is on the right just a few yards down the road.

Schroon Lake is a beautiful 9-mile-long mountain lake in the vast 6½-million-acre Adirondack State Park. It was a particularly popular summer resort in the early 1900s. At one point there were hotels and tourist homes lining the main street of the village and leading down to the lake that stretched for 2 miles. Few of these structures remain today, but the lake is as beautiful and as unspoiled as ever.

The neat beige Victorian farmhouse with white trim that's now known as Schroon Lake Bed & Breakfast was built in the 1920s, and it's rumored that the gangster Dutch Schultz once stayed here. A fire totally destroyed the house in the 1930s, but remnants of bootlegger bounty have been found in the brick foundation. The modest house was rebuilt in the 1930s. It was then a boarding house and later a private residence until it was converted to a B&B in the late 1980s. Bob and Rita purchased the B&B in 1995 and completed a top-to-bottom renovation before reopening it to guests. Bob is a retired systems analyst with IBM, and Rita was a New York–based food writer and stylist (at one time she was a columnist for *House Beautiful*).

The pretty house is fronted by a porch set with white wicker rockers and chairs. Ivy geraniums hang from the middle of each of the eleven arches created by the Victorian gingerbread surrounding the porch. The house sits on a knoll offering views of the mountains beyond Schroon Lake.

In the gracious living room, there are hardwood floors, Oriental rugs, a puffy sofa before a fieldstone fireplace, and Tiffany-style lamps. Upstairs, there's a den where books, magazines, board games, jigsaw puzzles, and a TV/VCR are available for guests to use.

The guest rooms include Yellow Iris, a large room with a king-size bed topped by an enormous painting of yellow and blue iris, an antique armoire, and Oriental rugs on polished oak floors. Leland has an antique brass queen-size bed and an antique curly maple dresser. The largest room is Monaco, which has an antique black iron and brass queen-size bed, a brocade settee in the sitting area, and a view of the Pharaoh Wilderness area. Each of these rooms has a sparkling new tiled private bath. The Pharaoh suite is in a separate wing.

Breakfast is served in the Victorian dining room, which is filled with antiques, or on the porch in summer. A food writer must know how to cook, and Rita has perfected her craft. She may prepare apple-walnut French toast with "burst of berries" fruit sauce or orange Belgian waffles with whipped cream and fresh raspberries, or perhaps Adirondack eggs Benedict, a light dish resembling little soufflés that she tops with hollandaise sauce.

Activities abound in all seasons. In the summer, lakeside beaches beckon as well as sailing and canoeing on Schroon Lake. In the fall, the brilliant foliage captures our romantic fancy, and its images fill the pages of photographers' scrapbooks. In winter, there are cross-country and snowmobile trails as well as downhill skiing at Whiteface and Gore Mountains.

Silver Spruce Inn Bed & Breakfast

Route 9
(mailing address: P.O. Box 157)
Schroon Lake, NY 12870
(518) 532–7031

FAX: (518) 532–7031
E-MAIL: progers358@aol.com
WEB SITE: www.silverspruce.com

INNKEEPERS: Phyllis and Clifford Rogers

ROOMS: 7, all with private bath, 2 with small kitchen, whirlpool tub, balcony

ON THE GROUNDS: On 16 acres with parking; gardens; gazebo; yard games; hiking trails

EXTRAS: Turndown with chocolates; tea, coffee, cheeses, and cookies available; telephone, fax, computer, dataport, office area available; one chocolate Lab named Lilly, one calico cat named Shacka and one Labrador retriever named Magen on premises; guest pets permitted with prior permission

RATES: $90–$110, double occupancy, including full breakfast; two-night minimum summer and holiday weekends

CREDIT CARDS ACCEPTED: MasterCard and Visa

HOW TO GET THERE: Take I–87 (the Northway) to exit 28. At the end of the ramp turn right and go ²/10 mile to the flashing red light. Turn left onto Route 9 north. The B&B will be on the left in 1⁸/10 miles.

Unique, fascinating, and an American original, the earliest portion of the Silver Spruce Inn, a 8,200-square-foot clapboard house built of post-and-beam construction, dates to 1846. After Mrs. Sallie Smith purchased it in 1926, however, it took on a whole new persona.

Mrs. Smith was the owner of Randolph and Clowes Foundry in Waterbury, Connecticut, which eventually became the American Standard Company. She purchased the house as an executive retreat for her employees. It already had six bedrooms and eight bathrooms when she bought it, but she added seventeen rooms and some fascinating architectural features. One room, for example, that was used for square dances could quickly be divided into three separate rooms by lowering hinged walls from the ceiling. A bookcase rolls back to reveal the liquor cabinet (this was during the reckless flapper days of Prohibition). Down a set of thick plank stairs, which are revealed by raising a hinged section of the living room floor, there's a tavern with a quarry-stone floor and walls, a massive stone fireplace, and beamed ceilings. A handsome bar, which was rescued from New York's old 34th Street Waldorf Astoria (where the Empire State Building now stands), is located here. The house must have been a showplace of Victorian furnishings and decor. After Mrs. Smith died, they were auctioned off by Sotheby's in 1954 in a sale that took an entire week to conduct.

The restoration of the house and grounds has been the passion of the current owners, Cliff and Phyllis Rogers, since 1981. They opened it as a B&B in 1994. The clapboard house is painted a creamy white, and it has black shutters and a slate roof. Across the front, there's a quarry stone porch filled with pretty antique wicker furniture. The walls of the living room are cedar, and there's a huge stone fireplace. In the dining room, the walls are sandblasted pine, and there's another huge stone fireplace as well as a woodstove. Phyllis is a quilter and weaver, and her artistry is found throughout.

There are seven guest rooms, all with private bath, and each is charmingly decorated with quilts. The rooms in the main house have cedar walls and fir plank floors topped by braided or woven rugs. The furnishings are of oak, mostly from the Arts and Crafts period. In Room #2, for example, there's a walnut headboard on the bed, an oak Morris reclining chair, and a pretty oak desk. The baths have cast-iron tubs with stenciled surrounds. Room #5, which is the largest, however, has a heated water bed with a half canopy, a combination not often seen in a B&B.

Breakfast is served in the dining room, where Phyllis brings out her fine silver, crystal, and china. The meal will include fresh fruits and juices, freshly baked muffins such as blueberry or raspberry, and an egg dish or maybe French toast served with New York State maple syrup.

The B&B sits on 16 acres in the heart of the 6½-million-acre Adirondack State Park. There are hiking and cross-country ski trails and trout fishing on the Schroon River.

What's Nearby
See "What's Nearby—Schroon Lake," page 231.

Candlelite Inn Guest House
3 South Ferry Road
(mailing address: P.O. Box 237)
Shelter Island, NY 11964
(516) 749-0676

FAX: (516) 749-0334

INNKEEPERS: John Sieni and Michael Bartholomew

ROOMS: 5, all with private bath and air conditioning

ON THE GROUNDS: On 1½ acres with parking and gardens

EXTRAS: Full-service hair and nail salon on premise; masseuse available

RATES: $175, double occupancy, summer season, including full breakfast; lower rates rest of year when no breakfast is offered; two-night minimum weekends mid-May–mid-October

CREDIT CARDS ACCEPTED: None

OPEN: Year-round, although by advance reservation only Sunday–Tuesday

HOW TO GET THERE: From New York City take I-495 (the Long Island Expressway) east to exit 73, where it terminates. Follow County Road 58 east to Route 25, then follow that east for about 30 miles to Greenport. Once in Greenport, follow the signs for the Shelter Island Ferry. After exiting the ferry on Shelter Island you will be on Route 114. Follow Route 114 south toward South Ferry. The B&B will be on the left in 2⁷/₁₀ miles. It is 2 miles north of South Ferry.

The house has been here for 160 years, but its unhappy state was hidden behind an overgrown hedge, and it barely attracted the eye of passing motorists. In 1998, however, new owners John Sieni and Michael Bartholomew had an ingenious plan. They decided to move their hairdressing salon to the ground floor and to create a bed-and-breakfast in the rest of the building.

They accomplished a thorough renovation that included repairing, cleaning, and replacing the corbels under the eves, building a new porch with a beadboard ceiling, repairing the fanciful gingerbread trim, and painting the outside. They virtually gutted the house, which enabled them to put in central air conditioning for the five bedrooms, which all have sparkling new baths. Then they built a side entrance for their hairdressing and nail salon and a front entrance for their bed-and-breakfast guests.

The B&B is welcoming and inviting. A pretty front porch contains wicker furniture. Guests enter a spacious living room, which has oak floors covered with Oriental rugs, a fireplace, and interesting antique oak furniture. There's a lion-head and clawfoot adjustable chair, a Hitchcock chair, an old oak yarn spinner, and a trunk that's used as a table. A TV is here for guests to use, as well as books, jigsaw puzzles, and board games.

The guest rooms are spacious and pretty and you will find fresh flowers on the nightstands. Room #1 has a bed with a metal frame and an antique oak dresser that was shipped to Shelter Island more than 200 years ago. The new bath has a tile floor with dramatic dark blue tiles and a pedestal sink. There's an antique mirror and fixtures made of chrome and crystal. Room #2 is decorated in shades of maroon. There's another metal-frame bed, an oak end table, and an oak armoire with a mirrored door. Two of the guest rooms have baths in the room, while the other three rooms have dedicated private baths, but they are accessed from the hallway.

In the summer a full breakfast is provided to B&B guests. It may include an egg dish or blueberry pancakes, or French toast and bacon, as well as freshly baked muffins or breads. The meal is served in a bright dining room that features a skylighted ceiling.

What's Nearby—Shelter Island

Shelter Island is cradled between the North and South Forks on the eastern end of Long Island and offers numerous watery pleasures, including swimming, boating, fishing, and canoeing. In addition, Shelter Island is home to Mashomack Preserve, a 2,000-acre expanse of marshes, freshwater ponds, tidal creeks, and forests owned by The

Nature Conservancy. There are hiking trails throughout the property. Shelter Island has numerous paved roads ideal for bicycling.

The House on Chase Creek

3 Locust Avenue
(mailing address: P.O. Box 364)
Shelter Island Heights, NY 11965
(516) 749–4379

E-MAIL: chasecreek@mindspring.com

WEB SITE: www.chasecreek.com

INNKEEPERS: Sharon and Bill Cummings

ROOMS: 3, all with private bath and air conditioning

ON THE GROUNDS: On creek with park benches

RATES: $65–$150, double occupancy, including Continental breakfast; two-night minimum weekends May–October and most holidays; three-night minimum Memorial Day, Fourth of July, Labor Day, and Columbus Day weekends

CREDIT CARDS ACCEPTED: American Express, MasterCard, Visa

OPEN: Year-round

HOW TO GET THERE: From New York City take I-495 (the Long Island Expressway) east to exit 73, where it terminates. Follow County Road 58 east to Route 25, then follow that east for about 30 miles to Greenport. Once in Greenport, follow the signs for the Shelter Island Ferry. After exiting the ferry on Shelter Island, you will be on Route 114, which becomes Grand Avenue. Stay on Route 114 south, as it turns the corner and goes down the hill. Just before crossing the bridge, turn right onto Locust Avenue. The B&B will be on the right, in about 2 blocks, on the corner of Locust Avenue and Meadow Place.

Located within Shelter Island Heights, which is the heart of Shelter Island, this little B&B is nevertheless tucked away on such a quiet little street that even in the height of the summer season it offers a peaceful refuge. Chase Creek, a pretty inlet off Dering Harbor, is just across the street, and a park bench offers a spot from which to view the birds that feed here. Or guests may wish to watch the activity from the white wicker swing on the front porch.

Guests enter through a large parlor, which is notable for the beautiful antique sofa and chairs found here. They are highly unusual because they have backs inlaid with mother of pearl and are upholstered in iridescent rust tapestry. A sitting room has a brick fireplace. Be sure to look at the collection of old postcards of Shelter Island that line the mantel.

There are three guest rooms. Room #2 has an iron bed and a beautiful large bath with a wood floor and a marble vanity. Room #1 is another spacious room with an iron bed and a beautiful bath with a pedestal tub. Room #3 is the smallest, and though it has a private bath, it contains only a shower.

A Continental buffet breakfast is served on a pretty porch filled with white wicker and antique tables. There are beautiful views of Chase Creek from the tall windows. A guest refrigerator provides space for sodas and wines collected along the North Fork Wine Route.

What's Nearby

For "What's Nearby—Shelter Island," see page 234.

Stearns Point House

Best Buy

7 Stearns Point Road
Shelter Island Heights
(Shelter Island), NY 11965
(516) 749-4162

INNKEEPER: Jan Carlson; managers: David Davignon and Maria Roberts

ROOMS: 5, all with private bath and air conditioning

ON THE GROUNDS: Parking

EXTRAS: Telephone available; dogs permitted with prior permission

RATES: $95–$150, double occupancy, including Continental breakfast; two-night minimum weekends May–October, three-night minimum holiday weekends

CREDIT CARDS ACCEPTED: None

OPEN: Year-round

HOW TO GET THERE: From New York City take I–495 (the Long Island Expressway) to exit 73, where it terminates. Follow County Road 58 east to Route 25, then follow Route 25 for about 30 miles to Greenport. Once in Greenport, follow the signs for the Shelter Island Ferry. After exiting the ferry on Shelter Island, you will be on Route 114, which becomes

Grand Avenue. Stay on Grand, which then becomes New York Avenue. At the end of the golf course, turn right onto West Neck Road and go up the hill. At the intersection with Shore Road, turn right onto Shore Road. Take the second left onto Stearns Point Road, and the B&B will be the second building on the left.

Shelter Island, reached by ferry from either the North or the South Fork of Eastern Long Island, is such a quiet, remote spot that it's seldom discussed in the same breath as its swank neighbor to the south, the Hamptons, or its up-and-coming wine country neighbor to the north. It lies in stark contrast to both, offering more sophisticated accommodations than the North Fork and a more relaxed pace than the Hamptons—a laid-back hideaway where the rich and famous and the rest of us can find a total escape.

Shelter Island Heights, a steeply hilled section on the northern bluff of the island, was developed in the 1870s when the Methodist Episcopal Church established the Grove and Camp Meeting Association here. Handsome Victorian houses welcomed the prominent lecturers and orators of the day, and many of these remain today.

Stearns Point House was built in Shelter Island Heights in the 1920s. The owners started taking in boarders in the 1930s, and in the 1950s the house was moved to the quiet country lane on which it sits today. Jan Carlson, who was an English instructor and dean at Nassau Community College, had summered on Shelter Island for many years. She had rented several rooms in her beachfront house, and she eventually purchased and renovated the old boarding house to create Stearns Point House.

The building is a handsome one—a white clapboard farmhouse with a porch across the front that rests in the center of $\frac{3}{4}$ acre of spacious lawns bordered by flower beds. A split-rail fence surrounds the property, and a parking area offers space for cars in back. The common room is furnished with painted tables and chairs. A buffet breakfast is set up here, and guests are free to eat in their rooms or to take their meal to the porch in summer. Jan prepares fresh muffins every day as well as platters of fresh fruit, juice, cereals, coffee, and tea. A guest refrigerator is available should guests wish to stock up on wine or soft drinks.

The rooms are crisp and charming, and the location ensures a quiet stay. They have either half-canopy beds with draperies that hang from the ceiling or canopy beds. Wicker chairs are covered with flowered chintz cushions. Each bedroom has its own private bath, but otherwise there are no amenities. One telephone is located in a phone booth near the common room.

Although not located in the village, the B&B has an excellent restaurant and country inn next door. Crescent Beach, the primary public swimming beach on Shelter Island, is an easy walk away.

What's Nearby

For "What's Nearby—Shelter Island," see page 234.

Hobbit Hollow Farm

3061 West Lake Road
Skaneateles, NY 13152
(315) 685-2791

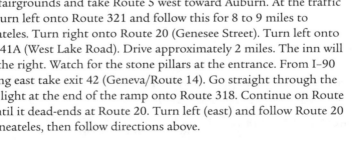

FAX: (315) 685-3426

E-MAIL: innkeeper@hobbithollow.com

WEB SITE: www.hobbithollow.com

INNKEEPER: Richard Fynn

ROOMS: 5, including 1 suite, all with private bath, air conditioning, telephone with dataport, radio, hair dryer, and robes; 2 with fireplace and whirlpool tub; 1 with private porch

ON THE GROUNDS: On 320 acres with hiking and cross-country skiing; parking

EXTRAS: Wine and cheese in the evenings; turndown with chocolates; one cat, Sam, on premises

RATES: $110–$270, double occupancy, including full breakfast and wine and cheese in the late afternoon

CREDIT CARDS ACCEPTED: American Express, MasterCard, Visa

OPEN: Year-round

HOW TO GET THERE: From I-90 (New York State Thruway) traveling west, take exit 34A and go south on I-481 to I-690. Go west on I-690 to exit 6 at the fairgrounds and take Route 5 west toward Auburn. At the traffic light, turn left onto Route 321 and follow this for 8 to 9 miles to Skaneateles. Turn right onto Route 20 (Genesee Street). Turn left onto Route 41A (West Lake Road). Drive approximately 2 miles. The inn will be on the right. Watch for the stone pillars at the entrance. From I-90 traveling east take exit 42 (Geneva/Route 14). Go straight through the traffic light at the end of the ramp onto Route 318. Continue on Route 318 until it dead-ends at Route 20. Turn left (east) and follow Route 20 to Skaneateles, then follow directions above.

I love discovering new B&Bs and this was one of my favorite 1998 finds. Located about 2 miles south of Skaneateles, the B&B sits high on a hill commanding a splendid view of Skaneateles Lake and the surrounding countryside. It's situated on a 320-acre farm and there are horses peacefully grazing in the pastures. The fields still produce corn.

This 1820 mansion was the centerpiece of the farm for many years, but in 1997 it was restored and improved with such incredible good taste that its rooms appear to have just stepped from the pages of *Architectural Digest.*

Guests enter a spacious reception hall. Along one wall a mural depicting the farm and all its outbuildings has been painted. There's a cozy little library where overstuffed chairs provide places to read a book borrowed from the shelves or to watch TV. The living room, which is separated from a hallway by pillars, has a fireplace and is decorated in green and peach. Wine and cheese are served here in the evenings. There's also a game room with a pumpkin-colored suede couch and wing chairs. An Oriental rug covers the oak floors. Best of all, however, there's a wide porch with white steel chairs that offers a wonderful vantage point for watching the sunrise over Skaneateles Lake and for admiring the late afternoon hues of gold and silver that play across the water.

The guest rooms, which are decorated with sophistication and style, are as lovely as the common rooms. All the beds are made with imported Italian sheets. The Chanticleer Room has a horsey theme, displaying red drapes with a horse motif. There's a red four-poster bed and a fabulous huge bath. The Lakeview Room is masculine in feeling. It has red-and-gold chintz drapes and a red matelassé spread on an ornately carved bed. A gas fireplace opposite the bed and a whirlpool tub in the bath evoke romance. The baths are all spacious and luxurious.

A full breakfast of perhaps eggs Benedict Hobbit style (prepared with Mornay sauce) or a Western egg roulade with breakfast potatoes is served in the formal dining room, which is painted a goldenrod yellow accented by gold drapes and upholstery on the chairs. Fine Wedgwood china, Waterford crystal, and Reed and Barton silver create elegant table settings.

What's Nearby—Skaneateles

Skaneateles is located in the Finger Lakes region of New York State. It is one of those picture-postcard towns with beautifully renovated turn-of-the-century brick buildings lining one side of Main Street. The other side arcs in a crescent around the head of Skaneateles Lake (the name means "long lake" in Iroquois), with parks edging the water. Clift Park, at water's edge, is where sightseeing cruises take place in the summer. Be sure to visit several of the excellent wineries in the Finger Lakes to sample their products. (See also Canandaigua and Ithaca.)

Evergreen on Pine Bed & Breakfast

89 Pine Street
Southampton, NY 11968
(877) 824–6600 or (516) 283–0564

WEB SITE: www.virtualcities.com/ ons/ny/l/ny/9701.htm

INNKEEPERS: Peter and JoAnn Rogoski

ROOMS: 5, including 1 suite, all with private bath, air conditioning, telephone with dataport, fax machine, radio, robes, hair dryer, iron, and ironing board

ON THE GROUNDS: Parking; gardens

EXTRAS: Telephone with dataport and modem; a Maltese named Michelle and a border collie named Lady

RATES: $110–$240, single or double occupancy, including Continental breakfast; two-night minimum weekends in June and July; three-night minimum weekends in August

CREDIT CARDS ACCEPTED: American Express, Diners Club, Discover, Master-Card, Visa

OPEN: Year-round

HOW TO GET THERE: From New York City take I–495 (the Long Island Expressway) to exit 70 (Manorville) and follow Route 111 south to Highway 27 (Sunrise Highway). Follow Highway 27 (which becomes County Road 39) east to Southampton. Turn right onto North Sea Road, which becomes Main Street. Follow Main Street through the shopping area of the village and turn left at the traffic light onto Meeting House Lane. Go 2 blocks and turn left onto Pine Street. The first driveway on the left leads to the parking area for the B&B, which is on the corner of Meeting House Lane and Pine Street.

ettled in 1640, Southampton is the oldest English settlement in New York State, yet today its shops, restaurants, and boutiques are the essence of twentieth-century chic. Evergreen on Pine is within a short 2-block walk of the fashionable shops of Main Street and Jobs Lane and almost next door to the Southampton Historical Museum, where guests can learn about Southampton's interesting history.

The white-shingled B&B is 250 years younger than the town. Built in 1887 and thoroughly updated by Peter and JoAnn Rogoski in 1996 (who moved here from Darien, Connecticut, for a lifestyle change), it's a modest Victorian with a front porch outfitted with wicker. A tall privet hedge surrounds the property, except for an arch cut to accommodate the gate that leads to the flower-bordered sidewalk. A parking area is located in back, and to the side, a tiled patio is surrounded by lawns and more flower beds. White iron chairs and tables with umbrellas repose here, a welcoming spot to sip a glass of wine and nibble the fresh fruit acquired at one of the local farm stands.

Inside, there's a handsome living room with Oriental rugs on oak floors, a white wooden fireplace mantel with scrollwork, and an antique camelback sofa. The decor is tied together in an English country theme.

There are two guest rooms on the main floor, and three upstairs. One room on the first floor has an elaborate high brass bed, a fireplace mantel (although the fireplace does not work), and a dressing table with a sculptured beveled mirror. There are oak floors and a paisley spread in gold, green, and rust on the bed. The other downstairs room is furnished with a sleigh bed that's covered with a green Laura Ashley fabric. The rooms upstairs are equally charming. A sunny corner room, furnished with white wicker and a pretty Laura Ashley fabric in yellows and blues, is a favorite. Although all the rooms have private baths, two of the rooms upstairs have baths off the hallway instead of in the room.

A Continental breakfast of fresh fruit, homemade muffins, croissants, and juice is served buffet-style in the dining room, which has another fireplace. The decor is light and fun. JoAnn covers the dining room table with a runner decorated with country animals and place mats featuring bunnies. She uses a white-on-white china, as well as crystal and silver. In nice weather guests often take their breakfast out to the patio.

What's Nearby—Southampton

Ocean and bay beaches beckon visitors throughout the summer, but there are many things to do here year-round. The Parrish Art Museum has an excellent collection of paintings by artists who lived and painted in the Hamptons, while the Southampton Historical Museum, which is housed in numerous buildings in a village setting, has a re-created country store with a post office, a blacksmith shop, and much more.

Southampton College of Long Island University, located in Southampton, has a Fine Art Museum and offers a wide array of cultural activities year-round. (See also Bridgehampton, and Westhampton Beach.)

The Ivy

Best Buy

244 North Main Street
Southampton, NY 11968
(516) 283-3233

FAX: (516) 283-3793
E-MAIL: theivy@earthlink.net
WEB SITE: http: //home.
earthlink.net/~theivy

INNKEEPERS: Melody and Philip Tierney

ROOMS: 5, all with private bath, air conditioning, telephone, radio, and desk; 1 with a TV

ON THE GROUNDS: On 1 acre with gardens and secluded swimming pool

EXTRAS: Afternoon refreshments of tea and cookies or wine and cheese available; 1 miniature American Eskimo dog named Iggy and Katie the kitty on premises

RATES: $99–$295, double occupancy, including full breakfast and afternoon refreshments; two-night minimum weekends in July; three-night minimum weekends in August

CREDIT CARDS ACCEPTED: American Express, MasterCard, Visa

OPEN: Year-round

HOW TO GET THERE: From New York City take I–495 (the Long Island Expressway) east to exit 70 (Manorville) and follow Route 111 south for 4 miles to Highway 27 (Sunrise Highway). Take Highway 27 (which becomes Montauk Highway) for approximately 18 miles to the traffic light in Southampton at North Main Street. Turn right onto North Main Street. The B&B is the seventh house on the left.

I love to sit on the lattice-covered brick courtyard draped with clematis and wisteria to sip a cup of coffee in the early morning while I watch the birds flit from branch to branch on the giant sycamore tree. This peaceful place to gather thoughts and daydream is far more effective than taking fistfuls of St.-John's-wort.

Melody and Philip purchased their B&B as part of a wonderfully romantic adventure. They had been high school sweethearts, but over the years they lost touch—until their thirty-year reunion at least. Undeterred by the fact that Melody had a career in the fashion industry in New York and Philip had just moved with his company to Arizona, they slowly wove their lives back together. Late in 1997 they launched a new joint business by purchasing this handsome 1860s house that is on the National Register of Historic Places.

Their home is distinguished by several unusual architectural features. The living room has a brick floor and exposed hand-hewn beams. Its barnwood walls are painted a cheerful butter yellow with white trim, and the ceilings are tall enough to accommodate several large pieces of pine furniture. The dining room, on the other hand, has been painted a "dare red."

The guest rooms are fresh and bright. They are entered along an upstairs hallway that has 11-foot ceilings. Room #3 has yellow walls and carpeting, a four-poster rice bed, and an English wardrobe. The terrific bath has exposed beams, a skylight, and white tile walls. Room #2, which has a cathedral ceiling, is done in black-and-white toile accented with a black-and-white stripe. There's a steel canopy bed and an antique wardrobe, as well as a cathedral ceiling with exposed beams.

Melody and Phil serve a full breakfast that might include a fluffy herb omelette with fresh tomatoes and cheese, along with homemade breads and jams and fresh fruits and juices.

The grounds are as lovely as the house. There are perennial beds next to brick pathways throughout the luxuriant lawns. In a secluded spot surrounded by a lattice fence, there's a beautiful pool with a brick apron.

What's Nearby

See "What's Nearby—Southampton," page 241.

Mainstay

579 Hill Street
Southampton, NY 11968
(516) 283–4375

FAX: (516) 287–6240
WEB SITE: www.hamptons.com/mainstay
INNKEEPER: Elizabeth Main

ROOMS: 8, including 2 suites, 5 with private bath and 3 sharing one bath; 5 with robes; 3 with TV and VCR; 1 with a fireplace

ON THE GROUNDS: Parking; swimming pool; gardens

EXTRAS: Decanter of sherry in guest room

RATES: $125–$350, double occupancy, including full or Continental breakfast; two-night minimum weekends May–October

CREDIT CARDS ACCEPTED: American Express, MasterCard, Visa

OPEN: Year-round

HOW TO GET THERE: From New York City take I–495 (the Long Island Expressway) to exit 70 (Manorville) and follow Route 111 south to Highway 27 (Sunrise Highway). Follow Highway 27 (which becomes County Road 39) east to Southampton University. At Tuckahoe Road, turn right and continue to Old Montauk Highway (Route 27A and Hill Street). Continue for ½ mile to the B&B, which will be on the left.

Although the shingled house on the outskirts of Southampton has been a B&B since 1985, it wasn't until Elizabeth Main began adding her clever and artistic wizardry in 1992 that it took on its alluring appeal. The house itself is an 1870s Colonial with a weathered-shingle exterior and white trim. Previously a country store for many years, it sits well back from the street behind a picket fence on an acre of land that's alive with flower gardens punctuated by secluded bowers with benches.

Elizabeth is a potter and artist who formerly was a photo stylist in New York. She has cleverly taken a simple house with narrow hallways and transformed it into a cute and hospitable B&B. This is not an elegant and fancy B&B, but one that is very comfortable and welcoming—the sort of place where you might sit with a cup of tea in the afternoon and curl up before the fire in the parlor or use it as a base for a weekend bicycle ride.

When you enter the foyer of the house, you'll see sponge-painted walls in spring green and flowers fancifully climbing the door frames. Over the entrance to the front parlor, there's an arrangement of dried flowers. The front parlor has bead board ceilings and a fireplace. In the country dining room, one side is dominated by a huge old woodstove, while another has a pine country cupboard displaying a colorful collection of Elizabeth's pottery. The walls here are sponged an ochre color, and there are grapes, apples, and pears painted across the walls above the wainscotting.

Guests are welcome to enter the bright, open, and light country kitchen at any time, and it would be a shame if they didn't. Painted across one wall is a marvelous mural of English climbing roses. In a little pantry off the kitchen, shelves hold stacks of Elizabeth's cups, saucers, bowls, and plates, ready to be used for breakfast or afternoon snacks.

The guest rooms are equally artistic. Room #5, the large master suite, has its own woodburning fireplace, a king-size iron bed, and a pine armoire. There are built-in shelves of books and in the bath, a clawfoot tub. In Room #6, there's an iron and brass bed and a pine armoire amid walls painted all over with climbing hydrangeas. The bath is modern and charming with bead board walls and ceiling and a clawfoot tub. Room #8 is the newest creation. In what was formerly the attic, Elizabeth has built a two-room suite. It has slanted ceilings, walls sponge-painted in yellow and gold, antique iron beds, lace curtains, and a skylight. One room has a cloud-filled sky on the ceiling. It has a terrific bath with wainscot walls. Other rooms have mirrors with wild dots, squiggles, and dashes splashed on the frame. Of the eight guest rooms, five have private baths, and the other three share one bath.

A Continental breakfast is served buffet-style. Cereals, fruits, and juices are set out on a sideboard and on the huge pine table in the center of the room. On weekends Elizabeth prepares a waffle batter that she sets on the old woodstove so that guests may prepare waffles at their leisure.

There's a swimming pool behind the house surrounded by a tall fence. The front porch holds wicker chairs, and there's plenty of parking for guest cars.

What's Nearby

See "What's Nearby—Southampton," page 241.

The 1708 House

126 Main Street
Southampton, NY 11968
(516) 287–1708

FAX: (516) 287–3593

INNKEEPERS: Skip and Lorraine Ralph; managers: Pete Reyer and Bernadette Meade

ROOMS: 12, including 3 suites and 3 cottages, all with private bath, air conditioning, TV, and telephone; 9 with desks; 2 cottages with mini-refrigerator and coffeemaker; 1 with VCR

ON THE GROUNDS: Parking

EXTRAS: Cheese and wine in afternoon

RATES: $165–$395, double occupancy, including Continental or full breakfast; two-night minimum weekends in May, June, September, and October; three-night minimum weekends in July and August; four-night minimum holiday weekends

CREDIT CARDS ACCEPTED: American Express, MasterCard, Visa

OPEN: Year-round

HOW TO GET THERE: From New York City take I-495 (the Long Island Expressway) to exit 70 (Manorville) and follow Route 111 south to Highway 27 (Sunrise Highway). Follow Highway 27 (which becomes County Road 39) east to Southampton. Turn right onto North Sea Road, which becomes Main Street, and proceed to #126, which will be on the left.

Antiques and historic houses go together, so antiques dealers who open B&Bs have definitely found their calling. Skip and Lorraine Ralph owned a bed-and-breakfast in Pittsburgh (where Skip was raised). Since they had also lived on Long Island for some time and had often spent summers in the Hamptons, they decided to open a B&B there for their next venture. Was it an uncanny instinct or fate that led them to their discovery of the rambling old house on Main Street?

The 1708 House is one of the most historic in Southampton, yet in 1993 it was in such disastrous shape that it didn't look as if it could possibly see 1994. There were squatters living in the cottages in back, the weeds were as high as a sly fox's eye, the foundation was crumbling, and the roof was falling in. Yet, Skip and Lorraine Ralph saw possibilities, particularly since it was on the village's premiere street and next door to a Saks Fifth Avenue store.

Thanks to the Ralphs' foresight and perseverance (it took three years to obtain the necessary permits), they are now proprietors of a classy new B&B in a historic old shell. From top to bottom, the B&B is fabulous.

In the living room, there are polished pine floors, an oak mantel over the woodburning fireplace, and tapestry-covered wing chairs. The library has pine floors, exposed hand-hewn oak beams, and a wood-burning fireplace. The dining room has burnished original beams and a ceiling of exposed floorboards. French doors lead to a spacious patio. Individual tables are used for games of cards in the evening and for breakfast in the morning. All the antiques are supplied from the couple's antiques shop around the corner, and are available for purchase.

Each of the nine guest rooms and three cottages is spacious and luxurious. Room #8, for example, has a wonderful, tall four-poster wheat-carved bed and a fabulous antique Governor Winthrop slant-top desk with a serpentine front and hidden compartments. One contains a note that a previous owner had written. It says, "Purch May, 1956. $91.90." This particular piece is now priced at $1,050.

My favorite rooms are the two in the front part of the oldest section of the house, although occupants of these may hear more street noise than those in the back. Room #2 is a two-bedroom suite that includes the original paneled walls and beamed ceiling. There's a needlepoint rug on the polished pine floor. The paneling in the second bedroom is painted with a garden of wisteria, pansies, tulips, and daffodils. Room #1 also has a paneled wall that includes a green pigment paint that is original to the early eighteenth century. In the bath the original knee braces have been exposed. There are three restored cottages in back, two with eat-in kitchens.

Downstairs, the utterly romantic wine cellar features brick walls, a terrific brick fireplace, and a tile floor. Old hand-hewn beams are supported by peeled locust posts. At one end, a bar is set up, and classical music gently plays while wine and cheese are served every afternoon.

On weekday mornings, guests may help themselves to croissants, bagels, juices, fruits, and coffee or tea. On Saturday and Sunday mornings, the Continental breakfast is supplemented by a quiche Lorraine (in honor of the innkeeper).

Besides offering shopping in the nearby excellent boutiques, galleries, shops, and ateliers, the B&B is close to ocean beaches and to Agawam Park, where concerts take place throughout the summer. The Parrish Art Museum has a fine collection of American Impressionist paintings, many of which were painted in the Hamptons.

What's Nearby

See "What's Nearby—Southampton," page 241.

Spencertown Country House, a Bed & Breakfast

1909 County Road 9
(mailing address: P.O. Box 279)
Spencertown, NY 12165
(888) 727–9980 or (518) 392–5292

FAX: (518) 392–7453

E-MAIL: info@spencertowncntryhouse.com

WEB SITE: www.spencertowncntryhouse.com

INNKEEPERS: Heather and John Spitzer

ROOMS: 8, all with private bath, air conditioning, and radio; wheelchair access

ON THE GROUNDS: On 5 acres with parking and gardens

EXTRAS: Afternoon tea and cookies; croquet

RATES: $60–$150, double occupancy, including full breakfast; two-night minimum weekends in July, August, and October, as well as on holiday weekends

CREDIT CARDS ACCEPTED: American Express, MasterCard, V isa

OPEN: February–December

HOW TO GET THERE: From New York City, take the Henry Hudson Parkway north to the Saw Mill River Parkway north, and then follow the Taconic Parkway north. Take the exit marked Austerlitz/Chatham/Route 203 and follow Route 203 for ½ mile. Turn left onto County Route 9 at East Chatham/Red Rock sign. The B&B is ⁹/₁₀ mile farther on the left.

Spencertown is a tiny village in the far eastern portion of the Hudson River Valley and in the foothills of the Berkshire Mountains. Your internal agenda might require some time out. If so, this is the perfect place to come to sit on the porch with a good book or to enjoy the beautiful gardens. On the other hand, there are excellent hiking trails nearby and back roads to explore by bicycle or car. Or you might visit the antiques shop in town. The Spencertown Art and Antiques Shop is a big, reasonably priced, eclectic store in a huge old building that's brimming with all sorts of items.

The Spencertown Country House was built in stages from 1803 to 1877. It was originally a simple farmhouse, but subsequent expansions gave it a curious Federal/Victorian appearance. Until the 1950s it served as the centerpiece of a productive farm, but it eventually was converted to a lodge noted for weddings and celebrations. It was purchased by the Spitzers in 1996. Following a total renovation they opened it as a B&B in 1997.

The pretty white-clapboard house with black shutters sits amidst gardens well back from the road. A wonderful columned porch across the back with a beadboard ceiling is furnished with wicker chairs and tables. An old oak sewing machine is used as a table.

Guests enter into a living room with wide-plank pine floors topped by Oriental rugs and a fireplace with a wooden mantel. A piano waits for a player. A parlor also has pine floors, but these are covered by kilims. There's a curved glass cabinet and a slate fireplace mantel.

The guest rooms have been beautifully furnished with antiques. One of my favorites is Gunda's Room, a room in which the Spitzers have ragged the walls in periwinkle blue. There's a blue-and-white striped duvet on the bed and a pretty oak armoire holds clothes. The bath has a painted blue floor and blue-and-white decorative tiles. Pierson has a four-poster bed and a painted beige floor, while Fisher has a taupe painted floor and a green-and-white check fabric on a Jenny Lind bed.

Heather prepares a full breakfast, which is served in the formal dining room. She might include French toast or perhaps blueberry buttermilk pancakes or a vegetable and cheese omelette in her menu.

What's Nearby—Spencertown

The Spencertown Academy is a 150-year-old schoolhouse that's on the National Register of Historic Places. You can purchase art or craft items in one of its galleries, or attend one of the fabulous folk or classical concerts held here. You might also attend a delightful Broadway-style musical at the charming Mac-Hayden Theatre-in-the-Round in nearby Chatham. Visit the Shaker Museum in Old Chatham or attend a concert at the Mount Lebanon Shaker Village. The area abounds with places to hike, cross-country ski, bicycle, and mountain bike, as well as fish in local streams. There's downhill skiing at Catamount. A bit farther afield, you could attend a concert by the Boston Symphony Orchestra at Tanglewood in Lenox, Massachusetts; visit the Norman Rockwell Museum in Stockbridge, Massachusetts; or spend a day at Hancock Shaker Village in Hancock, Massachusetts. (See also Canaan.)

Lakehouse Inn On Golden Pond

Shelley Hill Road
Stanfordville, NY 12581
(914) 266–8093

FAX: (914) 266–4051
E-MAIL: judy@lakehouseinn.com
WEB SITE: www.lakehouseinn.com
INNKEEPER: Judy Kohler

ROOMS: 10, including 8 suites, all with private bath, air conditioning, TV, VCR, telephone, stereo, coffeemaker, mini-refrigerator, robes, and CD player; 7 with wet-bar, balcony or patio, fireplace, and whirlpool tub

ON THE GROUNDS: On 22 acres with parking; lake swimming, boating, and fishing

EXTRAS: Turndown with truffles; bottled water, soft drinks, appetizer baskets provided in each room; fax, computer, copy machine available

RATES: $125–$650, double occupancy, including full breakfast; two-night minimum weekends; three-night minimum holiday weekends.

CREDIT CARDS ACCEPTED: MasterCard and Visa

OPEN: Year-round

HOW TO GET THERE: From New York City, take the Henry Hudson Parkway north to the Saw Mill River Parkway north and then follow the Taconic Parkway north. Take the exit marked Red Hook/Pine Plains/Route 199 and follow Route 199 west for ⁵/₁₀ mile. Take the first right onto Route 53 south and go 3½ miles. Turn right onto Shelley Hill Road and go exactly ⁹/₁₀ mile. Turn onto paved driveway. The Lakehouse Inn is at the end of the road.

When hearts turn to romance, few B&Bs can match the dreamy cocoons Judy Kohler has created for guests. Each is so huge and so secluded from one another that they feel like individual cottages sequestered away on private islands.

At first sight the cedar-sided house appears modest and unremarkable; even when we walked along the flying-bridge walkway to the entrance, we were unprepared for the gracious and urbane interior. The house envelops its guests in country charm but also offers luxurious and spacious private retreats. For a total getaway from the fast-paced city, I can't imagine a more relaxing sanctuary.

The living room is decorated with flair in gentle earth tones. The vaulted, rough-sawn pine ceiling and the wall of windows offering unobstructed views of tiny Golden Pond give the room a warm, inviting glow. It's furnished with antiques, Oriental rugs on oak floors, twig furniture, comfortable sofas, piles of magazines and books, and an ornately carved oak English bar on which Victorian flow blue china is displayed. It's surrounded by a wraparound deck with twig furniture overlooking the lake.

Each of the suties seems more amorous, more seductive, and more sybaritic than the last. The Casablanca Suite has its own fireplace laid with logs ready to be lighted and a private deck. There's a pink damask sofa on which to watch the flames with a loved one while sipping a glass of chilled wine. The canopy bed is swathed in lace. A TV, VCR, and CD player hide in a pine armoire. In the bath, a Jacuzzi for two has a serene view and is surrounded by a lip holding an array of fat candles. The equally spacious Master Suite, located downstairs, has a private deck offering a view of the lake. Oriental rugs cover oak floors, another lace canopy decorates the bed, fat shutters shield the windows, and the pink-tile bath has another Jacuzzi.

Every possible amenity is provided. As Judy explained, "We're so far out in the country that it's too far to go for a soft drink at a store, so we provide all of that in the room." Should guests wish to watch a movie on their in-room VCR, an extensive library offers nearly 150 options. In addition to soft drinks, the in-room refrigerators are stocked with bottled water, appetizers such as smoked salmon, and even Baby Watson cheesecakes (or perhaps a special treat prepared by Judy) in case someone has a late-night sweet-tooth craving. Snack baskets contain candy bars, cookies, potato chips, and more. Luscious truffles are offered at bedside.

In the morning, breakfast is delivered to the room in a covered basket. It may include cheese blintzes or French toast with cream cheese and pecans topped with an apricot sauce or heart-shaped frittatas with croissants. Of course, there will also be fresh fruit and freshly baked breads.

If guests do decide to venture forth, they will find rowboats and paddleboats for use on the lake, and swimming or fishing are also popular. There are hammocks and chaise longues on each of the decks and hiking trails cut through the twenty-two-acre property. Historic mansions, local wineries, and superb restaurants are located nearby.

What's Nearby—Stanfordville

Stanfordville is located just outside Rhinebeck. The Old Rhinebeck Aerodome, filled with vintage airplanes dating from 1908 to 1937, is one of the most interesting and unusual museums in the state. You can even take a ride in an open-cockpit biplane. Visit Montgomery Place in nearby Annandale-on-Hudson, a twenty-three-room, 1804 Livingston family mansion on a 434-acre estate, where you can walk nature trails and pick your own apples in season. (See also Millbrook and Rhinebeck.)

Westhampton Country Manor Best Buy

28 Jagger Lane
Westhampton Beach, NY 11977
(888) 288–5540 or (516) 288–9000

FAX: (516) 288–3292

E-MAIL: innkeeper@
hamptonsbb.com

WEB SITE: www.hamptonsbb.com/the manor

INNKEEPERS: Susan and Bill Dalton

ROOMS: 6, including 1 three-bedroom, two-bath cottage, all with private bath, air conditioning, telephone on private line, answering machine, TV, and radio; 1 with fireplace, porch, whirlpool tub, and coffeemaker

ON THE GROUNDS: On 2½ acres with parking; swimming pool; Har-Tru tennis court; gardens

EXTRAS: Plain-paper fax, copier, computer with modem available; notary public; a cat named Jill on premises; soda, bottled water, beer, and wine in guest refrigerator

RATES: $99–$225, double occupancy, or $79–$205, single occupancy, depending on season, with full breakfast; two-night minimum weekends; three-night minimum holiday weekends in spring, summer, and fall

CREDIT CARDS ACCEPTED: American Express, MasterCard, Visa

OPEN: Year-round

HOW TO GET THERE: From New York City take I–495 (the Long Island Expressway) to exit 70 (Manorville) and follow Route 111 south to Highway 27 (Sunrise Highway). Follow Highway 27 to exit 63 and go south on Old Riverhead Road to Highway 27A (Montauk Highway). Turn right (west) onto Montauk Highway and continue for 2 miles. Turn left onto Jagger Lane. The B&B is on the corner of Jagger Lane and South Country Road.

You can almost hear the hoofbeats of the horses and the passengers alighting from the stagecoach to refresh themselves at this former stagecoach stop, located on a quiet country lane. The handsome buff-colored Colonial clapboard house has seen numerous changes since it began life in 1810. In 1865, a wing was added to accommodate the waiting room and office of Dr. Jagger, for whom the nearby street is named. The 2½ acres still contain a picturesque old green barn and a cottage that also date to this period.

Westhampton Beach has the advantage of being the closest Hampton to New York City, and it is also near magnificent ocean beaches, outstanding restaurants, and peaceful bicycling and walking lanes. When Bill and Susan Dalton sought a lifestyle change after retiring (he as Deputy Commissioner for the New York City Department of Parks and she as a physician's assistant), they knew they wanted to open a B&B. The old homestead and outbuildings had been on the market for some time but were in reasonably good condition.

Today the manor house is a treasure-chest of antiques and interesting architecture. In the living room, there are oak floors, wainscotted walls, and sofas covered in floral fabrics sitting before a fireplace with a painted wooden mantel. French doors lead to a pretty porch with wicker chairs and a profusion of plants. On the grand piano rest a vase of fresh flowers, a Tiffany-style lamp, and a silver tray holding stemmed glasses and a decanter filled with an evening cordial. The separate TV room is so homelike that you feel comfortable eating popcorn and putting your feet up. A VCR and video library keep guests entertained for hours.

As an added plus, Susan and Bill Dalton have created a B&B that offers all the amenities a business traveler may need, including a comfortable office with ample desk space, a computer with a modem, a fax, and a copy machine. Shelves of books line one wall. This was once Dr. Jagger's office, and there's a handsome piece of stained glass here that dates to his time.

The guest rooms are equipped with antiques and featherbeds, and all the baths have been updated to reflect the needs of today's travelers. Room #1 has an antique spool bed, while #2 has an iron and brass bed with a pink-and-green quilt. Room #4 has a green iron bed.

Convivial conversation is assured in the dining room, which has a round table surveyed by a stained-glass chandelier. Susan bakes all her own breakfast scones, muffins, and cinnamon rolls. She also prepares a generous fruit plate and fixes entrees such as Dutch babies or a gourmet French toast made with coarse bread that's soaked overnight in a batter and then placed on top of fresh fruit in a casserole and baked.

There's a 20- x 40-foot heated swimming pool surrounded by a picket fence, a Har-Tru tennis court, and a three-bedroom, two-bath cottage on the property.

Westhampton Beach maintains two splendid ocean beaches (fee to park) with a pavilion offering rest rooms, showers, and concession stands. The pretty village Main Street is home to craft and antiques shops as well as restaurants and boutiques. The Quogue Wildlife Refuge in nearby Quogue is a wonderful place to take children. There are nature trails, scores of tame deer and ducks, and a refuge where rescued animals are nursed back to health. (See also Southampton.)

All Tucked Inn

Best Buy

53 South Main Street
(mailing address: P. O. Box 324)
Westport, NY 12993
(888) ALL–TUCK or
(518) 962–4400

FAX: (518) 962–4400
E-MAIL: haley+@westelcom.com
WEB SITE: www.alltuckedinn.com
INNKEEPERS: Tom Haley and
Claudia Ryan

ROOMS: 9, including 1 suite, all with private bath and radio; 3 with fireplace and desk

ON THE GROUNDS: On 2 acres with parking; gardens, yard

EXTRAS: Three collies, Turk, Aly, and Kelsey on premises

RATES: $65–$110, double occupancy, including full breakfast; two-night minimum weekends in summer and fall

CREDIT CARDS ACCEPTED: None

OPEN: Year-round

HOW TO GET THERE: From I–87 (the Northway) take exit 31 (Westport/Elizabethtown) and then follow Route 9N south for 4 miles to the village of Westport. Bear right onto Route 22 south at the village center. Route 22 is Main Street, and the B&B will be on the right.

Westport is located along a natural terrace encircling a deep bay off Lake Champlain. It developed as a fashionable resort in the late nineteenth century, and the stately homes with wide lawns and gardens, many of them fronted by ornamental iron fences and gates, have been well maintained over the years.

All Tucked Inn, a Dutch Colonial dating to 1872, was built to accommodate the staff of the old Westport Hotel, a grand structure that used to be located in Ballard Park. Tom and Claudia turned it into a bed-and-breakfast in 1993. This cozy B&B with its even cozier name is across from Ballard Park, which is on Lake Champlain.

With a name like this, you just know you're going to find comfortable beds dressed with lovely linens. You'll notice right away the beautiful quilts that cover each bed. I especially love #17, the suite. It has emerald green walls and a woodburning fireplace in the living room. The bedroom contains a bed with a wedding ring quilt and a cutwork duvet, as well as another woodburning fireplace. A crocheted topper covers a round end table. The floors are carpeted, so they are soft under foot and muffle sounds. Room #20 has a blue quilt and dormer windows.

The living room is comfortable and warm. There are sofas and wing chairs near the gas fireplace and books in a glass-fronted oak cabinet. Plump pillows can be tucked just right.

Breakfast is served in a formal dining room enhanced by oak chairs with pressed backs and colorful tablecloths. Tom is chef and he will prepare an egg dish as well as a bread entree such as blueberry pancakes or French toast. There will be freshly baked muffins and breads and fresh fruit. You'll certainly tuck into this hearty breakfast, and you may wish you could stay for several more days.

What's Nearby—Westport

Westport is located on Lake Champlain and near the Adirondack Mountains. On summer weekends you can listen to a concert in the village park or attend a show at the Depot Theatre. There's a lakeside beach for swimming and a marina for boating. Hiking, biking, golfing, and fishing are nearby. In winter there are excellent cross-country ski and snowmobile trails. (See also Crown Point.)

Albergo Allegria

Route 296
(mailing address: P.O. Box 267)
Windham, NY 12496
(800) 625–2374 or (518) 734–5560

FAX: (518) 734–5570

E-MAIL: mail@AlbergoUSA.com

WEB SITE: www.AlbergoUSA.com

INNKEEPERS: Lenore & Vito Radelich and Marianna & Leslie Leman

ROOMS: 21, including 6 suites, all with private bath, TV, VCR, and telephone; 9 with air conditioning; 8 with fireplace; 7 with balcony or deck; 6 with whirlpool tub; CD or tape player, iron, and ironing board; 5 with desk; 2 rooms with wheelchair access; cribs available

ON THE GROUNDS: On 2 acres with parking; wooden deck overlooking the river; gazebo; wildflower and herb gardens

EXTRAS: Afternoon tea on Saturdays and holidays with homemade cookies, hot chocolate, and spiced cider; fax, copier, modem hookup for business travelers; one "smiling" Samoyed named Shalom and a white bunny named Sunday

RATES: $65–$250, double occupancy, including full breakfast and afternoon refreshments; two-night minimum weekends; three-night minimum holidays

CREDIT CARDS ACCEPTED: MasterCard and Visa

OPEN: Year-round

HOW TO GET THERE: From I–87 (the New York State Thruway), take exit 21 (Catskill) and follow Route 23 west for 23 miles to Route 296. At the intersection, turn left (south) and go ¹/₁₀ mile. The B&B is on the left opposite La Griglia restaurant.

The air was crisp, leaves rested in piles beside the road, the mood was expectant. How else could it be when you're coming to a B&B whose names means "inn of happiness" in Italian?

Every time I visit Albergo Allegria, some wonderful new improvements have been made. The B&B, which is composed of two 1876 boarding houses joined together, is the creation of Lenore and Vito Radelich, who were the owners of La Griglia, the Italian restaurant across the street for many years. They are now ably assisted in their B&B venture by their daughter Marianna and her husband, Leslie. The B&B sits on two acres on the Batavia Kill

Creek, where the original Johnny Weismueller Tarzan movie was filmed in the 1920s.

In 1996 the family converted the carriage house into five luxurious suites. Each has a gas fireplace, whirlpool tub, king-size bed, and 15-foot ceilings with skylights. They are romantic and spacious.

The suites and rooms in the main part of the B&B are decorated in pine and oak. Each of the rooms is named for a month or season. July has a mini-cathedral ceiling with stained-glass windows, lace curtains, and an oak wardrobe and chest, while Summer has a king-size bed and an enormous double whirlpool tub in the bath.

The B&B has several cozy sitting areas. The downstairs parlor has a cherrywood mantel over the fireplace, and this is where afternoon tea is served. Upstairs, there's another parlor with a fireplace and a TV and VCR as well as an extensive video library. A lovely gift shop is located off the lobby.

Breakfast is served in the dining room, which has individual tables and oak chairs with pressed backs. Vito prepares incredible breakfasts. He may fix an Italian frittata or Belgian waffles, served with fresh whipped cream and berries, or spiced French toast.

In 1998 a gazebo was added to the gardens, where smokers are encouraged to indulge themselves. In addition, since a white bunny by the name of Sunday came to live at the B&B, the innkeepers decided he needed an appropriate home as well. Therefore, a delightful handcrafted "bunny mansion" was constructed. The elaborate house has real windows, flower boxes filled with flowers, and twinkle lights, and it's surrounded by a white picket fence. What more could a bunny desire?

The B&B offers ski packages and dinner packages in concert with the restaurant across the street as well as quiet-season packages.

What's Nearby–Windham

Albergo Allegria is located in the Catskill Mountains. Ski Windham is 1 mile away; Hunter Mountain is 7 miles; cross-country skiing takes place about a mile from the B&B. There are tennis and golf facilities next door, and a marvelous restaurant is just across the street. You can take the kids to the Supersonic Speedway Fun Park or the Zoom Flume Water Park in nearby Durham. Farther afield, Woodstock is an artsy village with a past. The famed 1960s rock concert took place near here. The town is still peppered with art galleries and museums, artist studios, and craft shops. Musical events take place in the summer at Byrdcliffe Arts Colony, as do photography exhibits at the the Center for Photography.

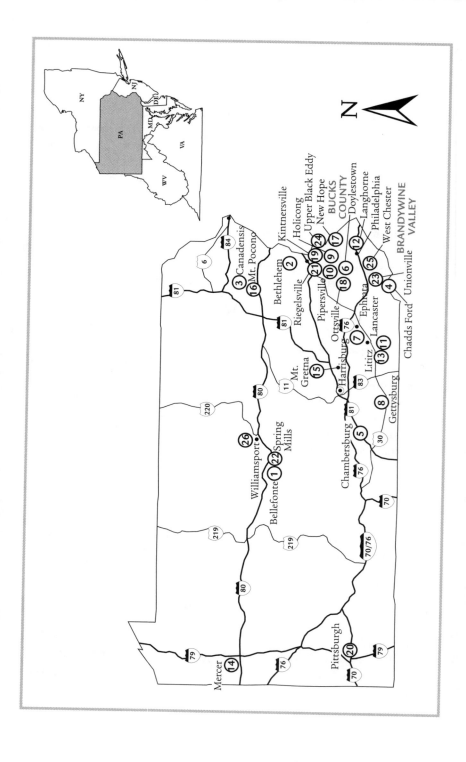

Pennsylvania

Numbers on map refer to towns numbered below.

Reynolds Mansion

Best Buy

101 West Linn Street
Bellefonte, PA 16823
(800) 899–3929 or (814) 353–8407

FAX: (814) 353–1530

E-MAIL: jheidt@bellefonte.com

WEB SITE: http://bellefonte.com/rmbb

INNKEEPERS: Joseph and Charlotte Heidt

ROOMS: 6, all with private bath and air conditioning, 5 with fireplace and Jacuzzi; 2 with desk; 1 with steam shower

ON THE GROUNDS: On 1 acre with gardens and parking

EXTRAS: Evening liqueurs and liquors such as brandy, blackberry brandy, and Jack Daniels; 2 cats named Melbourne and Sydney on premises

RATES: $95–$175, double occupancy, including full breakfast; two-night minimum on some Penn State weekends

CREDIT CARDS ACCEPTED: American Express, MasterCard, Visa

OPEN: Year-round

HOW TO GET THERE: From I–80 traveling east, take exit 24. Follow Route 26 toward Bellefonte until it reaches Route 550. At the junction with Route 550, turn right. Follow Route 550 to the third light and turn right onto Allegheny Street. Go to the second light and turn left onto Linn Street. Enter through the iron gates on the right to the inn's parking lot.

Is romance on your mind? Then come to the Reynolds Mansion and allow yourself to be carried away to the late nineteenth century, when gentlemen and ladies lived a luxurious life in grand and elegant mansions.

When you walk into a building as spectacular as the Reynolds Mansion, there's a sense of wonderment and joy. The twenty-seven-room 1885 high-Victorian home is so incredibly beautiful that you feel it should be a permanent decorator showcase, and in a sense it is—for those fortunate enough to stay here. It is constructed of red sandstone and has a combination of Gothic, Italianate, and Queen Anne styles, in a vaguely Richardsonian manner. Although a circular extension was added in 1901, it blends with the house as though it was there all along.

The house was built by Major William Frederick Reynolds, a wealthy businessman and banker (iron ore was the big local industry) who incorporated the finest materials of the day into his edifice. There are 12-foot ceilings on both the first and second floors, and incredibly, the walnut-paneled walls and ceiling in the vestibule (which also has a marble floor) have never been painted, nor have the doors (there are several sets of pocket doors) or moldings throughout the house. The most remarkable features of the house, however, in my opinion, are the floors. They are intricately inlaid in a variety of woods and patterns, and they remain in excellent condition.

The house contains some lovely common rooms. There's a large living room with a fireplace, as well as a billiards room, which also has a fireplace and a coffered Chippendale-style plaster ceiling that overlooks a slate billiards table. My favorite, however, is the snuggery or library, a cozy and intimate little room with another fireplace, where evening cordials are available. The dining room features an intricate floor of maple, mahogany, and walnut. Throughout, there are elegant antiques.

The guest rooms are equally beautiful. One of the most romantic is Louise's Cherub Room, which has an iron bed, a fireplace, and a patterned wood floor. There's a charming painting of cherubs on the ceiling, and a heart-shaped whirlpool tub is overseen by a beautiful chandelier. The Colonel's Green Room is more masculine. It has an iron canopy bed and a fireplace, as well as a black whirlpool tub in the room. It's lavishly decorated in green and brown Ralph Lauren fabrics.

Guests at the Reynolds Mansion will be served coffee and warm muffins outside their door when they are ready to rise. A full breakfast is served in the dining room. It may include poached pears with raspberry sauce, a baked French toast stuffed with cream cheese and apples and served with sausage, and a mini-Danish to finish the meal.

Joe and Charlotte Heidt, the caretakers of the house and the warm and friendly innkeepers, take great pride in showing off their B&B and their town. Both Penn State alums, they are intimately familiar with the area and love to advise their guests about things to do.

What's Nearby—Bellefonte

You might think that "what's nearby" can be summed up in two words— Penn State—but not true. In addition to all the activities on the campus, you can go downhill skiing at Tussey Mountain or see a play or concert, or attend a dinner-theater at the beautifully restored Garman Opera House. Be sure to save time, however, for a self-guided walking tour of this historic village and its wealth of wonderful buildings. The town has produced an excellent map complete with interesting histories. Although there are a variety of options for dinner, guests might want to try the historic Gamble Mill, a 1786 stone mill where wonderful French/American cuisine is served in style. (See also Spring Mills.)

Wydnor Hall Inn

Best Buy

3612 Old Philadelphia Pike
Bethlehem, PA 18015
(800) 839–0020 or (610) 867–6851

FAX: (610) 866–2062

INNKEEPERS: Charles and Kristina Taylor; manager: Norma Welsh

ROOMS: 5, including 2 suites, all with private bath, air conditioning, TV, private line telephone with dataport, hair dryer, and robes; cribs available

ON THE GROUNDS: On 2 acres with parking and gardens

EXTRAS: Afternoon tea (charge of $12 per person); room service house breakfast and newspaper; custom labeled sparkling water, pressed 100% cotton sheets, heated towel racks, crystal decanters of sherry and brandy; fax available, meeting room; three outdoor cats

RATES: $75–$140, double occupancy, including Continental breakfast; full breakfast $8.00–$9.00 additional; two-night minimum weekends May, June, September, and October

CREDIT CARDS ACCEPTED: American Express, Diners Club, Discover, MasterCard, Visa

OPEN: Year-round

HOW TO GET THERE: From I–78, take exit 21 (Route 412 Hellertown/Bethlehem) and turn left at the end of the ramp onto Route 412 south (this is Main Street, Hellertown). At the fourth traffic light, make a right onto Water Street. In about 1 mile, bear left at the V in the road, then continue 1 mile and turn right at Black River Road. Cross Route 378 at the traffic light. At the stop sign make a left onto Old Philadelphia Pike. Wydnor Hall is ¼ mile farther on the right.

Bethlehem was settled in 1741 by German immigrants who fled Moravia in current-day Czechoslovakia. The area rapidly became an important agricultural center. The Moravians were ingenious, industrious, and cultured, and several of the early Moravian buildings remain in Bethlehem's historic district.

Wydnor Hall is 3 miles south of Bethlehem. You'll know you've reached the right place when you see the American, Hungarian, and Pennsylvania flags gaily hanging at the front door. The handsome 1800s Georgian fieldstone manor house was restored by Charles and Kristina Taylor in 1988. Charles is a retired Bethlehem Steel executive, and Kristina a Hungarian-born artist. Examples of her extraordinary, luminous ceramic pieces will be found on display throughout the B&B, and the oversized cups and saucers she designs are used at breakfast.

The joy of being around this extraordinary couple is that their sense of curiosity and their desire to keep learning is infectious. Kristina started designing ceramics because she was fascinated by the process. Charles started baking because he loved the French bread he'd eaten in France and he couldn't find anything similar in America. Together, they poured their hearts and souls into this old house to create a B&B to equal the manor house inns they enjoyed so much in Europe. It's a serene and elegant retreat on two landscaped acres.

The living room has European oil paintings hanging on creamy ivory walls. A fireplace with a wavy wooden mantel warms the room in winter. A broad selection of books, many of which are leather bound, is available; cut crystal decanters of sherry and brandy sit beside stemmed glasses on a silver tray. Afternoon tea—which includes small sandwiches, light pastries, and a selection of teas—is served every afternoon for an additional charge of $12 per person. Guests generally sit at individual tables draped with heirloom cutwork cloths and eat on either the antique Herend or the Limoges china. The dining room is equally comfortable and inviting, enhanced by two magnificent Waterford crystal chandeliers and Oriental rugs on parquet floors.

The guest rooms are charmingly decorated with antiques and family heirlooms. Beds have handmade quilts and canopies; there are upholstered window seats. The South Room has lacy curtains, drapes made from a quilt, a pretty alcove with a desk, and a window seat. There's a stained-glass window in the bath. The North Suite has a tapestry headboard and a painted blanket chest. The marvelous bath is entered through double doors. It has a marble floor, tall ceilings, and a shower that converts to a steam bath.

Breakfast at Wydnor Hall is served in the dining room. It will consist of coffee, a glass of freshly squeezed orange juice, a selection of seasonal fruit with homemade yogurt, and several of Charles's freshly baked breads such as scones, muffins, or a European crusty roll, along with French fruit preserves. A hot entree, such as Irish oatmeal pancakes with Swedish lingonberries and maple syrup or an herb and cream cheese omelette with Lancaster County cured bacon, will be prepared on weekends for an additional charge.

What's Nearby—Bethlehem

At the Moravian Museum of Bethlehem, visitors see exhibits that illustrate the ideals, arts, and culture of the early Moravians who settled this area. The National Canal Museum at the Hugh Moore Historical Park in Easton has interactive displays that tell the fascinating story of the building and use of America's interlacing canals. There are also mule-drawn canal boat rides and a visit to a locktender's house. The Bach Choir of Bethlehem offers concerts seasonally that attract a large following. Renninger's Antiques and Farmers Market, an extravaganza that often attracts as many as 1,200 dealers, is located in nearby Denver (near Kutztown). The Nazareth International Speedway is nearby, as is the Lehigh Arts Center.

The Brookview Manor B&B Inn

Route 447
(mailing address: RR1, Box 365)
Canadensis, PA 18325
(800) 585–7974 or (570) 595–2451

FAX: (570) 595–5065

INNKEEPER: Mary Anne Buckley

ROOMS: 9, including 1 suite, all with private bath and air conditioning; 2 with Jacuzzi; 1 with fireplace and porch

ON THE GROUNDS: On five acres with hiking trails to "secret waterfall"; parking

EXTRAS: Turndown with chocolates; afternoon tea with cake/cookies

RATES: $110–$150, double occupancy, including full breakfast and afternoon tea

CREDIT CARDS ACCEPTED: American Express, Discover, MasterCard, Visa

OPEN: Year-round

HOW TO GET THERE: From I–80 traveling west go through the Delaware Water Gap toll booth. Then take exit 52 (Marshalls Creek) and make the first left onto Route 447. Follow Route 447 north for 16 miles to the B&B, which will be on the right.

ince Mary Anne Buckley purchased The Brookview Manor B&B Inn in 1995, it's taken on a whole new elegant and classy style. The crisp creamy white clapboard cottage has a forest green porch and shutters, a turret, and dentil trim. The wonderful big porch contains pretty white wicker chairs and tables and a glider with burgundy-and-green-striped cushions. This glider, apparently, has been a feature of the porch for many years, as one couple staying at the B&B brought photographs of themselves on their honeymoon many years earlier sitting on the glider.

The house was built as a summer home in 1911 by a banker from Scranton, and it remained in his family for more than thirty years. Since that time, it has been used as a seasonal summer resort and restaurant, but in the mid-1980s it was converted to a B&B.

The common rooms of the B&B are comfortable and interesting. There are pine floors covered with Oriental and other area rugs The den has a fireplace, while the parlor has another fireplace and a turret with curved-glass windows in which a baby grand piano sits.

The guest rooms include armoires with mirrored fronts and period reproduction four-poster beds of either pine or oak. One of the rooms in the main house has a fireplace. The newest rooms are in a handsome carriage house in back. These three lovely rooms have four-poster cherry beds and two of them (#10 and #11) have whirlpool tubs.

Breakfast is served in a series of pretty rooms. One has a fireplace, and it's furnished with oak tables and chairs; another room has ice cream tables and chairs. A full breakfast is served. Among Mary Ann's most popular entrees are a French toast casserole with sausage, and a ham and egg soufflé.

What's Nearby—Canadensis

The Pocono Mountains near Canadensis are rural and quiet, a bit off the beaten path that attracts the hoards of honeymooners seeking heart-shaped whirlpool tubs and water beds. This quieter and gentler Pocono offers golf courses and ski areas. Beautiful Lake Wallenpaupack has opportunities for boating and swimming, as does Promised Land State Park. The Pocono Playhouse in Mountainhome presents a long summer season of Broadway-style plays.

Hedgerow Bed & Breakfast Suites

268 Kennett Pike (Route 52)
Chadds Ford, PA 19317
(610) 388–6080

FAX: (610) 388–0194
E-MAIL: hedgerowbb@aol.com
WEB SITE: www.bbonline.com/pa/hedgerow
INNKEEPERS: Barbara and John Haedrich
ROOMS: 3 suites, all with private bath, air conditioning, TV, VCR, private line telephone with dataport, mini-refrigerator, hair dryer, desk, robes, iron, and ironing board; 1 with patio, fireplace, tape player, whirlpool tub, and microwave
ON THE GROUNDS: On 3½ acres with gardens; parking
EXTRAS: Snacks set on sideboard every afternoon; freshly baked cookies; turndown with chocolates
RATES: $135–$175, double occupancy, including full breakfast; two-night minimum
CREDIT CARDS ACCEPTED: American Express, MasterCard, Visa
OPEN: Year-round
HOW TO GET THERE: From I–95 take the exit onto Route 322 west. Continue on Route 322 for 7 miles to U.S. Route 1. Turn left onto Route 1 and follow this for 6 miles. At the intersection with Route 52 turn left. The B&B is ¼ mile farther on the right. Look for two large ivy-covered stone pillars at the entrance.

We longed for a weekend away in the beautiful Brandywine Valley. We would visit Winterthur Museum and Gardens and Longwood Gardens and also spend time at Nemours, the beautiful duPont mansion that is now open to the public. We would stay at Hedgerow Bed & Breakfast Suites, the lovely converted carriage house just off the Kennett Pike, in the heart of the lush chateau country of southeastern Pennsylvania.

The suites at Hedgerow are in an enormous 1860s post-and-beam barn/carriage house. John and Barbara live in the 1906 Victorian house in front, but the carriage house is in a peaceful spot in back, surrounded by lovely gardens, as well as holly trees and magnolia trees with huge pink blooms in spring. Massive poplar trees and a magnificent old sycamore add their comforting shade. Guests have the use of a gathering room, which has a gas fireplace and a pretty dining room, where breakfast is served. There's also a beautiful stone and brick patio.

The guest suites are spacious and luxurious. The Longwood Suite is on the ground floor. It has a private entrance with a slate entry and a sitting room with a gas fireplace. French doors lead to the patio. A rich cherrywood parquet floor is enhanced by an Oriental rug, and there's a wet bar with a microwave and a mini-refrigerator. The bedroom has a brass and enamel bed and the bath includes a Jacuzzi for two. The other two suites are located upstairs. Winterthur has two bedrooms—one with a pineapple-post four-poster bed and the other with two antique brass twin beds. Brandywine includes country oak furniture and a canopy bed.

Barbara prepares a full breakfast that will include her freshly baked scones, muffins, or coffee cake and a hot entree. One of her most popular is a baked apple French toast.

What's Nearby—Chadds Ford

Longwood Gardens, the magnificent 350-acre horticultural gardens that were formerly the preserve of Pierre S. duPont, has fantastic displays year-round. The glass-domed conservatories have blooms even on the darkest winter days, and from spring through fall the beautiful outdoor gardens display their wares. Winterthur Museum and Gardens is also located nearby. The former home of Henry Francis duPont contains America's finest and most complete display of decorative arts and antiques. There are 175 period rooms as well as spectacular gardens that cover much of the almost 1,000-acre estate. Chaddsford Winery offers tastings of excellent white and red wines and also a tour of the winery. The Brandywine River Museum, where the Wyeth family paintings are displayed in a Civil War–era grist mill, is in the village of Chadds Ford. (See also Unionville and West Chester.)

The Pennsbury Inn

883 Baltimore Pike
Chadds Ford, PA 19317
(610) 388–1435

FAX: (610) 388–1436
WEB SITE: www.pennsbury.com
INNKEEPERS: Chip Allemann
and James Pine

ROOMS: 5, including 1 suite, all with private bath, air conditioning, TV, telephone with dataport; 3 rooms with fireplace

ON THE GROUNDS: Parking; 8 acres of landscaped grounds, including woodland walking trails; gardens

EXTRAS: Afternoon refreshments; fax and VCR available; two Tibetan terriers named Ying and Yang; guest pets sometimes permitted with prior permission

RATES: $140–$225, double occupancy, including full breakfast and afternoon refreshments; two-night minimum weekends

CREDIT CARDS ACCEPTED: American Express, MasterCard, Visa

OPEN: Year-round

HOW TO GET THERE: From the NJ Turnpike, take exit 2 (Swedesboro). Take Route 322 west approximately 8 miles to the Commodore Barry Bridge and cross into Pennsylvania. Continue on Route 322 west for approximately 8 more miles to Route 1 (Baltimore Pike). Turn left onto Route 1 and travel south. Go through six traffic lights. The B&B is half a mile after the sixth traffic light on the right across from a large white barn.

In the days when horseback riders and dusty stagecoach travel were the norm, the Old Baltimore Pike (Route 1) was the primary link between Philadelphia and Baltimore. Stone taverns housed and fed travelers on their weary journey. Elegant plantation estates, stone villas, and clapboard mansions were joined by this modern new road.

The original portion of the Pennsbury Inn, which is listed on the National Register of Historic Places, was built of blue granite rubble stone from the Brandywine Valley in 1714. It was originally part of a plantation, then it became an inn, a tavern, a tannery, and a stagecoach stop.

The ingenious inspiration for the restoration of the creamy white clapboard-and-brick B&B originated because Chip and James wanted a house to showcase the elegant furniture their firm designs. Their design studio, Trade Secrets, is located just across the street in a big white barn. At Pennsbury Inn, the designs are showcased in complete room settings, and all the furniture is for sale.

Guests enter the B&B through the tavern, which has pine paneled walls and a stucco fireplace flanked by plush red sofas. The TV is hidden behind a cleverly made highboy that appears to hold drawers but instead has a hinged front that slides up to reveal the TV. The library is a blaze of crimson walls, furniture upholstered in red and white toile, and glass-doored cases holding shelves of books. Oil paintings hang on the walls The living room has an enormous arched stone fireplace, a sisal rug, and sofas in rust and green fabrics accented with needlepoint pillows.

The guest rooms are equally elegant. The Winterthur Room, for example, is the one most favored by brides. It has a center Palladian window with a view of the gardens, which include a little waterfall, a grape arbor, and a reflecting pool and pond with koi. Lutens-style benches sit on the clipped lawn under graceful trees. The room is decorated with red-and-cream chinoiserie paper that reaches to the top of the vaulted ceiling. There are Oriental rugs on the sisal-carpeted floors, a hallway lined with bookshelves, a Russian-style birdcage, French bergère chairs upholstered in watermelon, and a beautiful carved chest of drawers. The Longwood Room has twin beds with picket-fence headboards that are dressed in green and white, and in the Daniel Webster Room, there's an original 1749 paneled fireplace mantel and a tiger-maple queen-size bed. The baths are beautifully finished with tile. They have oversized sinks and in some cases, the tubs are surrounded with beadboard.

Breakfast is served in the dining room and also in the living room at a table overlooking the gardens. Fresh flowers dress the tables, which are set with fine china, linens, silver, and crystal. Guest may feast on strawberry pancakes, cinnamon muffins, fresh fruit, and juices. In the afternoon, guests are treated to freshly baked cookies. One time when we were visiting, a batch of coconut macaroons was just emerging from the oven.

What's Nearby

See "What's Nearby—Chadds Ford," page 267.

The Ragged Edge Inn

1090 Ragged Edge Road
(mailing address: P.O. Box 482)
Chambersburg, PA 17201
(888) 900–9555 or (717) 261–1195

FAX: (717) 263–2118

E-MAIL: raggededge@gettysburginns.com

WEB SITE: gettysburginns.com

INNKEEPER: Darlene Elders

ROOMS: 10, including 5 suites, all with private bath, air conditioning, TV, and radio; 8 with telephone; 4 with fireplace and Jacuzzis, CD/tape player, iron, and ironing board; 3 with mini-refrigerator and CD player; 2 with full kitchen and VCR; telephones are located on each floor

ON THE GROUNDS: On 6½ acres with lawns, gardens; parking

EXTRAS: Fax, computer, and copier available; meeting room; laundry room; dry cleaning pickup and delivery; pantry; two cats, Toby and Missy, on premises

RATES: $89–$179, double occupancy; including full candlelight brunch on weekends and full breakfast on weekdays; two-night minimum holiday weekends and all weekends in October

CREDIT CARDS ACCEPTED: American Express, Discover, MasterCard, Visa

OPEN: Year-round

HOW TO GET THERE: From I–81, take Pennsylvania exit 6 onto Route 30 east (Lincoln Way). Follow Route 30 toward Gettysburg for 2.5 miles to Ragged Edge Road. Turn left (north) onto Ragged Edge Road. The B&B is 1 mile on the right.

Innkeeper Darlene Elders has a theme for her bed-and-breakfast, and it goes like this: "If every day were Christmas, our hearts would be filled with loving, giving, caring, and sharing every day—not just at Christmas." So, I had Christmas in June. When I first visited this marvelous B&B, a fully decorated tree graced the grand front-to-back foyer, and others were scattered throughout the B&B—just as they are year-round.

This unique 13,000-square-foot 1900s brick mansion sits on a limestone hilltop surrounded by lawns and gardens. Behind the B&B, there's a 50-foot precipice of ragged rocks that drops to a creek below—giving the B&B its name. Built by Moorhead Kennedy, the president of the Cumberland Valley Railroad and vice president of the Pennsylvania Railroad, the mansion was often the setting for lavish parties. One imagines grand entrances down the three-story chestnut stairway with its elaborately turned spindles while the impressive arched window on the landing provided an impressive backdrop.

Darlene, who is an accountant, purchased the B&B in 1989 and has been restoring it ever since. Although she opened the B&B with one guest room in 1993, she feels it wasn't until 1997 that she could say the house was complete. Now she's working on the gardens.

The furnishings are as elegant as the setting. In the living room—which has rich mahogany walls, oak floors laid on a diagonal, heavy oak doors, and a fireplace with a marble surround—there are overstuffed sofas and chairs and a lovely mahogany china cabinet filled with Darlene's collectibles. The butler's pantry now serves as a guest pantry with a microwave, jars of granola and cookies, and a large plate of fresh fruit. On each floor, there's a refrigerator, a microwave oven, and corn for popping.

The guest rooms have lovely antiques as well. The Kennedy Suite, a favorite with honeymooners, has a brass bed, a fireplace, a rose velvet couch, and a bath with marbleized walls, a pedestal sink, and a whirlpool tub. Darlene calls the Ivy Room the "playful honeymoon" room. The sunny, bright room has a trellis headboard, a hot tub–like whirlpool with a skylight above, and a bath with a real throne and another skylight. The Rose Room has a king-size bed with iron posts and another fireplace. The lovely bath has a pedestal sink with glass knobs and a whirlpool tub.

During the week there's a full breakfast, but on weekends Darlene, who learned her terrific cooking style from her father ("I never use a recipe," she says), fixes a fantastic brunch. Guests eat in the dining room, which has a gorgeous handcarved French oak sideboard and table. Every meal is different, so there's no typical menu, but you may be assured that it will be unique. She will start with a whimsy (she calls it a "decadent")—maybe a chocolate pizza. For an entree she may prepare sherried sausages and eggs over an English muffin with a side dish of herbed potato casserole, but don't count on it. She'll really prepare whatever fits the mood of the day.

What's Nearby—Chambersburg

Chambersburg has the dubious distinction of being the only Northern town burned during the Civil War, and it was raided numerous times. Whitetail Ski Resort and Mountain Biking Center offers sports activities year-round, and the Whitetail Fly Fishing School is renowned as one of the best places to learn to fish for trout and smallmouth bass on the East Coast. In addition, there are about five golf courses within a short drive of the B&B. Wilson College is located in Chambersburg, and it is often the site of lectures and concerts, while the Totem Pole Playhouse, in nearby Fayetteville, mounts summer stock productions. Five antiques malls on Route 30 draw antique hounds from near and far.

Pine Tree Farm

2155 Lower State Road
Doylestown, PA 18901
(215) 348–0632

INNKEEPERS: Ron and Joy Feigles

ROOMS: 3, all with private bath,
air conditioning, telephone,
hair dryer, and desk

ON THE GROUNDS: Parking; swimming pool, pond, 16½ acres of lawns,
gardens, and nature areas

EXTRAS: Afternoon tea, wine, and cookies in the pantry

RATES: $160–$190, double occupancy, including breakfast and afternoon
refreshments; two-night minimum weekends; three-night minimum holiday weekends

CREDIT CARDS ACCEPTED: None

OPEN: Year-round except for Christmas

HOW TO GET THERE: From I–78 in New Jersey, take exit 29 onto I–287 south.
Then take exit 13 onto Route 202 south. Follow Route 202 across the
Delaware River and continue for about 10 miles to Doylestown. Stay on
Route 202 (do not take the Route 202 Bypass). Go through the first traf-
fic light and bear left at the second traffic light onto Court Street. Pine
Tree Farm is approximately 1¼ miles ahead on the left.

I will never forget my first visit to Pine Tree Farm. As I stood beside the
handsome stone farmhouse, admiring the clipped lawns beneath the
apple and pine trees, I sensed I was not alone. There, in the shade of an
apple tree, a pair of deer watched me expectantly, although they soon
resumed their feast of fallen apples. It's this sense of calm and peace that Joy
and Ron Feigles have created, where humans and wildlife live contentedly
side by side, that brings guests back again and again.

Joy and Ron have been welcoming guests to their 1730s fieldstone
manor house since 1987, and it's hard to imagine more gracious hosts. Joy
has a degree in hotel administration, she's a talented decorator, and she
loves to cook. Guests are treated as treasured friends at Pine Tree Farm
rather than as overnight travelers. While we became acquainted, we had a
glass of wine and nibbled on the cheese that had been set out for guests.

The living room, with an abundance of plants, is gracious and charming
and overlooks the pool and the gardens. The dining room has a fireplace in
the corner. The tiny library, which has another fireplace and stacks of

interesting books, is the cozy retreat that I like best. A patchwork cloth in rich velvet colors covers a round table, and puffy love seats face each other in front of the fireplace, which is faced with Mercer tiles. There's a French door that leads to the gardens and to the pond in the distance.

I love the enchanting guest rooms Joy and Ron have created. My favorite is the Pink Room, with its romantic white twig canopy bed draped in a mauve floral chintz. Upstairs a two-room suite has a white iron bed, and a pretty yellow room contains a pine pineapple-post bed and a window seat with views of the pond. The bathroom is stenciled. Each of the rooms has its own personality, but they are all crisp and bright with an abundance of attractive fabrics.

Joy's breakfasts are bountiful and convivial. We started with fresh fruit and homemade granola, a cranberry scone, and coffee cake made from a recipe that Joy's mother had used for years. It's a rich, buttery confection topped with brown sugar and nuts. Joy next served Grand Marnier French toast with maple syrup and German sausage. Other favorite offerings include puffed-apple pancakes and eggs Benedict.

Although we felt removed from all hint of civilization on this low-key estate, we especially appreciate that it's close to the many attractions of Doylestown. There are excellent restaurants nearby as well as antiques shops, boutiques, and museums.

What's Nearby—Doylestown

The James A. Michener Art Museum in Doylestown offers ongoing exhibits for adults and children. See art from the collection of James and Mari Michener and a permanent exhibit that celebrates Michener's contributions to American literature. Next door, the Mercer Museum contains exhibits important to Bucks County, including implements for more than sixty early American trades, such as woodworking and textile manufacturing, as well as Native American tools. The Moravian Pottery and Tile Works in Doylestown was started by Henry Mercer in 1912 to revive Bucks County's 1800s pottery-making industry. The handmade decorated tiles are still being produced and may be purchased at the factory store. There are self-guided tours of the foundry and of the beautiful building that houses it. Fonthill, Henry Mercer's fantastic mansion with 44 rooms, 18 fireplaces, 32 stairwells, and a lavishly embellished interior, was designed by Doylestown's Renaissance man between 1908 and 1910. It's now a National Historic Landmark containing art and decorative arts. It's open to visitors. (See also Holicong and New Hope.)

Clearview Farm Bed & Breakfast

355 Clearview Road
Ephrata, PA 17522
(717) 733-6333

WEB SITE: www.800PaDutch.com

INNKEEPERS: Glenn and Mildred Wissler

ROOMS: 5, all with private bath, air conditioning, and radio; telephone available in living room

ON THE GROUNDS: On 200 acres with parking; pond with swans and ducks; gardens

EXTRAS: Chocolates at turndown

RATES: $95–$145, double occupancy, including full breakfast; two-night minimum weekends

CREDIT CARDS ACCEPTED: Discover, MasterCard, Visa

OPEN: February–December

HOW TO GET THERE: From I–76 take exit 21 and go south on Route 222 for 5 miles to Route 322. Travel west on Route 322. At Pine Tree Motors turn right onto Clearview Road. The B&B is the first farm on the right.

On a rural country lane in the midst of a patchwork of neatly fenced fields, red barns, blue silos, and white houses, Clearview Farm stands out. The handsome limestone farmhouse has a spring-fed pond in its front yard, spacious lawns, brick pathways, and trim gardens, and it sits on a hill offering splendid views across the fields to the distant town. Glenn and Mildred Wissler raised their children here, tilled the land, and tended their 200-acre farm for thirty-nine years before opening it to guests.

When they first purchased the property, they decided they wanted a "modern" house and spent a great deal of effort covering the oak floors with wall-to-wall carpeting and removing the wainscotting from the walls. Over the years, however, they grew to appreciate the craftsmanship of their 1814 house, and when they converted it to a B&B, they restored much of the house's fine old features. Mildred confessed, "Glenn loves a construction project anyway."

Today the living room has a light green carpet, and the Victorian sofas and chairs are upholstered in a rainbow of pastel colors. There are an abundance of happy ferns in planters and a bay window with views of the fields. The den has a fireplace, books, and games. In the dining room, there's a rose rug, a brass chandelier, and a beautiful antique Victorian armoire with glass doors revealing the set of Royal Doulton china that's used for breakfast.

The guest rooms contain fine Victorian antiques as well. In the Royal Room, for example, there's an elaborately carved walnut Victorian bed, a Victorian étagère, and marble-topped Victorian tables. In the spacious bath, there's a clawfoot tub and a shower. The Princess Room has a canopy bed with a lacy canopy, a marble-topped Victorian dresser and a Victorian cradle filled with dolls. All the handmade quilts on the beds were made by Mildred. Guests especially appreciate the lovely Victorian chests and Colonial drysinks that Glenn used as bases for bathroom sinks.

Breakfast is a lavish repast that will begin with freshly baked muffins or cinnamon rolls, followed by perhaps a ham and cheese soufflé, which itself is followed by raspberry crêpes. The plates are among the prettiest you will see, decorated abundantly with bright edible flowers.

Guests love to meander around the 200-acre farm, which the Wisslers continue to farm.

What's Nearby—Ephrata

The Ephrata Cloister, one of Pennsylvania's most interesting attractions, is located here. Built of stone in a German medieval style in 1732, the Cloister was one of the earliest experiments in communal living. Designed as a retreat for Protestant men and women, it was renowned for its printing and publishing center and for the poetry and music its members produced. Today there are tours of twelve restored buildings, craft demonstrations year-round, and, on summer weekends, a musical drama depicting cloister life. The lovely stone buildings are on beautiful parklike grounds. Nearby you can tour the Pennsylvania Dutch countryside for handmade quilts or attend the famous Kutztown antiques fair. (See also Lancaster and Lititz.)

Historic Smithton Inn

900 West Main Street
Ephrata, PA 17522
(717) 733–6094

INNKEEPER: Dorothy Graybill

ROOMS: 8, including 1 suite, all with private bath, air conditioning, fireplace, flannel nightshirts, and desk; 6 with mini-refrigerator; 3 with whirlpool tub; telephone available; 1 room with wheelchair access

ON THE GROUNDS: Parking; award-winning dahlia garden, other gardens

EXTRAS: Snacks, including freshly baked cookies, available all day; chamber music piped into rooms; fresh flowers in rooms; guest pets allowed with prior permission; one rabbit named Peter on premises

RATES: $75–$170, double occupancy, including full breakfast and afternoon refreshments; two-night minimum if stay includes Saturday and on holiday weekends

CREDIT CARDS ACCEPTED: American Express, MasterCard, Visa

OPEN: Year-round

HOW TO GET THERE: From I–76, take exit 21 and follow Route 222 south. At the Ephrata exit, turn west onto Route 322 (Main Street) and travel 2½ miles, passing through the town of Ephrata. After passing the Ephrata Cloister, you climb a long hill. At the traffic light at the top of the hill, turn left onto Academy Drive and then immediately turn right into the B&B's parking lot on the corner of Academy Drive and Main Street.

When Dorothy Graybill purchased the Smithton Inn in 1983, she began a personal odyssey that has never stopped. Although the handsome 1763 fieldstone structure had been used as a stagecoach stop and stone tavern from its beginning, Dorothy had quite a different concept for her inn than one reminiscent of the rough and lusty meeting place of its earliest years. At some point during your stay, for example, do not fail to admire the recent additions of raised-stucco murals in the gables on the west wing and the northwest side. Executed by Dorothy's partner, Allen, one depicts the B&B's logo and the other shows the sun, moon, and stars with doves raining love and peace on the earth in the shape of heart raindrops.

Located in the heart of the Pennsylvania Dutch countryside—in an area of Mennonite, Amish, and Brethren homes complete with horse-drawn carriages and farm wagons—the inn is a showcase of local crafts and styles.

There's a painted chest in the entry; the canopy beds and desks were hand-made; the tiles surrounding the whirlpool tubs were glazed locally; there are handwoven bed canopies and drapes, hand-stitched quilts on the beds, and handpainted blanket chests on which to place your suitcase. The baths, however, are up to date and modern.

Dorothy loves to create an aura of an earlier time. Slip into one of the handmade flannel nightshirts provided in the closet, light a fire in the fireplace in your room, and select a book from the shelves nearby. Then you can immerse yourself in the charms of this B&B. For more authenticity, light some of the candles in the room and read by fire and candlelight.

Dorothy was raised in Lancaster County, and she has a wealth of information about local history. As you sit in the dining room admiring the display of quilts on the wall, the early Pennsylvania redware on the pine sideboard, the gift items on the harvest table, and the folk art on the windowsill, you appreciate Dorothy's dedication to local artistry and crafts.

Breakfast will include juice, fruit, and perhaps blueberry waffles or apple pancakes. In the snack area, guests can help themselves to raspberry lemonade or peach iced tea as well as hot tea, cookies, and pretzels.

There is almost an acre of gardens to explore and benches to sit on to absorb their beauty. Don't miss the incredible display of award-winning dahlias, the pond, and the fountain.

What's Nearby

See "What's Nearby—Ephrata," page 275.

The Appleford Inn

Best Buy

218 Carlisle Street
Gettysburg, PA 17325
(800) 275–3373 or (717) 337–1711

FAX: (717) 334–6228
E-MAIL: jwiley@cvn.net
WEB SITE: www.bbonline.com/pa/appleford
INNKEEPERS: John and Jane Wiley
ROOMS: 11, including 1 suite, all with private bath, air conditioning, and radio; 3 with desk; 2 with fireplace; telephone available in library
ON THE GROUNDS: Parking; gardens

EXTRAS: Freshly baked cookies, port, and sherry available; chocolates on pillow; fax, hair dryer, iron, and ironing board available; one golden retriever named Honeybunch, three cats named Magic, Cassie, and Orie on premises

RATES: $90–$160, double occupancy, including full breakfast; two-night minimum weekends from April to October and holiday weekends

CREDIT CARDS ACCEPTED: Discover, MasterCard, Visa

OPEN: Year-round

HOW TO GET THERE: From Route 15, take the York Street exit and travel 3 miles west on Route 30. Turn right at Lincoln Square onto Carlisle Street. The B&B is on the left in just over 2 blocks.

The Appleford Inn, which opened in 1984, was Gettysburg's first B&B. Located next to Gettysburg College, the 1867 Italianate Victorian brick mansion is in a quiet residential area of private homes and fraternity houses. Since 1995 it's been owned by John and Jane Wiley, experienced innkeepers who formerly operated a full-service inn in Eagles Mere, Pennsylvania. Friendly, helpful, and knowledgeable, they pamper their guests with personalized suggestions for local sightseeing, port and sherry in the evening, and freshly baked cookies on arrival.

Just off the wide entry hall, there's a tall reception desk backed by shelves containing Jane's antique bottle collection. In the living room, there's a grand piano and a fireplace, but the cozy library, which has shelves filled with numerous books about the Civil War, oak tables, and Oriental rugs on oak floors as well as games and puzzles, is the spot where most guests congregate. On the second floor landing, the antique violin collection attracts considerable guest attention, as do the many cross-stitch samplers throughout the inn. There's a sunroom, which is filled with pretty white wicker chairs with colorful floral cushions, an abundance of plants, a refrigerator filled with soft drinks, a little TV, and a Kitchen Queen cupboard with hot coffee and tea, a bowl of fresh apples, snacks, and cookies.

The guest rooms are charming, and they all have private baths, although these vary in size and accoutrements. The nicest is the General Pickett, which is also the largest room. It has two bedrooms, both with iron beds, and a terrific bath with a navy blue tile floor, navy towels, and an oak dresser holding the sink. The General Longstreet has an oak bed and an oak dresser with a sink in the room. The bath is small.

Breakfast is served in the formal dining room by candlelight. There's a lovely oak buffet and a corner cupboard filled with Jane's great-grandmother's Haviland china. Guests are seated around an oak table. Following fresh fruit and freshly baked muffins, Jane may serve tomato-basil eggs or cherry crepes.

The B&B sits on spacious lawns with a pretty garden in back. There are benches spaced among the flower gardens.

What's Nearby—Gettysburg

Gettysburg National Military Park is a 4,000-acre preserve dotted with almost 2,000 military monuments and more than 40 miles of roads. Stop to read the markers or take a tour with a guide. The park is guaranteed to have a lasting impact on both adults and children. Visitors to Gettysburg should plan to stay several days to experience the full historical impact. The only permanent home of Dwight and Mamie Eisenhower is also located here. A visit to their humble farm offers new insights into the life of one of America's most popular presidents.

Battlefield Bed & Breakfast Inn

2264 Emmitsburg Road
Gettysburg, PA 17325
(888) 766–3897 or (717) 334–8804

FAX: (717) 334–7330

E-MAIL: battlefieldinn@hotmail.com

WEB SITE: www.gettysburgbattlefield.com

INNKEEPERS: Charlie and Florence Tarbox

ROOMS: 8, including 2 suites, all with private bath and air conditioning; 4 with desk; 2 with fireplace; cribs available; portable telephone in summer kitchen available

ON THE GROUNDS: Parking; 46 acres of grounds including two ponds, a creek, and a wildlife preserve; barn, stable, and horses

EXTRAS: Civil War demonstrations; fax, telephone, copy machine available; tea and cookies offered all day

RATES: $135–$185, double occupancy, including full breakfast; two-night minimum if Saturday stay included

CREDIT CARDS ACCEPTED: American Express, Diners Club, Discover, MasterCard, Visa

OPEN: Year-round

HOW TO GET THERE: From Route 15, take the Steinwehr Avenue exit north toward Gettysburg. The driveway to the B&B is exactly 2⁴/₁₀ miles ahead on the right. Turn into the dirt road at the sign and drive ¼ mile to its end.

The battle of Gettysburg was a pivotal turning point in the Civil War. The Confederate and Union armies waged a three-day battle on July 1, 2, and 3 of 1863 that resulted in 51,000 American men either losing their lives or being wounded or captured. President Abraham Lincoln's eloquent tribute to these men still rings in our ears. "The brave men, living and dead, who struggled here have consecrated it [the ground] far above our poor power to add or detract. The world will little note nor long remember what we say here, but it can never forget what they did here." A visit to Gettysburg, and especially to Battlefield Bed and Breakfast Inn, makes these events come to life.

If you choose to stay at the Battlefield Bed and Breakfast, an 1809 clapboard and stone building tucked away at the end of a dirt road on forty-six acres in the heart of the battlefield, you will become totally immersed in the Gettysburg experience. In this quiet and peaceful setting with spacious lawns, stables and horses, a creek, walking trails through a nature preserve where deer and fox live, two ponds with Canada geese, snowy egrets, blue heron, and an abundance of bird feeders, you will be greeted by Charlie or Florence dressed in full Civil War–era attire. Following breakfast every morning you will be given a living history lesson or demonstration. Perhaps Charlie, who seems to live and breathe the Civil War era, will induct you into the infantry and issue you a uniform, or demonstrate a cavalry program on one of his horses, or teach you Civil War–era games and songs.

The former summer kitchen is now a gathering room with a square grand piano, a television and a VCR, and a huge old cooking fireplace with a racheting system for raising and lowering pots. The parlor has another fireplace and cabinets filled with interesting old china. There's a small gift shop containing books about the Civil War and small artifacts.

The guest rooms are all named for Civil War regiments or soldiers who were engaged in battle on these fields, and each door has a copy of the appropriate regimental flag on the door. In Graham's Battery, there's a braided rug on the floor, a quilt on the bed, an antique oak ice box used as an end table, and a fireplace. In General Merritt's Headquarters, the four-poster bed is covered with another quilt, there's a sitting room, and another fireplace. The baths are simple and functional and have stenciling on the walls. One of the most atmospheric rooms is the 2nd US Dragoons, which has rock walls, a beamed ceiling, an oak bed with a quilt coverlet, and a campaign desk.

A full breakfast is served in the dining room every morning. A typical menu might include freshly baked applesauce/pecan muffins with an apple crumble topping served with whipped cream, followed by apricot cream French toast accompanied by Italian sausage and dilled potatoes, or the menu may include an entree of cream cheese crepes with blackberry sauce. Florence garnishes all the plates with colorful edible flowers.

There are miles of trails to hike, and with even a semiactive imagination, the Civil War comes alive as you tramp the battlefields.

What's Nearby
See "What's Nearby—Gettysburg," page 279.

The Gaslight Inn
33 East Middle Street
Gettysburg, PA 17325
(717) 337–9100

E-MAIL: gaslight@mail.cvn.net
WEB SITE: www.bbonline.com/pa/
gaslight

INNKEEPERS: Denis and Roberta Sullivan

ROOMS: 9, all with private bath, air conditioning, telephone, TV, and radio; 6 with fireplace; 4 with spa/steam showers; 3 with private porch or patio; 2 with Jacuzzi, TV, and VCR; 1 room with wheelchair access

ON THE GROUNDS: Parking; large patio; garden

EXTRAS: Chocolates in rooms; tea, cakes, cookies, and sometimes beer and wine available in dining room every afternoon; dinners arranged on request; one chocolate Labrador named Aja; passes provided for nearby Y, which has a pool, exercise equipment, and racquetball

RATES: $100–$160, double occupancy, including full breakfast; two-night minimum holiday weekends

CREDIT CARDS ACCEPTED: American Express, Discover, MasterCard, Visa

OPEN: Year-round except Christmas

HOW TO GET THERE: From Route 15, take the Baltimore Street exit onto Route 97. Proceed 2⁷/₁₀ miles to the third traffic light. Turn right onto East Middle Street. The Gaslight Inn is at #33, the third house on the right. The parking area is in the rear.

In the summer, during the height of the tourist season, the streets of downtown Gettysburg throng with visitors. The small town swells to accommodate the 2½ million visitors who come annually. If at all possible, time your visit to avoid July and August. I visited Gettysburg one year in January, when the skies were a robin's-egg blue and it was possible to drive the entire battlefield circuit at a leisurely pace, with few other cars sharing the road.

The Gaslight Inn, a creamy-colored 1872 brick building, is Gettysburg's most upscale B&B. Guests enter through a wrought-iron gate and walk along a brick garden path bordered with tulips and lilies and lighted by a gas lamp.

When Denis and Roberta Sullivan purchased the building in 1994, it was a ramshackle apartment house. Following a total renovation, they opened it as a B&B. Crisp, fashionable, and stylish, the B&B blends antique and modern effortlessly.

The B&B has double parlors with pale buff-colored walls, Oriental rugs on narrow-strip oak floors, Oriental screens, and elaborate Lincrusta decor along the top of the walls. On the opposite side of the entry, the dining room is enhanced by a Victorian chandelier, stained-glass windows rescued from an old church, an inlaid cherry table, and a lovely china cabinet. Soft music plays throughout the rooms and can even be heard on the porch. A courtyard in the garden (which has a little pond) offers a place to relax in the afternoon or to take a cup of coffee in the morning before heading out to visit the sights. Upstairs, there's another sitting room with shelves stocked with books about the Civil War as well as a TV, a VCR, and a video library with Civil War documentaries and movie classics.

The guest rooms are serene oases. The Daisy Room, which is wheelchair accessible, has oak floors and a private brick patio. Upstairs, the Aster and the Sweet William Rooms both have gas fireplaces, handsome brass beds, and porches. The Ivy Room has ivy wallpaper and a bed with a lovely antique French Louis XIV headboard. All the baths are sparkling fresh with tile floors and tub surrounds. The Lily Room has a double Jacuzzi tub, and four of the rooms have double-sized steam spa/showers.

Roberta is a caterer as well as an innkeeper, and one of the first things you'll see when entering the dining room is the array of baked goods on the buffet. There will probably be a hot dish as well as several kinds of cookies, nuts, chocolates, soft drinks, hot coffee or tea, beer, and wine.

Breakfast is served in the dining room at the large cherry table. The meal will always start with six choices of juice, fresh fruit (perhaps a baked apple or a mélange of tropical fruit), and freshly baked breads such as feather-light scones or sticky buns. Roberta will then prepare one of her specialty entrees—perhaps gingerbread waffles with fresh fruit and whipped cream or orange buttermilk pancakes.

What's Nearby

See "What's Nearby—Gettysburg," page 279.

Barley Sheaf Farm

5281 York Road (Route 202)
(mailing address: P.O. Box 10)
Holicong, PA 18928
(215) 794–5104

FAX: (215) 794–5332

E-MAIL: info@barleysheaf.com

WEB SITE: www.barleysheaf.com

INNKEEPERS: Veronika and Peter Süess

ROOMS: 12, including 5 suites, all with private bath, telephone with data-port, and air conditioning; 5 with desk, patio, and robe; 3 with fireplace; 1 with a kitchen; 1 suite with wheelchair access

ON THE GROUNDS: On 30 acres with parking; swimming pool; pastures with grazing sheep; spring-fed pond; walking trails; volleyball, badminton, croquet, horseshoes

EXTRAS: Coffee, tea, and treats in the afternoon; fax available; one Swiss Bernese mountain dog named Barley Boy, one canary named Lovebug

RATES: $150–$250, double occupancy, including full breakfast; two-night minimum weekends; three-night minimum holiday weekends

CREDIT CARDS ACCEPTED: American Express, MasterCard, Visa

OPEN: Year-round

HOW TO GET THERE: From I–78 in New Jersey, take exit 29 onto I–287 south. Then take exit 13 onto Route 202 south. Follow Route 202 across the Delaware River and continue for about 6 miles. Watch for the B&B sign at a driveway on the left.

When George S. Kaufman, the eminent playwright, was in residence here in the 1920s and 1930s, it was the scene of lively entertainment. He worked on many of his plays here, although *Guys and Dolls* was much later. He probably met with neighbor Oscar Hammerstein on occasion here also.

The pretty farmhouse and outbuildings were converted to a B&B in 1976, making it the first in Bucks County. The original innkeepers, after a long and successful career, sold the property to Peter and Veronika Süess, a Swiss couple, in 1994, and the new innkeepers have been fortifying the high standards ever since. Friendly and outgoing, they have particularly concentrated on increasing their corporate business by converting a former outbuilding to a small corporate/executive center and by adding two luxury suites to the barn, one with a woodstove.

The B&B is located on thirty acres that include sweeping lawns, pastures with grazing sheep, walking trails through wooded areas, a pond for fishing, a flower garden, and a swimming pool. At a safe distance, there are hives of bees that produce honey for the B&B. We love the sense of peace and tranquility we feel here. The first sound you'll hear in the morning is the tinkling of the bells the sheep wear around their necks or birds singing merrily in the trees. Barley Boy, a Swiss Bernese mountain dog, will greet you and try to engage you in play. Lovebug, the canary, happily trills a pretty song in the breakfast room.

Guests enter through a reception area and small gift shop. Conversation areas are grouped around the fireplace in the living room and also in the small TV room. There are games, numerous books to choose from, puzzles, and a small table that's set in the afternoon with an interesting beverage, such as mulled cranberry juice, and a treat.

The guest rooms vary from those in the main house, which have simple, country decor, to the elegant suites in the barn. They have all been freshly painted in light, soothing colors and decorated with spritely floral fabrics. There are iron beds, sleigh beds, brass beds, and four-posters. Many of the baths have clawfoot tubs. I've always loved the cozy little cottage rooms reached by walking along a stone pathway with beds of waist-high tiger lilies on either side. They have beamed ceilings, brick floors, window seats, and fireplaces.

The multilevel conference center, which is complete with private interview offices, overlooks the pastures of grazing sheep. It seems to me that only congenial decisions could be made in such a relaxed setting.

A full breakfast is served in the sunny brick-floored dining room that's filled with plants and has a woodburning stove. Guests enjoy chatting around the long tables, and there are views across the lawns to the pool. Breakfast will begin with fruit (perhaps honey-steamed apples) and freshly baked breakfast breads. The entree might be a potato-onion frittata or croissant French toast topped with cranberry sauce.

Holicong is in the heart of Bucks County, midway between the museums in Doylestown and the shops and restaurants in New Hope.

What's Nearby—Holicong

Carousel World, located nearby in Lahaska, features a museum of carousel art, and visitors can ride an antique carousel. The Pearl S. Buck House is located nearby in Dublin. The 1835 stone house was the home of America's first woman to earn the Nobel and Pulitzer Prizes. (See also Doylestown and New Hope.)

The Bucksville House Bed & Breakfast

4501 Durham Road (Route 412)
Kintnersville, PA 18930
(888) 617-6300 or (610) 847-8948 (fax also)

WEB SITE: www.bbgetaways.com/bucksvillehouse

INNKEEPERS: Barbara and Joe Szollosi

ROOMS: 5, including 1 suite, all with private bath and air conditioning; 3 with fireplace; 1 room with wheelchair access

ON THE GROUNDS: On 4 acres with parking; two ponds; a screened gazebo; herb and flower gardens

EXTRAS: Afternoon refreshments of homemade cookies, tea, and cider; evening carafe of homemade wine; telephone, fax, copier available; one cat named Muffy on premises

RATES: $100–$130, double occupancy, including full breakfast; two-night minimum weekends; three-night minimum holiday weekends

CREDIT CARDS ACCEPTED: American Express, Discover, MasterCard, Visa

OPEN: Year-round

HOW TO GET THERE: From I-78, take the first exit in Pennsylvania (Easton). At the top of the ramp, turn left and then turn left again at the first road onto Cedarville Road. Go 1½ miles to its end. Turn right onto Easton Road (Route 611) south and go 12 miles to Ferndale. Turn right at the light onto Church Hill Road. Go 1½ miles to its end. The B&B is on the left on the corner of Durham Road (Route 412).

The handsome creamy-colored stucco house with grey-green shutters has been welcoming travelers for most of its 200-plus years. In the 1840s it was known as the Bucksville Hotel, and subsequently it became a stage-coach stop. It appears as if wagon wheels were repaired in the room that is now the dining room. During Prohibition, the building served as a speakeasy, and in the 1930s it was a tavern. Barbara and Joe Szollosi, former teachers, restored the gracious building in 1984 and opened it as a B&B.

They did a terrific restoration job. Barbara has been collecting fine antiques for years, and they now grace the rooms of the B&B. In addition, Joe is a carpenter/craftsman, and he has made numerous reproduction pieces. Guests enter a cozy brick-floored room with an extensive library in pine bookshelves, skylights, a spinning wheel, a Shaker-style bench, and tables for checkers and games. A brilliant red-and-white quilt hangs on the wall. The large living room has a gracious fireplace with a wood mantel and a lovely secretary, while the den has random-width pine floors, a coal stove, exceptional quilts hanging on the walls, and a collection of old games.

The guest rooms are beautifully furnished with beds with lacy fishnet canopies or pineapple or cannonball posts. There are braided and Oriental rugs on the floors, and three of the rooms have woodburning fireplaces. Barbara has an eagle's eye for gorgeous handmade quilts. Some of the more than seventy exquisite examples that she's purchased at antique auctions cover the beds and hang on the walls. She's supplemented the collection with intricate examples made by a local craftswoman. The baths are finished with wood or tile floors.

The little touches that Barb and Joe have thought of to pamper their guests include a plate of freshly baked cookies and cider in the afternoon and in the evening, a carafe of Joe's homemade wine (there are several nearby commercial wineries to visit also).

The B&B is located on four acres that include a spacious brick courtyard with stone and wood benches shaded by a massive maple tree. Neat brick pathways lead to a grape arbor, an herb garden, and a flower garden with azaleas, rhododendrons, perennials, annuals, and bulbs that also includes two ponds. A screened-in gazebo overlooks the gardens.

Breakfast is served in the dining room, which has another fireplace or, in summer, in the gazebo. A typical meal may include Angelic eggs casse-role—a cheese dish that contains three cheeses and puffs up like a soufflé—accompanied by ham and freshly made muffins or perhaps orange waffles with bacon and sausage.

What's Nearby—Kintnersville

The Bucks County Horse Park & Polo Club is located just around the corner. Guests can ride here if they bring their own horse or watch polo games if they have not. Nockamixon State Park offers plenty of summer fun including a huge swimming and diving pool, hiking and bicycling trails, picnicking areas, and a 7-mile-long lake with canoes, paddleboats, and rowboats for rent. Or stop at the Antique Hardware Store and Andrew's Furniture and Crafts in Kintnersville for a look at the interesting tools and local crafts. Sand Castle Winery is located nearby. Or head north to the Crayola Factory at Two Rivers Landing in Easton, which includes a 2,000-square-foot interactive exhibit area and a tour where you can see Crayola crayons and markers being made. (See also Ottsville, Pipersville, Riegelsville, and Upper Black Eddy.)

Lightfarm Bed & Breakfast ~Best Buy~

2042 Berger Road
Kintnersville, PA 18930
(877) 847–3276 or (610) 847–3276

FAX: (610) 847–8068
E-MAIL: litefarm@epix.net
WEB SITE: www.lightfarm.com
INNKEEPERS: Max and Carol Sempowski

ROOMS: 5, including 1 suite and 1 cottage, all with private bath, air conditioning, telephone, robes, TV, radio, hair dryer, and desk; 3 with fireplace; 2 with VCR, coffeemaker, iron, and ironing board; 1 with whirlpool tub and private porch

ON THE GROUNDS: On 92 acres with parking; spring-fed pond; hot tub; fields with sheep grazing; nature trails

EXTRAS: Archaeological dig and museum; fax available; turndown with Hershey Kiss and special note; pet accommodations available for a fee; six dogs, farm cats, two potbellied pigs, flock of sheep on property

RATES: $79–$175, double occupancy, including full breakfast; two-night minimum weekends

CREDIT CARDS ACCEPTED: American Express, Discover, MasterCard, Visa
OPEN: Year-round

HOW TO GET THERE: From I-78, take the first exit in Pennsylvania (Easton). At the top of the ramp, turn left and then turn left again at the first road onto Cedarville Road. Go 1½ miles to its end. Turn right onto Easton Road (Route 611) south and go 12 miles to Ferndale. Turn right at the light onto Church Hill Road. Go 1½ miles to its end. Turn right onto Durham Road (Route 412) north. Go 1 mile and look for the B&B sign on the right. Turn right onto Berger Road and continue for ¾ mile. The B&B is the second farm on the right.

Travelers who love to immerse themselves in the history of an area will find numerous things to fascinate them at Lightfarm Bed & Breakfast. Although most B&Bs in Bucks County are upscale and toney, Lightfarm offers a refreshing change of pace. Not only will guests learn from the artifacts collected in the archaeological dig on site and displayed in the B&B's museum, they will be treated to extraordinary stenciled walls created by innkeeper Carol Sempowski from old Colonial patterns and to colorful handmade log cabin and wedding ring quilts covering the beds, which were also made by Carol.

The museum is located in a stone-walled and beam-ceilinged lower-level room. Archaeology classes from Bucks County Community College are held here. The owners surmise, from the number of highly decorated fragments and shards of Pennsylvania redware and stub-stem pipes that have been found, that an early pottery manufactory may have been here.

Located on a ninety-two-acre working farm in a rural setting of barns, neatly fenced fields with grazing sheep, wooded areas, and a pond, the 1811 stone farmhouse offers beautiful views of the surrounding farmland. Inside there are wide-plank pine floors and beamed ceilings, and in the original old kitchen, there's a huge fireplace that still has its hinged shutter doors that close in front when it's not in use. The parlor boasts a Baldwin acrosonic piano, a grandfather clock, and an antique highboy. Museum-quality collections of Pennsylvania redware, Hummel figurines, and statues of border collies (the indispensable workhorse of a farm, according to Carol) line the shelves. On the walls, there's a collection of Wallace Nutting painted photographs.

The B&B has five rooms—all with beautiful stenciling in multiple colors. Solomon's Room has wide-plank pine floors, green-colored paneled walls, window seats with views of the fields, and a bed with a fishnet canopy. One of Carol's quilts in green shades is on the bed. John Jacob's Room has a bow-top canopy, walls that are highly stenciled, and a rag rug on the pine floor. Although the baths are neat, modern, and clean, they are not as up-to-date as at most of the B&Bs in this book. In 1998 a separate cottage was added also.

I love to wake to the smell of baking bread, and that lovely aroma wafts up to the guest rooms here as Carol prepares either fruit muffins or zucchini or banana bread in the morning. Breakfast may be taken at leisure, however. It is served in the formal dining room, which has a brass lamp, built-in cupboards, and a maple table. The table is set with linen, silver, and Johnson Brothers Old Britain Castles china. Carol may prepare a double-crust sausage pie with homemade applesauce or perhaps eggs with cream cheese and chives.

Because Lightfarm is still a working farm, Carol and Mike invite guests to help tend the garden and to feed the animals, if they desire. In addition to the two potbellied pigs, a flock of sheep, six dogs, and farm cats, there are two peacocks, two American turkeys, and white-crested black Polish chickens on the property. Guests also enjoy meandering along the nature trails that lead to a hollow where deer graze or that skirt Gallows Run Creek and run through the pine forest. For utter relaxation, however, they can just sit in a chair beside the spring-fed pond or loosen kinked muscles in the hot tub on the porch.

What's Nearby

See "What's Nearby—Kintnersville," page 287.

Gardens of Eden B&B

1894 Eden Road
Lancaster, PA 17601
(717) 393–5179

FAX: (717) 393–7722
E-MAIL: info@gardens-of-eden.com
WEB SITE: www.gardens-of-eden.com
INNKEEPERS: Marilyn and Bill Ebel

ROOMS: 4, including 1 cottage, all with private bath, air conditioning, radio, hair dryer, and robes; cottage with fireplace, small kitchen, coffeemaker, TV, and porch; 3 rooms with desk; portable phone available

ON THE GROUNDS: On 3½ acres bordering Conestoga River with parking; spacious gardens, walking trails, canoe and rowboat for use on river, fishing; bicycle storage

EXTRAS: Afternoon hot and cold drinks, freshly made cookies or cake; turndown with chocolates; fax available

RATES: $95–$130, double occupancy, including full breakfast; two-night minimum weekends; three-night minimum holiday weekends

CREDIT CARDS ACCEPTED: MasterCard and Visa

OPEN: Year-round

HOW TO GET THERE: From I-76, take exit 21 and follow Route 222 south for about 15 miles to Lancaster. Stay in the right lane and exit onto Route 30 east. At the next junction, exit onto Route 23 east toward New Holland. In less than $^8/_{10}$ mile, turn right onto Eden Road. In $^4/_{10}$ mile, just before the bridge, turn right into the B&B's lane and park below the stone wall.

Seldom do you find a B&B that's so perfectly named. Serendipitously located on Eden Road on a 3½-acre site that overlooks a waterfall on the Conestoga River, the B&B is surrounded by lush gardens. Lawns and flower beds rise behind the house, offering a perpetual kaleidoscope of color from early spring to late fall. In front, there are terraces and sloping hillsides planted with an abundance of daffodils and wildflowers that end in a grassy space at river's edge. Nature trails hug the river beyond and rise along the slopes behind the inn. Two county bicycle routes pass by. Along with their brochure, Marilyn and Bill Ebel send guests a pamphlet that begins with lines from Robert Browning's famous poem: "The lark's on the wing; / The snail's on the thorn; / God's in His heaven— / All's right with the world!" It lists the many birds (including the brilliant yellow winged-type Baltimore oriole), animals (including whitetail deer), and flowers (numbering almost seventy-five, all arranged and named by color) found on the property. Could there be a more peaceful and bucolic place?

The B&B is in a lovely 1867 brick Federal manor house with a slate roof, green shutters, and white pillars on either side of the door. The last time I was there a family of tiny Carolina wrens had made their nest in the front door decoration. They were undoubtedly so enchanted with Marilyn's design that they felt right at home. That's not surprising, since Marilyn is an acclaimed floral designer and instructor.

The common rooms are warm and inviting, just like the innkeepers. Burnished white pine floors are covered by Oriental rugs. The gracious living room has a white wooden fireplace mantel, floor-to-ceiling bookcases, and a 1907 Steinway grand piano. Other antiques, such as a tall-case clock made in Reading between 1799 and 1818, share space with a hooked rug made by Marilyn; paintings, photographs, and crafts by local artists; and Marilyn's dried floral arrangements.

In the guest rooms, there are antique beds. A wise old wooden owl sculpture sits on an old pump just beyond the stone terrace of the two-story Beecher Cottage, which was created from the original summer kitchen. Baskets hang from the ceiling, the fireplace burns logs in winter, a table sits by a paned window offering views of the barn. Upstairs, the bed is covered with another quilt.

The dining room is as welcoming as the rest of the house. Colorful place mats and china grace the Queen Anne–style reproduction table, and pieces of folk art sit on a shelf. An antique brass chandelier oversees the scene. Breakfasts are creative and healthful. There will always be fruit, juice, and muesli as well as either a baked egg dish or maybe waffles served with homemade violet syrup. Plates are decorated with edible flowers and fruit.

The East of Eden Pub, an excellent restaurant, lies on the opposite bank of the river, a short walk across the little bridge.

What's Nearby—Lancaster

To savor the delights of the Amish/Mennonite countryside, stop at the Mennonite Information Center. Guides can be hired to ride in your own car to direct you along the backroads as they describe the farm and religious life of the local families. Or they may take you to less commercial homes where quilts and furniture are made. The Lancaster Central Market is the nation's oldest publicly owned farmers' market. Open Tuesday, Friday, and Saturday starting at 6 A.M., this is the place to buy local produce, meats, bakery and craft items. Visit James Buchanan's home, Wheatland, for an insight into the life of America's fifteenth president. The American Music Theater opened in Lancaster in the spring of 1997; in the Heritage Center Museum of Lancaster County, there are exhibits that tell the story of the area's rich cultural history and a museum store where the work of current-day quilters, folk artists, and furniture makers can be purchased. (See also Ephrata and Lititz.)

The King's Cottage, A Bed & Breakfast Inn

1049 East King Street (Route 462)
Lancaster, PA 17602
(800) 747–8717 or (717) 397–1017

FAX: (717) 397–3447
E-MAIL: kingscottage@earthlink.net

WEB SITE: www.bbonline.com/pa/kingscottage

INNKEEPERS: Karen and Jim Owens

ROOMS: 9, including 1 suite, all with private bath, air conditioning, telephone, and radio; 6 with desk; 3 with hairdryer and TV; 2 with porch; 1 with a fireplace and a whirlpool tub; one room has wheelchair access

ON THE GROUNDS: Parking; garden with lily and fish pond

EXTRAS: Small gift shop; fax available; turndown with chocolates on the pillow; afternoon tea and evening cordials served in the library

RATES: $100–$250, double occupancy, including full breakfast; two-night minimum weekends; three-night minimum holiday and special event weekends

CREDIT CARDS ACCEPTED: MasterCard, Visa

OPEN: Year-round

HOW TO GET THERE: From I-76, take exit 21 and follow Route 222 south for 15 miles to Lancaster. Turn east onto Route 30 and follow this to Route 23 west (Walnut Street) to King Street. Turn right at the end of the exit ramp. At the second light, turn left onto Ranck Avenue. At the second stop sign, turn left onto East Orange Street. Follow East Orange Street for 1 block to Cottage Avenue and turn right. The B&B is the last building on the right, on the corner of East King Street and Cottage Avenue. Turn right into the lane just before the B&B and then turn left into the parking area.

You don't expect to see a golden stucco house with a Spanish tile roof in the heart of Amish/Mennonite country, but here it is. Built in 1913, the house is listed on the National Register of Historic Places. Instead of a strictly Mission-style interior, the house has architectural elements in both Victorian and Art Deco styles. Karen and Jim Owens opened the B&B in 1987.

Guests enter a Florida room with a tile floor that contains an extensive gift shop with quilts, pillows, and books, as well as a sitting area with wicker furniture. The living room has a traditional marble fireplace and comfortable sofas. Through a grand doorway flanked by fluted columns, there's a library that includes an Art Deco fireplace and a bay window as well as a TV, a VCR, and a video library.

The guest rooms are decorated with a combination of antiques and country pieces. The Princess Room, which uses Wedgwood blue Waverly fabric, has an antique four-poster cherry bed and a private tile-floored porch overlooking the lily pond and gardens. The bath is large and has a double sink with a marble counter and a clawfoot tub. The Contessa, on the ground floor, also has a private porch as well as a canopied bed with an antique mahogany headboard, a magnificent antique cherry secretary with a bookcase above, and an adjoining bath with a rose-colored marble sink.

The Carriage House, a separate little building entered through a barn door, is the most luxurious accommodation. It has an iron verdigris canopy bed draped with diaphanous white fabric and a purple floral spread on the bed. There's a gas fireplace, an antique armoire, pink walls, and an oak floor. The spacious bath features a tile floor, a Jacuzzi, and a sink in a marble counter.

Breakfast is served in the formal dining room, which has quilts on the walls, built-in Palladian-style china cabinets, a crystal chandelier, and pale green walls with white trim. Two large tables are set with fine linen and china. Karen has an extensive repertoire of breakfast menus. She may fix broiled grapefruit with spicy pear muffins, followed by ham and cheese crepes with hollandaise sauce. Or, it may be a fresh fruit salad followed by a plum torte with sausage.

Afternoon tea is served in the library. It features such delicacies as King's Delight, a tea cake with a nut crust and a whipped cream and cream cheese filling that's topped with fresh blueberries or strawberries, or Hummingbird Cake, a dense banana/coconut/pineapple cake with a coconut frosting. Few guests leave without purchasing one of the B&B's cookbooks.

What's Nearby

See "What's Nearby—Lancaster," page 291.

The Bridgetown Mill House

760 Langhorne-Newtown Road
(Route 413)
Langhorne, PA 19047
(215) 752–8996

FAX: (215) 741–1668

INNKEEPERS: J. Carlos and Kimberly DaCosta

ROOMS: 6, all with private bath, air conditioning, telephone with dataport (on request), and robes; 2 with fireplace

ON THE GROUNDS: On 8²/10 acres on Neshaminy Creek with parking; jogging track; English gardens

EXTRAS: Afternoon champagne with ladyfingers and strawberries; turn-down with chocolate truffles and sherry or port

RATES: $130–$185, double occupancy, including full breakfast; two-night minimum weekends; three-night minimum holiday weekends

CREDIT CARDS ACCEPTED: American Express, Diners Club, MasterCard, Visa

OPEN: Year-round

HOW TO GET THERE: From I–95, take exit 30 (Newtown) onto Route 332 west. Travel through 5 traffic lights. At the sixth traffic light, turn left (south) onto Route 413. Go through 1 more traffic light. At the next light turn right onto Bridgetown Pike. The driveway to the B&B is on the left before the bridge and just past the old stone grist mill.

It's always a pleasure to see a careful restoration accomplished with such perfection. The grand 6,000-square-foot fieldstone Colonial that Carlos and Kim converted to a B&B was almost ready for its first guest when I visited in May 1998. The circa 1719 stone house with black shutters and cream trim glowed softly in the springtime sun, while the giant 200-year-old sycamore trees stood guard, protectively shading it as they have for all these years. Down by the edge of the Neshaminy Creek, a romantic circa 1740 grist mill was awaiting restoration itself.

The house and mill were built by William and Mary Jenks, a prominent English Quaker family, who settled in America in the late 1600s. They operated the grist mill on the property and were influential in the political arena of Bucks County, as well as in the development of its agricultural importance. Carlos and Kim spent almost four years restoring the estate. Carlos, however, has more than twenty years' experience working in some of the finest hotels and restaurants in the area. He knows exactly what guests appreciate and want the most.

Today the house is approached from the parking area along brick pathways edged with stone walls. There's a beautiful English garden and a jogging trail beside the creek.

The main floor of the B&B contains a variety of rooms for guests to relax in. All are classically and elegantly decorated. There's a common room that has hand-hewn beams and pegged oak floors. Brown-colored sofas sit on Oriental rugs. Champagne, along with lady fingers and strawberries, is set out here every afternoon. A solarium just beyond has a brick floor, which leads to a covered porch with beautiful hanging baskets of verbena and dusty miller. A dining room has ivory shadow-striped paper on the walls and an elegant fireplace, while the library is as snug and cozy as a library should be. It features rich cranberry colors, numerous shelves of books, and another fireplace. The kitchen, where breakfast is served, is bright and welcoming. It has brick floors, beamed ceilings, and a huge walk-in brick fireplace.

The guest rooms are equally elegant. The beds are made with luxurious linens. Fine soaps and toiletries are found in the beautiful marble baths, as well as soft, fluffy towels made of Egyptian cotton. The rooms are named for the trees on the property. Locust has an iron bed that's dressed in silk damask in restful tones of grey and ivory. Sycamore has another iron bed and a fireplace, while Maple is decorated in reds and greens and it has a fireplace as well. Walnut has a walnut bed, and Bridgetown has a wonderful four-poster rice bed.

A full breakfast is served in the kitchen, where fine china and Christophle silver are used. The meal will start with fresh fruit and freshly made croissants or muffins. The entree changes daily, but a house specialty is an eggs Benedict dish with a truffle hollandaise sauce and fresh asparagus.

What's Nearby—Langhorne

The B&B is adjacent to Core Creek Park, which has a lake of more than one hundred acres. Guests can go boating, swimming, or fishing here. Historic Newtown is just two miles away. There are numerous antiques shops, art galleries, and gift shops for browsing, as well as several fine restaurants. A country club golf course is just 1 mile down the road.

Swiss Woods B&B

500 Blantz Road
Lititz, PA 17543
(800) 594–8018 or (717) 627–3358

FAX: (717) 627–3483

E-MAIL: innkeeper@swisswoods.com

WEB SITE: www.swisswoods.com

INNKEEPERS: Debrah and Werner Mosimann

ROOMS: 7, including 1 suite, all with private bath, air conditioning, telephone with dataport, balcony, and radio; 3 with desk, TV, and VCR, 2 with whirlpool tub; crib available

ON THE GROUNDS: On 30 acres with parking; abundant gardens; walking and hiking trails; canoe for use on a small adjacent lake

EXTRAS: Turndown with chocolates on the pillow; afternoon snacks with freshly baked cookies or pastries; two golden retrievers named Heidi and Gretl and cats outside only

RATES: $110–$175, double occupancy, including full breakfast; lower rates from January–March; two-night minimum weekends; three-night minimum holiday weekends

CREDIT CARDS ACCEPTED: American Express, Discover, MasterCard, Visa

OPEN: Year-round except December 24–26

HOW TO GET THERE: From I-76, take exit 21 and follow Route 222 south to Route 322. Take the Ephrata exit and travel west on Route 322 until it intersects with Route 501 in Brickerville. Turn left onto Route 501 and travel south to the first crossroads, which is Brubaker Valley Road. Turn right and go 1 mile to the lake. Just before the lake, turn right onto Blantz Road. The B&B is the first driveway on the left.

Lititz was founded in 1756 by Moravians (Moravia is now part of Czecho-slovakia), as was much of the surrounding countryside, and the hand-some stone buildings of the village give it the appearance of a Rhine River village. The entire town is a National Historic District.

Swiss Woods B&B is located 3 miles north of Lititz. On a 30-acre hilltop, the grounds are resplendently alive with colorful gardens from early spring, when the daffodils create a carpet of yellow, to late fall, when the maple trees wear their coats of red and orange. There are walking trails through the woods and down to small Speedwell Forge Lake, and benches through-out the glorious gardens offer guests tranquil places to enjoy the many birds, flowers, and animals.

The inn appears to have been plucked directly from a Swiss mountain-side, and it's no wonder. Werner Mosimann was raised in Switzerland, and he and Debrah lived there for several years. When they built their B&B in 1984, they fashioned it after the Swiss chalets they loved so much. Although Debrah was raised nearby, her family has a Swiss lineage also. She will point out the mantel in the Anker Stube, the warm common room, that was hand-hewn by her father and the wall of sandstones that were cut by Werner. Guests enter through this room, which has rag rugs on pine floors, persimmon and navy colored chairs and sofas, an upright piano, and tables and chairs by the wall of windows that looks out at the gardens.

One of the advantages of building a new B&B is that you can include features that might have been precluded in the transformation of an older building. At Swiss Woods every room has its own balcony or patio, allowing guests a bird's eye view of the gardens, which Werner, who has a degree in agronomy, tends from morning until night. Naturally, the railings hold planter boxes filled with bright blooms, just as in Switzerland, and the B&B is filled with vases of fresh flowers.

Some of the beds are on platforms, others are four-poster cherry beds, but my favorites are the new twisted-spindle pine beds. All are covered with feather-light down comforters with pretty chintz-covered duvets. My favorite room is Lake of Geneva, which has a pine bed with massive posts, a balcony with views of Speedwell Forge Lake, and a modern bath with a red-and-white tile floor, pine cabinets, and a Jacuzzi under a skylight.

Breakfast is served in Anker Stube at tables that overlook the gardens. It will begin with a fresh fruit platter and assorted freshly baked muffins—perhaps a selection of chocolate chip, strawberry, and pecan. This may be followed by a baked egg and cheese dish or by cinnamon raisin French toast stuffed with chocolate and strawberry cream cheese.

There's a little gift shop at the B&B that has beautiful quilts, quilted potholders and pillows, mugs, tote bags, and pretty children's and adult's pinafores in spritely colors. Nearby, there's a guest pantry with a refrigerator, and coffeemaker. A jar of chocolate chip cookies or snickerdoodles awaits on the buffet in the Anker Stube every afternoon.

What's Nearby—Lititz

Visit The Wilbur Chocolate Company's Candy Americana Museum & Store in Lititz for an education about the history of American candymaking. There are demonstrations, displays of antique molds, and candy at discounted prices. Also, visit the Sturgis Pretzel factory, founded in 1861, making it the oldest pretzel bakery in America. (See also Ephrata and Lancaster.)

Mehard Manor Bed & Breakfast   Best Buy

146 North Pitt Street
Mercer, PA 16137
(888) 606–2489 or
(724) 662–2489

E-MAIL: mehardmanor@
pathway.net
WEB SITE: www.pathway.net/
mehardmanor

INNKEEPERS: Lucille and Jerry Carlson

ROOMS: 4, all with private bath, air conditioning, and radio; 3 with desk

ON THE GROUNDS: On ½ acre with parking; gardens

EXTRAS: Telephone available; cookies and fruit in afternoon; a Maine coon cat, Lexi, on premises

RATES: $80–$90, double occupancy, including full breakfast

CREDIT CARDS ACCEPTED: American Express, Discover, MasterCard, Visa

OPEN: Year-round

HOW TO GET THERE: From I–80 take exit 2 and travel north for 2½ miles to the town of Mercer. Just before the second traffic light, turn right onto South Diamond Street. At the next intersection, turn left onto Pitt Street. The B&B is on the right in 1½ blocks.

The stately and gracious Mehard Manor was built in 1913 by Samuel S. Mehard, a prominent local attorney and judge. He chose a classic Georgian Colonial style with a hip roof for his home, adding a curved portico with fluted columns and dentil moldings and both fan and sidelights at the entrance door. The white-clapboard house with black shutters remains virtually the same as when the judge was living here. Lucille, who is a registered nurse, and Jerry, a retired chemist, have owned the property since 1995.

Guests enter a wide reception foyer with wainscot paneling on the walls and a molded plaster ceiling. A graceful stairway with carved newels and spindles rises to the second floor. It's overseen by a leaded-glass skylight, and on the second floor wonderful big Doric columns are incorporated into the design. The living room, a pretty room decorated in peach, pink, beige, and soft green tones, and boasting an ivory fireplace mantel, is classic in its proportions. It, the dining room, and the library, all of which lead off the foyer, have molded plaster ceilings and wide crown moldings. A solarium, on the other hand, has a clay tile floor and floor-to-ceiling windows offering magnificent views of the gardens. French doors lead to a patio. On the second floor a sitting room is reserved for guests to use. They will find a 35˝ screen TV and a VCR here.

The guest rooms are all on the second floor. They are decorated with a combination of antique and period reproduction pieces. The Williamsburg Room has a fabulous rococo-style bed and a handcarved teakwood armoire, as well as an antique dresser. The walls are decorated with pictures of Colonial Williamsburg. The Victoria Room has a bed with a fishnet canopy enhanced by elegant beige silk fabric and a burled walnut dresser and washstand. The impressive bath contains the original fixtures.

A full breakfast is served in the dining room in the morning. A typical meal will include fresh fruit and juices along with sweet breads such as muffins, scones, or sticky buns. Lucille might fix a zucchini quiche for an entree, and one of her most popular breakfast desserts is a white-chocolate bread pudding.

What's Nearby—Mercer

Mercer is about 20 miles east of the Ohio border and about 65 miles north of Pittsburgh. It's a charming Victorian town that is the county seat of Mercer County, and it boasts a very impressive courthouse. Visit the Mercer County Historical Society Museum to learn more about Mercer's history. In the summer you can enjoy summer band concerts or plan your visit when one of the Victorian weekends are underway. The Grove City Factory Shops, a complex of 140 outlet stores is just 7 miles away.

Mt. Gretna Inn

16 West Kauffman Avenue
Mt. Gretna, PA 17064
(800) 277–6602 or (717) 964–3234

FAX: (717) 964–3641
E-MAIL: inn@mtgretna.com
WEB SITE: www.mtgretna.com
INNKEEPERS: Keith and Robin Volker
ROOMS: 7, all with private bath, air conditioning, radio, hair dryer, and robes; 6 with fireplace; 2 with private porch
ON THE GROUNDS: On 1 acre with parking; gardens
EXTRAS: Adjacent to 4,000 acres of public and private forest land that offers hiking and cross-country ski trails; the B&B provides skis and mountain bikes; Socks, the cat, in owner's quarters
RATES: $95–$125, double occupancy, including full breakfast; two-night minimum weekends in summer, in October, and on Valentine's Day weekend
CREDIT CARDS ACCEPTED: American Express, Discover, MasterCard, Visa
OPEN: Year-round
HOW TO GET THERE: From I–76 (the Pennsylvania Turnpike) take exit 20 (Lancaster/Lebanon). Turn left onto Route 72 north and go 2 miles to the Mt. Gretna exit. At the stop sign at the bottom of the hill, turn left

onto Route 117 north. Go 2 miles to Boulevard. Turn left onto Boulevard and continue for 2 blocks to the end of the street. Turn left onto Kauffman. The B&B will be on the right.

The quaint and charming village of Mt. Gretna was established in the 1890s by the Pennsylvania Chautauqua Society. Victorian homes were built amidst the groves of pine trees and the campground. Many of the homes remain today to welcome back visitors whose families have been enjoying the educational and cultural offerings for more than one hundred years.

The Mt. Gretna Inn was constructed a bit later than the campgrounds. Designed in the Arts and Crafts style, it dates to 1921, when it was the showcase of a subdivision known as The Heights. It was converted to a B&B in 1988, and the Volkers became the owners in 1994. Since that time they've renovated all the guest rooms and added gas fireplaces to six of the rooms.

The B&B has a spacious parlor with a fireplace. Cases of books and numerous games keep guests occupied. The broad front porch is furnished with wicker rockers and chairs with floral cushions. A big wonderful glider is sought out by guests.

The guest rooms have been named for some of the area's most abundant trees. The Weeping Pines is one of the most popular. It has a canopy bed in burled maple and a private porch, as well as a gas fireplace. The Chestnut Suite has an antique bedroom set that includes a king-size bed and an armoire, as well as a gas fireplace, while Wild Cherry has a bed of inlaid woods and a marble-topped dresser. All of the rooms have private baths with showers. None of the baths has tubs.

Breakfast is served in two dining rooms. One of Robin's most popular entrees is a French toast strata that includes bread and cream cheese laced with a hot raspberry sauce. It's served with fresh fruit, sausage, and perhaps a blueberry coffee cake.

What's Nearby—Mt. Gretna

Mr. Gretna was established by the Pennsylvania Chautauqua Society in the 1890s, and a full range of educational and cultural events continue to be held here in the summer. You might attend a jazz or chamber music concert or a lecture or class. You can visit the Gretna theater for a live musical or theatrical performance. In summer you can hike the Horse Shoe Trail, which is part of the Appalachian Trail system. In winter you can cross-country ski on more than 20 miles of trails in the 4,000 acres of forest land that is partly owned by the state and maintained as game conservation property and is partly privately owned. The historic Cornwall Iron Furnace, a well-preserved example of an early glass furnace, is nearby and is open for tours.

Farmhouse Bed & Breakfast

Grange Road
(mailing address: HC1, Box 6-B)
Mt. Pocono, PA 18344
(570) 839–0796

FAX: (570) 839–0795

INNKEEPERS: Jack and Donna Asure

ROOMS: 4 suites and 1 cottage, all with private bath, air conditioning, fireplace, TV, VCR, telephone, radio, mini-refrigerator, and desk; 2 with private porch

ON THE GROUNDS: On 6½ acres with parking; gardens; horseshoe pits

EXTRAS: Coffee and coffeemakers in rooms; turndown with cookies; 2 cats, Boggy and Daisey, on premises

RATES: $95–$115, double occupancy, including full breakfast; two-night minimum weekends; three-night minimum holiday and race weekends

CREDIT CARDS ACCEPTED: American Express, Discover, MasterCard, Visa

OPEN: Year-round

HOW TO GET THERE: From I–80 take I–380 west. Follow this for 2 miles to exit 8 onto Route 940 east. Follow this for 2 miles to Mt. Pocono. After crossing Route 611, turn right off Route 940 onto Grange Road. The B&B is ⅛ mile farther on the right.

Jack Asure's parents lived in this charming 1850s farmhouse while Jack was growing up and they were operating Memorytown across the street. Since Memorytown includes a motel, as well as several restaurants, Jack learned the hospitality business at a young age, which comes in handy now since he and Donna converted the farmhouse to a B&B in 1989. Donna, by the way, is extremely knowledgeable about what's going on in the area. She's currently the township supervisor.

The Asures' living/dining room embraces a wide variety of antiques and collectibles the couple have acquired over the years. There are old rifles on the walls and a collection of Stengal pottery, among a variety of other items. Guests eat breakfast at one end of this room, where they can admire the collections. Donna may have baked an apple-sour-cream coffee cake or a pear tarte to begin the meal. For an entree there may be an omelette or perhaps French toast stuffed with cream cheese and raspberry sauce.

The six and one-half acres of property include numerous outbuildings, as well as the farmhouse, and Jack and Donna have converted several of them to guest suites already. We rather expect to see them utilize more. To date, the icehouse has been turned into a delightful cottage. It has a living room with a fireplace in one of the stone walls and a bedroom upstairs with a four-poster bed and a bath. A ranch house contains two suites. Both have sponge-painted and stenciled walls in warm colors. Sundown also has a fireplace and a sunken garden tub, while Sunup includes a full kitchen. The other two suites are found in the farmhouse. The Parlour Suite is on the main floor. It has paneled walls and a living room with a wall of library shelves and a stone fireplace. The Master Suite is upstairs, and it has a cast-iron fireplace in the living room.

What's Nearby—Mt. Pocono

The Pocono International Raceway here has NASCAR races during the season that attract thousands of people. Mount Pocono is near the Delaware State Forest, an area of more than 80,000 acres that includes 100 miles of trails and 5,000 acres of natural wooded and scenic areas. Together with the Lackawanna State Forest, these are wonderful spots to view brilliant fall foliage. Memorytown, which was owned by Jack's family for many years, is directly across the street. It features a village of shops, live entertainment, and paddleboats and fishing on a lake.

The Fox & Hound Bed & Breakfast of New Hope

Best Buy

246 West Bridge Street
New Hope, PA 18938
(800) 862–5082 or
(215) 862–5082 (fax also)

E-MAIL: foxhound@bellatlantic.net
WEB SITE: www.foxhoundinn.com
INNKEEPER: Dennis Cianci
ROOMS: 8, all with private bath and

air conditioning; 4 with fireplace; 2 with whirlpool tub and desk; wheelchair access

ON THE GROUNDS: On 2 acres with parking; gardens

EXTRAS: Guest pets permitted with prior permission

RATES: $120–$165 Friday and Saturday nights, double occupancy, including full breakfast; $65–$115, Sunday–Thursday nights, double occupancy, including Continental-plus breakfast; two-night minimum if Saturday stay included

CREDIT CARDS ACCEPTED: American Express, MasterCard, Visa

OPEN: Year-round

SMOKING: Smoking permitted; designated nonsmoking rooms

HOW TO GET THERE: From I-287 in New Jersey, take exit 13 onto Route 202 south. Follow Route 202 for 26 miles and cross over the bridge into Pennsylvania. Take the first Pennsylvania exit and follow Route 32 south for about ½ mile to New Hope. At the traffic light, turn right onto Bridge Street and proceed up the hill. The B&B will be on the right in ½ mile.

Although Dennis Cianci, the innkeeper at The Fox and Hound, has been operating his B&B since 1984, the recent renovations he incorporated have transformed it into a B&B of the 1990s. There's a bright and cheerful breakfast room, for example, with an oak floor, and green walls with white trim. Huge glass French doors lead to a terrace. A kitchen with a microwave and a supply of lovely dishes is available for guests to use.

The impressive 1850s grey stone building with its slate mansard roof is beautifully situated on two lush acres surrounded by glorious flower gardens. A barn occupies some space, and for a thoroughly whimsical touch, there's a huge cement pig on the lawn adjacent to the driveway.

Guests of this sophisticated and upscale B&B will enjoy the use of a graceful living room with green walls topped by beautiful crown moldings. There's a gas fireplace and a hooked rug on the polished oak floors.

The guest rooms are furnished with beautiful antiques and the baths are new and modern. Room #2, for example, has a king-size iron bed and a fireplace. The bath includes a pedestal sink. Room #3 has a gas fireplace and a whirlpool tub in the bath, and Room #5 has a bay window and pretty stenciling on the walls. There's a brown carpet and a bed with a red-plaid spread. The finest rooms, however, are Rooms #7 and #8. Room #7 has a canopy bed and some unusual and interesting antiques. There's a table with a ram's head and another table with a harp base and a flip top that can be used as a game or card table. Stenciling decorates the walls and there are shutters on the windows. My favorite antiques, however, are in Room #8, which has a fabulous highly carved bed that utilizes a pattern of inlaid woods.

Dennis has found that his guests prefer a lighter breakfast during the week than on the weekends. Therefore, on weekdays, he fixes fresh fruit and freshly baked muffins or croissants, as well as hot and cold cereals. On weekends, however, he supplements this with perhaps French toast made with homemade Italian bread or maybe a cheese quiche.

What's Nearby—New Hope

We love to rise early in the morning to take a brisk walk along the tow path that skirts the Pennsylvania side of the Delaware River. To see the Delaware Canal as it once was, take one of the mule-drawn barge rides that originate just down the street in New Hope. In addition, the Bucks County Playhouse, offering an array of live theater, concerts, musicals, and comedies, is just across the street. The Parry Mansion Museum on Main Street has displays of decorative arts from 1775 to 1900. Peddler's Village and Penn's Purchase Factory Stores are just down the street in Lahaska. The complexes include more than one hundred shops featuring everything from interesting antiques to factory outlet shops and restaurants. The New Hope Winery is also in Lahaska. It is open for visits and samples. (See also Doylestown, and Holicong as well as Lambertville, New Jersey.)

Mansion Inn

9 South Main Street
New Hope, PA 18938
(215) 862-1231

FAX: (215) 862-0277

E-MAIL: mansion@pil.net

WEB SITE: www.themansioninn.com

INNKEEPERS: Dr. Elio Bracco and Keith David

ROOMS: 9, including 5 suites, all with private bath, air conditioning, telephone, TV, clock/radio, hair dryer, desk, and robes; 5 with fireplace; 4 with whirlpool tub; 2 with porches or patios; wheelchair access

ON THE GROUNDS: Swimming pool; gardens with gazebo

EXTRAS: Turndown with fresh cookies, bottled spring water and ice; candy in common rooms; sherry in parlor; early morning coffee tray and newspaper delivered to room door; wine and cheese late Saturday afternoons

RATES: $160–$300, double occupancy, including full breakfast; two-night minimum weekends; three-night minimum holidays

CREDIT CARDS ACCEPTED: American Express, MasterCard, Visa

OPEN: Year-round

HOW TO GET THERE: From I–78, take Route 202 south. After crossing the Delaware River, exit onto Route 32 south and go to New Hope. At the traffic light at Bridge Street, turn right. Turn left immediately into the first driveway to reach the B&B's parking lot.

For years we walked along the streets of New Hope, browsing in the bookstore or in Katy Kane's antique clothing and linen shop, and wishing that someone would restore the unique Victorian mansion with its mansard roof that sits in the heart of the village. It had all the Victorian excesses we love—a porch embellished with gingerbread, a fanciful cupola, and a grapeleaf wrought-iron fence. At last it's happened, and best of all, it's a bed-and-breakfast that we can all enjoy.

When Dr. Kenneth Leiby decided to sell the house that had long been his home and office, the entire town was concerned about its possible fate. Although it was on the National Register of Historic Places, there was concern that it might be gutted for shops or offices. Not to worry. When Keith David and Dr. Elio Bracco toured the house and talked to Dr. Leiby, they knew what they had to do. And they did it right.

Today the house fairly gleams. It's painted a buttercup yellow with white trim that enhances its carved brackets, arched windows, and wooden cutwork. Inside, Dr. Leiby had carefully preserved doorways and hardware within the walls whenever he made changes, and the new partners, with Dr. Leiby's help, were able to return the house to its original configuration.

The central hall, with its magnificent mahogany staircase and darkly burnished wood floors topped with Oriental rugs, has a drawing room on one side and a double-length living room on the other. Arched mantels echo the arched entryway. A decanter of sherry with stemmed glasses sits on a silver tray on an antique side table.

On our first visit we were escorted to the Ashby Suite. The pretty blue-and-white room has a carved canopy bed hung with a blue-and-white French fabric that is repeated in the drapes and wallpaper. A Victorian love seat and chair are covered in the same fabric, and a beautiful silk Persian rug is on the floor. The featherbeds are dressed with starched white Porthault sheets and matelassé spreads. We slept like contented babies. Upstairs, the Windsor Suite contains a magnificent four-poster bed and a pretty sitting area. A fireplace and a two-person whirlpool tub make this a popular honeymoon destination.

The baths offer all the modern amenities we enjoy today. The floors are tile, as are the tub surrounds, and mirrors are liberally placed across the walls. The hosts have thoughtfully provided such extras as bath salts and oils sitting on a glass shelf.

The house is surrounded with flowers that bloom throughout the spring and summer, and there's a pretty private garden with a gazebo in back. A full-sized pool is located behind a picket fence.

For breakfast we feasted on a variety of sweet breads, muffins, and fresh fruit attractively displayed on an antique Dutch chest. For entrees there may be either French toast (perhaps using croissants and raspberries) or an egg dish (perhaps an omelette with tomato and brie).

New Hope is noted for its numerous antiques shops and fine restaurants, and because the crowds are often thick along New Hope's streets in the summer, it's especially nice to have a private place to park the car.

What's Nearby

See "What's Nearby—New Hope," page 304.

Auldridge Mead

523 Geigel Hill Road
Ottsville, PA 18942
(610) 847–5842

FAX: (610) 847–5664

WEB SITE: www.wsmg.com/auldmead

INNKEEPER: Craig Mattoli

ROOMS: 7, including 3 suites, 5 with private bath and 2 sharing a bath, all with air conditioning and robes; 5 with desk; 3 with TV; 2 with telephone, radio, mini-refrigerator, fireplace, and coffeemaker; 1 with VCR and private porch; telephone available for rooms without one

ON THE GROUNDS: On 14 acres with parking; swimming pool; hiking and walking trails; stables for horses, riding trails

EXTRAS: Guest refrigerator supplied with drinks; coffee and newspaper delivered to guest rooms before breakfast; beds dressed with fine cotton sheets, down comforters, and pillows; specially milled soaps; guest pets permitted with prior permission

RATES: $75–$225, double occupancy, including full breakfast; lower corporate rates available; two-night minimum most weekends; three-night minimum holiday weekends

CREDIT CARDS ACCEPTED: MasterCard and Visa

OPEN: Year-round

SMOKING: Permitted in common areas but not in guest rooms

HOW TO GET THERE: From I–78, take the Hellertown/Bethlehem exit onto Route 412 south. Travel about 12 miles until it intersects with Route 611. Follow Route 611 south for 2²/₁₀ miles and turn left onto Tohickon Valley Road at the Mobil Mini-Mart (on the left). Go 1 block to Durham Road and turn left. At the first crossroad, turn right onto Geigel Hill Road. Travel 2 miles to the B&B, which will be on the right.

Tucked away in a section of Bucks County seldom traveled by tourists, Auldridge Mead (which means "old meadow on the ridge") offers many reasons to make the journey. For one thing, innkeeper Craig Mattoli is a current-day Leonardo da Vinci. Is there anything he can't do? Graduating from college as a physicist in the 1970s, he became a Wall Street whiz in the 1980s. Today, however, in addition to his innkeeping duties, he makes exquisite wooden handcrafted furniture using rare woods that he personally selects for their coloration and graining. Starting as a designer of twig-style chairs and beds, Craig now makes furniture from polished hardwoods such as walnut, cherry, birch, and apple. He also happens to be a terrific cook, and there are frequent classes in Italian and French cooking at the B&B.

The B&B is located on top of a hill in a 200-plus-year-old stone house with a slate roof. A wonderful old stone bank barn with stables often has horses who are boarding. A picturesque stone smoke-and-bake house is a backdrop for a profusion of flowers, and a red granary building houses Craig's furniture workshop. The farm contains a score of fruit trees—including pear, peach, apple, and cherry. Although the complex is merely 4 miles from Route 32 and the Delaware River, it is a winsome rural retreat that's as far removed from the stresses of Wall Street as it can be.

The living room has stone walls, beamed ceilings, and pine floors with a huge braided rug. Craig mixed his own buttermilk-based paints to create the crackle finish he desired. A large-screen TV and VCR are located here along with a video library and a CD player and disks. There are six fireplaces in the B&B, and a massive stone example is located here. The dining room has another fireplace.

One of the guest rooms is located on the first floor in the original summer kitchen. The massive old fireplace is still hidden behind shuttered doors painted the original robin's-egg blue. There are stone walls, antiques, and a bed handcrafted by Craig of ebony, maple, and mahogany. Two more rooms are located on the second floor, reached by a narrow winding stair. He has beautiful stenciling of hanging bouquets on the walls, beamed ceilings, and quilts on the beds. These rooms share a bright little yellow bath with a clawfoot tub. On the third floor, Craig created a lovely, rustic room with a king-size twig bed, and in 1999 he added two new suites in a auxiliary barn building.

A newspaper and coffee are delivered to the door each morning. Breakfast, which is served in the dining room, will include freshly squeezed organic orange juice, fresh fruit, and an entree of perhaps croissant French toast (freshly baked the night before) or a baked egg soufflé with Jarlsburg cheese and smoked salmon served with homemade corn fritters and asparagus.

One of the joys of staying at Auldridge Mead is that there are fine restaurants, museums, cultural events, and shops within a ten-minute drive, but the peaceful, tranquil countryside surrounding the farm is seldom disturbed by even a passing motorist. Guests are welcome to bring their horses, and Craig will offer stable space and feed (there's a charge) as well as directions to the trails.

What's Nearby—Ottsville

The 611 Market nearby has a marvelous array of trash and treasures. On Tuesdays antique-lovers in the know head for Rice's Market on Green Hill Road north of Lahaska. The treasures here are renowned. In season you might go to Penn-Vermont Farm to pick fresh berries and fruit. (See also Doylestown, Kintnersville, Pipersville, Riegelsville, and Upper Black Eddy.)

The Victorian Peacock

Best Buy

309 East Dark Hollow Road
Pipersville, PA 18947
(215) 766–1356 (fax also)

E-MAIL: peacock @epix.net

WEB SITE: www.bestinns.net/usa/pa/
peacock.html

INNKEEPER: Lee Schmidt; proprietor: Lynne McAuley

ROOMS: 5, including 3 suites; 3 with private bath; all with air conditioning, hair dryer, iron, and ironing board

ON THE GROUNDS: On 5 acres with parking; gardens; swimming pool with
whirlpool

EXTRAS: Afternoon wine, tea, coffee, or sodas; billiard table; 3 dogs, Aja,
Chynna, and Indie, and 1 cat, Pricilla, on premises

RATES: $65–$150, double occupancy, including full breakfast on Sunday
and Continental breakfast rest of week, as well as afternoon wine; two-
night minimum weekends

CREDIT CARDS ACCEPTED: MasterCard and Visa

OPEN: Year-round

HOW TO GET THERE: From I–78, take exit 15 (Clinton) and turn left at the
end of the exit ramp. Follow the signs to Route 513 and go south on this
for 10 miles to Frenchtown, New Jersey. Go over the Frenchtown Bridge,
staying on Route 513, to Pennsylvania. Turn left onto River Road (Route
32) at the end of the bridge and follow this for 3²/10 miles to Dark Hollow
Road. Turn right and go 2⁹/10 miles to the B&B, which will be on the left.

I am always amazed at the surprises the back roads of Bucks County reveal.
My introduction to country inns was along the Delaware River on Route
32 in wonderful Bucks County. I have harbored a special affection for the
area ever since—and, of course, I never got over my unabashed love for country inns and bed-and-breakfasts.

The Victorian Peacock is certainly not just another B&B. Located on a
quiet country road that sees little traffic, it stands in stark contrast to the
old stone houses that predominate in Bucks County. Surprisingly, this gem
is not an old restored beauty, but a beauty that was built in 1992 as a private residence. It has three stories of fanciful shingles, gingerbread, and
clapboard, all painted just as a proper Victorian peacock should be in pale
green with grass green, ivory, and wine trim. Guests drive onto the property

along a circular driveway that encloses a pretty tiered fountain. The wrap-around veranda contains wonderful examples of antique wicker furniture. Lynne and Lee have owned it since 1996.

Guests enter a foyer with beautiful oak floors. The living room has a large oak and marble fireplace, and the oak floors are covered with Oriental rugs. One of the more unusual pieces of furniture in the house is a huge throne chair upholstered in burgundy. There's also a player piano here that guests enjoy using. The breakfast room has oak floors as well and another beautiful fireplace with a carved oak mantel.

The guest rooms are on the second floor, which also has oak floors. Victoria includes an antique wood bed and it's decorated with wallpaper featuring fans. Albert has a crown canopy bed with a wine-colored spread and green walls. There are watercolor paintings of floral still lifes of the walls. Victoria and Albert share a bath between them. Sense and Sensibility has a fabulous antique bedroom suite that includes a bed with turned posts and a Victorian dresser and loveseat. The private bath includes a clawfoot tub and a commode with a wall-hung water tank and a pull-chain. Lily Langtry has a burled walnut French bed with a cutwork spread, and Princess Diana features a French Provincial bedroom suite with blue-and-white decor.

There's a third-floor common room that features a billiards table and a TV and VCR, as well as a library of videos and books.

The grounds are as lovely as the house. There's a heated swimming pool and a spa and lovely perennial gardens that offer a kaleidoscope of colors from early spring to late fall.

Lee fixes a full breakfast on Sunday only, when she may serve French toast or waffles. The rest of the week guests will enjoy cereals, fresh fruit, muffins, and coffee or tea.

What's Nearby—Pipersville

Golfing and hiking are both nearby. Five covered bridges are close enough to this B&B to offer great bicycling destinations. Built between 1832 and 1874, they span a variety of styles. Bucks County River Country is also nearby in Point Pleasant. Canoes, tubes, kayaks, and rafts can be rented here for trips down the scenic Delaware River. (See also Kintnersville, New Hope, Ottsville, Riegelsville, and Upper Black Eddy.)

The Appletree Bed & Breakfast

703 South Negley Avenue
Pittsburgh, PA 15232
(412) 661–0631

FAX: (412) 661–7525

WEB SITE: http://deskshop.lm.com/appletree-bb

INNKEEPER: Louise H. Rosenfeld

ROOMS: 8, including 3 suites; all with private bath, air conditioning, telephone with dataport and voice mail, TV, VCR, radio, hair dryer, desk, iron, and ironing board; 7 with fireplace; 4 with whirlpool tub; wheelchair access

ON THE GROUNDS: Parking

EXTRAS: Freshly baked cookies, fruit, and beverages offered every afternoon and evening

RATES: $115–$150, double occupancy, including full breakfast and afternoon refreshments; two-night minimum most weekends

CREDIT CARDS ACCEPTED: American Express, Discover, MasterCard, Visa

OPEN: Year-round

HOW TO GET THERE: From I–76 (the Pennsylvania Turnpike), take exit 6 onto I–376 and follow this west to exit 9 (Edgewood/Swissvale), turning right onto Braddock Avenue. Follow Braddock to Forbes Avenue and turn left. Continue on Forbes Avenue for 3 lights and turn right onto Shady Avenue. Follow Shady Avenue for 3 more lights to Fifth Avenue and then turn left. Stay on Fifth Avenue for 3 lights and turn right onto Negley Avenue. Stay on Negley past Walnut Street and then in 2 short blocks turn right onto Elmer Street. The B&B is on the corner of South Negley and Elmer.

The Appletree is located in the heart of Shadyside, a beautiful area of art galleries, interesting shops, and fine restaurants, especially on Walnut Street. The houses on the side streets such as South Negley are gracious and charming, a beautiful place for a morning stroll past elaborate wrought-iron fences and brick or clapboard houses.

The Appletree was constructed in 1884 by the Reverend Thomas H. Chapman, the pastor of the Thirty-seventh Street Baptist Church. He was also a real estate developer, and for this house he used a combination of Italianate and Queen Anne styles. He only lived in the house for a year and one-half, however, before selling it to Fred and Susie Hoffman. Mr. Hoffman is notable because he was instrumental in developing Western Pennsylvania's natural gas industry. By the time he moved into 703 South Negley Avenue, he had already sold one company to George Westinghouse. The Hoffman family lived in the house from 1885 to 1964. The house was converted to a B&B in 1995.

The grey clapboard Victorian with white trim offers an immaculate streetside appearance. Bay windows are covered with lace curtains, and a beautiful Victorian side garden is alive with flowers. The main floor of the B&B is notable for its elaborately detailed 14-foot-high plaster ceilings and moldings. There are new polished walnut floors.

Guests can relax in a formal parlor, where a fireplace offers a warm welcome on cold winter days. There are numerous books for reading and a game table on which to play one of the board games that are provided. The formal dining room, where breakfast is served, has another fireplace. A gourmet breakfast might include a hot entree of the B&B's award-winning Appletree Breakfast Bake—a combination of eggs, cheese, and sausage. Or pumpkin pancakes or brie baked eggs might be offered.

The guest rooms are named for various types of apples. The MacIntosh has a fireplace, parquet floors, and a four-poster bed, while the bath features a clawfoot tub. The Golden Delicious has a sleigh bed and a fireplace. The Northern Spy suite includes a wrought-iron bed and parquet floors enhanced by Oriental rugs. A new room and two new suites were added in 1999. Braeburn, on the first floor, is wheelchair accessible. It has a four-poster bed and a fireplace. The Courtland Suite has floor-to-ceiling bay windows. There's a four-poster bed, a fireplace, and a whirlpool tub in the bath.

What's Nearby—Pittsburgh

Both of the B&Bs in this city that are mentioned in this book are located in the historic Shadyside district of Pittsburgh, an area known as "Mansion Row" for the wealth of grand mansions built nearby and now also a trendy area of upscale shops and restaurants. Nearby are the Carnegie Museums of art and history, the Carnegie Science Center, the Andy Warhol Museum, and the Frick Museum and Historical Center. The area is tucked between Carnegie-Mellon University and the University of Pittsburgh.

The Shadyside Bed & Breakfast

5516 Maple Heights Road
Pittsburgh, PA 15232
(412) 683–6501

FAX: (412) 683–7228

WEB SITE: www.pittsburgh.net/shadysidebb

INNKEEPERS: Richard, Gracianna, and
Allison Fennell; manager: Mary Beth Holan

ROOMS: 8, 6 with private bath and
2 that share 1 bath; all with air
conditioning, telephone with voice mail and dataport, and radio;
5 with desk, 2 with hair dryer

ON THE GROUNDS: On spacious grounds with parking; gardens

EXTRAS: Afternoon tea; guest kitchen with fruit, cookies, biscotti, and
sodas; evening wine and cheese; pets considered with prior inquiry

RATES: $120–$145, double occupancy, including Continental breakfast

CREDIT CARDS ACCEPTED: American Express, Discover, MasterCard, Visa

OPEN: Year-round

HOW TO GET THERE: From I–76 (the Pennsylvania Turnpike), take exit 6
onto I–376 and follow this west to exit 9 (Edgewood/Swissvale), turning
right onto Braddock Avenue. Follow Braddock to Forbes Avenue and
turn left. Continue on Forbes Avenue for about 2 miles to Beechwood
Boulevard and turn right. Follow Beechwood Boulevard for about 2
miles and turn left onto Fifth Avenue. Continue for ¹/₁₀ mile past the
Negley Avenue traffic light and turn left onto Maple Heights Road.
Maple Heights Road is between South Aiken and South Negley. Enter
the street through stone pillars that appear to lead to a private driveway.
Circle past two apartment buildings and continue up the steep hill
behind them. The B&B is the last house on the right, at the end of the
street.

What a wonderful B&B this is! I love the rich woods that are so elaborately used, elegant fireplaces, the spaciousness of the rooms, and the
grand front-to-back entry hall. As I approached the mansion on my
first visit, I must admit to an uncertainty. Was this approach, leading
through stone pillars to a parking area for two apartment houses and then
circling past a series of homes, really the entrance to so fine a mansion?

Indeed it was, for at the very end of the drive, I entered the stone porte cochere that offers shelter from the rain and snow to guests bound for this beige stone bed-and-breakfast. Built in 1903, the estate was converted to a B&B in 1991.

We entered a spacious entry hall. A grand stairway has fabulous stained-glass windows worthy of a church overseeing the landing. Off the entrance hall a library has a masculine and cozy feeling, with built-in bookcases with leaded-glass doors, leaded windows, and a huge fireplace. The oak floors are covered with a Bokhara rug and there are boxed beamed ceilings and a beautiful oak library table. A billiard room has another huge fireplace and elaborate moldings. A billiard table sits in the middle of the room, and there are views of downtown Pittsburgh.

The guest rooms are spacious and furnished with antiques. Room #1 has a four-poster reproduction bed, an antique secretary and dresser, and a chest with a marble top. There are oak floors and a crystal chandelier. Rooms #1 and #2 share a hall bath.

Breakfast is served in the formal dining room, which includes a beamed ceiling, ivory paneled walls, a beautiful carved built-in oak buffet, and an oak floor covered with an elegant Oriental rug. Dark wood tables are set with Ainsley china on English place trays. We were served delicious warm oversized muffins, fresh croissants, juice, and cereals.

What's Nearby

See "What's Nearby—Pittsburgh," page 312.

Stone Pond Bed & Breakfast

5846 Durham Road (Route 412)
Riegelsville, PA 18077
(610) 346–6236 (fax also)

WEB SITE: members.aol.com/stonepond1

INNKEEPER: Jerry Hanley

ROOMS: 5, including 2 suites; all with private bath, air conditioning, radio, and desk; 2 with robes, fireplace, and TV; 1 with whirlpool tub

ON THE GROUNDS: On 4 acres with parking; gardens; barn, "old milk house getaway"; swimming pool, hot tub

EXTRAS: Evening treats featuring double flourless chocolate cake with raspberry sauce, sherry, and handmade chocolates

RATES: $100–$145, double occupancy, including full breakfast and evening treats; two-night minimum weekends

CREDIT CARDS ACCEPTED: MasterCard and Visa

OPEN: Year-round

HOW TO GET THERE: From I–78 in Bethlehem take exit 21 (Hellertown) and follow Route 412 south for 8⁷/₁₀ miles. The B&B will be on the right.

Although Riegelsville is in Bucks County, it is located in a bucolic countryside far removed from the often glitzy and always upscale action of New Hope. This a peaceful country B&B where you can contemplate nature by admiring the beautiful gardens and the many birds and animals that visit them.

The land for Stone Pond was originally part of William Penn's holdings, and this particular parcel was deeded to William Crook in 1763 by Penn's sons. Innkeeper Jerry Hanley actually has a deed dated 1786, so parts of the current house may have been built at that time. It's a handsome two-story Federal stone house with a slate roof. A 1950s addition is made of clapboard. There's a huge stone barn and pond out back, as well as a picturesque milk house in which Jerry has created a quiet guest getaway. It's in a secluded and private spot, and it's outfitted with wicker furniture. On the other hand, there's also a hammock tied to some towering pines and a large Olympic-size swimming pool with a cobblestone surround and chaise longues for sunny summer days.

The B&B has a guest living room that includes a mammoth walk-in fireplace and Oriental rugs on wide-plank pine floors. The walls are white and there's mustard trim. Overstuffed sofas and chairs are creamy white. The sunroom is the happy abode of a greenhouse of plants that range from tropical orchids to rubber plants and ferns.

There are three guest rooms in the old section of the house, and all are decorated with antique or period reproduction furniture. The Brass Room has a brass bed and brass fixtures in the bath. White walls and green trim give it a crisp and restful appearance. The bath has wide-plank pine floors, and it's papered in a predominantly green color. There are two new suites. One has a four-poster cherry bed and a fireplace and TV, as well as a picture window overlooking the gardens. The other also has a four-poster cherry bed, a fireplace and a TV, but it has sliding glass doors to a private porch, as well as a whirlpool tub in the tiled bath.

Jerry has owned Stone Pond since 1991, but before that he owned a restaurant in Chicago. This man knows and cares about fine cuisine, as his breakfasts prove. Every breakfast menu is presented on a menu card that describes the offerings. One day the menu started with juices, coffee or tea, and homemade pumpkin and banana breads. Next he served baked pears in cream. This was followed by an entree of soufflé roulade with three-mushroom filling, beer batter potato pancakes, and hot cream biscuits. Another day the entree consisted of a country stack of Grand Marnier French toast with glazed breakfast ham and warm Vermont maple syrup.

Following a breakfast such as this, guests may wish to take a long and vigorous hike along the Delaware River tow path!

What's Nearby—Riegelsville

You might go for a horseback ride nearby or take a glider or hot air balloon ride across the patchwork of fields and forests meandering alongside the Delaware River. Or, for a change of pace, visit the Crayola Factory in Easton, where you can see Crayola crayons and markers being made and enjoy the interactive museum, or you might purchase Crayolas at the extensive Crayola store. Mostly, however, you should explore the quiet back roads of upper Bucks County to find the hidden treasures that keep us all coming back again and again.

Cooke Tavern Bed & Breakfast

Best Buy

RD #3, Box 218-A
Spring Mills, PA 16875
(814) 422-8787

FAX: (814) 422-8752
E-MAIL: cooketavn@aol.com
WEB SITE: www.virtualcities.com/ons/pa/c/pac2702.htm
INNKEEPERS: Mary Kay and Greg Williams

ROOMS: 3 rooms, 1 with private bath, the other 2 share 1 bath; all with air conditioning and telephone; 1 with two-person Jacuzzi

ON THE GROUNDS: On 40 acres bordering Penns Creek, with nature walk through wetlands to the creek; fishing

EXTRAS: Beverages and a snack such as cheese and crackers and fresh fruit served on arrival; turndown with homemade cookies or chocolates; Max, a border collie, on premises; guest pets possibly allowed with prior permission

RATES: $85–$125, double occupancy, including full breakfast and arrival snacks; two-night minimum during special event weekends

CREDIT CARDS ACCEPTED: MasterCard and Visa

OPEN: Year-round

HOW TO GET THERE: From I–80, take exit 24 onto Route 26 south. Follow this for 5 miles to Route 144 south. Follow Route 144 south for 3 miles to Route 45. Turn left onto Route 45 east and continue for 6 miles to the B&B, which is on the right.

Cooke Tavern, a grand two-story brick Georgian-style edifice, was built as a wayside tavern in 1808 by James Cooke. It operated as a stagecoach stop and tavern until 1863, when it was converted to a private residence. It must have been unused for a number of years, however, for when Mary Kay and Greg purchased it in 1991, it had never been equipped with a heating system or with indoor plumbing, and there was minimal electrical service. Fortunately, the original yellow pine floors and door hardware were still in place. Although it took four years, the historically accurate restoration the couple accomplished won them the Centre County Excellence in Historic Preservation award in 1995.

The august house boasts a winding staircase that reaches to the third floor and 11-foot ceilings on the main floor. The rich wide-plank pine floors are now burnished and mellow (although those in the original tavern room were not refinished, leaving them in a state the old stagecoach drivers would recognize today). The parlor has walls that were hand sponged in light pink, and it's decorated with antique furniture. The dining room walls were rag rolled to give them the ambience of an earlier time, and there's an antique dining room set here. In the kitchen, which still has its Colonial fireplace, the original woodwork remains. Mary Kay hand stenciled the walls, and the Williamses had cabinets custom built to look as if they were made in Colonial times.

The three guest rooms are spacious. The enormous ballroom, which measured 17 by 34 feet was divided in half to create two of the rooms. Both rooms are painted in authentic Colonial colors that include deep turquoise, burgundy, and gold. Ballroom North has a mahogany pineapple post bed, while Ballroom South has a cherry four-poster. Although these rooms share a bath, it is one of the most luxurious you will ever see. More like an elaborate Roman spa, it has a marble tile floor, wonderful big columns, and a two-person whirlpool tub. Water pours from the mouth of an ornate gargoyle, and there's a TV that's strategically placed to encourage utter relaxation. The other guest room, called the Cherub Room, is decorated in soft peach with accents of blue and yellow and contains a lovely antique iron and brass bed that belonged to Mary Kay's grandmother.

Breakfast is an event at Cooke Tavern. It's served by candlelight and will always include fresh fruit, homemade bread, and a specialty entree—two favorites are a mushroom cheese strata and baked French toast that's topped with bananas.

The B&B is surrounded by lovely gardens. Guests love to take the nature walk down to Penns Creek, where fishing is good, and there are spots for quiet picnics. The Williamses were in the midst of reclaiming some of the wetlands along the creek when I last spoke to them. They want to entice more birds and animals, although there are already several families of ducks and a variety of bullfrogs in the marsh grass. Butterfly enthusiasts love to come in August to see the beautiful Monarch butterflies who come to visit the milkweed on their annual migration.

What's Nearby—Spring Mills

Spring Mills is near State College, where a wealth of cultural, educational, and sports events take place year-round. In addition, it is also near the Mid-state Trail that traverses Poe Valley State Park, which is just south. It offers excellent hiking opportunities. In winter Tussey Mountain has trails available for downhill skiing, and there are golf courses nearby as well. A wonderful restaurant, The Hummingbird Room, serving fine French cuisine, is within walking distance. (See also Bellefonte.)

Liondale Farm

160 East Street Road (Route 926)
(mailing address: P.O. Box 339)
Unionville, PA 19375
(610) 444–7130

INNKEEPER: Linda Kaat

ROOMS: 4, all with private bath and air conditioning, telephone, fireplace, TV, VCR, radio, hair dryer, and desk; cribs available

ON THE GROUNDS: On 83 acres with parking; gardens; wooded trails, stream, barn, stable and ring for guests who bring their own horses; chicken coop with hens laying fresh eggs

EXTRAS: Tea, wine, beer, cookies in the afternoon; silver tray of cordials in living room; every bathroom amenity you may ever need; well-traveled pets permitted with prior permission; two barn cats and two dogs on premises

RATES: $125–$195, double occupancy, including full breakfast

CREDIT CARDS ACCEPTED: None

OPEN: Year-round

HOW TO GET THERE: From I–95 in Wilmington, Delaware, take exit 7 and follow Route 52 north, crossing the state line into Pennsylvania. After crossing Route 1, turn left (west) onto Route 926. The B&B is 2½ miles from Route 52 on the left.

Along a sleepy little highway in the Brandywine Valley, Liondale Farm sits on 83 acres of pasture, wooded acres, and farmland. The long lane to the farmhouse is bordered by majestic evergreen, ash, and copper beech trees interspersed with forsythia and other flowering trees and bushes. Fields of corn, soy beans, and wheat stretch on either side into the distance. To the left, there's a huge barn and stables where guests are invited to bring their horses for a ride in the B&B's ring or in the fields, and there's also a chicken house where chickens produce fresh eggs for the B&B's farm breakfasts. The fields behind the B&B are often used on Sundays by a local pony club for exhibitions.

This idyllic retreat is the newest adventure for experienced innkeeper Linda Kaat, whom we have long admired for her creation of the Brandywine's first elegant manor house B&B, Sweetwater Farm. After selling that several years ago and then living abroad, she returned to her roots, where she restored this historic 1770s farmhouse.

Guests enter the spacious living room, which has wide pine floors, tall bookcases, two fireplaces set in paneled walls with interesting built-in cupboards, a plush blue-and-white sofa, and a wonderful Scottish tall-case clock with ornate brass hands. Fresh flowers fill vases on tables and desks.

The guest rooms are reached by climbing a set of narrow winding stairs at either end of the house. Two rooms are located at each end, each with its own bath. There are canopy and wicker beds as well as antique desks and antique tables holding vases of fresh flowers. Linda has perfected the art of pampering her guests by thinking of all the little amenities and details that would make their stay memorable. Every room has a telephone and a

TV/VCR, and the baths are supplied with silver candlestick lamps, blue willow vases with fresh flowers, silver Revere bowls filled with loofahs, brushes, soaps, and bath salts, and medicine cabinets holding an array of perfumes, cotton balls, Band-aids, and much more.

Breakfast is served in the Colonial-style dining room, which has another woodburning fireplace and a built-in corner china cabinet oddly inserted into a straight wall. The brass chandelier burns candles. Guests are seated at a common table, where the conversation is bound to be fascinating. Linda fixes French toast with strawberry sauce or maple syrup and bacon as well as omelettes and other luscious dishes. One morning when I was there, she went next door and picked fresh mushrooms at the mushroom farm for omelettes and, of course, she uses her own farm-fresh eggs.

There are trails to hike through the woods and pastures to roam. The many attractions of the Brandywine Valley lie just beyond the peaceful farm.

What's Nearby—Unionville

The B&B's 83 acres are backed by Longwood Gardens, and the fields near the B&B are often used in spring and fall for equestrian competitions. The Willowdale Steeplechase & Gold Cup is run nearby, providing exciting viewing of nationally ranked horses leaping over spectacular jumps. There are also carriage parades and family activities. The Brandywine Valley labels itself the "Mushroom Capital of the World." Go to a nearby mushroom farm to pick your own or visit the Mushroom Museum at Phillips Place in nearby Kennett Square. The Franklin Mint Museum is located in nearby Franklin Center on US 1. See heirloom collector dolls and changing art exhibits showcasing the artists featured in Franklin Mint reproductions and view original art by Norman Rockwell and Andrew Wyeth. (See also Chadds Ford and West Chester.)

Bridgeton House on the Delaware

1525 River Road
Upper Black Eddy, PA 18972
(888) 982–2007 or (610) 982–5856

FAX: (610) 982–5080
E-MAIL: bestinn1@epix.net
WEB SITE: www.bridgetonhouse.com

INNKEEPERS: Bea and Charles Briggs

ROOMS: 11, including 3 suites; all with private bath, air conditioning, telephone with dataport, radio, and robes; 8 with private porch; 5 with TV and mini-refrigerator, 4 with VCR and desk; 3 with fireplace

ON THE GROUNDS: Parking; riverside terrace; dock for swimming, boating, canoeing, and fishing

EXTRAS: Turndown with chocolates; afternoon tea and sherry with cakes and cookies

RATES: $99–$325, double occupancy, including full breakfast and afternoon tea; two-night minimum weekends; three-night minimum holiday weekends

CREDIT CARDS ACCEPTED: MasterCard and Visa

OPEN: Year-round

HOW TO GET THERE: From I–78, take exit 15 (Clinton/Pittstown in New Jersey). Go to the light and turn left. Turn left at the end of the ramp onto Route 513 south and go for 11 miles to the New Jersey town of Frenchtown. Cross the Delaware River into Pennsylvania. Turn right onto Route 32 north and go 3½ miles to the B&B, which will be on the right.

Let your imagination run free, just as Bea and Charlie have, and you too can have a one-of-a-kind B&B. At Bridgeton House each room is an exuberant expression of artistic whimsy, but all are melded together into an amusing and original whole. Innkeepers Bea and Charles Briggs, working with Bea's cousin, artist Cheryl Raywood, have created a totally unique B&B.

Taking a circa 1836 terra cotta apartment house with shuttered windows that sits on the Delaware River, Charles, who happens be a master craftsman, created windows, French doors, and porches across the back to provide wonderful views of the river. Bea, who has a terrific decorating eye, coordinated fabrics and furniture, while Cheryl painted bold patterns on walls and ceilings.

Every guest room is as imaginative as a page from *Alice's Adventures in Wonderland.* In the River Suite, for example, red-plaid pillows accent the king-size bed. The top half of the walls are painted mustard yellow, while the lower half is a checkerboard of green, blue, and yellow. A bright blue-green chair rail separates the two. Other features include a corner fireplace and a screened porch. Another room has fuchsia-and-gold walls and a stenciled bath, while a third has a cobalt blue ceiling painted with gold stars. In the baths, Charlie has created polished mahogany cabinets and skirts for the tubs, which contrast with the tile floors and tub surrounds. The beds often have canopies or half-canopies. My favorite room is the cozy Garrett Room, which has pink sponge-painted walls embellished with squiggles, a half-canopy bed, and a romantic porch.

The penthouse suite, on the top floor, however, is stark by contrast. It has white walls, a 12-foot cathedral ceiling, and a fireplace of black-and-white marble. The king-size bed faces a wall of Palladian-style windows that offer breathtaking views of the river. Charlie created an Art Nouveau hanging bar with stained-glass doors and an enormous bath with a marble floor, a pedestal sink, and a deep tub with a marble surround.

Although the B&B sits close to the road, there is plenty of room in back for car parking, gardens, and a lovely, romantic terrace by the river. Down at the dock, guests can swim and fish, and there are canoes to rent nearby. Guests enter the B&B through a warm and comfortable common room that boasts stacks of books, magazines, games, and jigsaw puzzles.

The breakfast room has walls trimmed with stencils and a gas fireplace. Guests may choose from a menu of such delicacies as a baked pear in a light cream sauce and orange poppyseed waffles, or a baked apple with walnuts, oats, and brown sugar, followed by a frittata. Freshly baked breakfast breads include an apple/raisin bread, a lemon tea bread, and a pear bread.

What's Nearby—Upper Black Eddy

Take a hammer to Ringing Rocks Park, where the rocks ring like bells when struck. Take a stroll or a bicycle ride along the picturesque 60-mile-long Delaware Canal towpath as it meanders behind old stone houses and gardens adjacent to the Delaware River. Numerous picnic sites offer opportunities to rest and take in the beauty. (See also Kintnersville, Ottsville, and Riegelsville in Pennsylvania, and Milford, New Jersey.)

Whitewing Farm Bed & Breakfast

Valley Road (mailing address: RD 6)
West Chester, PA 19382
(610) 388–2664

FAX: (610) 388–3650
E-MAIL: info@whitewingfarm.com
WEB SITE: www.whitewingfarm.com
INNKEEPERS: Ed and Wanda DeSeta

ROOMS: 9, including 2 suites, all with private bath, air conditioning, TV, radio; 4 with patio; suites with a fireplace; 3 rooms with wheelchair access; telephone available in den; cribs available

ON THE GROUNDS: On 43 acres with parking; 10-hole pitch-and-putt golf course; swimming pool; tennis court

EXTRAS: Afternoon tea including freshly baked cookies; two cocker spaniels named Freckles and Margaret Quinn; outside cats, pet cows named Mickey, Oreo, and Double Stuff on premises

RATES: $115–$275, double occupancy, including full breakfast and afternoon tea; two-night minimum weekends

CREDIT CARDS ACCEPTED: None

OPEN: Year-round

HOW TO GET THERE: From I–95 in Wilmington, Delaware, take exit 7 and follow Route 52 north, crossing the state line into Pennsylvania. Continue on Route 52 for about 6 miles to Valley Road. Turn left onto Valley Road. The driveway to Whitewing Farm is on the right in ¾ mile.

Whitewing Farm is one of those secret treasures that's so special you hate to tell anyone about it for fear it may change in some way. Located on forty-three acres in the rolling rural countryside of Pennsylvania's Brandywine Valley, it's close to all the popular attractions and yet as far removed spiritually as if it were on another continent. It isn't just that the stream falls from the hillside in a stone-lined trough through a series of waterfalls into the pond or that the stone terraces offer views of the ten-hole pitch-and-putt golf course or that you can walk down to the pasture to feed the pet cows that come to the fence when called to nibble the carrots they love so much—it's also that Ed and Wanda DeSeta are some of the friendliest and nicest innkeepers you'll ever meet.

The rambling stone main house dates from 1796, but when it became the home of the treasurer of Dupont in the 1940s and 1950s, it took on an entirely updated character. He added the Pine Room, for example, which has beautiful wide-plank oak floors and corduroy-covered sofas before a pine-paneled wall containing a huge cooking fireplace. A pool table fills one end of the large room and gorgeous taxidermy pieces, including a bobcat leaping to catch a grouse and a fox with a fish in its mouth, stand on tables.

Guests enter the B&B through an open kitchen and immediately gravitate to the cookie jar, which is filled daily with a freshly baked offering—perhaps almond and lemon sugar cookies and chocolate buttermilk brownies. A big pine table sits in a bay window, offering a place to sip a cup of tea and gaze at the rolling countryside beyond the swimming pool. The formal living room has another fireplace and a wonderful Winterthur reproduction of a 1700s Rhode Island secretary with shelves above holding a collection of papier-mâché Santa Clauses. In the pine-paneled den, which has another fireplace, there's an Oriental rug on oak floors and shelves filled with books. This is where the telephone is located.

Throughout the B&B, there are huge pots holding cymbidium orchids and flowers. You understand the source, when you visit Nancy's whimsical greenhouse—a rambling structure in which she's painted the walls and cupboards with bouquets of daisies, coneflowers, lilies, and roses. Painted cascades of ivy topple over the doors and windows.

The guest rooms are furnished with nice reproduction pieces and include all the amenities both business and tourist travelers may need. The floors are carpeted, the closets are ample, the wing chairs before the TV are comfortable, and the beds have firm mattresses. There are vases of fresh flowers beside the bed and in the bath; a dish of candy sits on a nightstand. The baths have tile floors, marble counters, and showers large enough for two. There's a horsey theme throughout, with horse prints and oils on the walls and a leather statue of a horse in each of the rooms.

Breakfast is served in the formal dining room at a large table set with bright blue place mats. In winter a fire blazes in the fireplace. The meal will start with juice and several freshly baked breakfast breads such as lemon/poppyseed or blueberry/apple. The entree may include pancakes with raspberry sauce or eggs Benedict.

What's Nearby

Ride the Brandywine Scenic Railroad in West Chester for an excursion beside the Brandywine River or rent a canoe in Northbrook for a lazy ride on the river. Most of all, don't miss a trip to Baldwin's Book Barn, a unique collection of more than 400,000 rare and used books, maps, and prints, located in a historic 1822 stone bank barn on Routes 100 and 52 in West Chester. (See also Chadds Ford and Unionville.)

Snyder House Victorian Bed & Breakfast

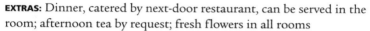

Best Buy

411 West Fourth Street
Williamsport, PA 17701
(570) 326–0411 or (570) 494–0835

E-MAIL: esnyder@csrlink.net

INNKEEPERS: Elizabeth Snyder-Slothus and Robert Slothus

ROOMS: 5, all with private bath, air conditioning, and TV; 1 with private porch; telephone available

ON THE GROUNDS: Parking; gardens

EXTRAS: Dinner, catered by next-door restaurant, can be served in the room; afternoon tea by request; fresh flowers in all rooms

RATES: $85–$150, double occupancy, including Continental breakfast; two-night minimum weekends

CREDIT CARDS ACCEPTED: MasterCard and Visa

OPEN: Year-round

HOW TO GET THERE: From I–80, exit onto I–180 and travel toward Williamsport. Take the Downtown/Basin Street exit and stay to the right. Go to the traffic light and turn left onto East Fourth Street. Stay on East Fourth Street through 6 traffic lights, and you will then enter the Historic District. The B&B is the third mansion on the left.

When Williamsport, which is in north-central Pennsylvania, was the heart of a bustling lumber region, lumber barons built their grand Victorian homes along the street now known as Millionaire's Row. The brick and brownstone double-turret mansion that houses the Snyder House Victorian Bed and Breakfast was built in 1889 as a wedding present for a bride. Lavishly furnished with the finest Victorian pieces of the day, the house and its furnishings have miraculously survived more than one hundred years intact. They passed from the original owner to Elizabeth's aunt, who lived here for more than fifty years. Elizabeth and Robert purchased the property in 1989, complete with the furnishings and an attic full of historic treasures.

Elizabeth and Robert seem perfectly melded into the time and place of their Victorian B&B. Elizabeth was raised on a nearby two-hundred-year-old farm, and she continues to maintain her flower and holiday shop, called the Strawberry Basket, there. She lavishly decorates the B&B in dried garlands and is rediscovering floral oil painting. Robert, who is a professor of radiography at Penn College, is also an accomplished pianist, writer, and copy-painter. He frequently entertains guests, especially during Sunday morning breakfasts, with piano pieces.

In the parlor, which is painted a deep green, there's a rose theme. Rose carvings accent the white wooden fireplace mantel, and roses appear in the lovely carpeting. Victorian chairs and love seats are covered in brocade and tapestry, and there's an electric pump organ and a lavish Victorian chandelier. In the music room/library the walls are painted oxblood, and there's a baby grand piano as well as a mahogany square grand piano. The unique furnishings, however, are in the dining room, which has creamy ivory walls that serve as a restrained backdrop for the elaborately carved dining room suite. The 14-foot table has club claw feet, and the sideboard is intricately carved with fantastical gargoyles. The matching server and china cabinet are equally elaborate. Exuberant stained-glass windows grace both the first- and second-floor landings.

In the guest rooms the antique Victorian furniture is also original to the house. The Wittenburg Bridal Suite has a bed with a high walnut Victorian head- and footboard, lavishly carved with daisies, ivy, and maple leaves. There's a matching marble-topped dresser and a marble-topped wash stand. The triple bowed stained-glass windows have hot pink jewels that cast reflections across the walls. The Snyder Anniversary Room also has a high Victorian handcarved headboard, this one embellished with dogwood blossoms. There's a matching full-length cheval mirror, a sitting area filled with antique wicker in the turret, and stained-glass windows with a fleur-de-lis design. Each room has a private bath, and in this one, the clawfoot tub has been marbleized.

No design detail skips Elizabeth's attention. For breakfast, she color-coordinates the food, place mats, and dishes, garnishing the plates with herbs and edible flowers from her gardens. She may prepare baked apples or poached pears with Chambord in the winter, while fresh fruit or berries are served in the growing season. Homemade muffins and breads are accompanied by homemade jams and jellies. The meal is either served from tiered sterling silver servers in the dining room or more informally in the kitchen, which contains a big old-fashioned stove.

What's Nearby—Williamsport

Williamsport is the home of the Little League World Series and the Little League Museum. The World Series, which is held toward the end of August, attracts teams and parents from all over the United States. The Lycoming County Historical Museum contains a wonderful history of the area and includes a diorama depicting the local logging industry, an exhibition of trains, and historical room settings.

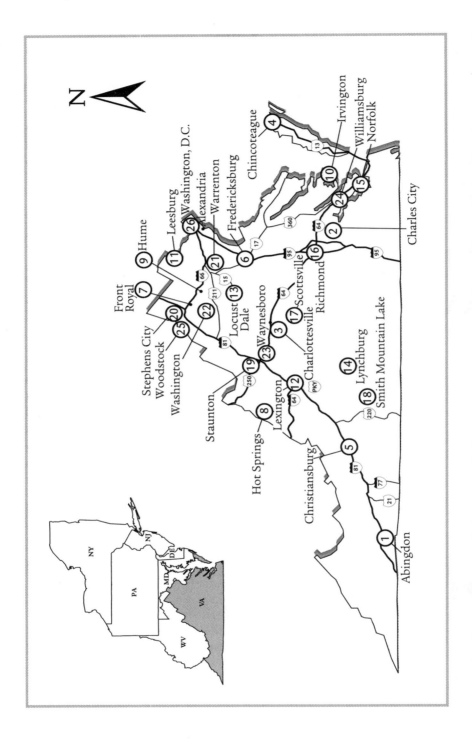

Virginia and Washington, D.C.

Numbers on map refer to towns numbered below.

Virginia

1. Abingdon,
   Summerfield Inn Bed &
     Breakfast, 330
   White Birches Inn, 332

2. Charles City, Piney Grove at
   Southall's Plantation, 334

3. Charlottesville, 200 South
   Street, 336

4. Chincoteague, The Watson
   House Bed & Breakfast and
   The Inn at Poplar Corner, 338

5. Christiansburg, The Oaks
   Victorian Inn, 340

6. Fredericksburg, Richard
   Johnston Inn, 342

7. Front Royal, Killahevlin B&B
   Inn, 344

8. Hot Springs, King's Victorian
   Inn Bed & Breakfast, 346

9. Hume, The Inn at Fairfield
   Farm, 348

10. Irvington, The Hope and Glory
    Inn, 351

11. Leesburg, The Norris House
    Inn, 353

12. Lexington, Brierley Hill B&B
    Country Inn, 355

13. Locust Dale, The Inn at Meander
    Plantation, 357

14. Lynchburg,
    Federal Crest Inn Bed &
      Breakfast, 359
    Lynchburg Mansion Inn Bed &
      Breakfast, 362

15. Norfolk, Bed & Breakfast at the
    Page House Inn, 364

16. Richmond, The Emmanuel
    Hutzler House, 366

17. Scottsville, Chester, 368

18. Smith Mountain Lake, The
    Manor at Taylor's Store
    B&B Country Inn, 370

19. Staunton, The Sampson Eagon
    Inn, 372

20. Stephens City, The Inn at
    Vaucluse Spring, 374

21. Warrenton, Black Horse Inn, 377

22. Washington,
    Middleton Inn, 379
    Sycamore Hill House and
      Gardens, 381

23. Waynesboro, The Iris Inn, 383

24. Williamsburg,
    The Cedars Bed & Breakfast, 385
    Inn at 802, 387
    Liberty Rose Bed & Breakfast
      Inn, 389

25. Woodstock, The Inn at Narrow
    Passage, 391

Washington, D.C.

26. Swann House, 393

Virginia

Summerfield Inn Bed & Breakfast

101 West Valley Street
Abingdon, VA 24210
(800) 668-5905 or (540) 628-5905

FAX: (540) 628-7515

E-MAIL: stay@summerfieldinn.com

WEB SITE: www.summerfieldinn.com

INNKEEPERS: Janice and Jim Cowan

ROOMS: 7; all with private bath, air conditioning, telephone with data-port, radio, desk, and robes; 5 with whirlpool tub; 3 with TV; wheelchair access

ON THE GROUNDS: On ¾ acre with rose garden

EXTRAS: Afternoon tea and cookies; evening wine or beer and light appetizer

RATES: $100–$140, double occupancy, including full breakfast and afternoon and evening refreshments; two-night minimum weekends and during local special events

CREDIT CARDS ACCEPTED: American Express, MasterCard, Visa

OPEN: Year-round

HOW TO GET THERE: From I–81, take exit 17 (Abingdon) and turn north onto Cummings Street. Follow this to its end and then turn right at the traffic light onto West Valley Street. The B&B is on the left in 2 blocks.

The Summerfield Inn is located within the historic district of Abingdon, just 1 block from Main Street. In a handsome ivory brick building with a cupola and a wraparound porch supported by boxed columns (complete with wicker chairs and rockers and a hanging swing), it is known as The Parsonage. It was built by John Bradley in 1921, but it soon became the general offices and parsonage for the Methodist Church, a role it sustained for 40-plus years—and it's still known by that name locally. The house has a porte cochere separating the main house from the carriage house and a large yard in back that contains a rose garden.

Janice and Jim Cowan purchased the B&B in 1998, and they completed a renovation of the inn and its bathrooms in 1999. Throughout the B&B, you will see examples of their elegant antiques and Jim's extensive collection of clocks. In the huge foyer, that's so big it can accommodate a 9-foot by 12-foot Oriental rug, for example, there's a German grandfather clock. The living room is notable for its substantial engraving of Rothenburg, Germany, above the fireplace, as well as for an open German grandfather clock, a rosewood cabinet, and a player piano. There are oak floors topped with Oriental rugs and paneled walls. At the end of the foyer, through beautiful pocket doors, a study has another fireplace.

The guest rooms are located on the second floor of The Parsonage and in the Carriage House. They are furnished with antiques, as well as period reproductions, including brass and four-poster beds. The pink room has an antique brass and porcelain bed and a charming painting of a beautiful young girl contemplating her new blue dress. The pastel colors in this room are taken from the painting. There are oak floors with Oriental rugs and a pretty mahogany wardrobe. The bath is fresh and new. The blue-and-white room in the Carriage House is decorated with white wicker furniture. There's a bed with a white wicker headboard, and the bath includes a whirlpool tub.

Breakfast is served in the formal dining room, or in the sunroom, or on the porch, depending on the weather. One of Janice's typical meals might feature cinnamon rolls with fresh fruit and orange pecan French toast with orange syrup and bacon.

What's Nearby—Abingdon

Abingdon is a charming and historic town in Virginia's southern panhandle, almost to the Tennessee border. The town dates to 1778 and is now the seat of Washington County. History buffs will want to take a walking tour of the historic district of this interesting town and to visit the Fields-Penn Museum House. Among the historic buildings in town are the Martha Washington Inn, which was built as a private home in 1830 and later expanded when it housed Martha Washington College. The historic Barter Theatre, in a building built in 1869, is the state theater of Virginia and it's just 1 block from the B&B. One of the oldest theaters in America, it's open year-round except for the month of January. For those who hike, the Appalachian Trail is nearby, as is the Virginia Creeper Trail, a 34-mile scenic trail suitable for hikers, bicyclists, and horseback riders. A more unusual adventure can be planned aboard a hot-air balloon that gently floats over the lush countryside.

White Birches Inn   Best Buy

268 Whites Mill Road
Abingdon, VA 24210
(800) BIRCHES or (540) 676–2140

FAX: (540) 676–2146

E-MAIL: stay@whitebirchesinn.com

WEB SITE: www.whitebirchesinn.com

INNKEEPERS: Michael and Paulette Wartella

ROOMS: 5, including 2 suites; all with private bath, air conditioning, telephone with dataport, fireplace, TV, VCR, radio, hair dryer, desk, and robes; 4 with whirlpool tub; wheelchair access

ON THE GROUNDS: On 1 acre with koi pond and gazebo in gardens; sheep graze in pasture behind

EXTRAS: Afternoon refreshments including cheese, fruit, wine or soft drinks; turndown with chocolates

RATES: $85–$110, double occupancy, including full breakfast and afternoon refreshments; two-night minimum weekends in August, October, and on holiday weekends

CREDIT CARDS ACCEPTED: American Express, MasterCard, Visa

OPEN: Year-round

HOW TO GET THERE: From I–81, take exit 17 (Abingdon) and turn north onto Cummings Street. Follow this to its end and then turn right at the traffic light onto West Valley Street. Go through one more traffic light and turn left at the second intersection onto Whites Mill Road. The B&B is the fifth house on the right.

The Barter Theatre in Abingdon was established in 1933, during the height of the Depression, in buildings formerly occupied by the Stonewall Jackson Institute, a girls' school founded in 1869. The name derives from the practice of "bartering" admission to a play with edible foodstuffs such as huckleberries and ham, which were used to pay the actors and playwrights.

Although the house was built in 1921, it celebrates the heritage of the Barter Theatre by naming its guest rooms after playwrights whose plays were performed there. All of the rooms are elegantly furnished with American and English antiques and beautifully appointed with designer linens. The Tennessee Williams Room, for example, has a mahogany sleigh bed and it's decorated in rich jewel tones of ruby, emerald, and gold. There are views of the gardens. The Noel Coward is a lush and tranquil oasis in browns and forest green, and it has a beautiful antique brass bed. All of the rooms have telephones with dataports, as well as TVs with VCRs, and all the baths have oak floors with Oriental rugs and tile tub and shower surrounds.

The house, which is an expanded cape, is a beauty. Its clapboards are painted sage green with forest green accents. It's fronted by glorious gardens that are an array of colors from spring through fall.

There's a spacious living room with a fireplace for guests to use. Polished oak floors are covered with Oriental rugs, and there are antique mahogany and walnut tables, all of which create a restful and elegant atmosphere. A library contains a player piano and there's a selection of musical rolls for guests to play. In addition to books, there is also a selection of videos for watching in the privacy of guest rooms. An outdoor room is furnished with beautiful antique wicker tables and chairs and painted furniture and cooled by ceiling fans. Here guests can enjoy the pond filled with koi that's fed by a small waterfall. Just beyond the pond, there's a pretty gazebo where guests love to sit and gaze at the sheep in the pasture beyond.

Michael is a restaurateur, and he still owns a restaurant in Tennessee. Breakfast here is unusual and appealing. It is served in the formal dining room, where a fire may be blazing in the fireplace in winter. Heirloom sterling silver, beautiful china, and pretty crystal are used. The table is lighted by romantic oil lamps. One of Paulette's most popular entrees is eggs Florentine.

Paulette, who is warm and welcoming, was formerly a registered nurse. She and Michael are long-time local residents, who know exactly how to help their guests plan their day.

What's Nearby

See "What's Nearby—Abingdon," page 331.

Piney Grove at Southall's Plantation

16920 Southall Plantation Lane
Charles City, VA 23030
(mailing address: P.O. Box 1359,
Williamsburg, VA 23187–1359)
(804) 829–2480

FAX: (804) 829–6888

E-MAIL: pineygrove@erols.com

WEB SITE: www.pineygrove.com

INNKEEPERS: The Gordineer family; manager: Joan Gordineer

ROOMS: 5, including 1 suite, all with private bath, air conditioning, radio, mini-refrigerator, coffeemaker, hair dryer, desk, fireplace, and robes; TV, VCR, iron, and ironing board available on request; telephone in main house reception hall

ON THE GROUNDS: On 7 acres with parking; swimming pool, croquet, badminton, volleyball; gardens; barn with farm animals; nature trail; porch swing on veranda

EXTRAS: Mint julep or hot toddy on arrival; Virginia wine or cider in refrigerators; fresh flowers in rooms; turndown with chocolates and brandy

RATES: $130–$170, double occupancy, including full breakfast; two-night minimum holiday weekends

CREDIT CARDS ACCEPTED: None

OPEN: Year-round

HOW TO GET THERE: From the north take I–95 to exit 84 and travel south on I–295. Take exit 22A to Route 5 east (Virginia Scenic Byway). One-half mile after the junction with Route 155, turn left onto Route 615 (watch closely for sign) and continue to the B&B, which will be in 7 miles. From the south take I–95 to exit 46 and travel north on I–295 to exit 22A. Follow remaining directions.

It was a sunny late-winter day when we first drove up to Piney Grove. Joan Gordineer was outside pulling weeds in anticipation of spring. As she showed us through her B&B, she said, "For years my family and I dreamed of restoring a period house. When we purchased this modest 1800s plantation house, it had no roof and some of the floor had deteriorated, but otherwise it was intact." The house includes the oldest log structure in Tidewater Virginia, and once inside it's hard to remember that we're actually in the twentieth century. To heighten the sense of an eighteenth-century welcome, Joan brought a hot toddy. Had it been summer, we would have been refreshed by a mint julep. As we sipped, we learned more about this remarkable family.

After the restoration of the main house was complete, the family—consisting of Joan and Joe, her husband; their son Brian (who is a historic preservation specialist) and his wife, Cindy Rae—saw an offer in *Preservation News* that they couldn't resist. The Ladysmith House, a two-story home built in 1857, was for sale for $1 if the new owners would move it. Today it occupies a spot beyond the gardens and contains five guest rooms. The entire property is now on the National Register of Historic Places.

The main house has four common rooms open to inn guests. The Log Room, which has log-and-chink walls and a huge brick fireplace, is used as a breakfast room. The family has dedicated themselves to finding artifacts that have a connection to the house. Old farm implements decorate the walls of the Log Room. In the dining room, which was added to the house in about 1850, there are Piney Grove artifacts and architectural maps. A display shows arrowheads found on the property which were left by the Chickahominy Indians, who had a settlement here in the seventeenth century. A parlor/library contains Virginia history books, while a reception hall reveals the Gordineer family history.

The appeal of the entire seven-acre property is the concerted attempt to create a B&B that's historically accurate and yet still provides the amenities guests appreciate today. The guest rooms in the Ladysmith House are simple but charming. Although furnished with period antiques and decorated with stencils, pots of garden-fresh flowers, down comforters, and painted floors, each room has a private bath, a fireplace, air conditioning, a radio, a refrigerator stocked with Virginia wine, and a coffeemaker. The newest room, located in the original summer kitchen, was created in 1997. It has the same amenities as the other rooms but also has a stone wall, a pierced-tin chandelier, hand-hewn oak beams, a cast-iron stove, and a brass bed covered with a woven coverlet. Antique kitchen accessories decorate the room.

The grounds include a barn that serves as shelter to the resident ponies, goats, chickens, sheep, ducks, and geese. The gardens are gorgeous, and a map describes specimens along a nature trail that meanders through the property. On a slight rise is a freeform pool surrounded by flower gardens and a gazebo.

In the morning we feasted on a plantation breakfast of juice, fresh fruit, Virginia ham, homemade breads, and an egg dish—a cheddar-cheese and egg strata. Another favorite entree is Joan's Piney Grove Baked French Toast. The meal is served by candlelight on pewter dishes.

What's Nearby—Charles City

Berkeley Plantation, the home of Benjamin Harrison, a signer of the Declaration of Independence, and of President William Henry Harrison, the ninth president of the United States, is located here. It was also the ancestral home of Benjamin Harrison, the twenty-third U.S. president. It is furnished with its original antiques and decor. Shirley, the oldest plantation in Virginia, is also nearby. The house is noted for its flying staircase and original portraits, silver, and furniture. Sherwood Forest Plantation was President John Tyler and Julia Gardiner Tyler's home after he left the presidency in 1845. The beautifully restored house is the longest frame house in America and is still occupied by Tyler descendants. Evelynton Plantation, the magnificent Georgian Revival ancestral Ruffin plantation, is also nearby. Belle Air Plantation is noted for its magnificent Jacobean stairway, interior decorative trim, and landscaped grounds. Westover, an elegant plantation built by William Byrd II, the founder of Richmond and Petersburg, is noted for its lovely eighteenth-century gates and its grounds that offer sweeping views of the James River. (See also Williamsburg.)

200 South Street

200 South Street
Charlottesville, VA 22902
(800) 964–7008 or (804) 979–0200

FAX: (804) 979–4403
E-MAIL: clancyb@cfw.com
WEB SITE: www.southstreetinn.com
INNKEEPERS: Brendan and Jenny Clancy

ROOMS: 20, including 3 suites, all with private bath, air conditioning, telephone with dataport, and radio; 9 with fireplace; 8 with desk; 6 with Jacuzzi; hair dryer, iron, and ironing board available; 1 room with wheelchair access; cribs available

ON THE GROUNDS: Parking; flower beds

EXTRAS: Wine and cheese in the evening; chocolates at turndown; health club available 2 blocks from B&B

RATES: $105–$195, double occupancy, including Continental breakfast, wine and cheese in the afternoon; two-night minimum weekends in April, May, and September–November

CREDIT CARDS ACCEPTED: American Express, Diners Club, MasterCard, Visa

OPEN: Year-round except Christmas Eve and Christmas Day

HOW TO GET THERE: From Washington, DC, take I-66 to exit 43 (Gainesville) and follow Route 29 south. In Charlottesville, take the Route 250 bypass east to the third traffic light. Turn right onto McIntire Road. At the second traffic light, turn left onto South Street. Travel ⅔ block and turn into the driveway on the right between 2 gateposts. Park in the inn's parking lot and come in the red door in back.

This in-city B&B is located in two gracious townhouses—one yellow brick with white trim, the other yellow clapboard with white trim—on a quiet side street in the city of Charlottesville.

The larger building was built in 1856 for Thomas Jefferson's first librarian at the University of Virginia. It is particularly notable for its stunning wraparound veranda and its solid-walnut, two-story serpentine interior stairway. Both buildings are surrounded by wrought-iron fences. They're separated by a driveway to a private parking lot that's entered between brick pillars.

The B&B is owned by Brendan and Jenny Clancy, expatriate New Yorkers, who have been doing a whirlwind of renovations. The B&B is a sophisticated blend of interesting colors, fabrics, and furnishings.

When I arrived one afternoon, wine and cheese were set out for guests in the library, which overlooks the gardens. This urbane retreat is painted a deep tomato red and has floor-to-ceiling bookcases. A handsome walnut gateleg table is a centerpiece. Breakfast is also served here, or you might prefer to eat on the veranda, which also overlooks the garden. In the summer this is filled with wicker furniture. A hideaway study is the perfect retreat in which to watch television or just to unwind. Unusual nineteenth-century oil paintings of exotic animals are on display in the main gallery. A front porch, which faces the street, is filled with antique white wicker furniture.

The guest rooms all feature English and Belgian antiques and have an English Country mood. There are canopy beds, gas fireplaces, fantastically carved armoires, and polished, wide-plank yellow pine floors topped with colorful kilims. The baths have tile floors and brass fixtures, and six have Jacuzzis. Room #6, for example, has a canopy bed, a walnut armoire (probably from one of the British channel islands), a carved Victorian desk, a fireplace, and drapes in wedgwood blue and white toile.

Brendan and Jenny serve a Continental breakfast that includes four or five freshly baked breads such as lemon-poppyseed or pumpkin-apple, scones, fresh fruit, and juices. There are a variety of excellent restaurants nearby as well as bicycle trails on which to work off the calories. Downtown Charlottesville has an eclectic, artsy population. There are a variety of art galleries, craft shops, bookstores, and boutiques in the downtown urban mall. In addition, the spectacular Charlottesville Ice Park—offering indoor ice skating, skating lessons, and lots of fun—is a short walk away.

What's Nearby—Charlottesville

The primary tourist attraction in the Charlottesville area is Monticello, Thomas Jefferson's stately architectural gem. The building and grounds are meticulously restored, and most of the furniture and household objects were once in the Jefferson family. Many of Jefferson's unusual inventions are on display. Ash Lawn-Highland, the country estate of James Monroe, is nearby also. There are a variety of cultural activities at the University of Virginia throughout the year. (See also Waynesboro.)

The Watson House Bed & Breakfast and The Inn at Poplar Corner

4240 and 4248 Main Street
(mailing address: P.O. Box 905)
Chincoteague, VA 23336
(800) 336–6787 or (757) 336–1564

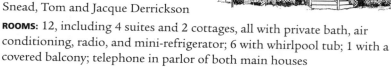

FAX: (757) 336–5776

WEB SITE: www.watsonhouse.com

INNKEEPERS: JoAnne and David Snead, Tom and Jacque Derrickson

ROOMS: 12, including 4 suites and 2 cottages, all with private bath, air conditioning, radio, and mini-refrigerator; 6 with whirlpool tub; 1 with a covered balcony; telephone in parlor of both main houses

ON THE GROUNDS: Parking

EXTRAS: Afternoon refreshments with cakes and cookies; complimentary use of bicycles, beach equipment, and binoculars

RATES: $69–$149, double occupancy, including full breakfast and afternoon refreshments; two- to three-night minimum weekends and holidays

CREDIT CARDS ACCEPTED: MasterCard and Visa

OPEN: Mid-March–November

HOW TO GET THERE: From Route 13, take Route 175 east just south of New Church. Follow this for 11 miles over several bridges and causeways and across the drawbridge to Chincoteague. At the traffic light on Main Street, turn left. The B&B is 4 blocks up Main Street on the right.

Chincoteague is a sleepy little village during the winter months, but in the summer the population swells with tourists who come for the vast stretch of beautiful ocean beaches, to eat the fresh local seafood, and to see the wild ponies made famous by Marguerite Henry's book *Misty of Chincoteague*. Chincoteague is the only village of note on both Chincoteague and Assateague Islands. It is located on Virginia's Eastern Shore just below the Maryland border.

When the Derricksons and the Sneads (parents, daughter, and her husband, all with long ties to Chincoteague) renovated The Watson House in 1992, they won a Chincoteague Restoration Award for their sensitive historic revival of this Main Street Victorian, which they painted a buff color with olive trim. But when their establishment was filled almost every night, they purchased two nearby cottages that can each sleep up to eight people. These come with Jacuzzis, washers and dryers, kitchens, cable TVs, telephones, and central air and heat. Still they had to turn people away. So in 1995 they built The Inn at Poplar Corner.

Both B&Bs offer broad front verandas and gabled rooflines dripping with gingerbread. It isn't often you see a newly built B&B that fits so perfectly into its environment. Yet The Inn at Poplar Corner, a rose-colored Victorian with white trim, slipped into the surrounding streetscape as neatly as if it had been here as long as its sister property, which harks to 1898. The two B&Bs are just across Poplar Street from one another.

The decor of The Watson House is restrained Victorian. Each of the rooms has its own private tiled bath, although several are quite small. The Inn at Poplar Corner, on the other hand, is much more grand. Each of the large suites has a refrigerator, and the spacious private baths have whirlpool tubs. One of the suites has its own private covered porch. There are parlors in both buildings for relaxation as well as wraparound porches, but the most popular spot is the third-floor sitting room in the Poplar Corner house. It has a reading area with a view of the marshes and of sunsets over Chincoteague Bay.

Both JoAnne and Jacque are wonderful cooks who love to share their recipes with their guests. In fact, few people leave without purchasing a copy of their cookbook, which is filled with interesting and inventive recipes. Breakfast may start with glazed lemon-almond bread and morning rolls, followed by Watson House peaches and cream French toast or a puffed crab roll with cheese sauce.

Afternoon refreshment time is never missed by guests in the know. It may include chocolate eclair cake, a brownie caramel pie, and salted peanut chews, among a myriad of other goodies.

What's Nearby—Chincoteague

The many recreational pleasures of Chincoteague are legendary. The Chincoteague National Wildlife Refuge (operated by the U.S. Fish and Wildlife Service) and the Assateague Island National Seashore offer 37 miles of beaches. Visitors can fish, crab, clam, hike (sightings of wild ponies are frequent), bike, beachcomb for shells, lay on the beach, or bird-watch (it's in the prime Atlantic Flyway). Tours with naturalists are also available. On the bay side, it's also possible to water-ski, boat, and canoe. Watch the annual wild pony roundup in July, when the ponies swim the inlet between Assateague and Chincoteague. There's an auction following where the foals are sold. (See also Snow Hill, Maryland.)

The Oaks Victorian Inn

311 East Main Street
Christiansburg, VA 24073
(800) 336–6257 or (540) 381–1500

FAX: (540) 381–3036

WEB SITE: www.bbhost.com/
theoaksinn

INNKEEPERS: Margaret and Tom Ray

ROOMS: 7, all with private bath, air conditioning, private-line telephone with dataport, TV, radio, stocked mini-refrigerator, desk, hair dryer, and robes; 5 with fireplace; 2 with Jacuzzi and VCR

ON THE GROUNDS: On 1½ acres with parking; perennial gardens, fish pond, fountain; garden gazebo with hot tub

EXTRAS: Complimentary refreshments in mini-refrigerator, decanter of sherry, cookie jar with homemade cookies and fresh fruit in every room; turndown with chocolates; complimentary bicycles to use; West Highland terrier named Kaile Bonnie Faire, a Scottie named Lulu, and two cats named Princess Mia and Prince on premises

RATES: $115–$165, double occupancy, including full breakfast; two-night minimum special event weekends at local universities

CREDIT CARDS ACCEPTED: American Express, Discover, MasterCard, Visa

OPEN: Year-round except first two weeks in January

HOW TO GET THERE: From I–81 take exit 114. Turn left if approaching from the south and right if coming from the north, and you will be on Main Street. Continue for approximately 2 miles to fork at Park and Main Streets. Bear right onto Park, then turn left into The Oaks driveway.

Christiansburg is in the beautiful highlands between the Blue Ridge and the Allegheny Mountains. More than 200 years old, the town was originally an outpost on the old Wilderness Trail, located on the edge of the American frontier. As civilization pushed westward, the town became a lumber and agricultural center, and at one time there were more than twelve fashionable Victorian hotels where guests could stay while "taking the baths" in the local hot springs. Today, it's a major university town, since both Virginia Tech and Radford Universities are nearby.

The Oaks, named for the seven magnificent white oak trees that shade the spectacular turrets and porches surrounding this classic Queen Anne Victorian beauty, is a gem by anyone's standards. It sits on a knoll surveying its domain of manicured lawns, boxwood hedges, and flower beds.

Romance pervades the elegant home, which was built by Major William Pierce as a wedding present for his bride, Julia. Together they raised seven children in their home. Nevertheless, by the time Margaret and Tom Ray saw it, the front door had fallen off and the basement was flooded. Today, after a caring and thorough restoration, the house is painted a daffodil yellow with white trim, and it's listed on the National Register of Historic Places.

Visitors first enter the grand entry hall, which has pine woodwork and an imposing staircase with a stunning stained-glass window on the landing. The B&B is furnished throughout with antiques. Here, there's an oak writing desk, a chiming clock, and a piano. The study, a magnet for conversation, has an outstanding Louis XV buffet and a gas fireplace. The parlor, which adjoins it, has multiple windows in a turret and another gas fireplace. In summer, however, guests love to congregate either on the massive wraparound porch with its rockers and wicker chairs or in the gardens in back, which have wrought iron tables and chairs on a brick terrace as well as perennial gardens, a fish pond, and a fountain. Tucked into a garden gazebo, the inviting hot tub offers a romantic starlit retreat.

The guest rooms are equally lovely—each with its own personality. Bonnie Victoria has a lace canopy bed with a crocheted coverlet and an Empire writing desk as well as a gas fireplace. There are adjoining his and hers baths with two showers and a clawfoot tub. Julia Pierce, a room that has five turret windows, has a handpainted slate fireplace mantel, a cherry chest dating to 1820, and a wonderful 7½-foot-tall 1860s Victorian walnut handcarved bed. It's decorated in soft green and peach fabrics. The bath has a Jacuzzi for two as well as a shower and a cherry vanity.

Breakfast is served in the former sunroom, which has a fireplace and windows on three sides overlooking the gardens and terrace. A marvelous heavily carved Flemish bookcase with leaded-glass doors holds the B&B's music system. Soft candlelight lends a glow to the lovely antique Dresden china that Tom inherited from his grandmother. The inventive Southern menu varies daily, but it may include cranberry/orange scones accompanied by fresh fruit and juice and followed by a pasta soufflé with baked salmon in lemon dill sauce and with fresh asparagus. The finale might be a pumpkin/pear strudel.

What's Nearby—Christiansburg

Located between the Blue Ridge and the Allegheny Mountains and near the Appalachian Trail, Christiansburg offers limitless opportunities for recreational fun. The New River State Park Bike Trail, the Huckleberry Bike Trail, The Dixie Caverns, and Chateau Morrisette Winery all present interesting diversions. The Long Way Home Outdoor drama is performed every summer in Radford. At Smithfield Plantation Historic Site in Blacksburg, the birthplace of two Virginia governors, costumed guides describe life on the frontier.

Richard Johnston Inn

Best Buy

711 Caroline Street
Fredericksburg, VA 22401
(540) 899-7606

E-MAIL: rjinn@aol.com

INNKEEPER: Susan T. Williams

ROOMS: 8, including 2 suites; all with private bath, air conditioning, and radio; 6 with desk; 3 with TV; 2 with mini-refrigerator and coffeemaker; telephone located in front hall

ON THE GROUNDS: Parking; brick patio shaded by two large magnolia trees

EXTRAS: Fax available; a Belgian sheepdog named Madeline and a Great Pyrenees named Beau on premises

RATES: $95–$150, double occupancy, including Continental breakfast

CREDIT CARDS ACCEPTED: American Express, MasterCard, Visa

OPEN: Year-round except at Thanksgiving

HOW TO GET THERE: From I–95 take exit 130A onto Route 3 east and travel 3 miles to Fredericksburg. Follow the signs to the Fredericksburg City Visitors Center. The B&B is across the street. It has its own parking lot behind the building, entered from Sophia Street.

Fredericksburg is a lovely gift from the past. There are more than 350 eighteenth- and nineteenth-century buildings in its 40-block National Historic District. The rosy brick facades look much as they did when George Washington and James Monroe walked these streets. A visit to the Fredericksburg Visitor Center, which is just across the street, is the first place to stop to pick up several of the excellent walking maps of the town.

Richard Johnston, who was mayor of Fredericksburg in 1809 and 1810, lived in these rosy brick buildings that were built in 1754 and 1780. The B&B is a serene retreat that faithfully re-creates the ambience of the Federal period while offering the amenities we crave today. When we arrived, we were glad the B&B has its own parking lot, as the town teemed with visitors, all vying for parking places on the street.

Susan Williams, proprietor and innkeeper since 1992, has created a lovely and historic spot in which to stay. Most guests enter the B&B via stairs from the courtyard near the parking area. The main floor has 12-foot ceilings, and there's a living room decorated in navy and rose with comfortable wing chairs, a fireplace, and an Oriental rug on the heart pine floors. Guests will find board games, jigsaw puzzles, and playing cards to use on tables in the dining room.

The guest rooms are furnished with lovely antiques and reproductions. My favorite is Room #9, which is located in the original kitchen. It has a brick floor and two antique double-sized beds. Room #11 has a canopy bed with rice-carved posts. Room #4, on the third floor, has a four-poster bed with pineapple-carved posts and a matching dresser, while Room #5, on the second floor, has a spectacular 1830s mahogany plantation-style bed. Two very elegant suites have private entrances off the brick courtyard in back. All the private baths are modern and up-to-date, although several are not en suite but located off the hallway.

A Continental breakfast of freshly baked breads and muffins, fresh fruit, juice, and coffee is served in the dining room at the cherry Duncan Phyfe table. Susan uses fine china, silver, and linens, and she serves the juice in stemmed glasses.

Caroline Street is filled with excellent antiques shops and boutiques; the sidewalks bustle with browsers. Next door to the inn, a charming little shop specializes in teddy bears. Several fine restaurants are located nearby. Merriman's is right next door, and Le Lafayette Restaurant, in a handsome landmarked 1771 Georgian building, is just down the street.

What's Nearby—Fredericksburg

History lives in Fredericksburg. For one thing, George Washington was born nearby at Ferry Farm, and Fredericksburg contains considerable Washington history. You can visit the Mary Washington House (the home George purchased for his mother in 1772); Kenmore, the beautifully restored and furnished estate of George's sister Betty Washington Lewis; and Rising Sun Tavern, the restored 1760s tavern where Lafayette once stayed that was at one time the residence of Charles Washington, George's youngest brother. In addition, the Fredericksburg and Spotsylvania National Military Park, chronicling the four major Civil War battles that took place over a two-year period here, offers moving insights into the encounters.

Killahevlin B&B Inn

1401 North Royal Avenue
Front Royal, VA 22630
(800) 847–6132 or (540) 636–7335

FAX: (540) 636–8694

E-MAIL: kllhvln@shentel.net

WEB SITE: www.vairish.com

INNKEEPER: Susan O'Kelly Lang

ROOMS: 6, including 2 suites; all with private bath, air conditioning, telephone with dataport, fireplace, hair dryer, and desk; 5 with whirlpool tub; 4 with private balcony or porch; 2 with TV; wheelchair access

ON THE GROUNDS: On 3 acres with gardens containing koi pond and waterfall and two gazebos; croquet, horseshoes, bocci ball

EXTRAS: Sherry and cookies in room; Irish pub with self-serve complimentary beer on tap, wine, champagne, soft drinks, and snacks; an outside cat named Oscar Wilde

RATES: $135–$250, double occupancy, including full breakfast, complimentary drinks in Irish pub, and sherry and cookies in room; two-night minimum if Saturday stay included and on holiday weekends

CREDIT CARDS ACCEPTED: American Express, Diners Club, Discover, Master-Card, Visa

OPEN: Year-round

HOW TO GET THERE: From I–66, take exit 6 and turn south (right) onto Route 522/340. Travel approximately 2 miles and turn left onto Fifteenth Street, which dead-ends at North Royal Avenue. Turn left onto North Royal Avenue and then turn right into the first driveway. (Watch for Killahevlin on the mail box.)

The brick Edwardian manor house was built in 1905 by William Edward Carson, an Irish immigrant, who came to Front Royal and made his fortune by quarrying local limestone. He placed his house high on a hill to take advantage of the spectacular views of the Blue Ridge and Massanutten Mountains, which guests still enjoy today. Mr. Carson was also a noted Virginia historian who is credited with the creation of the Skyline Drive, as well as with the placement of many of Virginia's historical markers.

It is fitting that another owner of Irish ancestry took on the task of restoring this beautiful house. Susan purchased the house in 1990 and began a thorough and accurate historic restoration with the help of local craftsmen and designers. The house has paneled walls enhanced by period reproduction wallpapers. There are maple floors and high ceilings throughout the first floor. A reception room has a fireplace, as does the formal parlor. The unique room, however, is the Irish Pub. Guests can step up to the oak bar with its brass footrail and help themselves to Irish draft beer on tap, as well as wine, soft drinks, and snacks, or they can watch a sports game on the TV.

There are four guest rooms located on the second floor of the main house. Each has a working fireplace with a mantel original to the house, spectacular mountain views, and a tiled bath. I love the restful Blue Room with its blue-and-white wallpaper and a four-poster bed facing the fireplace. There's an antique wardrobe as well as an antique marble-topped dressing table. A private porch is accessed through French doors, and there are wonderful mountain and sunset views. A fused-glass window overlooks a two-person indigo blue whirlpool tub. The Raspberry Room includes a wonderful antique four-poster bed and a French armoire. The fireplace is surrounded by antique tiles and an ornate columned mantel with a mirror.

The two suites are located in a three-story tower house behind the main house. This unique building was built originally to collect rainwater that was used to irrigate the property. The Jade Tree Suite is on the second floor. It has two balconies that afford mountain views, as well as both sunrise and sunset views. The living room has a fireplace and the carpeted bedroom has an antique brass bed. The bath has a jade green double whirlpool tub. Throughout the suite, there are Oriental art objects and decor.

Breakfast is served in the dining room, which has another fireplace. The meal will start with freshly baked muffins or coffee cake, along with fruit and juice. As an entree Susan may prepare eggs Benedict or Belgian waffles with country sausage.

What's Nearby—Front Royal

Front Royal is at the northern tip of the Shenandoah National Park and the beautiful Skyline Drive. There are endless opportunities for hiking and bicycling, as well as places to explore by car, and there are also numerous places to rent a canoe for a trip down the Shenandoah River. The Skyline Caverns, one of the area's major cavern attractions, is located here. You might visit Belle Grove Plantation, an exquisite small plantation on the grounds of Cedar Creek Battlefield, and a National Trust Property, that is open to the public. Or, you might visit one of the local wineries for a tour and samplings. (See also Hume and Stephens City.)

King's Victorian Inn Bed & Breakfast Best Buy

Route 220
(mailing address: Route 1, Box 622)
Hot Springs, VA 24445
(540) 839–3134 (fax also)

WEB SITE: www.inngetaways.com/
va.kingsvic.html

INNKEEPERS: Liz and Richard King

ROOMS: 6, including 1 suite and
plus 2 suites in a downtown cottage; 4 with private bath and 2 that share 1 bath; all with radio; 4 with air conditioning; and 3 with porch; telephone for rooms in main house in common area

ON THE GROUNDS: On 3 acres with parking; gardens

EXTRAS: Afternoon refreshments with cookies or cake

RATES: $85–$150, double occupancy, including full breakfast; two-night minimum in October and holidays weekends

CREDIT CARDS ACCEPTED: None

OPEN: Year-round except four days at Christmas

HOW TO GET THERE: From I–81 take exit 222 in Staunton and follow Route 254 west to Buffalo Gap. In Buffalo Gap take Route 42 south to Goshen. From Goshen follow Route 39 west to Warm Springs. At the junction with Route 220, turn south and stay on Route 220 for 4 miles. The B&B will be on the right. Enter the property by driving between two brick columns.

This pristine pearl grey Victorian with white trim was built in 1899, at the height of the Victorian era. It rests on its spacious lawns overlooking one of the Homestead's golf courses. Pretty benches sit under spreading old maple trees, and flower beds spill over with a kaleidoscope of color. Even in the chill of winter when I first spied the house, it was impressive. There are turrets and gables and bays and a veranda that almost encircles the house.

Liz and Richard King (he's with the postal service in Staunton, and she was a nurse) purchased their grand Victorian when it needed considerable work. Built by Dr. Henry S. Pole, a prominent local doctor, the house has also been used as a restaurant, a rooming house, and a leather shop. The Kings have meticulously restored the gracious building, and although they opened the B&B in 1988 with six rooms, they have added to it almost every year. The Ice House, located just behind the main house, contains a two-level suite, and they also have a downtown cottage with two two-bedroom suites.

The wraparound porch of the B&B is furnished with wooden rocking chairs and wicker tables and chairs—the perfect place to sip that final cup of coffee before setting out on a day of hiking or bicycling or "taking the baths" just as the famous, infamous, and not-at-all famous have done for years. But perhaps you'll be so enchanted by the gardens, which have tulips, daffodils, dogwood trees, and forsythia in spring, that you'll wander down to the boxwood garden to watch the birds bathing in the birdbath.

The common rooms of the B&B are decorated with high-quality reproduction furniture. The formal living room is quite elegant with plush sofas before a gas fireplace and a sunny turret area. Another parlor has Victorian love seats and chairs and a selection of board games and puzzles. Upstairs, there's a Garden Room with white wicker and a TV for guests to enjoy.

The guest rooms on the second floor include Room #4, which has a high rice-carved mahogany bed with a square canopy and a peach Oriental rug on the oak floor. Room #6 has a teal carpet and a powder room with a vanity table.

The formal dining room has another turreted sitting area and a nonfunctional fireplace. There are two mahogany tables—one with claw feet and the other a Queen Anne–style. They are both covered with fine linen, and breakfast is served on Royal Doulton china with sterling silver, unless it's during the holidays, when Liz brings out the Lenox holiday china. Guests feast on fresh juice and fruit, freshly made muffins or coffee cake, and either scrambled eggs with bacon, sausage, or ham, or maybe a French toast dish.

What's Nearby—Hot Springs

Hot Springs is nestled into a valley in the heart of the Allegheny Mountains. The hot springs in nearby Warm Springs attracted Native Americans long before white men arrived. The first rustic log inn was built in 1760. The famed Homestead Resort, on 15,000 acres, is within walking distance. There are numerous restaurants, three golf courses, renowned downhill and cross-country ski runs, a ski school, an ice skating rink, a bowling alley, carriage rides, a marvelous spa, and horseback riding. Guests of the B&B can use the Homestead's facilities, but there is an additional charge. The Garth Newel Music Center has concerts throughout the year. Visit the Bacova Guild Factory outlet in Bacova for a variety of silk-screened gifts.

The Inn at Fairfield Farm

Marriott Ranch, 5305 Marriott Lane
Hume, VA 22639
(877) 324–7344 or (540) 364–3221

FAX: (540) 364–2498
E-MAIL: irene@marriottranch.com
WEB SITE: www.marriottranch.com
INNKEEPER: Irene Voglsam; general manager: Jerry Cooper
ROOMS: 8, including 1 suite and 1 cottage; all with private bath, air conditioning, radio, and desk; 5 with fireplace, 4 with telephone and dataport,

and/or private porch, 2 with kitchen, 1 with whirlpool tub; wheelchair access

ON THE GROUNDS: On 4,500-acre cattle ranch, with gardens, pond, river for fishing, horseback riding, and hiking; scheduled trail rides, occasional cattle drives, river and mountain rides

EXTRAS: A light afternoon tea of coffee, lemonade, or cider (or beer or wine if requested), and a tray of cookies and scones; one calico cat named Trouble on premises

RATES: $125–$195, double occupancy, including full breakfast and afternoon tea

CREDIT CARDS ACCEPTED: American Express, MasterCard, Visa

OPEN: Year-round

HOW TO GET THERE: From Washington, D.C., take I–66 west for approximately 40 miles to exit 27 (the second Marshall exit). Turn left at the stop sign, crossing over I–66. Make an immediate right onto Route 647. Go 4 miles and turn right onto Route 635 and proceed 9½ miles to the main entrance of the ranch, which will be on the left.

J. Willard Marriott purchased Fairfield Farm in 1951. The vast 4,500-acre spread is used primarily as a ranch, where cattle that supply the beef for the Marriott hotel restaurants are raised. In addition, the ranch continues to serve as the site of Marriott meetings and seminars, as well as an annual management outing that includes a barbecue and family games.

The centerpiece of the farm is the distinguished brick James Marshall Manor House that was built in 1814 by James Markham Marshall, the brother of Chief Justice John Marshall. It had been vacant for thirty years when Marriott purchased the ranch, but he executed a marvelous historically accurate restoration of the house so that it looks today much as it did in Marshall's time. The house has 14-foot ceilings on the main floor and triple-hung Jeffersonian walk-out windows. The home is now the heart of the inn.

There are common rooms on the main floor of the house, including a dining room, a parlor, where a piano is located, and a library, as well as an entrance foyer. A large porch has white iron cafe tables and chairs, where guests enjoy sitting as twilight sets in to watch the sunset over the Blue Ridge Mountains. The second floor of the house has four guest rooms. They are elegantly furnished with four-poster beds and hardwood floors covered by Oriental rugs. Each of the rooms has a fireplace, and two of them have baths en suite; the other two have private baths accessed from the hallway.

The carriage house has three more rooms, and there's also the Baroness Cottage, a separate house named for Baroness Jeanne von Reininghaus Lambert of Belgium, who purchased the farm just before World War II. She converted a small log cabin that dates to the 1800s into this charming three-bedroom cottage for herself and her family. Decorated in a 1950s ranch style, it has beamed ceilings, an eat-in kitchen, a family room with a fireplace, three bedrooms, and two baths.

The old smokehouse, where hams and wild turkeys were cured over a slow hickory fire, has now been turned into a common room where guests might gather. There's a fireplace and the original beams of the room still impart a faint hickory smell. Guests are free to store a bottle of wine here in the lounge/bar, but no drinks are served.

A full breakfast is served in the manor house dining room. It will always begin with fresh fruit and homemade muffins or pastries. The entree of the day may be French toast stuffed with mascarpone and pecans.

Guests at the inn can make arrangements for a private guided jeep tour of the 4,500-acre Marriott Ranch and area vineyards, and they can even take a picnic lunch along. They may also wish to participate in one of the Western trail rides that take place on a scheduled basis at the riding center on the property. At round-up times, guests can also join a cattle drive and end the day with a chuck-wagon dinner, and there are scheduled moonlight, river, and mountain rides as well. The inn, which combines the elegance of a fine country inn with the informality of a dude ranch, offers a unique perspective into Virginia life.

What's Nearby—Hume

Hume is in the midst of an area that continues to support large farms and open space. Guests can visit Oasis Winery nearby, where fine wines can be sampled, and they can tour the winery. The Shenandoah National Park and the Skyline Drive are nearby as well, as is the Appalachian Trail. (See also Front Royal, Stephens City, and Washington.)

The Hope and Glory Inn

Best Buy

634 King Carter Drive
(mailing address: P.O. Box 425)
Irvington, VA 22480
(800) 497–8228 or (804) 438–6053

FAX: (804) 438–5362

E-MAIL: kenjo@rivnet.net

WEB SITE: www.1sttravelerchoice.com

INNKEEPER: Joyce Barber; proprietor: William Westbrook

ROOMS: 11, including 1 suite and 4 cottages; all with private bath and air conditioning; 5 with telephone; 4 with private patio or porch; 1 with TV, VCR, and fireplace; 1 cottage with wheelchair access; telephone on first floor of main house

ON THE GROUNDS: On 1 acre with parking; bicycles, tennis, gardens, including a moon garden with flowers that bloom at night; private, romantic, fully enclosed outdoor "bathing room" open to the stars

EXTRAS: Coffee, tea, lemonade in the afternoon; wine, cheese, and snacks in the evening; conference facility; complimentary bicycles to use

RATES: $95–$175, double occupancy, including full breakfast

CREDIT CARDS ACCEPTED: MasterCard and Visa

OPEN: Year-round

HOW TO GET THERE: From I–95 take exit 126 south of Fredericksburg and follow Route 17 south for about 55 miles to Tappahannock. Then follow Route 360 east for 6 miles to Route 3. Follow Route 3 south for about 40 miles to Kilmarnock. Watch for Irvington Road 200 and turn right toward Irvington. At the Texaco station, turn right onto King Carter Drive and the B&B will be on the right, just beyond the church.

What can I say? Bill Westbrook is an incurable romantic! Born locally and anticipating retirement, this Minneapolis/New York exec has created an utterly romantic B&B infused with exuberant playfulness and creative artistry. The impressive yellow Victorian building with its crisp white trim faces the street behind a snappy white picket fence. The building began life as a schoolhouse in 1890.

The whimsical decor of the B&B can partly be attributed to the creativity of local folk artist Brad Stephens, who made the folk art pieces and some of the furniture. His art is for sale at the B&B also. The entire B&B looks as if it's been plucked directly from the pages of Mary Emmerling's *New Country Collecting*.

The first floor, which has an open floor plan, is dominated by a grand center stairway. It has a floor painted in bold green-and-white squares and furniture cleverly arranged in conversation areas. In one corner there's one of Brad's folk art pieces—an armoire that looks like the front of the B&B. On the opposite side of the room, there's a massive fireplace surrounded by sofas and chairs. An oak table with a marble chess board holds pawns created of 1950s salt and pepper shakers.

Upstairs, the floors are also painted, and there's a pretty sitting area with spritely floral fabric on the chairs. The guest rooms have headboards that use "found" architectural elements—a fancifully shingled gable in one; a picket fence in another. Room #5, on the third floor, is a suite that has crackle-painted tables and chairs and a fence post headboard, while in Room #7 the curtains are hung from a birch limb. Each of the bedrooms has a private bath, although several are quite small.

In back of the B&B, there's a lovely brick courtyard with a fountain where breakfast is served in the summer. Several sweet Victorian cottages have been converted to cozy, charming guest rooms also. They each have private brick patios with pretty Victorian garden furniture, kitchens, and painted floors. The largest cottage has been made into a small conference facility, complete with a fireplace and audio/visual equipment.

The pièces de résistance of the B&B, however, are the romantic hideaways tucked away in the garden. In one secluded corner, there's a Moon Garden illuminated by low lights and candles. In another secluded spot, there's an open-air room enclosed by a seven-foot-high stockade fence. Inside, on the brick floor, there's a clawfoot tub, an elegant antique pedestal sink, and an outdoor shower. Fluffy robes hang on a hook, and a plethora of fat candles set the mood for this watery rendezvous for two.

For breakfast, Joyce may prepare her own special version of stuffed French toast, using a filling of cream cheese and orange marmalade and topping it with a pecan and orange-flavored syrup. The meal is accompanied by fresh fruit, juices, and perhaps freshly baked orange-poppyseed muffins. Creamy grits will always be offered.

What's Nearby—Irvington

Sailing and fishing on the Rappahannock River are both popular recreations, and there are numerous bicycle routes to follow along the flat, picturesque country roads. Several golf courses are close. Historic Christ Church, located here, was built in 1732 on the remains of a 1669 church by Robert "King" Carter, the ancestor of eight governors of Virginia and two U.S. presidents as well as General Robert E. Lee. The magnificent brick Greek-cruciform Colonial structure has a swag roof with four hips, aisles paved with slabs of sandstone, and a wine-glass pulpit. The church is almost entirely as it was in 1732. The adjacent Carter Reception Center and Museum contains historical displays about the life of King Carter.

The Norris House Inn

108 Loudoun Street S.W.
Leesburg, VA 20175
(800) 644–1806 or (703) 777–1806

FAX: (703) 771–8051

E-MAIL: inn@norrishouse.com

WEB SITE: http://norrishouse.com

INNKEEPERS: Pam and Don McMurray

ROOMS: 6, each sharing 1 bath; all with air conditioning, desk, and robes; 3 with working fireplace; telephone in library

ON THE GROUNDS: On ½ acre of gardens; grape arbor; croquet; Stone House Tea Room just across a pathway

EXTRAS: Decanters of port in the library; turndown with handmade chocolates; wine and cheese in the evening on weekends; music throughout common rooms; three cats available on request

RATES: $110–$150, double occupancy, including full breakfast; two-night minimum if Saturday stay included from April–December

CREDIT CARDS ACCEPTED: American Express

OPEN: Year-round

HOW TO GET THERE: From Washington, D.C., take I–495 (the Capital Beltway) to Route 267 (Dulles Toll Road), which terminates in Leesburg. Take exit 1A (Leesburg/Warrenton) and follow Route 15 (King Street) through 5 traffic signals. Turn left onto Loudoun and go 1½ blocks. The B&B will be on the right. Load and unload in front of the B&B, but park in the village garage.

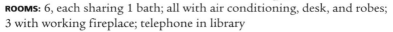

owntown Leesburg is a picturesque town with narrow streets shaded by oak and elm trees and bordered by brick and stone houses with ivy climbing their walls. The Norris House Inn, a 1760 brick Federal structure with tall windows, has a classic front door flanked by pillars with a fan light above. Its most notable owners were the Norris family, who built many of Leesburg's elegant buildings and who lived in this house for more than one hundred years.

Although the building has been operating as a B&B since 1981, it was purchased in 1991 by Pam and Don McMurray, former California marketing whizzes, who came to Virginia while researching their genealogy and never left. They have furnished it with lovely period antiques.

Guests enter a wide center hall flanked on one side by a front parlor, which has a fireplace and an antique china cabinet. Oriental rugs lie on gleaming wide-plank pine floors. On the opposite side, the library has another Colonial fireplace mantel and Eastlake Victorian cherry bookcases filled with books about travel, cooking, architecture, old houses, and antiques.

The guest rooms are lovely. The Norris Room has a four-poster bed with a fishnet canopy. Decorated in pink and blue, it has a Victorian love seat and a woodburning fireplace. The Old Dominion Room, which is decorated in shades of sage and ivory, has Eastlake Victorian furnishings, including a marvelous Victorian shaving stand. On the walls, there are hunt prints. Each of the rooms shares a modern, large tile bath. In the second-floor hallway, there's a refrigerator stocked with bottled water and juices. A bowl of fresh fruit is nearby.

The gardens are the glory of this winsome B&B. A 40-foot-long screened-in side veranda has wicker chairs. Behind the house lies a lovely lawn bordered by more flower beds and a rock garden. There's a swing under a grape arbor and white iron benches under a magnolia tree.

The Stone House Tea Room, located next door, is in the oldest stone house in Leesburg. It's also owned by the McMurrays. It has two romantic stone-walled rooms with an English cottage ambience. One room contains a spot where Henry Clay once scratched his name on the wall. Sandy Ruefer, who operates the tearoom, serves a traditional afternoon tea with sandwiches and pastries. She also has a shop where she sells tea cozies, loose tea, and tea accoutrements.

Breakfast is served in the historic dining room of the B&B, which has another woodburning fireplace, a Duncan Phyfe table, and a built-in china cabinet. Elegant linens cover the table, and Pam uses her beautiful Floradora patterned Royal Doulton china and her family antique Rosepoint silver. The meal starts with fresh orange juice and fruit. Then she may serve eggs Norris, a baked casserole dish with herbs and parmesan cheese that she serves over English muffins. The Norrises serve a coffee that's freshly roasted in Leesburg. The meal may end with a strawberry pound cake.

Brierley Hill B&B Country Inn   Best Buy

985 Borden Road
Lexington, VA 24450
(800) 422–4925 or (540) 464–8421

FAX: (540) 464–8925

E-MAIL: cspeton@cfw.com

WEB SITE: www.Brierleyhill.com

INNKEEPER: Carole Speton

ROOMS: 5, including 2 suites, all with private bath and air conditioning; 3 with fireplace, TV, and desk; 2 with whirlpool tub, mini-refrigerator, coffeemaker, hair dryer, iron, ironing board, and robes; 1 with private porch; portable telephone in upstairs hallway

ON THE GROUNDS: On 8 acres with parking; gardens

EXTRAS: Afternoon tea; fax available; one dog named Remi on premises

RATES: $95–$160, double occupancy, including full breakfast and afternoon tea; two-night minimum weekends in suites, and all rooms in October as well as holiday and special event weekends

CREDIT CARDS ACCEPTED: MasterCard and Visa

OPEN: Year-round

HOW TO GET THERE: From I–81 traveling north, take exit 188B onto Route 60 west. Follow Route 60 through Lexington (it becomes Nelson Street). Turn left onto Borden Road and continue for 1 mile to Brierley Hill, which will be on the left. From I–81 traveling south, take exit 191 onto I–64 west. Continue on I–64 to exit 55 and then follow Route 11 south to Lexington, passing Virginia Military Institute and Washington and

Lee University. At Nelson Street (Route 60) turn right and follow it west to Borden Road. Then follow directions above.

When Carole and Barry Speton, who then lived in Vancouver, British Columbia, began visiting their daughter at school in Virginia, they felt an immediate affinity for the area. On each visit they stayed in B&Bs and eventually decided to move here to open their own. So they purchased eight acres on a sunny hilltop just outside historic Lexington that offered views of the Blue Ridge Mountains and the Shenandoah Valley and built their dream B&B. The blue-clapboard English country farmhouse, which has crisp white trim and a spacious veranda, opened for business in 1993.

Guests enter a hall that has an antique oak reception table and an 1850s tall-case clock made in Brierley Hill, England, and for which the B&B is named. In the spacious upstairs hallway, there's a TV for guests to watch.

Each of the guest rooms is named for a flower that grows on the hillsides or in the gardens. The Primrose Room has a canopy bed and a floral-covered sofa. The pink-and-white striped wallpaper provides a pretty backdrop for the lacy curtains. The Cowslip Room is done is sunny yellows and has a canopy bed painted dark green. It offers views across the spacious meadows. The Peony Room is also done in yellow. It has a canopy bed painted townhouse ivory and a woodburning fireplace. Oriental rugs rest on oak floors, and there are views of the mountains on three sides. The Rose Suite features a fireplace and a bath with a whirlpool tub as well as a shower.

Afternoon tea is served either in the dining room or, in summer, on the veranda. There may be lemonade with cookies and cake or in winter perhaps tea with scones and little sandwiches.

Breakfast will be served in the formal dining room, which has a brass chandelier and a fireplace. Crisp English chintz in a rose pattern, candles, and fine crystal enhance the individual tables. A typical menu will include fresh juice and fruit and freshly baked breads such as Carole's apple turnovers or her oat-bran bread. Entrees may feature a wine and cheese baked egg casserole or Grand Marnier French toast. Accompaniments include Virginia lean ham or spicy sausage patties, pan fries, grits, or cornmeal patties with cheese and onions. On selected nights it may be possible to have dinner at the B&B also.

What's Nearby—Lexington

Lexington is filled with historic sites to visit. Start with a tour of Virginia Military Institute, which was established in 1839, and also of Washington and Lee University. The George C. Marshall Museum (he was author of the Marshall Plan) is on the VMI campus. You can also tour the Stonewall Jackson House, the home he and his wife purchased when he was an instructor at VMI. The Virginia Horse Center is located on 400 acres just outside Lexington. There are horse shows, auctions, lessons, riding demonstrations, and equestrian art and photography shows. Visitors should also plan a trip to Natural Bridge, a 215-foot-high, 90-foot limestone arch that spans a gorge created by Cedar Creek. It's one of the Seven Natural Wonders of the World and located just east of Lexington. Sound and light shows take place there in the summer.

The Inn at Meander Plantation

James Madison Highway (Route 15)
(mailing address: HCR 5, Box 460A)
Locust Dale, VA 22948
(800) 385–4936 or (540) 672–4912

FAX: (540) 672–0405

E-MAIL: inn@meander.net

WEB SITE: www.meander.net

INNKEEPERS: Suzanne Thomas, Suzie Blanchard, and Bob Blanchard

ROOMS: 8, including 5 suites and 3 cottages; all with private bath, air conditioning, telephone, radio, hair dryer, iron, ironing board, and porch; 5 with fireplace and dataport; 4 with desk; 1 with mini-refrigerator, TV, and VCR; wheelchair access

ON THE GROUNDS: Parking; boxwood and perennial gardens, herb gardens, 80 acres of lawns and meadows; croquet, volleyball, hammock; river for fishing, tubing or swimming; four horses on property

EXTRAS: Turndown with chocolates; evening cheese and crackers; afternoon cookies and fruit, coffee, tea, sodas, and juice; exercise room (personal trainer and massages by appointment); fax, computer, printer, copier available; dinner and picnic-basket lunches available by advance request; stable accommodations for horses available; guest pets permitted in some rooms with prior permission; two dogs named Honey and Sara and two cats named Bojo and William on premises

RATES: $105–$250, double occupancy, including full breakfast and afternoon refreshments; two-night minimum holiday and special event weekends and throughout October

CREDIT CARDS ACCEPTED: American Express, MasterCard, Visa

OPEN: Year-round

HOW TO GET THERE: From Washington, D.C., take I–66 west to exit 43 (Gainesville). Follow Route 29 south (it becomes Route 15/29) to a point just beyond Culpeper, where the routes split. Follow Route 15 south beyond Culpeper for about 9 miles. The B&B is on the west (right) side of Route 15.

How did a Texas native and a couple from Georgia and Michigan, who met in Chicago, happen to open a B&B together in Virginia, we asked? Well, it's a long story, but they did. It took several years of searching and a tremendous amount of patience and perseverance, but the historic manor house and buildings at a bend in the Robinson River and on an eighty-acre horse farm have developed into one of the finest places to stay in Virginia.

Meander Plantation was originally a 3,000-acre land grant to Colonel Joshua Fry, a member of the House of Burgesses and a professor at William and Mary College in Williamsburg. Colonel Fry and Peter Jefferson (the father of Thomas) were the first to draw an official map of Virginia Colony. A French copy of that map now hangs in the living room at Meander Plantation. Colonel Fry's son, Henry, built the brick Georgian manor house in 1766. Throughout Henry Fry's lifetime, the dignitaries of the day were entertained here. Thomas Jefferson was a frequent visitor; General Lafayette came often.

Narrowly escaping the hands of developers, the estate was purchased in 1991 by the current team. It had been vacant for many years and needed considerable restoration, but since Suzie had been Historic Preservation Officer of the Chicago suburb of Wilmette, she knew just what to do. They opened the property as a B&B in 1993.

In the main house, which has 11-foot ceilings, guests enter a reception area with a fireplace and a baby grand piano. An arched entry leads to a Georgian living room with another woodburning fireplace and chintz covered sofas. The manor house is joined to the summer kitchen by a covered brick passageway bordered by grand arches. Guests can sit on the two-tiered porch in back and gaze at the Blue Ridge Mountains. Or they can settle into a wooden rocker on the broad front veranda to sip a tall iced tea and watch the bluebirds, cardinals, and orioles eat from the feeder.

The guest rooms are stunning. The Master Bedroom, decorated in a rich pink, has a four-poster rice bed with a white Battenburg lace duvet over the down comforter, and a woodburning fireplace. The polished heart pine floors have hooked wool rugs. There's a modern tiled bath. The former summer kitchen is now a guest suite. It has a living room with chestnut floors and a bedroom upstairs with a four-poster bed and a woodburning fireplace. Three dependency buildings house charming private rooms with fireplaces.

Breakfast is served in the formal dining room, which is painted a Monticello rose with white trim. It has two antique buffets, a brass chandelier, a woodburning fireplace, and a black slate floor. Suzie fixes terrific meals (she also writes food articles). She may start with a moist Hawaiian bread containing pineapples, bananas, and nuts or with blueberry scones as well as fresh fruit and juice. She may follow this with a quiche of Vidalia onions and sausage, which itself will be followed by her special spicy multi-grain pancakes served with freshly made apple butter and topped with Vermont maple syrup.

What's Nearby—Locust Dale

One of the innkeepers will be pleased to make reservations for guests to take horseback riding or hunting lessons at a nearby farm or to take a hot-air balloon ride, which can leave right from the B&B's property. For a firsthand history lesson in the Civil War, visits to Brandy Station and Cedar Mountain battlefields are instructive. The nearby Skyline Drive in the Shenandoah National Park is a spectacular drive, especially in the spring when the rhododendrons are in bloom.

Federal Crest Inn Bed & Breakfast

1101 Federal Street
Lynchburg, VA 24504
(800) 818-6155 or (804) 845-6155

FAX: (804) 845-1445

E-MAIL: inn@federalcrest.com

WEB SITE: www.federalcrest.com

INNKEEPERS: Phil and Ann Ripley

ROOMS: 5, including 3 suites, all with private bath, air conditioning, telephone (4 have dataport), radio, and robes; 3 with TV and fireplace; 1 with a whirlpool tub and VCR

ON THE GROUNDS: On 1 acre with parking; gardens

EXTRAS: Mole Hole Gift Shop on premises; Fifties Cafe with jukebox; Eagles Nest Theater with 60˝ TV; fresh fruit and snack basket in every room; freshly baked snacks and soda on arrival; turndown with mints;

 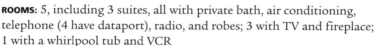

meeting space with stage; fax machine available; one dog named Carmel and one cat named Toni on premises

RATES: $95–$125, double occupancy, including full breakfast and afternoon snacks; two-night minimum weekends in May and October

CREDIT CARDS ACCEPTED: American Express, Discover, MasterCard, Visa

OPEN: Year-round

HOW TO GET THERE: From the Route 29 expressway, take the Main Street (downtown) exit. Continue on Main Street to Eleventh Street. Turn left onto Eleventh Street and go 6 blocks to Federal Street. The B&B is on the left corner of Federal and Eleventh Streets. Continue on Eleventh Street to the parking area beside the B&B.

Just like Rome, Lynchburg is built on seven steep hills affording spectacular views of the surrounding countryside. The town's industrialists and merchants built grand homes on the hilltops, each attempting to outdo the other. Along the streets of the Federal Hill Historic District, where the Federal Crest Inn is located, there are numerous fine nineteenth- and early twentieth-century mansions. Among the finest is this 8,000-square-foot brick Georgian Revival mansion with a tile roof that was built in 1909 for a prominent local lawyer.

Ann and Phil Ripley have created a delightful B&B here. Guests enter a foyer with gleaming heart pine floors and pink moire fabric on the walls, a crystal chandelier, and original moldings. The living room has a carved white wood fireplace mantel. Beautiful pocket doors lead to a library, which has the original bookcases with glass doors where the law books were kept. The Ripleys have added a lovely china cabinet filled with pink crystal, and there's also a gas fireplace.

The elegant dining room has paneled walls, a coffered ceiling, and another gas fireplace. One of my favorite rooms, however, is the original garden room, in which the Ripleys' have created a cafe with a 1950s theme. There's a tile floor and a great old jukebox complete with hits from the 1950s and 1960s. In addition, a little nook has been set aside as the Mole Hole Gift Shop, where lucky guests can purchase some of Ann's artwork. She's created paintings on damaged roof tiles and paints customized Christmas ornaments. Her original watercolored notecards are also available here.

Another unique room, which the Ripleys' call the Eagle's Nest, is found on the third floor. Created originally as the ultimate playroom, it has a stage where the owner's three daughters and two sons could perform their own plays. It's now used as a conference facility and has state-of-the-art audio/visual capabilities. High tech business presentations take place here. When not in use for a meeting, it's a terrific place to watch a special event on the 60-inch TV or a movie from the video collection.

The guest rooms are on the second floor, reached by climbing a grand stairway to an enormous landing. They are named for trees growing on the property. The grandest is Blue Spruce, which has marine blue walls, a mahogany canopy bed dressed with Battenburg lace, and a gas fireplace. The private porch, reached through a Jeffersonian window/door, has a library table, a queen-size sofa, and a TV set. The terrific bath has a tile floor and a Jacuzzi surrounded by a mural of the Blue Ridge Mountains that was painted by Ann. In the Dogwood Room, an iron canopy bed is swathed in yards of white lace, and there's a white cutwork spread. Pink-and-white dogwood branches stand in a corner, and there's a handsome gas fireplace and a walnut marble-topped dresser. The tile bath is modern and up to date.

Breakfast at Federal Crest is an event. It's served by candlelight with fine sterling silver. The meal begins with "message muffins," fruit muffins (perhaps blueberry) in which a message has been baked. When guests find the message inside their muffin, they read it aloud to the other guests. In addition, guests will be served a fruit cup or maybe a sugar-topped broiled grapefruit followed by Federal Crest egg casserole, a light soufflé dish served with cooked apples and bacon.

What's Nearby—Lynchburg

You can visit Thomas Jefferson's summer home, Poplar Forest, which he considered to be "the best dwelling house in the state, except that of Monticello." It's an extraordinary brick octagonal house with dependencies and landscaping. It was opened to the public recently, as it was in private hands until 1984, and it's still undergoing restoration. In addition, visit Red Hill, a home and plantation where Patrick Henry lived and died.

Lynchburg Mansion Inn Bed & Breakfast

405 Madison Street
Lynchburg, VA 24504
(800) 352–1199 or (804) 528–5400

FAX: (804) 847–2545

E-MAIL: mansioninn@aol.com

WEB SITE: www.lynchburgmansioninn.com

INNKEEPERS: Bob and Mauranna Sherman

ROOMS: 5, including 2 suites, all with private bath, air conditioning, telephone, TV, radio, hair dryer, iron, ironing board, and robes; 4 with desk; 3 with fireplace; 2 with porch; suites with kitchen; wheelchair access

ON THE GROUNDS: Parking; gardens, gazebo; hot tub

EXTRAS: Turndown with chocolates; newspaper at door in morning; lace bag of potpourri tied to bedposts; two miniature schnauzers named Happy and Krissy in owners' quarters

RATES: $109–$144, double occupancy, including full breakfast; two-night minimum weekends in May and October as well as holiday and college weekends

CREDIT CARDS ACCEPTED: American Express, Diners Club, MasterCard, Visa

OPEN: Year-round

HOW TO GET THERE: From Route 29 take exit 1 (Main Street/Downtown) and turn west onto Main Street. At Fifth Street, turn left and go 4 blocks. Turn right onto Madison Street. The B&B is the second house on the left on the corner of Fourth and Madison. It's the huge pillared mansion behind a 6-foot-high wrought-iron fence.

Thomas Jefferson considered the Lynchburg area "the most interesting spot in the state," so he built his summer home here. Soon, other dignitaries made it their permanent home. At the time, the primary crop grown on the surrounding plantations was "dark" tobacco, the leaves used for pipe and chewing tobacco. At first, bateaux transported the leaves on rivers and canals to Richmond, but eventually, a web of railroads that passed through Lynchburg contributed to the town's growth.

Lynchburg Mansion Inn, located in the Garland Hill Historic District, where the streets are still paved with brick, is certainly no shy violet. This mansion, sitting proudly behind its 6-foot-high wrought-iron fence and with its grand two-story columns, definitely makes a statement. The 9,000-square-foot white stucco Spanish Georgian mansion was built in 1914 by James R. Gilliam, the wealthiest man in Lynchburg. The building was built to impress. There are twenty-two massive columns circling the 105-foot Spanish-tiled veranda. Bob and Mauranna Sherman renovated this jewel and turned it into a B&B in 1990.

The double front doors of the house lead to a noble 50-foot grand hall with majestic cherry columns and wainscotting, oak floors, and a cherry and oak staircase that sweeps upward for three stories. The ceilings on the first floor are 11 feet high, while those on the second floor are 10 feet.

For guest relaxation, there's a living room with overstuffed sofas and chairs and a broad selection of books to read before the fireplace. Upstairs, there's a second-floor sunroom filled with plants. In addition, there are gardens to roam, a hot tub to relax in, and a sweeping veranda with wicker furniture where you can listen to the swish of the palm fronds as they sway gently in the breeze.

The entire B&B is furnished with fabulous antiques and original signed artwork. The first floor Veranda Suite, for example, has a bed with a 7-foot-tall burled walnut headboard and a matching dresser, as well as a fireplace. In the private solarium, there's a kitchen. The Garden Suite, which is in the original billiards room, has a paneled bedroom with boxed beams and a huge stone fireplace. The Raffles-style bed has Ralph Lauren linens. The French Country Room has Victorian fretwork decor and a bed made of light pine and covered with frothy white Battenburg lace. The baths feature a combination of turn-of-the-century accoutrements and twenty-first-century comfort. There are hexagonal tile floors, pedestal sinks, and clawfoot tubs.

Newspapers are delivered to doorways every morning, and coffee and juice are set out on a second-floor table. Breakfast is served in the formal dining room, which has a brass chandelier, oak floors, a fireplace, and a mauve-and-white rug. The large mahogany table is set with antique German gold-rimmed plates, silver flatware, linens, and crystal. Mauranna may start the meal with a Mediterranean medley consisting of grapes, plums, peaches, figs, sliced dates, and pineapple chunks warmed in fruit juices and then topped with coconut and sliced almonds and garnished with a fresh flower. Entrees may include peach French toast, which is allowed to stand overnight in a caramel custard sauce and baked for an hour in the morning, or a salmon and asparagus quiche.

What's Nearby

See "What's Nearby—Lynchburg," page 361.

Bed and Breakfast at the Page House Inn

323 Fairfax Avenue
Norfolk, VA 23507
(800) 599–7659 or (757) 625–5033

FAX: (757) 623–9451

E-MAIL: innkeeper@pagehouseinn.com

WEB SITE: www.pagehouseinn.com

INNKEEPERS: Stephanie and Ezio DeBelardino

ROOMS: 7, including 3 suites; all with private bath, air conditioning, telephone with dataport, TV, radio, desk, hair dryer, and robes; 4 with fireplace and tape player; 3 with whirlpool tub, VCR, and mini-refrigerator

ON THE GROUNDS: Parking; side yard

EXTRAS: Afternoon cappuccino and freshly baked cookies on arrival; soft drinks, juices, snacks, fruit, candy in common rooms throughout the day and night; fax/copier available; two Boston terriers named Charlie and Tootsie on premises

RATES: $120–$200, double occupancy, including full breakfast, afternoon refreshments, and snacks; two-night minimum weekends from April through October and some holidays, rest of holidays three-night minimum

CREDIT CARDS ACCEPTED: American Express, MasterCard, Visa

OPEN: Year-round

HOW TO GET THERE: From I–64, take the I–264 exit to downtown Norfolk. Continue on I–264 to exit 9 (Waterside Drive). Continue on Waterside (the name of the street will change to Boush) to Olney Road. Turn left onto Olney. Go 2 blocks and turn left onto Mowbray Arch. In 1 block turn right onto Fairfax. The B&B is the first building on the left. The parking area is behind the B&B.

In 1940 the authors of the WPA guide to Virginia described Norfolk as "a fusion of land and sea, of boats and brick houses, of civilians and sailors." Little has changed that dichotomy over the years. Still the home of the largest naval base in the world, Norfolk probably does have more sailors than civilians.

When Stephanie, who plays an active role in the Bed and Breakfast Association of Virginia, and Ezio, who is a retired contractor, first spied their dream B&B, it was in the last throes of devastation: condemned and ready for demolition. But they could see the beauty beyond the damage. Ezio worked his magic slowly but resolutely until all the woodwork was restored and the oak floors were polished to a soft glow. Then Stephanie called her aunt, who is a decorator, and together they combined family antiques and newly purchased items to create an elegant but comfortable B&B. Travelers who stay at Page House Inn have the good fortune to be staying in historic Ghent, a waterside neighborhood built between 1892 and 1912 and filled with wonderful old mansions.

On a recent afternoon visit, Stephanie opened the polished oak door to reveal a wide hallway with a sweeping stairway that climbs three stories. She invited us into the formal parlor with its marine blue walls, handsome floral window coverings, oil paintings, and puffy sofas before the fireplace. Soon steaming cups of cappuccino and a plate of luscious cookies were placed before us. As we nibbled and sipped, we looked at photographs of the restoration.

Other common areas for guest enjoyment include an informal parlor on the opposite side of the entrance hall that has a fireplace with an oak mantel and plaid sofas. Oak tables and chairs here provide a place to play a variety of supplied games or to complete a jigsaw puzzle. There's also a roof garden off the second-floor hallway with an iron swing and tables and chairs for spending a few relaxing minutes with that last cup of coffee before heading out to see the sights.

Our room for the night was a wonderful suite called Miss Diane. It has a navy blue carpet throughout and blue-and-white drapes and wall coverings. The bedroom has a white iron bed before a gas fireplace. There's a foyer with a table and chairs and a parlor with another fireplace and sofas and chairs covered in a blue and white fabric. The beautifully restored bath has a clawfoot tub. The newest room, created on the first floor in 1997, has a fireplace and a fabulous bath that includes a private hot tub for two as well as a huge shower that converts to steam. Some rooms even have wet bars, refrigerators, and VCRs. The ultimate romantic accommodation, however, is called Bianca Boat and Breakfast. One couple, or two couples traveling together, can stay overnight aboard the *Bianca,* a 43-foot nauticat built in Finland and moored just down the street.

Breakfast for B&B guests is served in the formal dining room, or, with advance notice, it can be served by candlelight on a table in the guest's room. Stephanie offers a full breakfast that will include fresh fruits and poached or baked fruit along with freshly baked sourdough bread and cream scones, followed by an omelette.

The Emmanuel Hutzler House

2036 Monument Avenue
Richmond, VA 23220
(804) 353–6900

FAX: (804) 355–5053

E-MAIL: be.our.guest@bensonhouse.com

WEB SITE: www.bensonhouse.com

INNKEEPERS: Lyn Benson and John Richardson

ROOMS: 4, including 2 suites, all with private bath, air conditioning, private-line telephone, TV, radio; 3 with desk; 2 with fireplace; and 1 with whirlpool tub

ON THE GROUNDS: Parking

EXTRAS: Fruit juices, coffee, sodas available all day

RATES: $89–$125, single occupancy; $95–$155, double occupancy, including full breakfast; two-night minimum holiday and special event weekends

CREDIT CARDS ACCEPTED: American Express, Diners Club, Discover, MasterCard, Visa

OPEN: Year-round except December 24–31

HOW TO GET THERE: From I–95, follow signs for I–64 east Petersburg (not I–295). From I–64, take exit 78 and turn right onto Boulevard and follow it for 1 mile to Broad Street. Turn left onto Broad and go approximately ½ mile past the Science Museum. Turn right onto Meadow and go 2 blocks; then turn right onto Monument. The B&B is on the corner of

Monument and Allison. You can unload in front, but overnight parking is in the rear.

Be sure to ask Lyn and John to show you pictures of the renovation of their magnificent B&B on Richmond's grandest boulevard. At one point it seemed to be nothing but structural members. Lyn and John stripped all the mahogany on the first floor themselves, including the walls of paneling and the intricate stair spindles. The painstaking work of restoration has paid off handsomely, as today the beige brick 1914 townhouse glows with warmth and vitality.

Located in Richmond's finest neighborhood, Monument Avenue is a broad boulevard with a grassy median incorporating magnificent statues of illustrious figures from Richmond's history. Among the most noteworthy is that of Jefferson Davis, which portrays the Confederate president as if giving a speech. He's backed by a huge semicircle of classical columns. Stonewall Jackson, J.E. B. Stuart, and Robert E. Lee are astride their horses. The most recent addition is a statue of tennis great Arthur Ashe, who was born here.

On entering The Emmanuel Hutzler House, guests find themselves in a grand 8,000-square-foot mansion with an entry hall dominated by a sweeping mahogany stairway. The staircase has the unusual distinction of rising in half-steps instead of full because the original owner had a congenital hip problem. To the right, a handsome living room is enclosed in mahogany paneling that includes a coffered ceiling, boxed beams, and bookcases on either side of the fireplace. An elegant French tapestry hangs above. Richmond history books sit on the large coffee table, illuminated with natural light from the bay of leaded-glass windows. TC, the friendly inn cat, loves to stretch out here on one of the damask sofas to bask in the warmth from the fireplace.

There are four spacious guest rooms on the second floor, and all are equipped with modern baths. My favorite is Marion's Room, which has watermelon-toned walls, a brass-and-iron bed, and an antique English desk. Henrietta's Room has hunter green walls, a decorative tiled fireplace, a bed with a cherry chairback headboard, and a Chippendale love seat. Isaac's Room has a four-poster bed. The Robinette Suite has a marble fireplace, a four-poster bed, and a cherry Sheraton dresser. The tiled bath includes a Jacuzzi and a separate shower.

Breakfast is served in the formal dining room on a massive common table that's overseen by a handsome pier mirror. It will include fresh fruit, cereals, muffins or breads, and a hot dish such as French toast with bacon or scrambled eggs with sausage and fried Virginia apples.

The small parking lot is just outside the back door. When you come in, you leave your keys so that John can move your car if someone needs to leave before you do.

What's Nearby—Richmond

Richmond is a beautiful and resilient Southern city with a proud heritage and significant architecture. The city was the site of the treason trial of Aaron Burr (presided over by John Marshall). Capital of the Confederacy from 1841–1845, it is now the capital of Virginia and has one of the most impressive capitol buildings, partly designed by Thomas Jefferson, of any state. Other interesting sites to see are the Confederate Museum, the Edgar Allan Poe Shrine (he spent much of his boyhood here); St. John's Church, where Patrick Henry gave his famous "Give me Liberty or Give me Death" speech; and Shockoe Slip and Shockoe Bottom, the oldest sections of Richmond, which now contain upscale restaurants and shops. Above all travelers to Richmond should plan a visit to the Virginia Historical Society, which is just down the street. They have terrific exhibits about Virginia and Richmond history.

Chester

243 James River Road
Scottsville, VA 24590
(804) 286-3960 (fax also)

E-MAIL: chester@cstone.net
WEB SITE: www.chesterbed.com
INNKEEPER: Jean Stratton
ROOMS: 5; all with private bath, fireplace, air conditioning; guest telephone in library, portable telephones available; wheelchair access
ON THE GROUNDS: On 8 acres with extensive gardens and walking trails
EXTRAS: Wine or soft drinks on arrival; a dog named Lucy Rose and two tabby cats, Alexander and Madeline, on premises
RATES: $150–$165, double occupancy, including full breakfast and welcoming beverage; two-night minimum in October and on some holiday weekends

CREDIT CARDS ACCEPTED: MasterCard and Visa

OPEN: Year-round

HOW TO GET THERE: From I–64 just outside Charlottesville, take exit 121 (Scottsville) onto Route 20 south. Travel 17 miles to State Route 726 (James River Road) and turn right. The B&B is on the left in 2½ blocks.

Chester was built in 1847 in the Greek Revival style, with a pitched gable roof and a porch across the front. Its builder, Joseph C. Wright, was a retired landscape architect from Chester, England. He designed his home in the style of a handsome English country manor house, and he embellished the grounds with exotic flowers, shrubs, and trees. They say that the largest holly tree in Albemarle County is on the grounds, and there are tall stands of English boxwoods, as well as over fifty different varieties of trees, shrubs, and flowers. The grounds include a natural lily pond, a garden patio pond, and fountains.

The house was purchased by Jean and Craig Stratton in 1995, and although it had been operating as a B&B since 1983, it was the Strattons who restored it to the grand style it had originally known. Jean is an interior designer and her expert hand can be seen in the beautiful new tiled baths, as well as in the lush furnishings.

Guests can relax in utter comfort in the library, which is complete with books in built-in cases. This is where the guest telephone is located and a desk for guests to use. A living room has a fireplace with a painted mantel, as well as an aubergine damask sofa and a baby grand piano. There's a Tibeten carpet on the heart pine floor.

The guest rooms are sophisticated and elegant—reminiscent of those found in English country houses. Room #1 has a four-poster bed so high that a step-stool is necessary to reach it. It's covered with an ivory spread, and there's a fireplace as well. The tiled bath is bright and new. Room #4 is the largest. It has a four-poster bed and a fireplace. The bath has a pine floor.

Breakfast is served in the formal dining room, which has another fireplace and beautiful floral paper on the walls. Guests are seated at individual cherry tables. The meal will begin with fresh juices and fruit, as well as homemade breads. Among Jean's most popular breakfast entrees, guests may feast on popover pancakes or perhaps Grand Marnier French toast.

Scottsville is in the heart of Virginia's beautiful and historic Albemarle County. The countryside is rural and bucolic—offering the epitome of gracious Southern living, a perfect spot for a country outing. Ash Lawn-Highland, the charming home of James Monroe, is nearby, and it is open for tours, as is Thomas Jefferson's home, Monticello. You can golf on a number of nearby courses, or you can canoe, raft, or tube on the James River.

The Manor at Taylor's Store B&B Country Inn

Best Buy

Route 122
(mailing address: P.O. Box 510)
Smith Mountain Lake, VA 24184
(800) 248–6267 or (540) 721–3951

FAX: (540) 721–5342

E-MAIL: taylors@symweb.com

WEB SITE: www.symweb.com/taylors

INNKEEPERS: Lee and Mary Lynn Tucker; manager: Gloria Scott

ROOMS: 6, including 4 suites and 1 cottage; all with private bath, air conditioning, radio, and robes; 3 with private porch; 2 with fireplace

ON THE GROUNDS: On 120 acres with multitudes of hiking opportunities; formal Colonial gardens with gazebo; 6 spring-fed ponds for swimming, fishing, canoeing, etc.; volleyball, badminton, croquet on property

EXTRAS: Guest kitchen with coffee, iced tea, lemonade, etc., turndown with handmade special gift; fully equipped exercise room

RATES: $85–$175, double occupancy, including full breakfast

CREDIT CARDS ACCEPTED: American Express, MasterCard, Visa

OPEN: Year-round

HOW TO GET THERE: From I–81 in Roanoke take exit 143 onto I–581/Route 220 south, which will take you through Roanoke. Continue on Route 220 south through Boone's Mill to the Route 122/40 exit and then go north on Route 122 toward the Booker T. Washington National Monument and Smith Mountain Lake. Pass through Burnt Chimney and continue for exactly 1⁶/10 miles to the inn, which will be on the right.

Mary Lynn and Lee Tucker have beautifully converted an 1820s manor house that was originally the centerpiece of a large plantation into a lovely and very tranquil B&B. But the most atypical aspect of the inn is not the buildings themselves, but the dedication of the innkeepers to keeping their guests healthy. Not only do they have an exercise room, but they prepare breakfasts for their guests that are absolutely "heart-healthy." Here you'll receive fabulous meals, but the entire menu will be low in cholesterol and fat. Lee is a physician and pathologist and Mary Lynn a family nurse practitioner, so they were all too familiar with the consequences of improper diets. Now guests can purchase a copy of their *Heart Healthy Hospitality* cookbook and learn to cook healthy themselves. In addition to operating this B&B, the couple owns a gourmet food and wine shop in Roanoke.

Taylor's Store was a significant landmark to early pioneers who bartered farm goods for other items here as early as 1799. Located on a westward trail known as the Old Warwich Road, it was also a provisioning center for folks headed west. The building later became an ordinary and eventually the general post office for the area. The store was located directly in front of the B&B, and its signpost is still there. Regrettably, the old store was torn down in 1979.

The gracious white-clapboard manor with black shutters that Lee and Mary Lynn converted to their B&B is on 120 acres that are laced with six ponds and a multitude of hiking trails. Swimming docks provide sunning and swimming possibilities, there are canoes to use, and fishing poles are available for the fisherfolk. Brick pathways lead through gardens to a gazebo, and there's another gazebo by a pond. Vineyards beside the house attest to Lee's adventures into Chardonnay production.

The manor house has several guest retreats. A formal parlor is distinctive for a fabulous tall-case clock said to have been designed by Stanford White, as well as for the European oil paintings on the wall. It has a fireplace and a piano as well. The great room is more informal, with a huge brick fireplace, a billiards table, and a large-screen TV. A sunporch, which offers a happy habitat for plants as well as people, has a bright and cheerful aspect.

Some of the guest rooms are located in the manor house, and these are elegantly furnished with antiques and a sophisticated decor. Castle Suite, for example, has a canopy bed, two antique throne chairs, and prints of English castles on the walls. The bath includes a sunken tub for two. The Toy Room has another canopy bed. It's decorated with antique quilts and toys. A French door leads to a balcony that affords sunset views.

Additional rooms are located in the West Lodge, a hand-hewn log cabin set away in the woods. A private cottage, which has three bedrooms and two baths, as well as a full kitchen and a den with a fireplace, is a secluded retreat for families or several couples traveling together.

Mary Lynn and Lee serve breakfast in the sunroom. They will start with fresh fruit and juice and a selection of freshly baked breads such as lemon yogurt muffins or Mark's Walnut Coffee Cake. As an entree, Mary Lynn might prepare manor moon pies, a dish in which cheese and strawberry preserves are tucked into pita pockets, dipped in a batter and sautéed. They are then topped with fresh strawberries. These might be accompanied by turkey sausage and followed by a breakfast dessert such as bread pudding topped with rum sauce.

What's Nearby—Smith Mountain Lake

Smith Mountain Lake is 5 miles away. You can go boating, fishing, or swimming here, and golfing and tennis are also nearby. Waterfront restaurants offer several options for dining. Roanoke is merely twenty minutes away. The Mill Mountain Theater is a year-round professional theater that offers a range of adult and children's programs. At Center in the Square you can visit the Science Museum of Western Virginia or the Art Museum of Western Virginia or the Roanoke Valley History Museum.

The Sampson Eagon Inn

238 East Beverley Street
Staunton, VA 24401
(800) 597-9722 or (540) 886-8200

E-MAIL: eagoninn@rica.net
WEB SITE: www.eagoninn.com
INNKEEPERS: Frank and Laura Mattingly

ROOMS: 5, including 2 suites; all with private bath, air conditioning, telephone with dataport, TV, VCR, radio, desk, magnifying mirror in all bathrooms, iron, and ironing board; 4 with decorative fireplace; 2 with CD player

ON THE GROUNDS: Parking; gardens with benches

EXTRAS: Snacks such as fruit, mineral water, coffee, sodas available 24 hours; fax and copier available; fresh flowers in rooms; one cairn terrier, Jeepers Creepers, on premises

RATES: $95–$130, double occupancy, including full breakfast; two-night minimum weekends, April–November

CREDIT CARDS ACCEPTED: American Express, MasterCard, Visa

OPEN: Year-round

HOW TO GET THERE: From I–81 take exit 222 and follow Route 250 west to Staunton. Turn right onto Route 11 (Coalter Street) and continue past the traffic light. The B&B is on the left, at the corner of Coalter and Beverley Streets.

It's hard to describe such perfection. It isn't just that Laura and Frank Mattingly have completed a superb restoration of their 1840s Greek Revival mansion in the Gospel Hill Historic District, and it isn't just that they've filled it with gorgeous American Federal and Empire antiques from their outstanding collection. Nor is it the fact that these friendly, knowledgeable innkeepers have included all the guest amenities one could imagine for absolute guest comfort. It's the combination of all their expertise and thoughtfulness that makes this B&B stand out above the rest.

The handsome creamy-colored house with its columned portico sits behind a stone wall across the street from the home in which Woodrow Wilson was born. The Mattinglys have a passion for history and historic preservation that shows in the restoration of the polished pine floors and moldings that surround the 12-foot-high ceilings on the main floor. The moldings particularly stand out against the peach-colored walls in the parlor, which has been furnished with an 1840s butler's desk, fine American and English oil paintings, and an Oriental rug.

The guest rooms are named for people who lived in the house, and each room is furnished in the period of its namesake. The Kayser Room, for example, harks to the mid-1800s when the Kayser family owned the house. It has a magnificent carved New York State four-poster Empire canopy bed draped with creamy damask and accented with teal blue. There's a two-tier crystal chandelier and an ornate fireplace mantel with columns carved to match the bed. The mantel is topped by a late Victorian pier mirror. (Alas, although each room once had a working fireplace, none are currently functional.) The Holt Room is furnished in Colonial Revival style, reflecting the taste of the Holt family, who lived here in the 1920s. The fireplace is surrounded by blue-and-white Delft tiles; the four-poster mahogany bed and a matching highboy date to the 1930s. The room is lavishly swagged in cream-and-blue French toile. Thoroughly modern bathrooms include pedestal sinks, and in Tam's Suite the original brass-and-glass towel bars remain.

The dining room is one of the most memorable rooms in the house. It is furnished with a mid-nineteenth-century Duncan Phyfe pedestal table, a Sheraton sideboard, and Chippendale chairs that date to the 1760s. Breakfast is served on antique Royal Doulton china accompanied by family sterling silver and Waterford crystal glasses. Laura's specialty breakfast is Grand Marnier soufflé pancakes, which she serves with a strawberry sauce, country sausages, and freshly baked breads or muffins.

A side garden is filled with flowers in summer that guests may enjoy while sitting on benches in their midst or from a slightly loftier perch on the side porch, which has a swing for two.

What's Nearby—Staunton

The Woodrow Wilson Birthplace and Museum is across the street. Although Wilson only lived here in his infancy, the excellent museum traces his life as a professor and president of Princeton University as well as through his presidency. The Museum of American Frontier Culture offers excellent living history exhibits of life on the frontier, including costumed guides who demonstrate farming, crafts, and domestic chores. Staunton is in the Shenandoah Valley, tucked between the Shenandoah Mountains and the Blue Ridge Mountains, close to both the Blue Ridge Parkway and the Skyline Drive. (See also Waynesboro.)

The Inn at Vaucluse Spring

140 Vaucluse Spring Lane
Stephens City, VA 22655
(800) 869–0525 or (540) 869–0200

FAX: (540) 869–9546

E-MAIL: mail@vauclusespring.com

WEB SITE: www.vauclusespring.com

INNKEEPERS: Mike and Karen Caplanis; Neil and Barry Myers

ROOMS: 12, including 2 suites and 2 cottages; all with private bath, air conditioning, and fireplace; 11 with whirlpool tub; 7 with desk; 4 with private porch; 1 with wheelchair access; telephone available for all rooms

ON THE GROUNDS: Parking; swimming pool, gardens, 103 acres of pastures and open land; stream; cross-country skiing when adequate snow

EXTRAS: Afternoon refreshments; fax and limited wordprocessing available; meeting rooms; newspapers available; a Gordon setter named Miss MacIntosh and a cat named Toby on premises

RATES: $145–$250, double occupancy, including full breakfast; two-night minimum weekends mid-April through mid-June and mid-September through mid-November plus certain holidays

CREDIT CARDS ACCEPTED: MasterCard and Visa

OPEN: Year-round except Thanksgiving and Christmas

HOW TO GET THERE: From Washington, D.C., take I–66 west to its end and exit onto I–81 north. Take exit 302 (the first exit) off I–81 and turn left onto Route 627, traveling west toward Middletown. Continue to the end of Route 627 and turn right (north) onto Route 11. Drive 2 miles on Route 11 and turn left onto Route 638 (Vaucluse Road). Drive ¾ mile and turn left at the inn sign. Follow signs to check-in.

When John Chumley had his art studio and gallery here, the tumble of buildings may have been as dynamic as they are today, but it's doubtful they were any more picturesque. Anchored by Vaucluse Spring Pond, the 103 acres that now comprise The Inn at Vaucluse Spring has a fascinating history that begins even before the Chumley family lived here.

The grand brick Federal manor house that sits on a distant hill was built by Strother Jones on land he purchased from his father, Gabriel Jones, known as the "Valley Lawyer," in about 1785. The Civil War impoverished the Jones family, however, and they lost Vaucluse, which was named after the Vaucluse region of France. By the time the Caplanis and Myers families discovered the property, the manor house had been abandoned for some 50 years and only the chimney was left of Mr. Jones's original law office.

Restored and decorated in a sophisticated style, the inn now consists of B&B rooms in the manor house and the Chumley Homeplace as well as in Chumley's former gallery and studio. Throughout the B&B there are original Chumley paintings hanging on the walls (he painted realistic scenes of the Shenandoah Valley), and all rooms have beds dressed in brilliant Ralph Lauren-type designer fabrics, gas fireplaces, and (all except one) whirlpool tubs in modern bathrooms. We love the two-level Mill House Studio, which has its own stone terrace beside the mill pond, a gas fireplace in the living room, an upstairs bedroom with an enchanting view, and the soothing sound of water rushing through the mill race to lull guests to sleep.

The keeping room in the Chumley Homeplace—which has walnut log and chink walls, exposed beams, a large stone fireplace, tufted oxblood leather and natural-wicker furniture, and Oriental rugs on polished heart pine floors—offers a cozy and inviting spot to read or talk to other guests. B&B telephone is in an alcove. A sunporch overlooks the millpond.

The manor house was fully restored and opened to guests in 1997. The reception area for guest check-in is located here. The building, which has 11-foot-high ceilings and massive triple-hung 10-foot-high Jeffersonian walk-out windows, is dramatic and spectacular. Cherry and walnut doors rise almost to the ceilings. The deep claret red living room has an 1830s Greek Revival fireplace mantel, a chintz sofa, and piles of books on the coffee table.

There are two dining rooms in the manor house, and this is where breakfast is served every morning. Dinners are offered on Saturday night as well. Karen and Neil may start breakfast with lemon-poppyseed muffins followed by Mike's dramatic six-fruit muesli, which is layered with whipped cream in a parfait glass. Next comes a quiche Shenandoah accompanied by applewood-smoked trout or maybe banana-pecan pancakes with cider-glazed sausages and fans of bananas and strawberries.

There's a lovely heated swimming pool surrounded by a stone wall in front of the gallery building. The pastures are often populated with Holstein cows.

What's Nearby—Stephens City

Do not leave the area without picking up a bag of Route 11 Potato Chips, natural chips made just up the road in Middletown that are the best chips you'll ever eat (you can watch them being made, too). Belle Grove Plantation, a National Trust property, is a beautiful restored 1700s stone mansion that should be included on any visit to the area. Thomas Jefferson influenced its design. Other scenic diversions include Fort Valley with its Woodstock tower for spectacular vistas and the State Arboretum of Virginia, which has the most extensive boxwood collection in North America. You can drive a circular route through its 170 acres.

Black Horse Inn

8393 Meetze Road
Warrenton, VA 20187
(540) 349–4020

FAX: (540) 349–4242
E-MAIL: blackhrs@citizen.infl.net
WEB SITE: www.blackhorseinn.com
INNKEEPER: Lynn Pirozzoli

ROOMS: 9, including 2 suites; all with private bath; 8 with air conditioning; 4 with fireplace and whirlpool tub; 2 with TV and VCR; telephones with dataports available for 4 rooms

ON THE GROUNDS: On 20 acres with gardens and gazebo; barns, riding ring, and pastures with horses, jogging trail

EXTRAS: Afternoon "hunt country tea" with international cheese and fruit display, as well as wines and nonalcoholic beverages; turndown with chocolates; exercise room; guests are welcome to bring their horses (prior permission required); black Labrador, Zoe, on premises, as well as thoroughbred horses

RATES: $125–$350, double occupancy, including full breakfast and afternoon tea; two-night minimum April–July and September–November

CREDIT CARDS ACCEPTED: American Express, MasterCard, Visa

OPEN: Year-round except Christmas

HOW TO GET THERE: From I-66, take exit 43A (Warrenton) and travel south on Route 29 for approximately 13 miles to the second exit for Warrenton, which is Route 643 (Meetze Road). Turn left and go 1⁶/10 miles. The B&B is on the left.

Lynn Pirozzoli traveled a fascinating path to reach her B&B—from Washington to California and back again. She had diligently worked in corporate America for eighteen years, while also becoming an accomplished horseback rider. And then she struck gold—literally—in the hills formerly mined by the '49ers in California Gold Rush country. By utilizing an advanced technology, she and her partners were able to extract additional gold from mines that had long ago been abandoned. Lynn took her proceeds and purchased this fabulous inn, and she's never looked back.

After Lynn bought her B&B in 1993, she undertook a top-to-bottom renovation of the 1850s white-clapboard mansion, not opening it to guests until 1995. She calls it the Black Horse Inn in memory of the Black Horse

Cavalry, a mounted unit that originated in Warrenton in 1838 and played a significant role in the Civil War. The house was used as a hospital during that period.

Guests enter the B&B through an impressive double-height columned veranda. A grand circular stairway winds from the entry hall to the second floor of the mansion. Guests can relax in a living room that has a fireplace and comfortable overstuffed chairs and sofas. The B&B has a horse-country theme, and there are statues, lamps, and objets d'art throughout in either a horse or a dog motif. A library has cherry paneling and an abundance of books, as well as another fireplace. There is also a porch that offers views of the gardens and gazebo.

The guest rooms are romantic, intimate, and alluring. All are filled with beautiful antiques. Great Expectations is a favorite that is often requested for honeymoons. It has a terrific bedroom with a fireplace, a beautiful antique cubbyhole desk, and an ivory damask sofa. There's a private porch reached through French doors that offers romantic sunset views over the Blue Ridge Mountains and a marble bath with a whirlpool tub for two and a glass-enclosed shower. Hunter's Heaven has a more masculine appeal. The room features rich green colors that Lynn has used to create a hunting-lodge motif. A spread on the gorgeous Chippendale-style canopy bed and in a wallpaper border along the ceiling carry out this theme. There's a rock fireplace, and the tiled bath has wainscotted walls.

Breakfast is served in the formal dining room, where a lovely antique buffet is located. One of Lynn's most popular entrees is Little Washington French Toast (a recipe she received from The Inn at Little Washington) in which the French bread is stuffed with mascarpone cheese, brown sugar, and pecans before baking.

One of the glories of this B&B is its grounds. The inn has its own hunter stables, and guests are encouraged to bring their equine companions along. Lynn is an accomplished rider who will describe the best rides and advise guests when to come to see a fox hunt or a point-to-point race. She'll even prepare picnic lunches and tailgate baskets so that those guests who want to keep their feet firmly planted on the ground can still participate. Regardless of the season, there's something tranquil and reassuring about a pasture full of grazing horses, and that's a sight you're bound to see here.

What's Nearby—Warrenton

The big activity in these parts is fox hunting and steeplechase racing. Lynn is an expert on the times and places, so be sure to ask. Several excellent Virginia wineries nearby offer tours and tastings. A Rails-to-Trails path is across the street—the perfect place to bicycle or cross-country ski, depending on the weather. For Civil War buffs, Manassas Battlefield is nearby to explore. Warrenton is just 45 minutes from Washington, D.C.

Middleton Inn

176 Main Street
(mailing address: P.O. Box 254)
Washington, VA 22747
(800) 816–8157 or (540) 675–2020

FAX: (540) 675–1050

E-MAIL: middlein@shentel.net

WEB SITE: www.middleton-inn.com

INNKEEPER: Mary Ann Kuhn

ROOMS: 5, including 1 cottage, all with private bath, air conditioning, telephone, TV, hair dryer, fireplace, robes, CD player, iron, and ironing board; 2 with desk; 1 with a Jacuzzi, stereo, mini-refrigerator, and coffeemaker

ON THE GROUNDS: On 6 acres with parking; gardens; open fields, barn, stables, paddocks, horses

EXTRAS: Afternoon tea and cookies; wine and cheese in the evening; port and chocolates at turndown; fax available; dogs named Prince Charles, Lady Carolina, and Hannah on premises; horses named Belle and Gambler in stables; five outside cats

RATES: $195–$425, double occupancy, including full breakfast, afternoon tea, evening wine and cheese, port and chocolates; two-night minimum weekends in October and on holiday weekends

CREDIT CARDS ACCEPTED: American Express, MasterCard, Visa

OPEN: Year-round

HOW TO GET THERE: From Washington, D.C., take I–66 west to exit 43A (Gainesville). Follow Route 29 south for 12 miles into Warrenton and turn right onto Route 211 west. Go 23 miles and turn right at the sign for the Washington Business District. Turn left at the stop sign onto Main Street and go 2 blocks. The B&B is on the left.

We love the rural quiet of "Little Washington." The cluster of old houses and the clutch of shops, the old post office and library belie the sophistication beneath the surface. To all outward appearances this is a rural farm village that's changed little since the nineteenth century. But we all know better.

Middleton Inn was created in 1995 by Mary Ann Kuhn, a former *Washington Post* reporter and producer for CBS-TV news. On a 1996 trip through Virginia, I heard persistent reports about her terrific new B&B, so I couldn't wait to see it for myself. I was not disappointed.

The 1850s brick Federal manor house sits on a six-acre knoll just outside the town. It was built originally by Middleton Miller, who designed uniforms for the Confederate Army—thus the name.

The B&B is a dream. Mary Ann proudly greeted me in the spacious center hall and took me to the living room, where wine and cheese were set out for her guests. (In summer guests relax in the afternoon on one of the spacious porches.) The living room has sunny daffodil yellow walls, plaid sofas, and a creamy marble fireplace. Oil paintings and sporting prints of foxhounds, horses, and hunters line the walls. The focal point, however, is a magnificent carved-rosewood square grand pianoforte from the 1830s with a bust of George Bush on its polished surface.

Mary Ann showed me to the Hunt Room, a spacious room with hunter green walls, a beautiful antique carved four-poster bed with its own steps to reach it, an antique Empire bureau, a French-horn chandelier, and a fireplace. The marble bath is exquisite, with a tiny soaking tub and a full shower. All of the rooms have working fireplaces.

For those who want total privacy, a charming guest cottage is located nearby. It also has a fireplace, and the living room holds shelves of interesting books. Upstairs, a loft bedroom has a sleigh bed, and the marble bath contains a Jacuzzi.

For dinner I treated myself to a marvelous meal at The Inn at Little Washington, where the impressive food never disappoints. When I returned, I found a decanter of port and delicious chocolates awaiting me.

The next morning I awoke to the tantalizing smell of hot-from-the-oven muffins. In the elegantly dressed dining room, we savored fresh fruit and eggs Benedict. Mary Ann prepares them with smoked trout instead of Canadian bacon, and they were delicious. On other days she might fix raspberry pancakes.

What's Nearby—Washington

Come in the spring or fall to watch the Virginia foxhunting or steeple-chase events. Little Washington Theater has performances of plays, readings, and concerts that take place year-round. The Skyline Drive and the Appalachian Trail follow the crest of the mountains in Shenandoah National Park. Spectacular vistas from both the drive and the trail are awarded to travelers, especially in the spring when the rhododendrons are in bloom. You can pick your own strawberries, raspberries, apples, and peaches at nearby farms or visit Oasis Vineyards, Naked Mountain Vineyard & Winery, and Linden Vineyards & Orchards to sample the local wines. Come in December and select your Christmas tree from a local tree farm.

Sycamore Hill House and Gardens

110 Menefee Mountain Lane
Washington, VA 22747
(540) 675–3046

WEB SITE: www.bnb-n-va.com/
sycamore.htm

INNKEEPERS: Kerri and Stephen
Wagner

ROOMS: 3, all with private bath,
air conditioning, and hair dryer; 2 with radio; 1 with TV, desk, and robes; guest telephone on a separate line in the living room

ON THE GROUNDS: Parking; extensive flower gardens; 52 acres on a mountain top; 65-foot veranda with spectacular views

EXTRAS: Turndown with mints; chocolate chip cookies in guest rooms on arrival; fresh flowers in guest rooms; one huge white shaggy dog named Mollie Bean, one white cat named Zippy, and one calico cat named Pansy on premises but not on guest floor

RATES: $115–$200, double occupancy, including full breakfast; two-night minimum holiday weekends and all weekends in spring and fall

CREDIT CARDS ACCEPTED: MasterCard and Visa

OPEN: February–December

HOW TO GET THERE: From Washington, D.C., take I–66 west for 23 miles to exit 43A (Gainesville). Follow Route 29 south for 12 miles into Warrenton and turn right onto Route 211 west. Go 23 miles and turn right at the sign for the Washington Business District. Immediately turn right again onto Route 638. Follow this road past the library to the white pillars and turn left. The B&B is about 1 mile up the hill.

As you wind higher and higher up Menefee Mountain, you pass beyond the pine trees and meadows, where perhaps you'll see deer grazing or a red fox dart across a field (this is also a National Wildlife Habitat).

Wrapping the Virginia fieldstone house, which sits on 52 acres at 1,043 feet, are gardens in a kaleidoscope of colors to delight the eye. You become so enchanted by the bluebirds flitting into their special houses, the hummingbirds sampling the nectar in their red garden, and the beds of more than fifty varieties of flowers—including roses, daffodils, zinnias, and more than 2,000 iris—that you don't even notice the view. It's only after you enter the house that you become aware of it—that overwhelming, top-of-the-world view that stretches across the south side of the house, looking directly across at the Blue Ridge Mountains.

Many B&Bs have wraparound porches; this one has a wraparound view. The bowed windows above a 65-foot projecting veranda furnished with Kennedy rockers seem to reach out and bring the outside in. And the gardens don't stop at the front door, either. Stretching down the hillside are dogwood and redbud trees, a vegetable and herb garden, and a perennial bed filled with peonies, columbines, and day lilies. Inside there are pots of orchids, African violets, ivy, and spectacular clivias, which have brilliant orange flowers in the spring.

The gardens are the creation of Kerri Wagner, who has been adding to them ever since she and her husband, internationally acclaimed illustrator Stephen Wagner, purchased the house in 1987. Steve's original art, some of which he executed as covers for Time-Life Books, *National Geographic,* and others, decorates the walls of this extraordinary B&B. Be sure to pull yourself away from the view long enough to study his work. The B&B is decorated in a smart contemporary style—blond oak floors are covered by Oriental rugs. In winter, a fireplace warms the living room.

The three guest rooms are on the same level as the common rooms. The Master Bedroom has a 6-foot picture window with a fantastic view across the valley. In a private setting at one end of the house, it has a high four-poster pineapple-post pine bed dressed in a beautiful Amish quilt in shades of pale green and rose, and it also has a dressing room and a private bath. The Peach Room and Wicker Room are at the opposite side of the house. The Peach Room has a brass bed and built-in cases of books. It has views that stretch out in three directions and an in-room bath. The Wicker Room, which also has a view, is furnished with white wicker. It has soft grey walls and contains light pink accent pieces. It has a bath just across the hallway.

Breakfast is served on glass-topped tables in the dining room. Kerri prepares a vegetarian menu that includes a marvelous array of fresh fruit and home-baked breads such as cinnamon raisin bread or country biscuits. She may fix a cinnamon-apple puff (rather like a soufflé) for an entree or perhaps scalloped eggs, a combination of eggs, scallions, and cheese.

What's Nearby

See "What's Nearby—Washington," page 381.

The Iris Inn **Best Buy**

191 Chinquapin Drive
Waynesboro, VA 22980
(540) 943–1991

FAX: (540) 942-2093

E-MAIL: irisinn@cfw.com

WEB SITE: www.irisinn.com

INNKEEPERS: Wayne and Iris Karl

ROOMS: 9, including 2 suites, all with private bath, air conditioning, telephone with dataport, TV, radio, mini-refrigerator, hair dryer, robes, CD player; 8 with deck or patio and desk; 3 with coffeemaker, iron, and ironing board; 2 with VCR, whirlpool tub; 2 with fireplace; and 3 rooms with wheelchair access

ON THE GROUNDS: Parking; gardens with more than 3,000 iris; 21 acres of grounds; observation tower; hot tub

EXTRAS: Treadmills and bicycles in suites; freshly baked cookies available at all times; beverages at check-in; small conference room

RATES: $85–$150, double occupancy, including full breakfast; two-night minimum weekends

CREDIT CARDS ACCEPTED: MasterCard and Visa

OPEN: Year-round

HOW TO GET THERE: From I–64, take exit 96 (Waynesboro-Lyndhurst) and go south on Route 624 toward Lyndhurst. Take an immediate left onto Chinquapin Drive. The driveway to the B&B is approximately ³/₁₀ mile up the hill on the left.

The Iris Inn is appropriately named for two reasons: A brilliant display of iris covers the bank beside the driveway leading to this hilltop aerie, and Iris Karl, along with her husband, Wayne, is one of the innkeepers.

This unique B&B was built by the Karls in 1992. The cedar-and-brick building, with its arched entrance, has decks or balconies off each of its guest rooms except one, offering woodsy vistas of trees, birds at numerous feeders, and gardens. Sitting on twenty-one acres, the architecturally dramatic original structure is now complemented by a new building, which was completed in 1997. It contains two suites and a small conference/meeting facility. A three-story tower includes a treetop cupola with views of the Shenandoah Valley, and there's a hot tub on the first-floor deck that offers evening sunset views over the valley.

The great room of the main building continues to be the focal point of the B&B. At one end, a fieldstone fireplace soars to the 20-foot cathedral ceiling. On another wall, a mural, painted by wildlife artist Joan Henley, includes gentle deer, fearless rabbits, bold raccoons, bluebirds and robins, chipmunks and squirrels, and a carpet of flowers. In a loft overlooking the room, there's a library, a piano, and easy chairs offering views of the real fields of wildflowers, trees, mountains, and the Shenandoah Valley—a panorama that lies just beyond the windows. It's in the midst of a designated "forever wild" area. Filled with sunlight that streams in the walls of windows, the great room is where guests gather to read, to converse, and to eat breakfast every morning.

The guest rooms have woodland themes as well. Each is identified by a handpainted sign framed and hung by a rope. In the Bird Room, which has wallpaper featuring birds and bird watercolors on the walls, there's a pineapple-post pine bed and a lovely pine armoire, while the Duck Room, which is wheelchair accessible, has a bed with an oak headboard and a sitting area with a wicker sofa. The private baths have handpainted tiles that reflect the room's theme as well. The newest suites have fireplace, private decks, lofts reached by spiral stairways, canopy beds, kitchens, and baths with whirlpool tubs. Joan painted woodland creatures on the furniture here. In one room there's a squirrel painted on a cabinet who is waiting to crawl inside to retrieve his acorns, which are painted inside.

Iris prepares a full breakfast that will start with fresh fruit and freshly baked breads such as apple-nut muffins and coffee cake. The entree may feature an egg strata with browned potatoes and bacon.

What's Nearby—Waynesboro

Waynesboro is the home of the P. Buckley Moss Museum, a museum devoted to the work of one of America's most celebrated living artists. See her charming watercolors, etchings, and prints of Amish and Mennonite families, farms, and buildings. Virginia Metalcrafters is also headquartered in Waynesboro. Visitors to the factory can watch as molten brass is poured into sand molds. Trivets, candlesticks, sconces, chandeliers, and much more can be purchased in the shop. The Skyline Drive, the Blue Ridge Parkway, and the Appalachian Trail are just 3 miles east of the B&B. (See also Charlottesville and Staunton.)

The Cedars Bed & Breakfast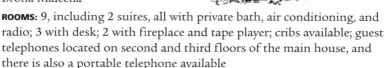

616 Jamestown Road
Williamsburg, VA 23185
(800) 296–3591 or (757) 229–3591

FAX: (757) 229–0756

E-MAIL: cedars@widomaker.com

WEB SITE: www.ontheline.com/cedars

INNKEEPERS: Carol, Jim, and
Bróna Malecha

ROOMS: 9, including 2 suites, all with private bath, air conditioning, and radio; 3 with desk; 2 with fireplace and tape player; cribs available; guest telephones located on second and third floors of the main house, and there is also a portable telephone available

ON THE GROUNDS: Parking

EXTRAS: Refreshments in afternoon; sherry and nuts in evening; fax, iron, and ironing board available

RATES: $95–$185, double occupancy, including full breakfast; two-night minimum holiday weekends and all weekends in April, October, and December

CREDIT CARDS ACCEPTED: MasterCard and Visa

OPEN: Year-round

HOW TO GET THERE: From I–64, take exit 242A (Busch Gardens) onto Route 199. Follow Route 199 for 5 miles. Turn right onto Route 5/Route 31 east (Jamestown Road). Go 1²/₁₀ miles. The Cedars will be on the right. The parking lot is behind the B&B.

The Cedars has been welcoming guests since the 1930s, but when Carol, Jim, and Bróna Malecha purchased it in 1993, they transformed it into a bed-and-breakfast of the 1990s. Located just across the street from the College of William and Mary and within walking distance of Merchant Square and Colonial Williamsburg, the Cedars is a great choice in its location, style, and friendliness.

Carol greeted me in the gracious Colonial sitting room of her home, where guests often relax in the evening before the fireplace. The soul of the inn, however, is the handsome, tile-floored tavern porch. An all-season room filled with sunlight, plants, and flowers, it has eighteenth-century, scallop-legged tables set with novelty candles in hurricanes. Tea, hot chocolate, and soft drinks are set out in the afternoon. In the evening this is a favorite place to read, play cards, or enjoy one of the many board games.

We were staying in the George Washington Suite, located on the first floor. It's a beauty. The high ceilings give dimension to the carved-mahogany canopy bed and antique armoire. A sunny sitting room contains a lovely antique writing desk, and the tile-floored bath has a tile shower.

Most of the guest rooms are located upstairs, where a decanter of sherry and a dish of macadamia nuts await on a table on the landing so that guests can help themselves to a snack before or after dinner. The Plantation Room has an arched bed with a fishnet canopy and a bow-front dresser, while the Christopher Wren Room, on the top floor, has windows on three sides, a four-poster bed draped in a plum floral fabric, and a dormer window with a window seat. A charming brick carriage house behind the main house was most recently renovated to provide two additional rooms. The Lord Botetourt Room has a slanted ceiling, a pine wardrobe, and a corner gas fireplace as well as a modern white-tiled bath.

Carol's hobby is food and wine, so breakfast here is one of those "don't miss" affairs. She sets out an assortment of items on a hand-hewn huntboard on the tavern porch. The array is astounding and includes some of the most inventive breakfast items I've encountered. There will always be an assortment of freshly baked breads (perhaps cranberry muffins or monkey bread) as well as a tray of fresh fruit. In addition, she might create an oatmeal-pudding entree. This unusual dish is made with oatmeal, eggs, milk, cottage cheese, nutmeg, and cinnamon. Brandied raisins and maple syrup are served on the side. Another specialty is a mushroom egg puff or a sausage-and-apple casserole. To accompany the entree, there will be Virginia ham biscuits or perhaps baked or poached fruit. You definitely will not go away hungry.

What's Nearby—Williamsburg

Walk along the restored streets of Colonial Williamsburg and visit the numerous shops where candles, hats, shoes, and furniture are made. Take a tour of the Governor's Palace, the Capitol, Raleigh Tavern, Bassett Hall, the George Wythe House, the Abby Aldrich Rockefeller Folk Art Center, and the DeWitt Wallace Decorative Arts Gallery. Eat in the reconstructed taverns operated by the Colonial Williamsburg Foundation. Other nearby attractions include Jamestown Settlement, the first English settlement in America; Carter's Grove Plantation; and Busch Gardens, a 360-acre family amusement park adjacent to the Anheuser-Busch brewery, which also offers tours. (See also Charles City, Virginia.)

Inn at 802

802 Jamestown Road
Williamsburg, VA 23185
(800) 672–4086 or (757) 564–0845

FAX: (757) 564–7018

WEB SITE: www.innat802.com

INNKEEPERS: Don and Jan McGarva

ROOMS: 4, all with private bath, air conditioning, TV, radio, hair dryer, and desk

ON THE GROUNDS: Gardens

EXTRAS: Refreshments such as cookies, brownies, fruit, candy, cheese, wine, mixed drinks, soft drinks available; two dogs, Aaron and Emily, and one cat, George, in separate building; guest pets permitted with prior permission

RATES: $135–$155, double occupancy, including full breakfast and all refreshments; two-night minimum weekends and during special events

CREDIT CARDS ACCEPTED: American Express, Discover, MasterCard, Visa

OPEN: Year-round

HOW TO GET THERE: From I–64, take exit 242A (Busch Gardens) onto Route 199. Follow Route 199 for 5 miles. Turn right onto Route 5/31 east (Jamestown Road). Go 1 mile to the B&B, which will be on the right.

It was Christmas and we had come to Colonial Williamsburg to spend the holiday in eighteenth-century fashion, where everything new is old again and time stopped in 1770.

From 1699 to 1780 Williamsburg was the political, social, and cultural center of Virginia. But in 1780 the capital was moved to Richmond and Williamsburg's importance slowly slipped away. In 1926, however, John D. Rockefeller came for a visit and appreciated the wealth of Colonial buildings that were still intact. He spearheaded the restoration of some eighty-eight original structures and the reconstruction of fifty others, and today the streets of Williamsburg look and feel much as they did in Colonial days.

At Christmastime the cobblestone streets take on a special magic. Homes and stores have beautiful and unusual wreaths on their doors, and in the evening, huge torches of twigs are lighted by a runner, just as they were in Colonial days, to illuminate the streets. Every evening a different historic mansion is also illuminated in the same fashion and an interpreter recites its history.

The Inn at 802 is one of those perfect little B&Bs. It's located about ¾ mile from the historic district, which makes it easy to leave your car right here and walk. A pretty brick cape with a slate roof and dormers, the house was renovated into a B&B in 1998 by Don and Jan McGarva. Don, who was formerly a teacher, also had a construction company, so he understood exactly what to do to convert the home into a gracious B&B. Jan is a flight attendant. The pampering couple have provided just about everything to make their guest's stay enjoyable. There are cookies, brownies, fruit, candy, and cheese available for snacking and soft drinks, wine, and mixed drinks for sipping.

The B&B has several attractive common areas that are furnished with antiques and period reproduction pieces. The living room, which has a woodburning fireplace, polished oak floors, and wainscotting on the walls, is formal and elegant. It has a brass chandelier and wallpaper in wine and cream colors. A library has another fireplace and built-in shelves of books. There's also a sunporch, which has pretty wicker furniture and overlooks the gardens.

The guest rooms are equally elegant. The King George has a mahogany rice-carved four-poster bed and a dark green carpet. A Waverly fabric in burgundy and white is used on the bed and the windows. There's a private bath. The Duke of Gloucester has a cherry pencil-post bed with a frame canopy, and it's decorated in a blue-and-white Waverly fabric. An Oriental rug graces the oak floor. The bath for this room has a tile floor and a cast-iron tub.

Jan serves a full breakfast every morning in the dining room, where guests sit around a beautiful, large mahogany table. She will start with freshly made muffins or bread and then serve an entree such as baked

German apple pancake or Grand Marnier French toast, along with bacon, ham, or sausage.

What's Nearby

See "What's Nearby—Williamsburg," page 387.

Liberty Rose Bed & Breakfast Inn

1022 Jamestown Road
Williamsburg, VA 23185
(800) 545–1825 or (757) 253–1260

WEB SITE: www.libertyrose.com

INNKEEPERS: Brad and Sandra Hirz

ROOMS: 4, including 2 suites; all with private bath, air conditioning, telephone with dataport, TV, hair dryer, robes, iron, and ironing board; 3 with desk; 1 with fireplace

ON THE GROUNDS: On 1 acre with parking; gardens; swings in 100-year-old trees

EXTRAS: Freshly baked chocolate chip cookies on arrival; soft drinks and juice always available; afternoon tea and snacks; turndown with a long-stemmed papersilk rose on the pillow

RATES: $140–$225, double occupancy, including full breakfast; two-night minimum May–October and in December; three-night minimum some holidays and on weekends May–October and in December

CREDIT CARDS ACCEPTED: American Express, MasterCard, Visa

OPEN: Year-round

HOW TO GET THERE: From I-64, take exit 242A (Busch Gardens) onto Route 199. Follow Route 199 for 5 miles. Turn right onto Routes 5/31 east (Jamestown Road). Go ½ mile to the B&B, which will be on the left. Watch for the long white picket fence and drive between the brick entrance pillars.

If you feel as if you've been in a Colonial time warp in Williamsburg, the Liberty Rose will be a welcome change. Definitely not Colonial in ambience, the B&B has an eclectic style that might best be described as Southern Victorian. One thing is for sure, however: Each guest room is a thoroughly romantic retreat—a couple's paradise.

The Liberty Rose is located about a mile from Colonial Williamsburg on the way to Jamestown. On a hill surrounded by venerable beech, oak, and poplar trees, the slate-roofed clapboard house offers a serene and relaxing retreat after visiting the numerous local historic sites.

Sandi and Brad Hirz have owned Liberty Rose since 1987. Warm and gracious, Sandi is the perfect hostess. In addition to her bed-and-breakfast, she is also an interior designer and a wedding consultant. She greeted us and immediately offered a plate of freshly baked chocolate chip cookies. Who could resist?

There's a grand Victorian parlor with a fireplace and a piano for the use of all the guests as well as a pretty and sunny morning porch that overlooks the gardens. This opens to a bluestone courtyard that is surrounded by lush flower beds.

The guest rooms at Liberty Rose are a reflection of Sandi's imaginative design ideas. Rose Victoria, for example, where we were staying, has an elaborate cherry French canopy bed swagged in fringed and tasseled bed curtains. It has red damask wall coverings, a tin ceiling, and ivory woodwork. A television is hidden in an exquisite French antique walnut armoire. The bath is incredible. One wall was taken from a Victorian turn-of-the-century townhouse that was torn down. There's an oversized clawfoot tub (the perfect size for two-person bubble baths) and a red marble shower.

Suite Williamsburg contains a massive carved ball-and-claw tester bed with curtains and valences in copper silk stripes and a bed cover in a rose-colored jacquard fabric. A working fireplace and a bath that contains cherry paneling, a clawfoot tub, and a black Italian-tile shower make this a popular sanctuary for honeymooners. The television in this room is cleverly concealed in a swiveled box painted to look like an elaborate doll mansion. Magnolia Peach and Savannah Lace contain similarly romantic decor. The elaborate rosewood tobacco-post bed in Savannah Lace is incredible.

Breakfast is either served on the morning porch or in the courtyard. Brad is a great cook. One day he fixed a breakfast that included French toast stuffed with cream cheese and marmalade and topped with fresh strawberries. Alongside, he served eggs and bacon. Another day he filled a croissant with thickly sliced Virginia ham, Swiss cheese, and honey mustard, and heated it. This was served with country-fried potatoes, fresh fruit, and freshly baked muffins. He also makes Granny Smith apple-fritter hotcakes topped with roasted pecans. With this he serves scrambled eggs with cheese-and-sausage patties.

The Inn at Narrow Passage

Best Buy

Route 11 South
(mailing address: P.O. Box 608)
Woodstock, VA 22664
(800) 459–8002 or (540) 459–8000

FAX: (540) 459–8001

E-MAIL: innkeeper@innatnarrowpassage.com

WEB SITE: www.innatnarrowpassage.com

INNKEEPERS: Ellen and Ed Markel, Jr.

ROOMS: 12, all with private bath, air conditioning, and radio; 9 with telephone, hair dryer; 7 with fireplace; 1 room with wheelchair access; crib available; guest telephone in living room

ON THE GROUNDS: Parking; 5 acres of lawns and gardens with views of river and mountains; herb garden; fishing on the river; horseshoes

EXTRAS: Lemonade, tea, or cider and cookies in the afternoon; soft drinks in refrigerator at all times; conference room; a golden retriever named Holly on premises

RATES: $95–$145, double occupancy, including full breakfast; two-night minimum holiday weekends and spring and fall weekends

CREDIT CARDS ACCEPTED: Discover, MasterCard, Visa

OPEN: Year-round except Christmas and two weeks in January

HOW TO GET THERE: From I–81, take exit 283 to Route 11 south. Follow Route 11 for 2 miles south of Woodstock. The B&B is on the left side of the road at the junction with Route 672 (Chapman Landing Road).

Historic Route 11 follows the trail forged by post riders and stagecoach drivers along the Great Wagon Road that led through the Shenandoah River valley, which is tucked between two rugged mountain ranges. The road eventually took travelers to the western frontier through the mountains at the Cumberland Gap in the southwest corner of Virginia. The route is still dotted with old stagecoach taverns and wayside stops, and the rustic, atmospheric Inn at Narrow Passage is one of the most engaging. It sits on a five-acre plot that overlooks the Shenandoah River.

The oldest section of the B&B, which has thick log-and-chink walls that could withstand attack from Indians, was built in 1740. At this spot in the road, the trail snaked through a limestone ridge so narrow that there was only room for passage of one wagon at a time, making the journey quite dangerous. Travelers were often subjected to Indian attacks here. In 1862 during the Civil War, Stonewall Jackson made the B&B his headquarters while he conducted his Valley Campaign.

Ellen and Ed Markel have done an excellent job of retaining the rustic, old-fashioned mood while giving us all the modern comforts we enjoy today. They added a wing to the original B&B constructed in such a harmonious style that all parts seamlessly blend together.

Guests have a number of options for relaxation. The original log living room has exposed beams, log walls, wide-plank pine floors, and a huge limestone fireplace. Plaid sofas and wing chairs and Early American tables and chests are arranged in conversation areas. In the newer wing, the Markels used old pine flooring and paneling to create a gathering room that's hard to distinguish from its neighbor, which is 250 years older. A broad porch across the back has white cedar rockers where guests can sit in the afternoon with a cool drink to watch the lazy passage of the Shenandoah River against the outline of the Massanutten Mountains just beyond the B&B's lawns and gardens.

The guest rooms are furnished with Early American reproduction pieces. Room #8, for example, has a handmade pine bed with a fishnet canopy and a brick fireplace. Room #S-2 is spacious and comfortable. It also has a pine bed with a fishnet canopy and a fireplace as well as handcrafted pine chests with shafts of wheat carved into the doors. Every room has a private, modern bath. The new section also contains a handsome conference room that's ideal for small meetings.

Breakfast is served in the Colonial-style dining room, which has woodplank pine floors, pine paneling, and another stone fireplace. There are beamed ceilings, tin chandeliers, Windsor tables and chairs, and mullioned windows dressed with country-cotton ball-fringed curtains. Ellen serves a bevy of fruits and breads, including perhaps a cherry-almond or a cinnamon-walnut coffee cake. The entree may consist of bacon, eggs, and hashbrowns or French toast with sausage and apples—hearty fare well-suited to the many visitors who come here to hike, fish, or bicycle.

Washington, D.C.

Swann House

1808 New Hampshire Avenue, NW
Washington, D.C. 20009
(202) 265–4414

FAX: (202) 265–6755

E-MAIL: swannhouse@aol.com

WEB SITE: www.swannhouse.com

INNKEEPERS: Mary and Richard Ross; manager: David Story

ROOMS: 11; all with private bath, air conditioning, private-line telephone with dataport and voice mail, TV, radio, hair dryer, desk, iron, and ironing board; 6 with VCR and tape player; 5 with fireplace; 4 with mini-refrigerator; 3 with balcony and coffeemaker; 2 with whirlpool tub; 1 with hot tub

ON THE GROUNDS: Patio with pool; gardens; roof deck

EXTRAS: Afternoon snacks such as tea, lemonade, cookies, candies, party mix

RATES: $135–$275, double occupancy, including Continental breakfast; two-night minimum weekends

CREDIT CARDS ACCEPTED: American Express, Diners Club, MasterCard, Visa

OPEN: Year-round

HOW TO GET THERE: From I–95, take I–496 (the Beltway) west to exit 30B (Colesville Road—Route 29). Follow this south toward Silver Spring and continue for 2 miles past Silver Spring until you reach Sixteenth Street. Turn left onto Sixteenth Street south. Follow this for 5 miles until you reach New Hampshire Avenue, NW, at the intersection with "U" Street, just past "V" Street. Make a 45-degree right hand turn onto New Hampshire Avenue, NW. Stay on New Hampshire through the traffic light at Seventeenth Street. The B&B is on the right, on the corner of New Hampshire Avenue, NW, and Swann Street, NW. Park in front.

I have been hoping for the restoration of a marvelous mansion such as this in Washington, D.C. for many years, so I am delighted to be able to include the Swann House in this book. The house is in a delightful and safe, yet quiet, neighborhood, and the restoration has been done with absolute perfection. Mary and Richard Ross purchased the house in 1996, and although they opened their first rooms that year, they waited to renovate eight of the rooms until previous tenants moved out.

The grand brick mansion was built for Walter Paris, an architect and artist, in 1883. It was his intention to live there himself, although he never did. He sold it in 1886 to Colonel Theodore Tyrer, who lived there until 1901. Mr. Tyrer made major alterations to the house, including removing the original wood porch and replacing it with the impressive brick-and-stone porch we see today—giving it a weighty Richardson Romanesque facade. In the 1940s the house was converted to a boarding house, but although it declined substantially after that, the ornate stairway, moldings, paneling, inlaid wood floors, and doors are the originals.

Guests enter a broad entry hall. To the left, a charming parlor has a fireplace with an ornate plaster mantel and a crystal chandelier. There are peach walls, navy drapes, and Oriental rugs covering the polished oak herringbone parquet floors. A sitting room has another fireplace and a silver tray of stemmed crystal glasses and a decanter of sherry. The ceilings on this floor reach to 12 feet.

The guest rooms are spacious and elegant. The Regent Room, where we stayed one night, has a king-size bed covered with a luxurious flowered damask spread and shams. The walls are periwinkle blue. There's a beautiful fireplace with a plaster mantel and one of the most impressive baths I've ever seen. There's a marble and mirrored vanity room and an additional room with marble floor and walls that contains a two-person whirlpool tub, as well as multiple shower heads on the walls for two-person showers. A stairway leads to a private deck that contains a hot tub. Another of my favorites is Il Duomo, a room on the third floor with an iron bed, a mirrored fireplace, a wet bar, antique Gothic windows, and a cathedral ceiling containing a skylight. The bath in this room has a whimsical and charming mural of angels painted above the clawfoot tub.

A Continental breakfast is served in the handsome dining room, which has a fabulous crystal chandelier and an elaborately carved marble fireplace mantel. The wonderful and grand antique English buffet provides plenty of space for the breakfast foods. They offer freshly baked pastries, juices, fruits, and cereals or homemade granola.

What's Nearby—Washington, D.C.

The B&B is located in the eclectic and charming section of Washington, D.C. known as Dupont Circle. There are numerous shops, restaurants, and galleries to explore, as well as a terrific bookstore/cafe. A Metrorail stop in Dupont Circle provides access to all attractions. The White House is within walking distance, and a tour should be on the schedule for any first trip to Washington. The museums in the Smithsonian complex are varied and extensive. It would take weeks to see them all, but several buildings can be visited on a weekend trip.

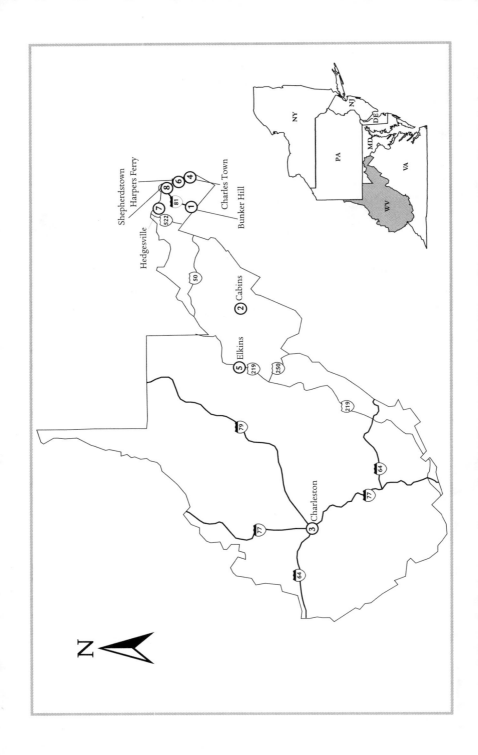

West Virginia

Numbers on map refer to towns numbered below.

Edgewood Manor B&B

Route 11, Rural Route 2, Box 329
(mailing address: P.O. Box 509)
Bunker Hill, WV 25413
(304) 229-9353

E-MAIL: edgewood@intrepid.net

WEB SITE: wvweb.com/www/EDGEWOOD

INNKEEPERS: Sharon and John Feldt and Birdie Lamkin

ROOMS: 6, including 1 suite; 4 with private bath and 2 that share a bath, and all with air conditioning and robes; 3 with fireplace; 2 with desk; telephone in library, although there are jacks in every room and a portable telephone as well

ON THE GROUNDS: Parking; 52 acres with gardens, a pond, and wooded areas; croquet, horseshoes, badminton

EXTRAS: Snacks including cookies or brownies, tea, coffee, cappuccino, and lemonade; turndown with chocolate candies, warm cookies, and hot chocolate; afternoon tea, including scones, finger sandwiches, and desserts, available with reservations (extra charge); a picnic lunch for two prepared April through September with advance notice (extra charge); fax, telephone, copier, computer with Internet access available; gift shop; two cats named Fat Boy and Muffin, in owners' quarters only

RATES: $110, double occupancy, including full breakfast; two-night minimum holiday and special-event weekends

CREDIT CARDS ACCEPTED: American Express, Discover, MasterCard, Visa

OPEN: Year-round

HOW TO GET THERE: From I–81, take West Virginia exit marked Whitehall/Route 11 and follow Route 11 north. The B&B is about 3½ miles ahead on the left. You will see the B&B sign beside a Civil War monument.

West Virginia contains many Civil War reminders, but few buildings have witnessed as many historical events as Edgewood Manor. General Stonewall Jackson headquartered here; General Robert E. Lee and his troops camped here; the Civil War battle of Bunker Hill was fought here; John Boyd, who was raised here, was accused of spying and arrested here; and General James Pettigrew drew his last breath here.

When the 1839 brick mansion was purchased by John and Sharon Feldt and Sharon's mother Birdie Lamkin in 1995, it needed considerable work. In the process of doing the repairs, John, an attorney, and Sharon and Birdie, both educators, conducted extensive historical research. Today their guests enjoy the fruit of their work, and the building is on the National Register of Historic Places.

The Civil War seems to come alive at Edgewood. There's a library with a cozy fireplace surrounded by a wooden mantel and an extensive collection of Civil War books on the bookshelves. The music room has another fireplace and an 1839 pianoforte. The Tuscarora Brass Band, of which Mr. Feldt is director and whose members play with period saxhorns, is headquartered here. There's a parlor with a fireplace and an 1810 carved Virginia sofa that is original to the house. In a cupboard, the innkeepers display their scone mix, lemon and lime curd, and apple butter, which are for sale.

The guest rooms are beautifully furnished. One is dedicated to General Pettigrew and contains a fireplace, an elegant leaded crystal chandelier, a bed dressed in a burgundy quilt with a crocheted ecru coverlet and a fishnet canopy as well as maps, artifacts, and a portrait of the General. The Texas Room celebrates the Feldt and Lamkin heritage, as the trio were all raised in that state. The theme features bluebonnets (the Texas state flower) and the yellow rose of Texas, and there are books and magazines about Texas. This room has twin wicker beds dressed in yellow and blue fabrics. All the baths have tile floors and new fixtures.

A light breakfast of homemade muffins, juices, fresh fruits, and coffee or tea is set out on the upstairs porch in warm weather, which is furnished with wicker chairs, a dining table, and a porch swing. Guests can sit here overlooking the rose garden and fountain before starting out for a day of sightseeing.

For those who enjoy a larger breakfast, it is served in the formal dining room, which has an elegant mahogany pedestal table and sideboard and a grandfather clock in the corner. Sharon and Birdie own twelve sets of china, so it's always fun to see which pieces they will use. The meal may start with baked apples or pears accompanied by homemade peach muffins or honey oatmeal bread. The entree may be a spinach quiche or perhaps a Texas scramble, a dish that began as a mistake and has become a best-request item. Every afternoon high tea is served, with freshly baked scones, finger sandwiches, dipped fruits, and pastries.

The grounds of Edgewood Plantation include a stone-lined pond filled with koi and surrounded by day lilies, a stream, and a carriage path to a secret bower.

What's Nearby—Bunker Hill

People come from miles around to visit the Bunker Hill Antiques Mall, which is located just down the lane from the B&B in an old brick three-story mill. There are more than 200 dealers, and the facility is open seven days a week. Bunker Hill is close to Winchester, Virginia, where the Victorian cottage that served as Stonewall Jackson's headquarters in the winter of 1861–1862 is filled with maps, photographs, and memorabilia. (See also Charles Town.)

North Fork Mountain Inn

Best Buy

Smoke Hole Road
(mailing address: P.O. Box 114)
Cabins, WV 26855
(304) 257-1108

FAX: (304) 257-2008

E-MAIL: nfi@access.mountain.net

WEB SITE: wvweb.com/www/northfork-inn

INNKEEPERS: Joan and Art Ricker

ROOMS: 8, including 2 suites and 2 cottages; all with private bath; 6 with air conditioning and tape player; 3 with balcony or porch and desk; 2 with kitchen, fireplace, robes, and whirlpool tub

ON THE GROUNDS: On 15 acres with hiking trail, jogging trail; archery range, horseshoes, lawn bowling; herb garden; and hot tub

EXTRAS: Afternoon and evening refreshments with homemade cookies, candy, snacks, and nonalcoholic beverages; turndown with cookies and beverage; two poodles named Smokey and Domino, and a cat named Blackie, on premises; guest pets under 20 pounds permitted in cottages with prior permission

RATES: $85–$115, double occupancy, including full breakfast and afternoon refreshments; two-night minimum throughout the year

CREDIT CARDS ACCEPTED: MasterCard and Visa

OPEN: February–November

HOW TO GET THERE: From I-81, take exit 296 onto Route 55 west. Continue on Route 55 west for 65 miles to Petersburg. In Petersburg continue west on Route 55 for 7 miles. Turn left at the first bridge and watch for the signs to the Smoke Hole Caverns and the Big Bend area. Climb up the mountain road for 7 miles. The B&B will be on the right.

North Fork Mountain Inn, in an area known as the Potomac Highlands of West Virginia, makes no exaggerations in its literature when it claims it offers "fresh air, solitude, and deliverance from the common to the extraordinary." Joan and Art Ricker (he a refugee from corporate life near Washington, D.C., where he was vice president and director of marketing for Ringling Bros. Barnum and Bailey Circus) constructed their remote mountain B&B in 1995. It's on the eastern slope of the North Fork Mountain in the 908,000-acre Monongahela National Forest, where it has breathtaking views of Smoke Hole Canyon.

Their intention was to "create a secluded wilderness getaway, but at the same time offer some of the amenities you would expect from a fine hotel in the city," and they've exceeded the expectations of the most jaded urbanite. The B&B is built of Pennsylvania white pine logs and has five fieldstone fireplaces and a broad porch that extends along the second floor, populated by a herd of Tennessee rockers. From this perch you're likely to see deer, rabbits, wild turkey, and perhaps a bear, as well as a myriad of other small animals. Birds frequent the feeders the Rickers have placed throughout the grounds, and eagles can be seen soaring above the rocks.

The B&B has a Great Room with a wall of native stone that enfolds a fireplace and walls and ceiling of natural pine. There's a stereo here. A game room includes a pool table, darts, maps, hiking information, and a TV and VCR. A video library offers numerous selections. Outside, guests can play horseshoes or shoot archery or try their hand at lawn bowling. A network of hiking trails leads from the B&B's door, and there's also a jogging trail. Joan encourages travelers to explore her garden, where she grows herbs for breakfast dishes; there's also a hot tub under the stars—the best possible way to loosen the kinks earned on the hiking trail.

The guest rooms are unpretentious but comfortable. They were not designed for luxury, but to provide all the comforts guests expect today, with few of the frills. There are no telephones or TVs in the rooms, for example. Each of the rooms is charmingly decorated with quilts and there are braided rugs on the pine floors. The walls and ceilings are of pine, as well, and all the baths have tiled floors. The Eagle's Nest has a cathedral ceiling and a bed and chairs made of willow; others have beds made of oak or are designed in a twig style. Both the North Fork and the Seneca Rock Rooms have fireplaces, and the Seneca Rock Room and the Smoke Hole Room have whirlpool tubs in the rooms.

Joan fixes a hearty country breakfast designed to prepare her guests for a day in the mountains. She will offer juice, fruit, and homemade breads, as well as pancakes, or waffles, or an omelette with bacon or country sausage.

Guests of the North Fork Mountain Inn are sure to be on a West Virginia mountain high by the time they leave—renewed and rejuvenated—and anticipating a speedy return.

What's Nearby—Cabins

The Monongahela Mountains near Cabins are rugged and wild—the ideal spot for those seeking outdoor recreation. The North Fork of the South Branch of the Potomac River flows through the area, offering wonderful fishing. The region is known for its hiking, horseback riding, rock climbing, hunting, and canoeing. The Dolly Sod Wilderness Area, which contains unusual highland barrens and upland peat bogs, and Seneca Rocks National Recreation Area are nearby. Guests should plan to explore Smoke Hole Caverns, a series of large caves with vents to the outside that are open for tours. For golfers, there's a course 20 miles away.

The Brass Pineapple Bed and Breakfast

1611 Virginia Street East
Charleston, WV 25311
(800) CALL WVA
(304) 344–0748 (fax also)

E-MAIL: pineappl04@aol.com

WEB SITE: wvweb.com/ brasspineapplebandb

INNKEEPER: Sue Pepper; manager: Bobbie Morris

ROOMS: 7, including 1 suite; all with private bath, air conditioning, private line telephone with dataport and voice mail, TV, VCR, radio, hair dryer, desk, and robes; 1 with mini-refrigerator, stereo, and CD player

ON THE GROUNDS: Parking; small rose terrace

EXTRAS: Afternoon tea with pastries, fresh fruit, cheese or tea sandwiches; turndown with chocolates or milk and cookies; snack basket and sherry in hallway; fax, copier available; bicycles provided for touring historic area

RATES: $69–$109, double occupancy, including full breakfast and afternoon tea

CREDIT CARDS ACCEPTED: American Express, Diners Club, MasterCard, Visa

OPEN: Year-round except major holidays

HOW TO GET THERE: From I–64 take exit 99 (Greenbrier Street), turn south onto Greenbrier Street, and continue to the Kanawha River. Turn right onto Kanawha Boulevard, go 1 block and turn right onto Elizabeth Street, go 1 more block and turn right onto Virginia Street. The B&B is in the middle of the block on the right. Park behind the B&B.

The Brass Pineapple is located in the historic district of Charleston, near the beautiful and impressive, 293-foot-high gold-domed state capitol building, which was designed in 1921 by Cass Gilbert, architect of the U.S. Supreme Court Building in Washington, D.C., and the Woolworth Building in New York City. Overshadowed by two massive oak trees, the house was built in 1910 by real estate developer E. C. Bauer. Nothing but the best would do. He incorporated Italian tile, oak paneling, and exquisite stained- and leaded-glass windows into the design that combines both Art Nouveau and Victorian elements.

When Sue Pepper first saw the house, it had long before been converted to apartments. The oak paneling had been painted white, spacious rooms had been dissected, and the lower portion of the grand stairway had been removed to make room for a bathroom. Today, however, the golden paneling gleams, the rooms are spacious and inviting, there are Oriental rugs on polished oak floors, and, thanks to the discovery of the original stairway balustrades in the basement, the stairs once again climb grandly upward from the entry hall.

The formal parlor, which has an oak floor with an Oriental rug, a Victorian chandelier, and antique Victorian furniture, is an inviting place to sit. A covered veranda in front, which has a hexagonal tile floor and black wrought-iron tables and chairs, is a summer outdoor living room. Baskets of flowers hang from the ceiling and candles are lighted in the evening, giving it a romantic, dreamy effect.

The guest rooms are charming and original. The English Gentleman is furnished with a beautiful antique walnut carved Victorian bedroom set that includes a bed with a high headboard and footboard and a marble-topped dresser that contains a sink. The masculine room is paneled in elegant raised walnut and has marble baseboards. An oak Morris chair sits beside the decorative fireplace. In the Hearts & Flowers Bridal Suite, there's a king-size white iron-and-brass bed and a separate sitting room with a TV, a VCR, and a video library stocked with romantic movies. The newest room, Charleston Manor, has an iron bed with frothy white coverings and an antique desk and dresser.

Breakfast and afternoon tea are served in the formal dining room, which has richly grained tiger oak wainscotting, an oak floor with an Oriental carpet, and a crystal chandelier. Golden-toned stained glass in the bay windows gives the room a warm and sunny feeling. Sue and her staff have an extensive breakfast repertoire. Solicitous of her guests' wishes, she offers an option of a Continental or a full breakfast. There will always be fresh or cooked fruits, such as vanilla-scented pears or cinnamon fried apples, fruit breads such as banana walnut or blueberry streusel muffins, and perhaps hot oatmeal or cold cereals. This may be supplemented by a sausage-and-egg casserole or chocolate waffles.

Sue supplies bicycles to pedal through the historic district and over to see the capitol grounds.

What's Nearby—Charleston

Charleston is located on the Kanawha River, where there are jogging trails that border the river and sternwheeler cruises. You may wish to visit Sunrise Museum and Science Hall, the 1890s mansion and gardens of Governor William MacCorkle. Located on sixteen acres, it includes a science hall, planetarium, nature trails, gardens, and a furnished mansion, Torquilstone. The state capitol houses a cultural center, a craft shop, and a theater as well as the West Virginia State Museum, where West Virginia's history is traced from the earliest Native American inhabitants to the twentieth century. And it's free!

The Carriage Inn

417 East Washington Street
Charles Town, WV 25414
(800) 867–9830 or (304) 728–8003

FAX: (304) 728–2976
E-MAIL: carriage@intrepid.net
WEB SITE: www.carriage inn.com
INNKEEPERS: Al and Kay Standish
ROOMS: 6, including 2 suites; all with private bath, air conditioning, and radio; 4 with fireplace; 2 with TV; 1 with mini-refrigerator; telephone located in main hall at reservation desk
ON THE GROUNDS: On 1 acre with parking; gardens
EXTRAS: Coffee or tea available all day
RATES: $85–$165, double occupancy, including full breakfast; two-night minimum weekends in October and winter holiday weekends
CREDIT CARDS ACCEPTED: American Express, MasterCard, Visa
OPEN: Year-round

HOW TO GET THERE: From I–81, take exit 12 east onto Route 45 and continue for about ½ mile until it becomes Route 9. Follow Route 9 east for 14 miles toward Charles Town. At the intersection with Route 51, turn west (right). Route 51 becomes East Washington Street in Charles Town. Continue for ½ mile. The B&B will be on the left on the corner of Seminary Street. Turn left onto Seminary Street to enter the parking area.

The handsome grey brick 1836 mansion sits proudly on an acre of manicured lawn behind a black wrought-iron fence. Black shutters frame the windows, and a broad porch with four fluted columns creates a grand entrance. Located near the Charles Town Races, the B&B is an easy walk from town.

You'll undoubtedly be greeted by the friendly innkeeper, Kay Standish, who is justifiably proud of her B&B. She and her husband, Al, have owned the B&B since 1996, and they've furnished it with many lovely family antiques. The attractive parlor has high ceilings, a gas fireplace, a piano, and family antiques that include a lovely old desk. Oriental rugs cover the narrow-board oak floors. Be sure to read the yellowed old newspaper accounts of the nearby battles hanging on the walls. On the opposite side of the entry, the dining room is in what was the original east parlor. This is where General Ulysses S. Grant and General Philip Sheridan met to discuss their Shenandoah Valley strategy in 1864 during the Civil War. Another sitting room is located upstairs, where there's a refrigerator for guests to use as well as a TV.

The guest rooms are appealing. In the Green Room, there's a four-poster bed with a fishnet canopy and a gas fireplace, while in the Porch Room, there's both a canopy bed and a gas fireplace as well as a sitting porch furnished with a TV. Were I to choose a favorite (which is difficult), I believe it would be either the Blue Room, which has large windows that fill the room with light and a very high four-poster rice bed, or the Rose Room, which has a four-poster maple bed with a fishnet canopy. Both these rooms have sunken baths with steep steps that may be difficult for some people to negotiate.

The Carriage House has been converted into a lovely suite, which is a nice place for families to stay. There are light pink sponged walls and a sitting area with a fireplace. Upstairs there's a bedroom decorated in green and yellow that contains a pretty brass bed.

Breakfast is served in the formal dining room, which has another fireplace. A beautiful 1890s family silver coffee and tea set stands on the buffet.

Kay uses her family sterling flatware and lovely ivory Lenox china with a gold rim to serve breakfast. Come prepared to have a scrumptious meal. Cooking has long been one of Kay's favorite activities. She's received awards in cooking contests, and her recipes have been featured in newspaper articles. A typical breakfast may include cranberry apple juice, strawberries with Devonshire cream, cheese blintz soufflé, bacon, and lemon poppyseed bread. Refills of Starbucks coffee are encouraged while guests become acquainted around the table.

What's Nearby—Charles Town

Charles Town is noted for several unusual attractions. The Charles Town Races, a thoroughbred race track, has been open since 1933. There are live races Wednesday, Friday, Saturday, and Sunday, and simulcast races the rest of the week. Charles Town is also the place where abolitionist John Brown was tried and hung for treason in 1859. You can visit the Jefferson County Courthouse, where the trial took place, and also see where he was executed. There are historical markers identifying other Civil War events throughout the town. At the Old Opera House, live theatrical performances take place year-round. (See also Harpers Ferry and Shepherdstown.)

The Cottonwood Inn

Mill Lane
(mailing address: Route 5, Box 61-S)
Charles Town, WV 25414
(800) 868–1188 or (304) 725–3371

FAX: (304) 728–4763

E-MAIL: travels@mydestination

WEB SITE: www.mydestination.com/cottonwood

INNKEEPERS: Joe and Barbara Sobol

ROOMS: 7, all with private bath, air conditioning, and desk; 4 with TV; telephone located in living room; 1 with fireplace and porch

ON THE GROUNDS: On 6 acres with walking trails and a stream crossed by a wooden bridge; large picnic pavilion; parking

EXTRAS: Cold drinks or hot cider in afternoon; fax and computer with limited Internet access available; two dachshunds named Sadie and Higgins and two cats named Spot and Shadow in owners' quarters

RATES: $75–$110, double occupancy, including full breakfast; two-night minimum holiday weekends, all weekends in October, and festival weekends in June and September

CREDIT CARDS ACCEPTED: American Express, MasterCard, Visa

OPEN: Year-round

HOW TO GET THERE: From I–81, take exit 12 (Charles Town/Martinsburg) onto Route 51 and travel east toward Charles Town. At the junction with Route 9, take Route 9 east toward Leesburg. In about 1 mile turn right (south) onto Kabletown Road. Go 3²/10 miles to Mill Lane and turn right. The B&B's driveway is ²/10 mile down Mill Lane.

If you prefer your B&Bs to be quiet retreats from the noise of horns and sirens and from the rush and bustle of city life, then you must come to The Cottonwood Inn. Tucked away on six acres in a remote setting of ponds and streams and gardens and lawns, this heavenly spot is at the end of a peaceful lane. As you cross the little bridge across Bullskin Run and see the pristine farmhouse beyond, you know you're in for a treat. Joe and Barbara Sobol have owned the B&B since 1994 and have made many improvements to the established property.

The 1840s white-trimmed yellow brick farmhouse is fronted by a broad porch just made for relaxation. Sit here in a rocker or on the porch swing in the cool of a summer evening and listen to the rush of the stream, the chirp of the crickets, and the breeze through the cottonwoods, and watch the fireflies dance through the night. Wake in the morning to the joyous sound of the birds.

The B&B has a warm and comfortable ambience. One thing you'll notice immediately are the extraordinary quilts throughout. There's one with an intricate pattern by an award-winning artist in the entry hall, and another in the living room. A cozy reading area and a brick fireplace in the living room invite perusal through the bookshelves, while the piano will appeal to musically talented guests.

The guest rooms are charming, with various nooks and crannies that add to their interest. Room #1 has a four-poster pine bed and green walls, while Room #2 contains a sleigh bed, natural pine floors, a fireplace, and plank walls. Room #3 has a brick wall and a four-poster maple bed as well as a bath with a clawfoot tub, while Room #4 has a beamed ceiling and a pedestal sink in the bath.

Breakfast is served in the breakfast room, which was the original farmhouse kitchen. The huge cooking fireplace can still be stoked up on cold winter days, and the beamed ceiling and plank walls give the room a warm glow. Barbara and Joe prepare a breakfast that begins with fresh fruit and juice and perhaps an apple-cherry coffee cake. For an entree they may fix a potato-cheese casserole and smoked turkey puffed pastry.

In addition to running the B&B, Joe and Barbara are video experts. They own a company called Destination Images, and they write and produce video tours of European destinations, specializing in driving tours beyond the cities. They also produce corporate videos.

What's Nearby

See "What's Nearby—Charles Town," page 406.

Tunnel Mountain Bed & Breakfast

Old Route 33 (mailing address: Route 1, Box 59–1)
Elkins, WV 26241
(888) 211–9123 or (304) 636–1684

WEB SITE: www.wvonline.com/shareourbeds/tunnelmtn

INNKEEPERS: Anne and Paul Beardslee

ROOMS: 3; all with private bath, air conditioning, iron, and ironing board; 1 with fireplace; guest telephone in office; portable telephone available

ON THE GROUNDS: On 5 acres with hiking trails, benches in woodland settings

EXTRAS: Two golden retrievers named Molly and Jessie, on premises

RATES: $65–$80, double occupancy, including full breakfast; two-night minimum holiday and festival weekends

CREDIT CARDS ACCEPTED: None

OPEN: Year-round

HOW TO GET THERE: From I-79 traveling south, take exit 99 (Weston/Buckhannon) onto Route 33 east. Follow Route 33 through Elkins and for 4 miles beyond. Follow the signs for the Stuart Recreation Area, and turn off onto Old Route 33. The B&B is on the left in $^2/_{10}$ mile.

Tunnel Mountain Bed and Breakfast, located on the slopes of Tunnel Mountain (which is a nickname for this section of Cheat Mountain because of the 1890 railroad tunnel that runs beneath the mountain), is one of those homespun B&Bs that remind us of the way our grandparents lived—but with considerably more sophistication and style. It's a congenial-looking house with a fieldstone foundation and clapboards above. A log fence surrounds the property, and a stone patio offers a spot to sit outdoors, where guests regularly see a variety of animals and birds—sometimes as many as seven or eight deer will meander through the property in a single evening. The B&B is nestled amidst tall spruce and tulip poplar trees on five acres, just minutes from the Stuart Recreation Area.

The house was constructed in 1939 as a private residence, and it has a warm lodgelike appearance. Anne and Paul, who are both former college administrators, purchased it in 1990 and converted it to a B&B.

The house has a living room with knotty pine paneling and a fireplace. Paul's collection of antique iron toys is on display here, and a chemistry cabinet stores games for guests to play. Antique tools hang on the walls. In the foyer a pie safe contains samplers and baskets that Anne has made.

There are merely three guest rooms—two on the main floor and one on the top—and each has a view of the surrounding mountains. The favorite is on the third floor. It has walls paneled in wormy chestnut and a private bath. The remaining two rooms are on the second floor, where all the floors are oak. One has a rope bed with a maple headboard that had been in Paul's family; the bath has a tiled floor. The other has a pre–Civil War canopy bed that Anne inherited, and the bath here has an oak floor. There are pretty quilts on the beds, antique tools on the walls, and throw rugs on the floors.

Anne fixes a full breakfast that is served at one end of the living room. The meal will begin with fresh fruit and juice, but for an entree Anne may prepare herbed eggs or French toast stuffed with cream cheese and apricot preserves, soaked in an orange-laced batter and served with maple syrup.

What's Nearby—Elkins

Elkins is located in the Monongahela National Forest, an unspoiled wilderness of 908,000 acres that includes rivers and streams for fishing, forests and plateaux for bird watching, rock climbing, hiking, rafting, canoeing, and camping. Davis and Elkins College is located here, and this is where the famed Augusta Heritage Festival—a five-week celebration of the music, dance, folklore, and crafts of Appalachia—takes place.

You can take instruction in and participate in such varied activities as bead embroidery, twig furniture construction, playing the fiddle, or clog dancing. In the 1½-acre Elkins City Park, just across Buffalo Street, there are tennis courts and horseshoes, and every Wednesday night local fiddlers gather for "Pickin' in the Park," an impromptu fiddle fest.

The Warfield House

318 Buffalo Street
Elkins, WV 26241
(888) 636–4555 or (304) 636–4555

FAX: (304) 636–1457
WEB SITE: www.bbonline.com/wv/warfield
INNKEEPERS: Connie and Paul Garnett
ROOMS: 5; 3 with private bath and radio; 2 with fireplace and robes; 1 with a Jacuzzi
ON THE GROUNDS: Parking; gardens
EXTRAS: Complimentary soft drinks and coffee; cookie jar of freshly baked cookies; dog named Boo and cat named Red on premises
RATES: $75–$85, double occupancy, $65–$75, single occupancy; including full breakfast; two-night minimum holiday weekends, three-night minimum during Forest Festival, six-night minimum during Augusta Heritage Festival
CREDIT CARDS ACCEPTED: None
OPEN: Year-round
HOW TO GET THERE: From I–79, take exit 99 (Weston/Buckhannon) and travel east on Route 33 into Elkins, where Route 33 is called Randolph Avenue. Turn left at the Iron Horse Statue onto Sycamore Street. The B&B is in 1 long block on the right—on the corner of Sycamore and Buffalo Streets.

The Warfield House, a grand 1901 late-Victorian beauty, boasts spectacular stained glass, elaborate moldings and woodwork, a sweeping stairway with carved spindles, and a dramatic terra cotta fireplace wall that has elaborate ornamentation. Prosperity came to the rural town of Elkins, whose economy had been based on coal and timber, via the railroad. When railroad owners Senator Henry Gassaway Davis and his son-in-law Senator

Stephen Elkins designated Elkins as the primary hub, the quiet little village blossomed into a full-fledged town, and elaborate mansions soon lined the streets. This particular mansion was built by Harry Warfield, the president of the Elkins National Bank.

When Connie and Paul Garnett purchased the building in 1995, however, it had fallen on hard times. Nevertheless, with a tremendous amount of work and painstaking attention to detail, they meticulously polished the rich oak and cherry woodwork and refinished the oak floors. Today, if Mr. Warfield walked in the front door he'd feel right at home.

The yellow-shingled house with its pristine white trim has a broad 70-foot wraparound porch filled with inviting furniture. Green wicker chairs have pretty floral cushions, and there are an abundance of tables and a green porch swing. Beyond the entry hall, where you can admire the ornate stairway and the fantastic stained-glass windows on the landing, there's a parlor with a piano and oak moldings and a pocket door leading to the living room, which has a spectacular terra cotta fireplace, walls of bookshelves, cherry moldings, an elegant Oriental rug on the polished oak floor, and a patchwork quilt on a table.

Connie and Paul have turned the former butler's pantry into a guest pantry. It's complete with a microwave, a guest refrigerator, a coffeemaker, and shelves filled with glasses and cups. It seems as if there's nothing they've forgotten in their efforts to make their guests comfortable.

The guest rooms are spacious and inviting—each with its own personality. I would have to say my favorite is the Maple Room, which has a marvelous maple quarterposter bed draped in lace and a curly maple French armoire as well as a yellow-painted corner cupboard. At present, this room shares a bath with the Pine Room, but there are plans to give it its own. The Walnut Room has an elaborate Victorian walnut bed and a private bath with a shower, while the Pine Room has white iron beds covered with matelassé spreads and wicker chairs. The oddest room in the house is the hallway bathroom for the Pine and Maple Rooms. Instead of harmonizing with the rest of the Victorian house, this bath is a study in Art Deco. There are shiny black walls and blue fixtures.

Breakfast is served in the formal dining room, which has an oak table, oak pressed-back chairs, oak wainscotting, and a built-in oak china cabinet. Lace curtains cover the windows in the bay. The full breakfast will start with fresh fruit and juice as well as home-baked cinnamon rolls or fruit starburst roll-ups and an entree of Dutch apple pancakes or French toast stuffed with cream cheese, ricotta cheese, and jam.

Paul and Connie are knowledgeable about the goings-on in Elkins and happily direct their guests to fine restaurants and cultural activities. The couple are both cellists who met while performing with the Georgetown Symphony, and they continue to play on occasion, although Paul also owns a local computer company.

What's Nearby

See "What's Nearby—Elkins," page 409.

Harpers Ferry Guest House

Best Buy

800 Washington Street
(mailing address: P.O. Box 1079)
Harpers Ferry, WV 25425
(304) 535-6955

E-MAIL: alsdorf@harpersferry.wv.com

WEB SITE: www.harpersferry-w.v.com

INNKEEPERS: Al and Allison Alsdorf

ROOMS: 3; all with private bath, air conditioning, TV, radio, coffeemaker, and desk; 1 room with wheelchair access

ON THE GROUNDS: Parking; gardens

RATES: $70–$98, double occupancy, including full breakfast

CREDIT CARDS ACCEPTED: None

OPEN: Year-round

HOW TO GET THERE: From Washington, D.C., take I–270 north to Frederick, Maryland, and then take Route 340 south. In about 20 miles you will cross the Potomac River Bridge into Virginia. Proceed for 2 more miles on Route 340 to the Shenandoah River Bridge to West Virginia. About 200 yards after crossing the Shenandoah bridge, turn right onto Union Street (you are in Harpers Ferry) and continue for a little over a ¼ mile to Washington Street. Turn right onto Washington. The B&B is 1 block up the hill on the corner of Washington and Jackson Streets.

Harpers Ferry is located at the intersection of two powerful rivers, the Potomac and the Shenandoah, and at the juncture of Maryland, Virginia, and West Virginia. Picturesque and European in appearance, the village seems poised for an artist's canvas or a photographer's film. Built on a steep hill, the village grew after Robert Harper established a ferry to cross the river at this point. Eventually, mills powered by the fierce waterpower were built along the riverbanks. Even today, narrow streets made more for riders on horseback than those in cars climb the impossibly steep hills, making you very glad to have a place behind your B&B in which to park. The lower village has been beautifully restored by the National Park Service, and there are lovely trails along the riverfront and throughout the village.

The Harpers Ferry Guest House strikes the perfect balance between a casual place for hikers and bicyclists and an upscale spot for those visiting the town for its cultural activities. Each of the rooms is spacious and attractively decorated, and the baths are fresh and sparkling clean.

On my first visit to Harpers Ferry Guest House, I was greeted by a hiker who was walking the 2,160-mile Appalachian Trail from its start in Georgia. Now, some 965 miles later, he welcomed the comfort of this relaxed B&B. With no pretensions, this very neat and very clean B&B, which is located across the street from the Appalachian Trail Conference headquarters, even has a place in the basement for hikers to stow and repack their gear.

Al and Allison built the grey-clapboard B&B, which has white trim, in 1993. The style is vaguely Victorian. While Al continues to work for Lockheed, Allison, who formerly ran a diner in the Hudson River Valley, handles the innkeeping duties. There's a living room with pine furniture and a handsome brick fireplace. Polished yellow pine floors gleam, covered by braided rugs. Lovely quilts hang on the walls. The couple fix breakfast in a large open kitchen, which overlooks an oak table in the eating area "so guests can see me make all my mistakes," Al jovially told me. A typical morning breakfast will include fresh juice and fruit, a vegetable omelette accompanied by home fries or French toast with stuffed mushrooms. Homemade muffins might be of the blueberry, raisin bran, or poppyseed variety.

There is one guest room on the main floor. The Lincoln Room, which is wheelchair accessible, has twin beds and a shower in the bath. There are two guest rooms upstairs, each with yellow pine floors and tall ceilings. In the Lee Room, there's a queen four-poster bed covered with quilts. In a little alcove, there's a table with a coffeemaker; a TV and a desk are in the room. The Jackson Room has a four-poster cherry bed with a canopy top and a colorful quilt covering it. The spacious bath includes all the amenities.

Were I to hike the length of the Appalachian Trail (which I've always imagined I'd do some day), this is the kind of B&B in which I'd like to stay each night.

What's Nearby—Harpers Ferry

Harpers Ferry National Historical Park is the scene of the confrontation between abolitionist John Brown and troops led by Robert E. Lee. The National Park Service has completed an extraordinarily fine restoration of the mellow brick buildings in the Lower Town, where you can walk along streets lined with preserved shops, buildings, and houses. The recreational possibilities of the area are limitless. There's rafting and canoeing on the Shenandoah River. Alongside the old Chesapeake and Ohio Canal, which passes through Harpers Ferry, there's now a hiking and bicycling trail that stretches from Washington, D.C., to Cumberland, Maryland. Harpers Ferry is the headquarters of The Appalachian Trail Conference, and the Trail marches through here also. (See also Charles Town and Shepherdstown.)

The Farmhouse on Tomahawk Run   Best Buy

1828 American Fruitgrowers Road
Hedgesville, WV 25427
(304) 754–7350 (fax also)

E-MAIL: tomahawk@intrepid.net
WEB SITE: www.information.com/
wv/farmhouse
INNKEEPERS: Judy and Hugh
Erskine

ROOMS: 5, including 1 suite and 1 cottage; all with private bath, air conditioning, coffeemaker, and radio; 4 with porch; 4 with dataport capabilities; 2 with hair dryer and desk; cottage with TV, VCR, kitchen, telephone, and fireplace; 1 room with wheelchair access; telephone in great room

ON THE GROUNDS: Parking; on 280 acres with walking paths through the hills, woods, and meadows; flower gardens, patio with arbor and benches; stone spring house; tobogganing and cross-country skiing in winter

EXTRAS: Turndown with chocolates; afternoon tea with homemade fruit breads; one outside cat, Mr. Tumnus

RATES: $85–$150, double occupancy, including full breakfast and afternoon refreshments; two-night minimum holiday weekends

CREDIT CARDS ACCEPTED: American Express, Diners Club, Discover, Master-Card, Visa

OPEN: Year-round

HOW TO GET THERE: From I–81, take exit 16 west and follow Route 9 for 6 miles (2 miles beyond the Hedgesville traffic light) to Route 7 (Tomahawk Road). Turn left and go 2½ miles on Tomahawk Road. Turn right between the Tomahawk Christian Church and the Tomahawk Valley Store onto American Fruitgrowers Road. Go ½ mile to the B&B, which will be on the left.

In a very rural setting, this lovely B&B is a welcome surprise. When Judy Erskine inherited the overgrown 280-acre farm with its dilapidated farmhouse and stone springhouse, she had fond memories of coming here as a child. The land was first granted to Israel Robinson in 1750 by Lord Fairfax, who was then British governor of Virginia. Judy is a direct descendant of Robinson, so this land has been in her family for more than 250 years—surely one of the longest of any English land grant in the United States.

Judy and her husband Hugh began their restoration odyssey in 1991 and were ready to open the doors to guests by 1994. When comparing the pictures of the farmhouse before the restoration with the finished B&B, you marvel at their vision.

Guests enter a wide stone hallway that contains a weasel—a yarn winder that emits a "pop" when it has finished a skein—initiating the old saying "pop goes the weasel." Hugh is retired from the U.S. government, but while he was an active employee, the couple lived all over the world. Many of the decorative items and the furniture in the B&B were collected in their travels. In addition, Hugh's grandfather was a missionary to Japan, and the magnificent carved dining room table and black walnut buffet are his legacy. A quilt that hangs over the upstairs stair railing was made by Judy's grandmother.

At the end of the hallway, in a new wing, a gathering room has been created. It has a pine floor, tall ceilings, and a massive fieldstone fireplace. An English regimental drum serves as a table. Beyond the French doors, there's a wraparound porch with a West Virginia mahogany floor and a hot tub. The view of the meadows, the old privy, the stone spring house (it still encloses the spring, which is in the shape of a tomahawk, giving the entire area its name), and the woods beyond are peaceful and still. The quiet is interrupted only by the songs of the birds that flit from birdhouse to birdhouse.

Hester's Room, which is located on the first floor and is wheelchair accessible, is presided over by a stern picture of its namesake, an ancestor of Judy's. There's a four-poster bed with blue bed coverings and a very pretty new bathroom with a tile floor and a shower. There are two more guest rooms upstairs, and each has its own wide porch. They are decorated with lovely quilts or cutwork duvets and interesting furniture, such as a chest made from the house's attic floorboards that now contains a sink. The baths are absolutely top quality. The two rooms in the Carriage House are ideal for a family. There is a kitchen and a living room with a fireplace as well as two bedrooms and two baths. French doors off the living room open onto a large deck, and the bedrooms share a large balcony.

Breakfast is served in the dining room on the Japanese table (and also in a smaller room if the B&B is full). A typical meal may include a fresh fruit cup or a baked apple, homemade muffins (perhaps blueberry-yogurt or cranberry-apple), and a main course of maybe a cheese strata with roasted rosemary potatoes, Canadian bacon, and homemade Colonial bread toast or black walnut pancakes (from the B&B's trees) with fresh local sausage and maple or blueberry syrup.

What's Nearby—Hedgesville

Hedgesville is located between Berkeley Springs and Martinsburg. In Martinsburg, the Boarman Arts Center specializes in the work of West Virginia artists. Come here to purchase original art. People come from miles around to go to the extensive outlet mall located in a converted woolen mill in Martinsburg. In Berkeley Springs you can bathe in the warm mineral waters at Berkeley Springs State Park. Massages and heat treatments can accompany a therapeutic bath. Cacapon Resort State Park is a 6,000-acre preserve with a lake for swimming, fishing, and boating; an eighteen-hole golf course; hiking trails; and horseback riding.

Thomas Shepherd Inn

Best Buy

300 West German Street
(mailing address: P.O. Box 1162)
Shepherdstown, WV 25443
(888) 889–8952 or (304) 876–3715

FAX: (304) 876–3313

E-MAIL: mrg@intrepid.net

WEB SITE: www.intrepid.net/thomas.shepherd

INNKEEPER: Margaret Perry

ROOMS: 7; all with private bath and air conditioning; 1 with a fireplace; guest telephone upstairs in library and downstairs in sitting room

ON THE GROUNDS: Parking; gardens

EXTRAS: Sherry in the evening; fax, meeting room available; a Lhasa apso, Walter, on premises

RATES: $85–$135, double occupancy; $75–$125, single occupancy, including full breakfast; two-night minimum all holiday weekends and also if stay includes Saturday from March to Thanksgiving

CREDIT CARDS ACCEPTED: American Express, MasterCard, Visa

OPEN: Year-round

HOW TO GET THERE: From I–81, take exit 16 onto Route 9 east and follow signs to Route 45. In Martinsburg take Route 45 east to Shepherdstown. Route 45 becomes West German Street in Shepherdstown. The B&B is at the intersection of West German and Duke Streets in the center of town.

Shepherdstown, which was founded in 1727 by German settlers, is the oldest town in West Virginia, but it wasn't until Thomas Shepherd arrived in 1734 that the town began to grow. The entire town is a historic district and listed on the National Register of Historic Places. The B&B, a creamy-colored brick Federal building with green shutters, was built in 1868 to house the parsonage of the Lutheran Church. It was converted to a B&B in 1984, and Margaret Perry purchased it in 1989.

Margaret is a friendly, outgoing innkeeper who is a font of information about Shepherdstown. You might sit in the lovely back garden where her adorable Lhasa apso plays while she tells you about the best access points to the C&O Canal bicycle path or the Appalachian Trail. And she will certainly fill you in about the town's newest restaurants, galleries, and shops.

The B&B is appropriately furnished in a Colonial style. Guests can relax in a formal living room, which has wide-plank pine floors covered with Oriental rugs, green-checked sofas, and cranberry-colored wing chairs before a fireplace. A decanter of sherry and glasses sit here. The extensive gift shop in the dining room reflects Margaret's varied interests. It includes cookbooks, flower seeds, jams, and bags of potpourri. There's also a library on the second floor that has a TV, a VCR, a video library, and a selection of books. Off the library, there's a covered treetop porch that is complete with white rockers, a braided rug, and a romantic trelliswork wall. An array of flowering plants flourishes here.

The guest rooms are simply decorated with comfortable Colonial furnishings that include canopy and poster beds and other antiques. The nicest rooms are Room #2, which has a sleigh bed and a new bath, and Room #7, which has a sitting area with a fireplace, a bedroom with a lovely Victorian half-tester bed, and a nice bath. It's all decorated in Laura Ashley fabrics. Although each of the rooms has a private bath, several are very tiny, and Room #3 has a bath across the hallway.

Margaret has a culinary background, and she loves to cook. She serves breakfast in two small and cozy dining rooms. One has a handsome brass chandelier, polished pine floors, a pretty corner cupboard where segments of the gift shop repose, and a fireplace. Guests eat on antique tables that seat six. She may include blueberry sour cream muffins, juice, fresh fruit, and strawberry pancakes with homemade sage sausage and Vermont maple syrup. The repast is served by candlelight on china that is coordinated with the linens and using stemmed glasses. Every plate is garnished with bright edible flowers and herbs.

What's Nearby—Shepherdstown

A walking tour of historic Shepherdstown will take you past buildings dating to 1790. Visit the Historic Shepherdstown Museum and the Rumsey Steamboat Museum to learn more about the village. In recent years, Shepherdstown has developed an artsy following. There are upscale art galleries, craft shops, restaurants, clothing boutiques, and antiques shops along the streets. (See also Charles Town and Harpers Ferry, West Virginia, as well as Sharpsburg, Maryland.)

Indexes

Alphabetical Index to Bed & Breakfasts

Best Buy B&Bs

B&Bs Especially Suited to Children

B&Bs Especially Suited to Business Travelers

B&Bs with Wheelchair Access

B&Bs That Accept Pets (with Prior Permission)

B&Bs with Swimming Pools

B&Bs That Permit Smoking

B&Bs Near Skiing, Hiking, or Mountain Biking

B&Bs Near Fishing, Boating, or Rafting

Mansion Inn, 304
Pine Tree Farm, 272

Virginia
Hope and Glory Inn, The, 351
Inn at Fairfield Farm, The, 348
Inn at Meander Plantation, The, 357
Inn at Narrow Passage, The, 391
Manor at Taylor's Store B&B Country
Inn, The, 370

Watson House Bed & Breakfast, The,
and Inn at Poplar Corner, The, 338

West Virginia
Farmhouse on Tomahawk Run, The,
414
Harpers Ferry Guest House, 412
North Fork Mountain Inn, 400
Warfield House Bed & Breakfast, The,
410

B&Bs in or near Cities

Maryland
Ann Street Bed & Breakfast, 28
Celie's Waterfront Bed & Breakfast, 30
Gramercy Mansion Bed &
Breakfast, 83
Mr. Mole Bed & Breakfast, 32

New York
Bed & Breakfast on the Park, 210
428 Mt. Vernon—A Bed & Breakfast
Inn, 221
Inn at Irving Place, The, 212
Inn New York City, 214
Inn on 23rd, The, 216

Pennsylvania
Appletree Bed & Breakfast, The, 311
Shadyside Bed & Breakfast, The, 313

Virginia
Emmanuel Hutzler House, The, 366
Page House Inn, 364

Washington, D.C.
Swann House, 393

West Virginia
Brass Pineapple Bed & Breakfast,
The, 402

Mountain B&Bs

Maryland
Antietam Overlook Farm Bed &
Breakfast, 62

New York
Albergo Allegria, 256
Lamplight Inn Bed & Breakfast,
The, 202
Schroon Lake Bed & Breakfast, 229
Silver Spruce Inn Bed & Breakfast, 231

Pennsylvania
Brookview Manor B&B Inn, The, 264
Farmhouse Bed & Breakfast, 301
Mt. Gretna Inn, 299

Virginia
Inn at Narrow Passage, The, 391
Iris Inn, The, 383
King's Victorian Inn Bed & Breakfast,
The, 346
Oaks Victorian Inn, The, 340

West Virginia
North Fork Mountain Inn, 400
Tunnel Mountain Bed &
Breakfast, 408
Warfield House Bed & Breakfast,
The, 410

B&Bs by Bays, Lakes, or Rivers

B&Bs by the Ocean

B&Bs on the Delaware Peninsula

B&Bs in the Hamptons

B&Bs in the Finger Lakes Region of New York

ABOUT THE AUTHOR

Suzi Forbes Chase has been writing about food and travel longer than she likes to admit. As the author of *Country Inns and Back Roads*, she traveled from east to west and back again researching, inspecting, and writing about bed and breakfasts and inns from British Columbia to Florida. Today, however, she confines most of her research to the states closest to home. She is a resident of New York State. Suzi is also the author of *Recommended Country Inns®: Mid-Atlantic and Chesapeake Region* (The Globe Pequot Press) and *The Hamptons Book: A Complete Guide* (Berkshire Press) and the editor of *ZagatSurvey to Long Island Restaurants*.